Tradition and Reflection

Tradition and Reflection

Explorations in Indian Thought

Wilhelm Halbfass

State University of New York Press

Published by
State University of New York Press, Albany

Printed in the United States of America

For information, address State University of New York
Press, State University Plaza, Albany, N.Y. 12246

Library of Congress Cataloging-in-Publication Data

Halbfass, Wilhelm.
Tradition and Reflection: Explorations in Indian Thought /
Wilhelm Halbfass.
p. cm.
Includes bibliographical references.
ISBN 0-7914-0361-0.—ISBN 0-7914-0362-9 (pbk.)
1. Philosophy, Indic. 2. Vedas—Influence.
3. Philosophy, Hindu. 4. Vedas—Criticism,
interpretation, etc. I. Title.
B131.H28 1991
181′.4—dc20 89-29795
CIP

10 9 8 7 6 5 4 3 2 1

Contents

Preface

This book continues and supplements the investigations presented in *India and Europe: An Essay in Understanding* (SUNY Press, 1988). It combines ten interrelated essays on fundamental issues of traditional Indian self-understanding. Its topics include the idea of dharma, karma and rebirth, the role of man in the universe, the structure of society, the relation between ritual norms and universal ethics, as well as questions concerning the motivation and justification of human actions, and reflections on the goals and sources of human knowledge. Above all, the book deals with the relations and tensions between reason and Vedic revelation, and with philosophical responses to the idea of the Veda.

The essays found in this book examine the self-understanding of Śaṅkara, Kumārila, Bhartṛhari, Udayana, and other leading exponents of "orthodox" Hindu thought. But they also explore more remote and apparently marginal phenomena, for instance, the traditions concerning the mysterious "liberators from samsāra" (*saṃsāramocaka*) and the notorious Thags (*ṭhaka*). The approach is partly philosophical and partly historical and philological. To a certain extent, it is also comparative. The essays deal with indigenous Indian reflections on the sources, the internal structure and the inherent meaning of the Hindu tradition, and with traditional philosophical responses to social and historical realities. They do not deal with social and historical realities per se. They are, however, based upon the premise that for understanding these realities the reflections and constructions of traditional Indian theorists are no less significant than the observations and paradigms of modern Western historians and social scientists. Indian thought has its own ways of dealing with, or compensating for, the realities of Indian life. In trying to understand these modes of thought, we are dealing with the reality of the Indian tradition through the medium of Indian theoretical and soteriological reflection.

In spite of their mutual affinities and their thematic associations with *India and Europe*, the ten chapters which make up this volume are different and mutually independent, as far as their actual genesis is concerned. Chapters 3, 4, 5, and 6 constitute the core of the book. These chapters are thoroughly revised and greatly enlarged versions of my four *Studies in Kumārila and Śaṅkara*, which were published in 1983 and have been out of print for some time. Chapter 8 includes materials first presented in my article "Anthropological Problems in Classical Indian Philosophy" (*Beiträge zur Indienforschung, Ernst Waldschmidt zum 80. Geburtstag gewidmet*. Berlin, 1977). Chapter 9 is based upon my article "Karma, *apūrva*, and Natural Causes" (*Karma and Rebirth in Classical Indian Traditions*, ed. W. D. O'Flaherty. Berkeley, 1980). Chapter 10 is the revised and enlarged English version of a monograph originally published in German: *Zur Theorie der Kastenordnung in der indischen Philosophie* (Göttingen, 1976). Chapters 1, 2, and 7 have no direct predecessors, apart from lecture manuscripts and related materials.

Some of these chapters are more easily accessible to the general reader than others. Specialized philological investigations predominate in some chapters, while others pose questions of broad philosophical and comparative interest. Chapter 6 is clearly the most technical chapter, while chapter 7 is probably the least technical one. Such differences reflect the nature of the sources and our state of research. In some central instances, the resolution of technical problems, and the attention to minute philological details, are indispensable in order to approach the broader issues. Philology and philosophical reflection cannot be separated in such cases.

Finally, it is my pleasant duty to acknowledge the help and encouragement I have received from friends, colleagues, and students. In particular, I want to thank Dr. John Baker for his share in preparing the English version of chapter 10. Lynken Ghose has helped to produce the manuscript of the book. The Department of South Asia Regional Studies, University of Pennsylvania (Philadelphia), has provided financial support and a congenial atmosphere.

Berlin, Wissenschaftskolleg/
Institute for Advanced Study

CHAPTER 1

The Idea of the Veda and the Identity of Hinduism

Introduction

1. Louis Renou has characterized the role of the Veda in traditional Hinduism in a memorable and familiar statement: Even in the most orthodox circles of Hinduism, reverence for the Veda was nothing more than a "tipping of the hat," a traditional gesture of saluting an "idol" without any further commitment ("un simple 'coup de chapeau' donné en passant à une idole dont on entend ne plus s'encombrer par la suite").[1] Against incautious identifications of Vedic and Hindu religiosity, Renou invokes Max Weber's observation that "the Vedas defy the *dharma* of Hinduism."[2]

Indeed, the role the Veda has played in Indian tradition appears paradoxical, ambiguous, and no less elusive than the "teachings" of the Veda itself. There seems to be a blatant contradiction between the proclamations of its sacredness and authority, and its factual neglect by the Hindu tradition. While it is often invoked as the criterion of Hindu "orthodoxy," its actual presence in Indian thought and life seems to be quite limited. Its oldest and supposedly most sacred sections, in particular the *Ṛgveda* itself, have become most obscure and obsolete. For the "reality" of later Hinduism, they seem to be nothing more than a distant, barely recognizable echo of a different world.

The Vedic texts contain no Hindu dogma, no basis for a "creed" of Hinduism, no clear guidelines for the "Hindu way of life." They offer only vague and questionable analogues to those ideas and ways of orientation that have become basic presuppositions of later Hinduism. It may suffice to recall here the cyclical world-view, the doctrine of karma and rebirth, the ethical principle of *ahiṃsā* and the soteriology of final liberation. For all of this, the oldest and most fundamental Vedic texts provide no clearly identifiable basis. The Hindu pantheon, the forms of worship and devotion, and the temple cult are not Vedic. The traditional "order of castes and stages of life" (*varṇāśramadharma*) is far removed from the Vedic beginnings. Regardless of all retrospective glorification of the Veda, even the "orthodox" core of the tradition, as represented by the exegetic Mīmāṃsā and the Dharmaśāstra, follows largely unvedic ways of thought and is oriented around a projection or fiction of the Veda. This is also true for those philosophical systems of Hinduism whose "orthodoxy" is defined by their recognition of the authority of the Veda. While proclaiming the sanctity of the Veda, the Hindu tradition seems to be turning away from the Vedic ways of thought and life. The preservation and glorification of the text seem to coincide with its neglect and the obscuration of its meaning.

Renou himself says that the history of the Veda in India is ultimately a history of failure and loss ("déperdition"), and that the recitation of the text, in particular the mantras, and the preservation of its phonetic identity, occurred at the expense of a living exegesis and appropriation. From an early time, the Veda ceased to be "a ferment of Indian religiosity" ("un ferment de la religiosité indienne"); in the end, the Vedic world was nothing but "a distant object" ("un objet lointain").[3] Is this the final word on the role of the Veda in India? Are Vedism and Hinduism essentially different religions and world-views, held together only by an ideology of continuity and correspondence? Is the Veda, which the Dharmaśāstra and the "orthodox" systems of Hindu philosophy present as a measure of orthodoxy, actually a projection and a fiction?

In addition to his research on the Veda as such, Renou has done much to document and explore the ways in which the Veda is present in the later Hindu tradition. His study *Le destin du Veda dans l'Inde* ("The Destiny of the Veda in India") contains much useful information on the role of the Veda in post-Vedic India, such as the forms in which the Veda was preserved, the attitudes towards the Vedic word, and the application, interpretation, and critique of the Veda at various levels of religious life and philosophical reflection. Regardless of his statements on the merely ceremonial role of the Veda, Renou also refers to its "real extensions" ("prolongements réels") in later Hinduism.[4] Somewhat casually, he notes that the very essence of the Vedic world found its way, in a process of transformation ("en se transformant"), into "the living substance of Hindu practice and speculation" ("la chair même des pratiques et des spéculations hindouistes").[5] What is the meaning of these "real extensions," and how do they relate to the ceremonial gestures and retrospective projections? How can the statements concerning the real "transformation" of the Vedic world be reconciled with those about its loss and obscuration? Renou's survey provides helpful clues, but not much explicit hermeneutic reflection concerning these questions.

2. What Renou calls "the destiny of the Veda in India" is a wide-ranging phenomenon of extraordinary complexity and ambiguity. His survey makes reference not only to the literary traditions of the Hindu sects, Tantrism, Dharmaśāstra, the Epics, Purāṇas, iconography, rituals, traditions of secular learning, methods of preserving the Vedic texts, techniques of recitation and memorization, Vedic schools and auxiliary sciences, Vedic commentarial literature, and the "orthodox" systems of Hindu philosophy, but also to the anti-Vedic critique and polemics of the Buddhists, Jainas, and Materialists. We are dealing with semantic as well as nonsemantic approaches, with ritual and magical usages of Vedic words and formulas, with myths and theories concerning the unity and totality of the Veda, with forms of archival preservation, with definitions and reinterpretations, and with comprehensive attempts to establish the Veda as the source and framework of the entire tradition. In spite of the growing distance and obscuration, an idea and vision of the Veda emerges not only as a focal point of Hindu self-understanding, and a center for the precarious unity and identity of the tradition, but also as a prototype for its inner variety and potential universality.[6]

In dealing with the Veda, the Hindu tradition combines strict commitment to textual and phonetic details with an extraordinary freedom of speculation. In one sense, the Veda is the sum total of its words and sounds. In another sense, it can be summarized in a few "great sayings" (*mahāvākya*), or fundamental ideas. On the one hand, there is the idea that no single sound or syllable is dispensable. On the other hand, there is a persistent belief that this verbal multiplicity may be reduced to an original unity (such as the Ṛgvedic *akṣara*),[7] or transcended towards one ultimate essence, that is, the *brahman* and its closest linguistic approximation, the *om* or *praṇava*.[8]

The orthodox traditionalists of the Mīmāṃsā and of some related schools try to establish the Vedic texts as timeless, unalterable linguistic constellations, texts without divine or human author, and thus beyond the range of error and deception. They also try to demarcate once and for all the extent of genuine Vedic "revelation" (*śruti*), and to distinguish it from merely human and traditional additions or accretions. According to the most common definition, "revelation" in the strict sense comprises the Mantras and Brāhmaṇas; that is, the collections of hymns and ritual formulas in the Ṛg-, Yajur-, and Sāmaveda, together with their accompanying Brāhmaṇas, Āraṇyakas, and Upaniṣads. While the status of the Atharvaveda remains somewhat precarious, more significant debates focus on the internal differentiation of the Vedic revelation, its modes of discourse, the different kinds of linguistic entities contained in it (*vidhi, arthavāda, mantra, nāmadheya*), and the different types of meaning and levels of authority associated with its injunctive and factual statements.[9]

The theistic traditions, on the other hand, view the Vedas as the word of God, and as a stage in an open-ended process of revelation.[10] In this view, they are susceptible to, and even call for, continued revisions, explications, adaptations, and other forms of divine supplementation and renewal. Furthermore, there is also room for the idea that the present Vedas are not the Veda per se, that is, its true and real archetype.[11] The "real" and original Veda is thus contrasted with the extant Vedic texts and invoked against their "orthodox" and inflexible guardians, and a dynamic sense of tradition is brought into confrontation with a static and archival one.

The Veda as Text and Reality

3. Understanding the role of the Veda in Indian thought involves more than textual hermeneutics. It also involves what we may call the hermeneutics of an event. The different approaches to the Veda are not just different interpretations of a text, and commitment to the Veda is not only, and not even primarily, acceptance of a doctrine. In another and perhaps more fundamental sense, it means recognition of a primeval event, and a response to a fundamental reality. In the understanding of those who accept it, the Veda itself is beginning and opening par excellence. It not only speaks, in its own elusive fashion, about the origin and structure of the world and the foundations of society; it is also their real and normative manifestation and representation.

The language of the Veda *is* primeval reality. Bhartṛhari says that the Veda is the "organizing principle" (*vidhātṛ*) of the world, that is, not only its "teacher" or principle of instruction (*upadeṣṭṛ*), but also its underlying cause and essence (*prakṛti*).[12] This may be an extreme and somewhat unusual form of expression, but the basic viewpoint it articulates is by no means isolated. The *Manusmṛti*, as well as other dharma texts, characterize the Veda as an organizing and sustaining principle, and even as the real basis of the social and natural world.[13] It would be wrong to view such statements as merely metaphorical. The Veda *is* the foundation of language, of the fundamental distinctions and classifications in the world, and of those rituals which are meant to sustain the social and natural order. It is itself the primeval manifestation of those cosmogonic occurrences which establish the dharma.[14] Text and world, language and reality, are inseparable in this world-view and self-understanding.[15] The "text" itself opens and sustains the "world" in which it appears, to which it speaks, and by which its own authority has to be recognized and sustained.

Commitment to the Veda in this sense means, above all, accepting one's ritual obligations, one's dharma; that is, one's duty to renew and perpetuate the primeval occurrences represented by the Veda, and to uphold the structure of the world established by it. The recitation, memorization, and exegesis of the Vedic texts, just as the correct usage of the Sanskrit language in general, has ritual implications. The "rehearsal" (*svādhyāya*) of the Veda not only supplements the actual physical rituals, but to some extent may even replace them.[16]

In a sense, the Veda precedes or transcends the entire semantic dimension. This applies specifically, but not exclusively, to its mantra portions. According to Kautsa's controversial thesis, the mantras have no semantic status at all. Authoritative advocates of the tradition, such as Yāska, Śabara, and Sāyaṇa, reject Kautsa's notion of the "meaninglessness" (*ānarthakya*) of the mantras.[17] Yet even they recognize the protosemantic dimension of the Vedic language, specifically of the mantras, a reality of the Vedic word that is more fundamental than any semantic functions, and that precedes the dichotomy of "word" and "meaning." Even though the mantras may not be "meaningless," the amount of information they provide is not their most significant aspect. They are, above all, "real" components of a mythical and magical world, and basic ingredients of the rituals necessary to uphold this world. As such, they have to be employed and enacted, not "understood."[18]

From the perspective of later Hindu thought, the entire Veda is sometimes associated with the idea of a protosemantic presence of "words" and "sounds." In this view, the Veda is "primarily word" (*śabdapradhāna*) and thus distinguished from the Purāṇas, which are said to be *arthapradhāna*, that is, texts in which "meaning" and "information" predominate.[19]

4. What then is the role and "destiny" of the Veda in later Hindu thinking and self-understanding? What are the basic hermeneutic positions and presuppositions in dealing with the Veda? What are the basic forms and patterns of its preservation and neglect, its interpretation and misinterpretation? What is implied in the "transformations" of the Vedic world to which Renou refers? What kind of continued presence does the Veda have within such transformations? What is the relationship between preservation, transformation, obscuring, and loss? Are there modes of presence and elements of continuity that remain unaffected by the growing distance and obscuring, and inherent in all the later fictions and superimpositions? In what sense is the relegation of the Veda to the distant past, this inapplicability and obsoleteness, compatible with its continued recognition and authority? Is such withdrawal from the actual world of living Hinduism, such remoteness and transcendence, perhaps a peculiar manifestation of sanctity and authority?

How can we distinguish the "real extensions" ("prolongements réels") of Vedic thought and life from later projections and reinterpretations? Is there any inherent connection between these "real extensions" and the later myths and fictions *about* the Veda? Why did the Veda become the focus of so many fictions and superimpositions? Why were so many ideas that seem to be foreign to, or even incompatible with, "real" Vedic thought projected into the

Veda? Does the Veda provide a genuine basis for the processes of superimposition?

In order to deal with these questions, and to account for the fictions and projections that post-Vedic India has associated with the Veda, inevitably, one must examine the extra-Vedic components of later Hinduism. But regardless of such external accretions,[20] how does the Veda lend itself to these later developments? Is there a sense in which the Veda itself has been conducive to the superimpositions and fictions attached to it? Are there reinterpretations, fictions or myths, and perhaps even forms of rejection and neglect, that are at the same time genuine effects and "real extensions" of the Veda?

Whatever the answer to these questions may be, and regardless of the highly elusive and ambiguous nature of the historical relationship between the Veda and Hinduism, the Hindu tradition has, for many centuries, defined itself in relation to the Veda. The Veda, or the idea of the Veda, has provided one indispensable focus for Hindu self-understanding. It may be true that "the Vedas defy the *dharma* of Hinduism";[21] yet it is also true that they have provided this dharma with its most significant point of reference and departure, and with a basis for its tenuous continuity and identity. We may even say: There would be no Hinduism without the Veda; its identity and reality depends upon the idea, or fiction, of the Veda. But what is the "reality" of Hinduism?

"Orientalist Constructions" and the Problem of Authenticity

5. It has often been stated that Hinduism has neither a well-defined, clearly identifiable creed nor a coherent organizational structure, and that it is not a religion in the sense of Christianity and Islam. More recently, this observation has been radicalized in various ways. There has been a tendency to call the reality of Hinduism itself into question, or to challenge the legitimacy and authenticity of the concept of Hinduism. W. Cantwell Smith says: "There are Hindus, but there is no Hinduism."[22] In his view, this concept is nothing but a foreign—Islamic and European or Christian—superimposition upon the "luxuriant welter" of a tradition that "is not a unity and does not aspire to be," and an inappropriate attempt "to systematize and congeal the spontaneous."[23] Similarly, H. von Stietencron states that "Hinduism" is a European invention, "an orchid bred by European scholarship. . . . In nature, it does not exist."[24]

Von Stietencron's statement echoes P. Hacker's observation that Hinduism is nothing but a "collective label" ("Sammelbezeichnung"), which was produced by Western scholars of religion in order to have a common designation for "the innumerable, partly cognate, partly divergent religious phenomena of one geographical and historical region" ("die zahllosen, teils verwandten, teils divergenten religiösen Erscheinungen eines geographisch-geschichtlichen Raumes").[25] According to Hacker, the similarities and common denominators that can be found in this "group of religions" are primarily due to contacts and coexistence in the same area of South Asia.[26]

From a different angle, various Indian authors have also rejected or criticized the concept of Hinduism, as well as its characterization as a religion.[27] Yet, since the early nineteenth century many other Indians have asserted the unity and identity of Hinduism, and they have tried to establish it as a religion fully commensurable with Christianity and Islam.[28] Others (and this may be the more characteristic approach) have tried to define the "essence" of Hinduism not in terms of a specific religion, but as a more comprehensive and inclusive constellation of religious thought and life, and as a potentially universal framework for religious plurality. According to this view, such religions as Islam and Christianity should not be compared to Hinduism itself, which appears as a kind of "metareligion," but to the sects or sectarian "religions" within Hinduism, such as Śaivism and Vaiṣṇavism.[29]

Are both of these modern conceptions radical deviations from the tradition? Are they expressions of a nonauthentic self-understanding, a borrowed sense of identity, an adoption of Western ways of objectifying the life and thought of the Indians? Is such a sense of "religious" identity and such an allegiance to "Hinduism," or "the Hindu way," without genuine precedent in premodern or at least pre-Islamic, India? This is indeed the case, according to critics like P. Hacker. In Hacker's view, questions concerning the "essence" of Hinduism have meaning only from the standpoint of Neo-Hinduism; the idea of such unity and essence is motivated by, and inseparable from, the modern Indian search for national identity.[30]

6. Other, even more radical denunciations of the concept of Hinduism are associated with the critique of "Orientalism" and scholarly "discourses of domination," which has gained momentum in recent years. This movement of critique and "deconstruction" tries to expose links between the scholarly exploration and the political subjugation of India and the "Orient," to identify and eliminate Western constructs and superimpositions, and to provide a comprehensive revision of the conceptual apparatus of Oriental and Indian studies. Western Orientalists, according to such critics, have tried to "represent" the Orient, to deprive it of a genuine self-understanding, to project it as a sphere of "otherness," to objectify, categorize, and classify it in accordance with European interests of domination. More specifically, Indologists have categorized, redefined, or even invented "much of India's ancient past."[31] In a more or less explicit alliance with the British colonial administration, and in consonance with such measures as the census reports, they created the "caste system" in its currently accepted sense, and "Hinduism" as a clearly definable religious category. If there is a connection with premodern India, it is through the conceptualizations and theoretical norms of the brahmins, whose writings provided the source materials for the scholars as well as the colonial administrators. Through this unholy alliance, colonialism "elevated Brahmanic formulations to the level of hegemonic text,"[32] while "Indological discourse" continued to project "the essence of Indian civilization" as "just the opposite of the West's"; that is, as the caste system and the "religion that accompanies it, Hinduism."[33] In the hands of the colonialists, "caste became an administrative tool to arrange and register Indian society into a definable sum of parts," and "helped to transform brahmanical hypocrisy into an established social fact."[34]

There can be no doubt that the time for such critique concerning the premises, goals, and ramifications of Indian and "Oriental" studies has come. Yet it is equally obvious that its own premises and procedures, too, call for critical reflection and clarification. This may be exemplified by referring to the most famous and influential contribution in this field, Edward Said's *Orientalism* (first published in 1978).

7. In a broad and general sense, Said claims "that all academic knowledge about India and Egypt is somehow tinged and impressed with, violated by, the gross political fact,"[35] and that Orientalism as an academic discipline is "a kind of Western projection onto and will to govern over the Orient."[36] "Orientalism overrode the Orient. . . . Can any other than a political master-slave relation produce the Orientalized Orient?"[37] The positivism of Western research appears itself as an ideology of domination; philology is a symptom of the Western will to power: "There is an unmistakable aura of power about the philologist."[38] Europeans have not tried to understand the Orientals; they have tried to articulate or prescribe a self-understanding for them: "They cannot represent themselves; they must be represented."[39]

Said's book deals specifically with certain French and British approaches to the Islamic "Orient" since the end of the eighteenth century. However, these approaches appear as symptoms of much more pervasive European attitudes and of much deeper links between thought, speech, and power. In Aeschylus's drama *The Persians*, which was written after the battle of Salamis in 480 B.C., Said finds a programmatic summary of the central motifs of Orientalism: "Europe is powerful and articulate; Asia is defeated and distant. Aeschylus *represents* Asia. . . . It is Europe that articulates the Orient."[40] What is more, F. Nietzsche and M. Foucault are invoked to enhance such critique with even more general suggestions concerning the nature of truth and the inherent connections between language, power and illusion.[41]

The rhetorical qualities of Said's procedure are obvious; its contribution to historical understanding and conceptual clarity is, however, questionable and elusive. Said merges different levels of argumentation and analysis; he confounds highly selective historical observations with broad philosophical generalizations. The specter of "Orientalism" he conjures up is a combination of very specific and very general traits. Much of what he says applies only to the European treatment of Islam, but not of other parts of Asia or the non-Western world; other statements, though meant to depict "Orientalism," apply equally to European ways of dealing with Occidental, European phenomena. And finally, a very substantial part of what he says applies by his own admission to the encounter of civilizations and to human group behavior in general, and thus to "Oriental" as well as "Occidental" ways of dealing with "the other" and his otherness.[42] At the end, "Orientalism" emerges as a historical and conceptual hybridization that is no less a construct and projection than the so-called Orient itself.

8. Said does not deal explicitly with European approaches to India. This has been done by other authors. For instance, R. Inden has criticized "Orientalist constructions of India" and ways in which "Indological discourse" has denied to Indians "the power to represent themselves" and thus reinforced processes of alienation and subjugation.[43] Indology, too, has projected its objects into a sphere of "otherness," has "reified" and "essentialized" them in its own way, and "has appropriated the power to represent the Oriental, to translate and explain his (and her) thoughts and acts not only to Europeans and Americans but also to the Orientals themselves."[44] In particular, it has construed the caste system as the "essence of Indian civilization."[45]

Inden's critique of Indology is by no means a mere extrapolation of Said's procedure, yet it raises some analogous questions. It, too, blends specific historical issues, concerning specific European misinterpretations and false "essentializations" of Indian phenomena, with fundamental epistemological and metaphysical questions concerning the role of essentialization and conceptual representation and construction in general. Such specific issues as the role and meaning of "castes" in medieval India require empirical historical research and efforts of understanding; so does the genesis of European constructions or misconstructions of the "caste system." The epistemological and metaphysical issues concerning "representation" and "construction" per se; that is, ultimately the very structure of our world of appearance, demand an essentially different approach. The commensurability and mutual applicability of the two sets of problems can certainly not be taken for granted; greater efforts of reflection and clarification are called for. Moreover: What is the role of essentialization and representation in the critical process itself? What are the standards to expose false constructs and superimpositions? To what extent are "Orientalism," "Indology," and the other targets of criticism themselves constructs and imposed essences?

Another question to be addressed is: What is the relationship between European and non-European, specifically traditional Indian modes of conceptualizing and "representing" others in their otherness? It may be true that there is something unprecedented about the European ways of objectifying and representing others, and this something may have to do with what has been called the "Europeanization of the Earth." Yet in order not to be parochial and naive, "xenological," "heterological" reflection requires a comparative perspective.

Self-questioning and the critique of Eurocentric preconceptions are necessary ingredients of any responsible study of India. However, the attempt to eliminate *all* Western constructs and preconceptions and to liberate the Indian tradition from all non-Indian categories of understanding would not only be impractical, but also presumptuous in its own way. Although it would seem to be diametrically opposed to the Hegelian Eurocentric method of subordinating and superseding non-European traditions, it would raise the problem of a "reverse Eurocentrism."

"The capacity to have true knowledge and to act have to be, as it were, returned to the many Others from whom Western practices have taken it. We cannot claim to accord independence of action to a sovereign, independent India while still adhering (whether intentionally or not) to presuppositions that deny the very possibility of it."[46] The West has imposed its methods of research, its values and modes of orientation, its categories of understanding, its "epistemic absolutism"[47] upon the Indian tradition and alienated the Indians from what they really were and are. It now takes the liberty to remove such superimpositions, to release the Indians into their authentic selfhood, to restore their epistemic and axiological sovereignty. This self-abrogation of Eurocentrism is at the same time its ultimate affirmation.

9. What kind of "authenticity" would the Indian civilization have once it has been freed from "Orientalist constructions" and Western "discourses of domination"? Would it be a reality and identity free from all constructs and essentializations? Would it be a reality left to indigenous, Indian, and thus "legitimate" constructions? Could it still be subject to inappropriate and illegitimate, though indigenous, constructions and superimpositions? Does the tradition itself have its own modes of alienation and epistemic subjugation?

We have referred to the argument that there has been an unholy alliance between the brahmins and the colonialists, and that brahminical constructions of Indian society were adopted and translated into social reality by colonial administrators or misinterpreted as truthful descriptions of Indian society by Indological scholars. Accordingly, the exposure of Western "Orientalist constructions" would have to be combined with a critique of internal, brahminical superimpositions and "discourses of domination," as found, for instance, in the Dharmaśāstra texts or the Mīmāṃsā literature.[48]

The desire of the early "Orientalists" to find in the normative and theoretical dharma literature factual accounts of Indian society and its governance was obviously mistaken. But does this mean that such texts and their teachings are inauthentic and insignificant as far as the *reality* of the Indian civilization is concerned? Where the earlier reading may have been too literal and naive, more recent approaches have gone into the opposite extreme, tending to explain and dismiss these texts as documents of wishful thinking and theoretical constructs, and to overlook their real authentic role in the multilayered totality of the Indian tradition.

At this point, we cannot and need not discuss to what extent the norms and precepts found in these texts have been applied or implemented, and in what sense their schemes and theories correspond to actual occurrences in society. Whatever the answer to these questions may be, the texts themselves, as well as their "theoretical" constructions, have an overwhelming presence among the extant records of the Indian civilization. Whether or not they have much value as "descriptions" of this civilization, they certainly are its products and reflections. They may be expressions of wishful thinking, attempts to legitimize divisions of society and relationships of exclusion and subordination. Yet, they are also expressions of a sense of identity and community that transcend such divisions and relationships of exclusion. They reflect a commitment to a shared structure of mutual relations, which assigns different forms of participation to different groups; that is, they are expressions of a self-understanding and sense of identity which is characterized by the idea of dharma.

The Idea of Dharma and the Coherence of Hinduism

10. What are the premodern antecedents of the modern ideas of "Hinduism," the "Hindu way," etc.? Is there a traditional sense of identity or coherence that pervades what Hacker calls the "innumerable religious phenomena" of South Asia? Is there, or was there, a "reality" of Hinduism over and above the "reality" of individual Hindus? In order to answer or clarify these questions, no concept is more significant than the concept of dharma.

"In the history of traditional Hinduism, *dharma* is one of the most pivotal, most symptomatic concepts. It is the key-term of 'Aryan' self-understanding. Its uses exemplify the basic orientation, but also major changes, reinterpretations, and tensions in the tradition. The term refers to the primeval cosmogonic 'upholding' and opening of the world and its fundamental divisions, and then to the repetition and human analogues of the cosmogonic acts in the ritual, as well as the extension of the ritual into the sphere of social and ethical norms. Subsequently, there is increasing emphasis on the 'upholding' of the social and religious status quo, of the distinction between hereditary groups and levels of qualification (i.e., the *varṇāśramadharma*), and on the demarcation of the *ārya* against the *mleccha*. The rituals and social norms which were once associated with the upholding of the universe are now primarily a means of upholding the identity and continuity of the Aryan tradition. An ancient cosmogonic term becomes a vehicle of traditionalism and ethnocentrism."

"We cannot reduce the meanings of *dharma* to one general principle; nor is there one single translation that would cover all its usages. Nevertheless, there is coherence in this variety; it reflects the elusive, yet undeniable coherence of Hinduism itself, its peculiar unity-in-diversity. There is no *one* system of understanding *dharma*, but a complex network of interactions and tensions between different usages. Various groups and movements have laid claim to this fundamental term. They have reinterpreted it in different ways, and they have used it in order to challenge the 'orthodox' core of the tradition. Yet these reinterpretations and competing usages were in most cases indebted to, and oriented around, the 'orthodox' brahmanocentric usages. It is easy to argue that Mīmāṃsā and

Dharmaśāstra do not represent the totality of the Hindu tradition; but it is also easy to underestimate their central and paradigmatic role."[49]

This is not the place to discuss the specific developments that have led to the modern notion of "Hinduism," to its interpretation as a "religion," to the Neo-Hindu reinterpretations of dharma, and to the lexicographic equation, or at least coordination, of dharma and "religion."[50] The changes are obvious and significant. It is important, however, not to overlook the traditional, premodern dimensions of unity and identity, contextuality and coherence, and the centripetal and inclusive elements in what W. Cantwell Smith calls the "luxuriant welter" of traditional Hindu life.[51] To be sure, this is not the dogmatic and institutional identity of an "organized religion"; but on the other hand, it is neither an "Orientalist construction," nor can it be reduced to a brahminical fiction or projection.

11. It has often been suggested that in traditional India a sense of religious identity and allegiance comparable to what we have in Christianity and Islam may be found in the "sectarian" movements of Śaivism and Vaiṣṇavism, but not with reference to "Hinduism" as such.[52] Indeed, such movements may represent self-contained religious constellations and much more immediate and obvious domains of religious commitment and identification than the wider field of "the Hindu tradition." Yet the manner in which the theoreticians and literary representatives of these theistic formations relate and refer to one another, juxtapose or coordinate their teachings, and articulate their claims of mutual inclusion or transcendence, indicates the presence of this wider field. It reflects a wider sense of identity, a sense of coherence in a shared context and of inclusion in a common framework and horizon, and it refers us to some fundamental implications of the elusive reality of "Hinduism."[53]

The commitment to unity and identity, and the idea of one comprehensive structure and framework for the variety of Indian religious thought and life, is much more explicit and compelling in the work of such "supra-sectarian" theoreticians and ideologists of the Hindu tradition as Bhartṛhari, Kumārila, Śaṅkara, Sāyaṇa, and Madhusūdana Sarasvatī.[54] In all these cases, the idea of a comprehensive unity of the tradition, and of a common ground of orthodoxy, is inseparable from a vision of, and commitment to, the Vedic revelation. The Veda is invoked as the source and focus of the unity and identity of the tradition, but also as the prototype of its inner variety. It is invoked against the internal, sectarian disintegration of the tradition, as well as against the "external" (*bāhya*) and "heterodox" (*nāstika*) challenges of Buddhism, etc.[55]

The modern idea of "Hinduism," or of the "Hindu religion," is a reinterpretation of the traditional ideas and, in a sense, a hybridization of the traditional self-understanding. Yet it is by no means a mere adaptation of Western superimpositions. It is also a continuation of the tradition, an expression and transformation of that self-understanding which articulates itself in its commitment to the Vedic revelation. It is this commitment that provides the focus for traditional Hindu self-understanding, and that provides a paradigm and exemplary precedent even for those movements that pay little attention to the Vedic revelation, or try to supersede and replace it.

12. The following essays deal with theoretical aspects of the Hindu tradition, and with central issues of traditional Indian self-understanding. They deal with such topics as dharma, karma, and saṃsāra, with conceptualizations and rationalizations of the system of "four castes" (*varṇa*), with questions concerning the motivation and justification of human actions, and with reflections on the goals and sources of human knowledge. They deal, above all, with the relationship between reason and Vedic revelation, with theoretical reconstructions of traditional norms and concepts, and with philosophical responses to the idea of the Veda.

These essays are primarily based upon philosophical and normative literature in Sanskrit, that is, on texts which were for the most part composed by brahmins. They explore the self-understanding and the complex traditionalism of such thinkers as Kumārila, Śaṅkara, Bhartṛhari, Jayanta, Vācaspati, Udayana, etc. Their approach is partly philosophical, partly historical and philological; their goal is, above all, to contribute to a better understanding of some representative manifestations of traditional Indian self-understanding.

These essays deal with indigenous Indian reflections on the sources, the structure and meaning of the Hindu tradition, and with traditional philosophical responses to social and historical realities. They do not deal with social and historical realities per se. They are, however, based upon the premise that for understanding these "realities," the reflections and "constructions" of traditional Indian theorists are no less significant than the observations and paradigms of modern Western historians and social scientists.

Chapter 1: Notes

1. L. Renou, *Le destin*, 2. Renou's study has been translated into English by D.R. Chanana (*The Destiny of the Veda in India*. Delhi, 1965). This translation is so awkward and unreliable that it seemed advisable to disregard it.

2. Cf. M. Weber, *The Religion of India*, trans. H.H. Gerth and D. Martindale. New York, 1967, 27. The German original quoted by Renou (*Le destin*, 3, n. 3) expresses such "defiance" even more strongly: ". . . der Veda schlägt dem Dharma des Hinduismus geradezu ins Gesicht."

3. *Le destin*, 77.

4. *Le destin*, 3.

5. *Le destin*, 77.

6. See below, chs. 2 and 3 (especially the sections on Bhartṛhari).

7. Cf. J.A.B. van Buitenen, "Akṣara." *Journal of the American Oriental Society* 79 (1959), 176–187.

8. On the history and meaning of the sacred syllable *om*, cf. A. Parpola, "On the Meaning and Etymology of the Sacred Syllable *Ōm*." *Studia Orientalia* 50 (1981; Proceedings of the Nordic South Asia Conference, Helsinki), 195–213; V. Svaminathan, "On Auṃkāra-Maṇḍanamiśra and Śaṅkarācārya." *Journal of Oriental Research* (Madras) 40/41 (1970/72), 105–116.

9. On the definition and analysis of the Veda, see, for instance, Medhātithi on Manu II, 6; Sāyaṇa's introduction to his commentary on the Ṛgveda (together with H. Oertel, *Zur indischen Apologetik*. Stuttgart, 1930); Madhusūdana Sarasvatī, *Prasthānabheda*; Laugākṣi Bhāskara, *Arthasaṃgraha* (with translation and notes by A. B. Gajendragadkar and R.D. Karmarkar, Poona, 1934).

10. Cf. G. Oberhammer, "Die Überlieferungsautorität im Hinduismus." *Offenbarung, geistige Realität des Menschen*. Vienna 1974, 41–92; in the

same work, see also 29–40: J. C. Heesterman, "Die Autorität des Veda."

11. See, for instance, *Bhāgavata Purāṇa* IX, 14, 48: *eka eva purā vedaḥ praṇavaḥ sarvavāṅmayaḥ.*

12. Cf. Bhartṛhari, VP I, 10 (with his own Vṛtti); and below, ch. 3, § 8 f.

13. Cf. Manu II, 76 ff.; III, 75; XII, 99. But see also II, 7, where the epithet *sarvajñānamaya* should be construed with *veda,* not *manu;* cf. A. Wezler, "Manu's Omniscience: The Interpretation of Manusmṛti II, 7"; *Indology and Law* (J.D. M. Derrett Felicitation Vol.), Wiesbaden, 1982, 79–105; specifically 90 ff., on Medhātithi's explanation of the Veda as *sarvajñānamaya.*

14. Cf. *India and Europe,* ch. 17.

15. The Veda itself frequently presents itself as a cosmic or cosmogonic reality. See, for instance, *Ṛgveda* X, 90, 9; for numerous other references, cf. Muir III, 3, ff.

16. Cf. Ch. Malamoud, *Le Svādhyāya.* Paris, 1977.

17. On the Kautsa controversy, cf. Renou, *Le destin,* 68 ff. The most important references are Yāska, *Nirukta* I, 15 f.; Śabara on MS I, 2, 31–53; on Sāyaṇa, cf. H. Oertel, *Zur indischen Apologetik.* Stuttgart, 1930, 15–26; 53–72. See also *Understanding Mantras,* ed. H. P. Alper. Albany, 1988.

18. Cf. the role of the *dhāraṇī* in Tantrism; in various significant ways, the Tantric approach to the reality and real power of words, and their association with cosmogonic events, continues the Vedic tradition.

19. Cf. Renou, *Le destin,* 83; see also 25, n. 8.

20. We should, of course, not forget that the Vedic texts do not necessarily present a full picture of the religious thought and life of the Vedic period. What we tend to regard as "later" elements of Hinduism may, to some extent, have coexisted with what is documented in the Vedic texts.

21. See above, § 1.

22. W. Cantwell Smith, *The Meaning and End of Religion.* New York, 1962, 65.

23. Op. cit., 66. Above and beyond his specific critique of the concept of Hinduism, Smith rejects any attempt to "reify" or "essentialize" the personal faiths of human beings, and he considers the very idea of "religions," and of "religion" itself, as inadequate; see R. D. Baird, *Category Formation and the History of Religions.* The Hague, 1971, 91–106.

24. Cf. H. von Stietencron in: H. Küng and H. von Stietencron, *Christentum und Weltreligionen II: Hinduismus.* Gütersloh, 1987, 25 f.: "Heute weiss man, ohne dies zugeben zu wollen, dass der Hinduismus nichts ist als eine von der europäischen Wissenschaft gezüchtete Orchidee. Sie ist viel zu schön, um sie auszureissen, aber sie ist eine Retortenpflanze. In der Natur gibt es sie nicht." For further valuable and challenging comments on this issue, see H. von Stietencron, "Hinduism: On the Proper Use of a Deceptive Term." *Hinduism Reconsidered,* ed. G. D. Sontheimer and H. Kulke, New Delhi, 1989, 11–27.

25. P. Hacker, *Kl. Schr.*, 480; see also 290, n. 43.

26. Cf. *Kl. Schr.*, 496; 790 (with references to L. Renou).

27. Cf. *India and Europe*, ch. 18 (on Bankim Chandra Chatterji and S. V. Ketkar); see also L. S. Joshi, *A Critique of Hinduism*, trans. G. D. Parikh. Bombay, 1948 (originally published in Marathi, Nagpur, 1940).

28. Cf. *India and Europe*, 341 ff.

29. Cf. *India and Europe*, 341 ff., and below, ch. 3; see also S. Radhakrishnan, *The Hindu View of Life*. London, 1968 (first ed.: 1927).

30. Cf. P. Hacker, *Kl. Schr.*, 790.

31. Cf. D. A. Washbrook, "Progress and Problems: South Asian Economic and Social History c. 1720–1860," *Modern Asian Studies* 22 (1988), 57–96; ibid., 83.

32. Cf. G. G. Raheja, "India: Caste, Kingship, and Dominance Reconsidered." *Annual Review of Anthropology* 17 (1988), 497–523; ibid., 498.

33. Cf. R. Inden, "Orientalist Constructions of India." *Modern Asian Studies* 29 (1986), 401–446; ibid., 402.

34. Cf. J. Rösel, *Die Hinduismusthese Max Webers*. Munich, 1982, 101.

35. E. W. Said, *Orientalism*, New York, 1979, 11.

36. *Orientalism*, 95.

37. *Orientalism*, 96.

38. *Orientalism*, 132.

39. This quote from *The Eighteenth Brumaire of Louis Bonaparte* by K. Marx serves as the motto of Said's book. In Marx's own context, the sentence has no reference to the "Orient."

40. *Orientalism*, 57.

41. Cf. *Orientalism*, 203 (Nietzsche on language and truth); 94 (Foucault's concept of discourse); but see also 23: "Yet unlike Michel Foucault, to whose work I am greatly indebted, I do believe in the determining imprint of individual writers upon the otherwise anonymous collective body of texts constituting a discursive formation like Orientalism."

42. On p. 204, Said himself notes casually that "imperialism, racism, and ethnocentrism," which his book associates very specifically with the *European* phenomenon of "Orientalism," are, in fact, common attributes of the way in which "human societies, at least the more advanced cultures" have dealt with "other" cultures.

43. Cf. R. Inden, "Orientalist Constructions" (see above, n. 33), 440.

44. Ibid., 408.

45. Ibid., 402.

46. Ibid., 445.

47. Ibid., 444; Inden wants "to produce a world that is more egalitarian and multi-centered" (445); this project in itself is obviously rooted in European ideals and ideologies and "Eurocentric" in its own way.

48. The idea of an internal Indian "Orientalism" has, indeed, been suggested by S. Pollock in an unpublished paper on "Deep Orientalism: Sanskrit and Power beyond the Raj."

49. *India and Europe,* 332 f.

50. Cf. *India and Europe,* ch. 18.

51. See above, § 5.

52. For their part, Indian authors have often argued that the Western notion of religion has fundamentally sectarian connotations and corresponds to what has been called *sampradāya* in the Indian tradition; see, for instance, S. V. Ketkar, *An Essay on Hinduism.* London 1911 (reprint Delhi, 1988 under the title: *Hinduism—Its Formation and Future*), 155.

53. Cf. *India and Europe,* ch. 19.

54. Among these authors, Śaṅkara himself has become one of the symbols of the fundamental unity of Hinduism; he appears in this role, perhaps in response to the Islamic challenge, in such works as the *Śaṅkaradigvijaya* by Mādhava-Vidyāraṇya.

55. On the use of the term *bāhya* see, for instance, Medhātithi on Manu II, 6 (ed. J. H. Dave, Bombay 1972 ff., 168); on the distinction between *nāstika* and *āstika,* see *India and Europe,* ch. 19.

CHAPTER 2

The Presence of the Veda in Indian Philosophical Reflection

Apologetics and Exegesis in the "Orthodox" Systems

1. The distinction between "orthodox" (*āstika*) and "heterodox" (*nāstika*) systems is among the most basic and familiar features of the Indian philosophical tradition. It is as common in traditional Indian doxographies as it is in modern surveys of Indian philosophy. Six or more "orthodox" systems of Hinduism are usually contrasted with the "heterodox" teachings of the Buddhists, Jainas, and Materialists.[1]

Among the criteria of Hindu "orthodoxy," recognition of the validity and authority of the Veda is by far the most significant one. However, within this "orthodox" domain of acceptance of the Vedic revelation, or at least the nonrejection of it, there is much room for variations. On the one hand, there is an intense apologetic and exegetic commitment to the Veda; on the other hand, there are very loose and casual references, or mere avoidance of obvious contradictions, even explicit disregard for the Veda. The positions of classical Sāṃkhya and Yoga, Nyāya and Vaiśeṣika, Pūrvamīmāṃsā and Uttaramīmāṃsā (i.e., Vedānta), as well as the numerous systems of theistic thought, in particular Vaiṣṇava Vedānta, illustrate the wide range of attitudes towards the Veda in traditional and orthodox Hindu philosophy.

The traditions of Nyāya and Vaiśeṣika on the one hand, and of Mīmāṃsā on the other hand, are of special and exemplary significance. In a learned and useful investigation, G. Chemparathy has compared and contrasted the role of the Veda in these systems.[2] He has characterized the basic differences as follows: The traditions of Pūrvamīmāṃsā and Uttaramīmāṃsā emanate from the Vedic tradition itself, and have developed "in dependence on the Veda" ("en dépendance du Veda").[3] Nyāya and Vaiśeṣika, on the other hand, were not originally and genuinely affiliated with the Veda. They recognized the Veda as a "source of knowledge" (*pramāṇa*), and committed themselves to its defense, in a retroactive manner, after they had established themselves as philosophical systems. "Pour les premiers systèmes, le Veda était la base même de leur spéculation; alors que pour les derniers, le Veda n'était qu'un des moyens de connaissance valide."[4] Furthermore, and in accordance with their different genealogies, Nyāya and Vaiśeṣika are primarily concerned with apologetics, while Mīmāṃsā and Vedānta are genuinely exegetic traditions.

Chemparathy notes that this characterization agrees with the self-understanding of classical Nyāya. Jayantabhaṭṭa states that the Mīmāṃsā is not a science of the *validity* of the Veda (*pramāṇavidyā*), but only an exegetic discipline, a science of the meaning of Vedic sentences (*vākyārthavidyā*), and that its references to the problem of the validity of the Veda (*vedaprāmāṇya*) are derivative and secondary (*ānuṣaṅgika*).[5] With this demarcation against the Mīmāṃsā, the Nyāya asserts its own special role and relevance as an orthodox system. It claims for itself a part in the defense and maintenance of the Vedic tradition which is more fundamental than mere exegesis.

It is obvious that the Nyāya system thus assumes a role for which it was not originally designed. It puts concepts and methods of thought that have no special and authentic association with the Veda into the service of Vedic apologetics. It attempts to establish and clarify the superhuman Vedic revelation by relying on extra-Vedic sources, "merely human" means and methods of thought and argumentation. As is well known, its basic assumption is that the Veda is the reliable word of God (*īśvara*), and that such reliability can be supported by generally accepted "means of knowledge" (*pramāṇa*).[6] By committing itself to the authority of the Veda, and by assuming apologetic responsibilities, the Nyāya system detaches itself from all traditions of merely "worldly" thought and argumentation (*yukti, tarka, ānvīkṣikī*). The Nyāya itself is *ānvīkṣikī*, "investigative science" and "reasoning"; but it is also *ātmavidyā*, "science of the self" that is based upon the Veda and committed to soteriological goals. Numerous explicit statements in the *Nyāyabhāṣya* by Vātsyāyana Pakṣilasvāmin and other texts exemplify this self-understanding and self-definition of classical Nyāya.[7]

2. Within the context of this presentation, there is no need for a detailed discussion of Nyāya and Vaiśeṣika apologetics, or for an analysis of their arguments concerning the authority of the Veda. We may limit ourselves to a few basic reminders, and, for further details, refer to Chemparathy's survey.

It is first of all the alleged analogy of the Veda with the *āyurveda*, the medical science, that characterizes Nyāya apologetics. It presupposes that God is the author of the Veda as well as of the original *āyurveda* teachings. The truth and effectiveness of the divine teachings, which appear in the *āyurveda*, is supported by empirical evidence. Since the Vedic texts are by the same divine author, analogical reasoning leads us to the conclusion that their ritual and soteriological teachings, even though they cannot be verified empirically, are also true, effective, and beneficial. In this connection, the Nyāya develops a tradition of "proving" the existence and goodness of God, which culminates in the work of Udayana.[8]

After the period of Uddyotakara, most conspicuously in Vācaspatimiśra, another argument for the validity of the Veda becomes more important and prominent—the argument that it has been accepted by "great" or exemplary people (*mahājanaparigraha*).[9] Since *mahājana* may also be read in the sense of *bahujana*, "many people," this argument amounts basically to an invocation of the views of the factual majority of (Indian) people, that is, those who are committed to the *varṇāśramadharma*.[10] Udayana tries to avoid the potential circularity, as well as the conventionalism, inherent in this reference to the "great" or "many people." He redefines *mahājana* as *sarvadarśanāntaḥpātipuruṣa*, "persons belonging to all systems," that is, in a sense which postulates an "acceptance" of the Veda even by its opponents. Followers of all religious and philosophical schools in India recognize certain Vedic premises, though implicitly and unknowingly. Even the Buddhists fall within the range of that totality of systems (*sarvadarśana*) which is ultimately dependent upon the Veda: the Veda is valid insofar as it is the origin and framework of the entire Indian tradition, the condition of its possibility.[11] For this line of reasoning, Udayana had predecessors in Nyāya as well as in Mīmāṃsā. Above all, we have to mention the name of Kumārila.[12]

Apart from the existence of God, the following "Vedic" themes and teachings are especially conspicuous in Nyāya apologetics: the existence of the *ātman*, for which the Nyāya also tries to provide independent, extra-Vedic proof, the "order of castes and stages of life" (*varṇāśramadharma*), and the efficacy and legitimacy of the Vedic rituals, which have to be defended "rationally" against criticism from the Buddhists and other groups.[13]

The Nyāya defends the Veda from a certain distance. It does not try to find its means and methods or its origin within the Veda. In spite of Udayana's reference to the Veda as the framework and basis of the entire Indian tradition, the Nyāya does not normally present itself as a "real extension" of the Veda.

3. To be sure, the Nyāya does not presume to ratify or rediscover through its own methods the specific norms and regulations of the *varṇāśramadharma*. It does not try to establish or reestablish that or why the brahmin should not drink wine.[14] As far as such special dharmic obligations and prohibitions are concerned, the Nyāya, just as the Mīmāṃsā, regards the Vedic tradition as the sole authority. What it tries to establish rationally and empirically is the framework of the *varṇāśramadharma* and the fundamental reliability of its source, the Veda. It invokes the doctrine of real universals in support of the *varṇa* system. It tries to demonstrate that the arguments against Vedic ritualism are inconclusive, and that the efficacy of the rituals cannot be disproven. It presents, above all, the existence of God (*īśvara*) and the soul (*ātman*) as truths within the reach of inferential reasoning (*anumāna*). Those who deny the existence of the soul are not so much in conflict with the sacred texts as with the verdict of reason that provides this scriptural truth with an endorsement and definitive "ratification" (*pratisandhāna*).[15] In other cases, the scriptural indications are ambiguous, even contradictory, and it is inference alone that can bring about a conclusion. As an example, we may mention the much-debated issue of the eternity or noneternity of meaningful "sound" (*śabda*); according to Vācaspati, both views can adduce the testimony of Vedic passages.[16]

Referring to Vātsyāyana Pakṣilasvāmin's concordance between the "means of knowledge" (*pramāṇa*) and the "members" (*avayava*) of the "fivefold syllogism," Vācaspati also remarks that the sacred Vedic tradition (*āgama*) in general functions as a "thesis" (*pratijñā*), for which the orthodox Nyāya ought to provide valid argumentation and inferential proof.[17] In assuming this role, the Nyāya asserts its orthodoxy as well as its own accomplishments and its identity as *ānvīkṣikī*. The ideal situation is, of course, the full concurrence of sacred tradition and inference (*āgamānumānayoḥ sahakāritā*). Udayana's *Pariśuddhi* illustrates this by correlating a series of scriptural passages, mostly from the Upaniṣads, with basic Nyāya teachings.[18]

The Nyāya tries to establish itself as a soteriologically relevant science of the self (*ātmavidyā, adhyātmavidyā*), that is at the same time an analytical, investigative science (*ānvīkṣikī*); it tries to integrate both roles into that of an *ānvīkṣiky ātmavidyā*.[19] It provides the Vedic truths with a dimension which they do not have simply as parts of the Vedic tradition, that is, with the element of analysis and reflection. It accepts, even proclaims the notion that argumentation, analysis and reflection should be conducive to the "human goal" (*puruṣārtha*) of liberation; but it also assumes and proclaims that the attainment, even the very idea of such a goal depends upon reflection and examination. As Udayana says, it would not be possible for a "human goal" to be what it is without being achieved through a "means of knowledge" (*pramāṇa*). Moreover, "since all purposes of prudent people are based upon means of knowledge, which have to be accounted for by the analytical science (*ānvīkṣikī*), therefore, there can, indeed, be no suspicion that final liberation, which is the ultimate human goal, would not conform to the condition of having this basis; for if it would not have this basis, it would, as an undesirable consequence, lose its status as a human goal." (*na hy asti sambhavaḥ puruṣārthaś ca-apramāṇahetukaś ca-iti . . . yataḥ sarvaṃ prekṣāvatprayojanam ānvīkṣikīvyutpādyapramāṇamūlam, ato niḥśreyasasya paramapuruṣārthasya tanmūlatāyāṃ viparyayaśaṅkā-eva na-asti, atanmūlatve puruṣārthatvahāniprasaṅgād iti*).[20]

4. Udayana's statement on the relationship between *puruṣārtha* and *ānvīkṣikī* draws a subtle, yet radical conclusion from ideas that have been associated with *ānvīkṣikī* since ancient times. In the introduction to his *Arthaśāstra*, Kauṭilya cites a verse that is obviously taken from an older source: "The analytical science has always been considered as a source of light for all sciences, a tool for all activities, a foundation for all religious and social norms" (*pradīpaḥ sarvavidyānām, upāyaḥ sarvakarmaṇām / āśrayaḥ sarvadharmāṇāṃ śaśvad ānvīkṣikī matā*). It is well known "that the verse quoted by Kauṭilya appears also, with a variant appropriate to the new context, in the *Nyāyabhāṣya* by Vātsyāyana Pakṣilavāmin," and that the Nyāya itself is presented as the fulfillment of the idea of *ānvīkṣikī*. Vātsyāyana and his commentator Uddyotakara "define ānvīkṣikī as an 'investigative,' 'reflective' science which reconsiders, re-examines what has been grasped through sense-perception and sacred tradition, and which applies valid criteria (*pratyakṣāgamābhyām īkṣitasya-arthasya-anvīkṣaṇam; pramāṇair arthaparīkṣaṇam*), and they assert that without its peculiar discipline of reasoning and argumentation the Nyāya would not be different from the Vedic-Upaniṣadic 'science of the (supreme) self' (*ātmavidyā, adhyātmavidyā*)."[21]

The "investigative," "analytical" science accompanies and enhances all other sciences, including the threefold Vedic science (*trayī*); they have to be explained, clarified, and accounted for by means of *ānvīkṣikī*. It is once again Udayana who provides the most intriguing articulation and interpretation of this idea: "Although the reliance on the means of knowledge is the same (in *ānvīkṣikī* and the other sciences), . . . these (other sciences) rely on the means of knowledge as something to be accounted for by it (i.e., *ānvīkṣikī*), but this does not likewise (rely on the means of knowledge) as something to be accounted for by those (other sciences)" (*pramāṇopajīvane samāne 'pi . . . etadvyutpādyam upajīvanti tāḥ, na-evam tadvyutpādyam iyam api*).[22]

On the other hand, Udayana emphasizes that the Veda is by no means dispensable for the Naiyāyika. The "concordance with the sacred tradition" (*āgamāvirodha*) legitimizes the inferential knowledge of the self, etc.; there is no purely secular "science of the self" that could be pursued by anybody regardless of his access and commitment to the Veda. To be sure, a śūdra, who is by definition excluded from the study of the Veda, may be as qualified to use sense-perception and inference as a brahmin. But since he does not have access to the Veda, he cannot achieve the "ascertainment of concordance" (*avirodhaniścaya*) between inference and the sacred texts; therefore, he is "unqualified" (*anadhikṛta*) for the study of the Nyāya.[23] For a proper assessment of the role and limits of critical reflection in the Nyāya system, we should also recall its tendency to include itself in a timeless framework of traditional knowledge. According to Jayantabhaṭṭa, all legitimate branches of traditional learning (*vidyā*), including such sciences as grammar, Mīmāṃsā and Nyāya, are coeval with the Veda itself; that is, they have been in existence since the beginning of the world (*ādisargāt prabhṛti*).[24] In this sense, the Nyāya, though not a part or "real extension" of the Veda, is firmly embedded in that traditional framework of which the Veda is the center and prototype.

5. The Nyāya does not try to compete with the Mīmāṃsā in the technical field of Vedic exegesis. It does not engage in a specialized investigation of Vedic words and sentences. It accepts the Veda as a source for our knowledge about the ātman, the hereafter, the validity of rituals and soteriological striving, and, above all, as the basis of the *varṇāśramadharma*. Recognition and defense of this dharma, the social status quo, the ritual norms of the Āryan, is an essential aspect of Nyāya and Vaiśeṣika apologetics. As far as the contents of dharma are concerned, and the special norms which it implies, Nyāya and Vaiśeṣika adopt the views of the orthodox Dharmaśāstra tradition. They do not question or examine these views measuring them against their alleged Vedic sources; nor do they try to justify or criticize them in the name of reason. There are, however, attempts to explain and legitimize the most basic conceptual premises of the varnāśramadharma by including them, and trying to account for them, in the framework of the Nyāya and Vaiśeṣika system of categories. In particular, the theory of real universals (*sāmānya, jāti*) serves to explain and support the system of four main castes (varṇa). The concepts of dharma and adharma themselves appear under the title adṛṣta in the list of "qualities" (*guṇa*), i.e. as instances of the second "category" (*padārtha*) of the classical Vaiśeṣika system of Praśastapāda.[25] They are, however, absent from the older list of seventeen "qualities" found in the *Vaiśeṣikasūtra*. This retroactive addition illustrates how teachings which are not inherently affiliated with the "Vedic," or "Vedicizing," traditions, and are at least potentially neutral, serve an increasingly apologetic function.

In the history of Mīmāṃsā, the development seems to have been the reverse. A genuinely and originally exegetic and text-oriented tradition opens itself increasingly to epistemology and logic, and to inherently "neutral" and universal methods of thought and argumentation. In its origins, the Mīmāṃsā is inseparable from the Vedic "auxiliary sciences" (*vedāṅga*), specifically the Kalpasūtras, and its initial role is a strictly "intra-Vedic" one. From these origins, it proceeds into the open forum of philosophical argumentation and debate. Its gradual adoption and reconstruction of the doctrine of "means of knowledge" (*pramāṇa*) provides the most significant illustration of this process of philosophical reconception and universalization, and of the concurrent amalgamation of philosophy and exegesis. The very modest beginnings we find in the Sūtras of Jaimini are systematically expanded and developed first of all by the Vṛttikāra and Śabara, and subsequently by the great commentators of Śabara. The central and symptomatic notions of the "self-evidence" or "self-sufficient validity" (*svataḥprāmāṇya*) of valid cognition and of the "authorlessness" (*apauruṣeyatva*) and "eternity" (*nityatva*) of the Veda, are presented in an increasingly articulate and elaborate manner.[26]

The contributions which Kumārila, Prabhākara and Maṇḍana, as well as Śaṇkara and other leading exponents of Advaita Vedānta, have made to these developments are among the most significant and challenging episodes in the history of Indian philosophy.

The Definition of the Veda and the Status of the Mīmāṃsā

6. Regardless of the differences between Nyāya apologetics and Mīmāṃsā exegesis, the Mīmaṃsā, too, does not try to find its own peculiar methods and teachings in the Veda. Although it assumes a very intimate association with the Veda, it does not claim Vedic, i.e. "revealed," status for itself. According to Kumārila, the Mīmāṃsā is a "constellation of rules and arguments" (*yuktikalāpa*) that has been produced by a long tradition of human thought and teaching; in this respect, it is basically comparable with the "extended Nyāya" (*nyāyavistara*).[27] Likewise, Śabara, Kumārila, and Prabhākara do not try to derive their teachings on epistemology, ontology, categoriology, and the philosophy of language from the Veda. The Vedic revelation does not provide any help when it comes to arguing and debating about such matters. The Veda reveals the dharma; it does not reveal the factual nature of the world, nor does it teach the proper rules and methods of human argumentation.

All knowledge about dharma, the ritual norms and duties, is ultimately obtained from the Veda. The Veda alone has absolute, unconditional authority in this respect. This is the basic premise of the exegetic enterprise that the Mīmāṃsā pursues in extraordinary breadth and detail. It is, however, also a premise for apologetics; exegesis and apologetics can hardly be separated in this case. Relegating the dharma radically and exclusively to the Veda, yet trying to justify such relegation through argumentation and reasoning: this is the basic apologetic procedure of the Mīmāṃsā. The knowledge of dharma may be *vedamūla*, "based upon the Veda"; but the insight that this is so is supposed to be *nyāyamūla*, "based upon reason."[28] Reasoning is used to remove the dharma from the domain of reasoning, and to safeguard it against rational and empirical critique. In this respect, the apologetic dimension, that is, the establishment of the irrefutability and validity of the Veda, is by no means secondary (*ānuṣaṅgika*),[29] instead, it appears as the condition of the possibility of legitimate exegesis. For leading thinkers, such as Kumārila, apologetics in this sense takes clear priority over all specific exegesis.

Chemparathy notes correctly that the Mīmāṃsā tradition of exegesis has developed "in dependence on the Veda"[30] and has not been attached to it in a secondary and retroactive manner. Does this mean that the Mīmāṃsā is a genuine continuation and emanation, a "real extension," of the Vedic world? In spite of the roots of the Mīmāṃsā in the tradition of Vedic "auxiliary sciences" (*vedāṅga*), the answer has to be negative in the following sense: The Mimāṃsā is not, not even in its own self-understanding, an expression or manifestation of Vedic thought and life. Rather, it deals with the Veda, or a certain idea of the Veda, in a retrospective, objectifying manner. It uses the idea of the Veda for ideological purposes, and invokes this idea in order to uphold certain social and religious constellations, specifically the *varṇāśramadharma* and the identity of the Āryan tradition, in an era of philosophical argumentation. On the other hand, it uses philosophical argumentation to support its idea of the Veda. What then is the relationship between philosophy and Vedic exegesis and apologetics in the Mīmāṃsā? How genuine, or how vicarious, is its interest in philosophy? How serious is its commitment to truth? To what extent does it produce philosophical arguments, concepts, and theories ad hoc and merely for strategic purposes?[31] To what extent has it succeeded in integrating philosophy and exegesis? Does its conception of the Veda itself have genuinely philosophical implications?

7. Kumārila is the most important representative of classical Mīmāṃsā thought and apologetics, as well as the most effective advocate of Āryan and brahminical identity. He uses the philosophy of his time, such as Nyāya, Vaiśeṣika, and the philosophy of grammar, adopts what is suitable to his purposes, and modifies and expands it in accordance with the requirements of apologetics.[32] Are his epistemology, ontology, philosophy of language, etc., projections of brahminical ideology? Or do they present us with genuine philosophy in the guise of apologetics and ideology? Does Kumārila's philosophy play a merely secondary, instrumental role for the defense of the Veda and the *dharma*, or is his Vedic apologetics just an arena for the pursuit of truly philosophical questions?

A nonambiguous answer may neither be possible nor called for in this case. Regardless of Kumārila's apologetic motivation, his conceptual ability and commitment are obvious from his writings. Exegesis and apologetics become vehicles of radical philosophical reflection. The Veda itself is invoked and projected as a response to fundamental problems of epistemology, semantics, ethics, etc., and to questions concerning the limits of rationality and philosophy itself. This is true not only for Kumārila, but also for Prabhākara and Maṇḍana, as well as for the great commentators of Prabhākara and Kumārila, above all Śālikanātha and Pārthasārathi.

The following examples may illustrate the connection and integration of philosophy and exegesis. The theory of *svataḥprāmāṇya*, the "self-sufficient validity," "self-validating authority" of valid, specifically Vedic, cognition, is obviously motivated by apologetic concerns; yet it also makes a genuine contribution to the epistemological debate of its time and beyond.[33] Such concepts as *bhāvanā, vidhi*, and *niyoga* all deal primarily with the causal and motivating power of the Vedic word, and with the sense of obligation arising out of the commitment to the Veda; but they also refer to problems concerning ethics, the causality of human actions, and the motivating power of language in a far more general sense.[34] This is expanded upon further in the debates between the schools of Prabhākara and Kumārila about an unconditional, "categorical" commitment to "what ought to be done" (*kārya*), that is, primarily ritual duty, and the instrumental, "hypothetical" role of actions as "means to reach desired ends" (*iṣṭasādhanatā, abhimatasādhanatā*).[35] In the philosophy of language, the competing theories of *abhihitānvayavāda* (which emphasizes the semantic primacy of the word) and *anvayābhidhānavāda* (which takes the sentence as the fundamental semantic unit and is inseparable from Prabhākara's view that the prototypical rank of the Vedic language is manifested by its indivisible, unconditional injunctions) reflect different premises of Vedic exegesis; beyond that, they also deal with general problems and possibilities of semantic theory and linguistic analysis.[36] Likewise, in the field of ontology, the different explanations of "being" are associated with exegetic positions. While Kumārila adopts and modifies the Vaiśeṣika notion of the highest universal *sattā*, Prabhākara and Śālikanātha explain it as *pramāṇasambandhayogyatā*, "suitability for being connected with valid cognition," in order to accommodate *kārya*, "the ought," as a reality sui generis. Maṇḍana, who rejects Prabhākara's *kārya* and wants to support his own interpretation of the nature of *vidhi*, "injunctions," proposes *vartamānatā*, "being present," or *vartamānakālasambandhitva*, "connectedness with the present time."[37] Yet, at the same time, these definitions are contributions to the general ontological debate. As such, they have been recognized not only within the Mīmāṃsā, but also in the wider arena of Indian philosophical debates.

8. Unlike the Nyāya and Vaiśeṣika, the Mīmāṃsā does not have to assert and defend its alliance with the Veda. Its genuine affiliation with, and commitment to, the Veda are generally accepted. There is even a familiar notion that the Mīmāṃsā is included in the Veda and may itself be referred to by the term "Veda." This is, for instance, documented in Jayanta's *Nyāyamañjarī*. Discussing the status of the Vedic "auxiliary sciences" (*vedāṅga*), Jayanta states that the Mīmāṃsā cannot be regarded as a separate *vedāṅga*, since it is, by virtue of its special proximity, a section of the Veda itself (*pratyāsannatvena vedaikadeśabhūtatvāt*).[38] Prior to this statement, Jayanta cites a verse that he ascribes to the "Bhaṭṭa" and that is probably taken from Kumārila's lost *Bṛhaṭṭīkā*; the verse, which appears also in Śālikanātha's *Prakaraṇapañcikā* and Vācaspati's *Nyāyavārttikatātparyaṭīkā*,[39] describes the Mīmāṃsā as a Vedic supplement designed to complete the scriptural injunctions with regard to their specific "modes of operation" (*itikartavyatā*). Nonetheless, the Mīmāṃsā is then also listed as one of the fourteen traditional branches of learning (*vidyā*).[40]

Another verse quoted in Vācaspati's *Tātparyaṭīkā*, possibly also from Kumārila's *Bṛhaṭṭīkā*, states that "the reasoning which is called *mīmāṃsā* is derived from the Veda in its entirety. Therefore, it is (of the nature of the) Veda, comparable to the saltiness of a piece of wood extracted from a salt mine" (*mīmāṃsāsaṃjñakas tarkaḥ sarvavedasamudbhavaḥ/ so 'to vedo rumāprāptakāṣṭhādilavaṇātmavat*).[41] In the relevant section of his *Pariśuddhi*, Udayana refers to "the opinion that the Mīmāṃsā is not separate from the Veda" (*mīmāṃsāyā vedād abhedavādaḥ*).[42]

9. According to Pāraskara's *Gṛhyasūtra*, the Veda comprises *vidhi, vidheya*, and *tarka* (*vidhir vidheyas tarkaś ca vedaḥ*).[43] There is widespread, though not complete agreement among the interpreters of this statement that *vidhi* refers to the Brāhmaṇas, specifically the injunctions contained therein, and *vidheya* to the Mantras.[44] There is, however, much less agreement on the meaning of *tarka*. Although Pāraskara's commentators generally prefer to explain it as *arthavāda*, they also know and mention its interpretation as *mīmāṃsā*, which is, indeed, well documented outside of the *Gṛhyasūtra* tradition.

Bhartṛhari's autocommentary on the first part of the *Vākyapadīya* is among the many texts that cite Pāraskara's definition.[45] Without considering alternatives, Vṛṣabhadeva's *Paddhati* simply paraphrases tarka as *mīmāṃsā*.[46] Kumārila also cites Pāraskara and says that, according to this definition, the Mīmāṃsā itself, being essentially a summary of all Vedic reasoning (*samastavaidikatarkopasaṃhārātmikā*), can be referred to by the word *veda* (*mīmāṃsā-api vedaśabdavācyā bhavati*).[47] However, he adds that this does not give the Mīmāṃsā a truly Vedic status, that is, a status comparable to that of the Mantras and Brāhmaṇas. Likewise, the *Kalpasūtras*, which Kumārila discusses at length, should not be considered as Vedic, that is, as being included in the Veda itself.[48]

The Kalpasūtras as well as the Mīmāṃsā are of human origin, products of human thought about the Veda—extracts, explications, restatements and extrapolations—but not parts or emanations of the eternal, authorless Veda itself. To be sure, the Mīmāṃsā is such an extensive and complex "constellation of rules and arguments" (*yuktikalāpa*) that it could not have been produced by one single author. It presupposes an ancient tradition which goes back to time immemorial. Yet it proceeds from a "worldly" basis, from the successive and continuous efforts of lineages of scholars who used their worldly means of knowledge, such as perception and inference.[49] Kumārila's commentator Someśvara, by the way, paraphrases Pāraskara's *tarka* as *upaniṣad*, thus discarding the idea that the Mīmāṃsā might be included in the definition of the Veda.[50]

For Kumārila and his followers, there is no compromise and no transition between the eternal and authorless language of the Veda, and the expressions of human reasoning, even if it is reasoning about the Veda itself. Unlike Bhartṛhari,[51] they do not recognize a dynamic extension of the Veda into the world of human speech and thought. Insofar as it is the result of human reasoning, the Mīmāṃsā is neither a part, nor is it an emanation of the Veda. It may be allied with and committed to the Veda. Yet, it also keeps its distance, and claims, in a sense, its sovereignty vis-à-vis the Veda.

Human Reason and the Authority of the Veda

10. At this point, we may recall Śaṅkara's critique of the Mīmāṃsā, specifically of its views on the relationship between reason and Vedic revelation.[52] According to Śaṅkara, the Pūrvamīmāṃsā misunderstands the nature and origin of what it presents as its own metaphysical discoveries, and adopts false ideas concerning the potential sovereignty of human cognition. In this respect, it is not different from the Nyāya. Both of them reflect on Vedic themes and truths, but they miss the meaning of the Veda as well as the meaning of their own efforts. They fail to see to what extent the insights for which they claim credit have been received from the Veda, and to what degree their reasoning and reflection needs to be guided by the Veda.

In various sections of his works, most memorably in his commentary on the *Bṛhadāraṇyaka Upaniṣad*, Śaṅkara criticizes the Mīmāṃsakas as well as the Naiyāyikas (whom he calls *tārkika*) for their false reliance on human reasoning. Both of them imagine that insights such as that into the existence of the ātman, which have been derived from Vedic references, are accomplishments of their own worldly intelligence (*svamatiprabhava*).[53] They rely on the "power of their own thought" (*svacittasāmarthya*) and "follow the (deceptive) skills of their own intellects" (*svabuddhikauśalānusārin*), but not the "path which has been shown by revelation and authoritative teachers" (*śrutyācāryadarśitamārga*).[54] In the sections on Sāṃkhya and Yoga within his *Brahmasūtrabhāṣya*, Śaṅkara develops his critique of the false claims of autonomous human cognition in greater detail, and he exemplifies his own understanding of the relationship between reason and revelation.[55]

According to Śaṅkara, Vedic revelation cannot be restricted to a special and limited domain, outside of which human reason and experience would have their full sovereignty. In the view of Pūrvamīmāṃsā, the Veda has absolute authority with reference to the "deontological" sphere of *dharma*. Here, human reason has no mandate whatsoever. But it does not exercise such authority, as far as merely factual, even metaphysical matters are concerned. Here, human thought is basically on its own. Śaṅkara accepts that the Veda reveals the dharma; but it also reveals brahman, the ultimate essence and origin of the world. This means that, according to Śaṅkara, there is no realm of merely factual truth that would be entirely excluded from the jurisdiction of the Veda. And there is no metaphysically valid and soteriologically significant knowledge that would not require the light and guidance of the Veda. The Veda provides human thought with valid archetypes and with a goal and direction. It is an objective epiphany, a sun which shines upon reality and appearance.[56] Human insight, human access to ultimate truth, is rendered possible by the Veda. It has to accept itself, its own validity and legitimacy, as a gift of the Veda.[57]

11. With this radical commitment to Vedic revelation, Śaṅkara withdraws ultimately from the open arena of philosophical debate, which the philosophers of the Pūrvamīmāṃsā, in particular, Kumārila, had entered so resolutely. As a matter of fact, the role of Kumārila in this arena, specifically in the debates with Buddhism and Nyāya-Vaiśeṣika, is much more conspicuous than that of Śaṅkara.

Although Kumārila defends the Vedic dharma by presenting it as a domain inaccessible to common experience and argumentation, he does so in a language which is meant to be fully accessible to those with whom he disagrees. He stays within the sphere of human communication and interaction (*vyavahāra*) which he shares with his opponents. Śaṅkara, on the other hand, does not commit himself to this sphere; and his radical nondualism, which he derives from the Veda, ultimately supersedes and annuls the entire context of innerworldly, intersubjective communication. The readiness to transcend the realm of *vyavahāra*, of worldly practice and orientation, and to discontinue any kind of communication and debate which is committed to this realm is an integral part of Śaṅkara's Vedic self-understanding.[58] From this entire sphere, he may withdraw into the nondual certainty of his knowledge of brahman; it provides him with a "secure fortress" (*abhayaṃ durgam*) to which the "reasoners" and "dialecticians" (*tārkika*) who are "without the grace of the sacred texts and authoritative teachers" (*guruśāstraprasādarahita*) will never gain access.[59] Śaṅkara's way of finding patterns of valid reasoning in the Veda itself, specifically in the Upaniṣads, exemplifies his own reflection on the relationship between reason and revelation. Yet, as we have seen, the inclusion of tarka in the Veda, or its derivation from the Veda, has a certain tradition.[60] In addition to our earlier references, we may mention the idea of an *ānvīkṣikī parā*, which occurs in the Mahābhārata, that is, the idea of a "supreme reasoning" that is contained in, and can be extracted from, the Upaniṣads.[61] An appendix (*pariśiṣṭa*) to Yāska's *Nirukta* states that the gods themselves provided post-Vedic men with tarka, in order to replace the Vedic *ṛṣi* and his visionary abilities (*tarkam ṛṣiṃ prāyacchan*).[62]

However, nobody among Śaṅkara's predecessors in this field has made more suggestive and significant contributions than Bhartṛhari, who has, moreover, produced a much more comprehensive and systematic metaphysics of the Vedic word (and of language in general) than Śaṅkara himself.

12. Unlike Kumārila, Bhartṛhari does not draw a strict border between the uncreated Veda and the traditions of human thought and exegesis. And unlike Śaṅkara, he does not postulate a radical dichotomy between absolute and relative, empirical-practical truth (i.e., *paramārtha* and *vyavahāra*). Bhartṛhari's Veda is brahman's unfolding into the world; it extends into the social and natural world as its underlying structure and basis. The Veda itself is a dynamic process, initiating its own division into different parts, branches, and recensions; this process of differentiation and expansion is continued and extrapolated in the work of human exegesis. Not only the "seers" (*ṛṣi*) who manifest the Vedic texts, but also their exegetes and interpreters, are agents and instruments of the self-manifestation, self-differentiation and self-explication (*vivarta*) of the absolute "word-brahman" (*śabdabrahman*). The different interpretations of the Vedic texts, in particular of the *arthavādas* and Upaniṣads, form the basis and starting point for the different philosophical systems of the monists, dualists, etc.[63] These teachings are not only more or less adequate statements about the Vedic brahman, but also further manifestations and differentiations of its potential. Both the expanded Veda itself, and the traditions of thought and exegesis which are rooted in it, are expressions of the "principle of the word" (*śabdatattva*), the *akṣara* which is celebrated in the introductory verses of the *Vākyapadīya*.[64] Due to its inherent powers (*śakti*), this one and undivided principle projects itself into the world of multiplicity and separation (*pṛthaktva*); and the primeval "seers" who divide the Veda into its basic "paths" and "branches," as well as the authors of subsequent traditions of *smṛti* and exegesis,[65] carry out and continue what is inherent in brahman itself. As such, they are not only speakers about, but agents and representatives of the reality of the Vedic word, and they are participants in cosmic and cosmogonic processes. The Veda, in whose manifestation they participate, is not just a text *about* brahman, but its actual "imitation" and representation (*anukāra*).[66]

The language which is prototypically present in the Vedic revelation, as well as the world of meanings which go with it, is the condition of the possibility of human thought and insight. Thinking and reasoning (*tarka*) have to be supported and upheld by the Vedic tradition. They are "permeated" (*anuviddha*)[67] by the Vedic words; legitimate human reasoning is ultimately nothing but the "power" and manifestation of these words (*śabdānām eva sā śaktis tarko yaḥ puruṣāśrayaḥ*).[68] It provides insight only if it is in accordance with the Vedic teachings (*vedaśāstrāvirodhin*).[69] Any kind of reasoning which tries to deny or disregard its Vedic roots and conditions can only be "dry," fruitless reasoning (*śuṣkatarka*). A few centuries later, Śaṅkara himself uses this term in his own way.[70]

13. In dealing with the Veda, Bhartṛhari and the great thinkers of the Pūrva- and Uttaramīmāṃsā articulate genuine philosophical concerns. The idea of the Veda is the vehicle of intense reflection on fundamental problems concerning human thought and action. They invoke this idea as a response to epistemological problems, and to the dangers of religious and ethical pluralism and relativism. Bhartṛhari and Śaṅkara are aware of the instability of human reason; they know to what extent it can be used and misused as a mere instrument. Kumārila has a keen sense of the problems of ethical relativism.[71] Prabhākara's concept of *kārya* exposes crucial questions concerning human action and motivation.

Why did they not face and articulate these problems as such, instead of relegating the answer to a particular text, the Veda? Their reliance on the Veda may be associated with a genuine sense of the limits of human thought and understanding, an awareness of the confusions, the aporias, and the existential and spiritual vacuum human reasoning may produce. Yet the question remains: Why did they rely on the Veda, and only on the Veda? Why not on any other kind of "revelation"? Why did they not simply recognize the need for "revelation," or "objective epiphany," as such and in general? Are there any truly philosophical reasons, apart from cultural, psychological and ideological motivations? Even within its historical and cultural context, the orthodox decision for the Veda has been problematic and controversial. There have been great advocates of other, extra-Vedic revelations. Abhinavagupta's reliance on the Śaivite Āgamas is certainly as much motivated by philosophical concerns and accompanied by reflection on the conditions of human thought as Śaṅkara's decision to rely on the Veda.[72] And, according to its Buddhist critics, the "light of the Veda" is in reality no light at all, but utter darkness.[73]

What then is the connection between the Veda and Indian philosophical reflection? Is the "Veda of the philosophers" essentially a fiction and projection? Is there any significant connection between the "Veda itself" and the notion of the Veda in later epistemological reflection? Is the "Veda itself," the "real" Veda, a real and essential source of classical Indian philosophy?

14. The Veda itself does not teach a coherent philosophical doctrine; it does not contain a system. It addresses few, if any, of the more specific questions and concerns of the philosophical systems. There are, of course, important doctrinal correspondences and obvious historical continuities between Vedic-Upaniṣadic thought and the teachings of Advaita Vedānta and other schools of Hindu philosophy. There are patterns of Vedic mythology, such as its recurrent schemes of immanence-in-transcendence, or of unity-in-diversity, which have become precedents and presuppositions of philosophical thinking. There are, above all, those elusive, yet distinctive and suggestive teachings concerning ātman and brahman which thinkers such as Bhartṛhari and Śaṅkara tried to recover as an anticipation of their own thinking and as a primeval response to the Buddhist challenge.[74] But regardless of the extent and nature of these correspondences and continuities, they cannot account for the later philosophical usages and retrospective conceptualizations of the Veda. They cannot explain or justify the way in which the entire Veda, that is, the collection of Mantras, Brāhmaṇas, Āraṅyakas and Upaniṣads, has been presented as a "source of knowledge" (*pramāṇa*), as one meaningful revelation, and as the final standard for philosophy itself.

The Veda in this comprehensive sense contains a multitude of different, apparently incompatible layers and sections. It contains a "works portion" (*karmakāṇḍa*) and a "knowledge portion" (*jñānakāṇḍa*), and a great variety of forms of expression and instruction. It documents the thought of many centuries, and reflects fundamental changes in orientation. But, in a sense, it is this internal multiplicity and variety itself, this challenging and suggestive chaos, that accounts for the significance of the Veda in Hindu philosophy. It provides an elusive and ambiguous guidance, an open, yet authoritative framework, with suggestive hermeneutic patterns and precedents and inherent appeals to human reflexivity. This applies, most specifically, though in different, yet equally significant ways, to Bhartṛhari's and Śaṅkara's understanding of the Veda.

There is a certain structure in the chaos. There are mutual references and explicit interrelations and hierarchies between different parts of the Veda; there is also a great deal of self-reference, self-proclamation and self-reflection in these texts. All this provides hermeneutic suggestions and prototypes for later approaches to the Veda, and for the orthodox understanding of the relationship between human thought and Vedic revelation. In its structured multiplicity, through its different layers and types of statements, the Veda seems to anticipate basic possibilities of human thought and orientation, of reflection, debate, and disagreement; it appears as a framework that can accommodate and neutralize the challenge of Buddhism and other traditions of "merely human" origin. It seems, moreover, to separate and integrate more or less relevant, more or less authoritative statements, and to encompass and interrelate provisional and ultimate truth; and it seems to show ways of soteriological progression from lower to higher stages.[75] Thus, the Veda represents not only prototypical variety, but also an elusive, yet highly suggestive orientation towards unity and identity and an inherent tendency to transcend and supersede itself.

The Veda itself exhibits a paradigmatic commitment to an absolute origin and foundation, and seems to provide clues for its own later role in Hindu thought. It has its own retrospective and reflexive dimension and refers back to the Ṛgveda as its center and source. The epistemological and cosmological "priority" (*prāthamya*) of the Ṛgveda within the Vedic corpus[76] somehow foreshadows the sanctity and authority of the entire Veda within the orthodox Hindu tradition. Yet, in addition to such a retrospective commitment to an absolute origin, the Veda also seems to suggest that the "earlier" may be a preparation for the "later," that the Atharvaveda transcends the other Vedic Saṃhitās, and that the Upaniṣads supersede the Brāhmaṇas.[77]

All this does not explain the intriguing and disturbing alliance between the Veda and philosophical reflection in orthodox Hinduism, but it might help us to recognize and accept it.

Chapter 2: Notes

1. Cf. *India and Europe*, ch. 19, on the doxographic schemes of traditional Hinduism.

2. Cf. G. Chemparathy, *L'autorité du Veda selon les Nyāya-Vaiśeṣikas*. Louvain-la-Neuve, 1983. For a very different and rather idiosyncratic attempt to interpret the relationship between Vedic "gnosis" and philosophical thought, see J. G. Arapura, *Gnosis and the Question of Thought in Vedānta*. Dordrecht, 1986.

3. *L'autorité du Veda*, 7.

4. Ibid.

5. Cf. Jayanta, NM, 4.

6. Cf. *L'autorité du Veda*, 19 ff.; 28 ff. (on the development of the theory of the divine authorship of the Veda in Nyāya literature); for the Vaiśeṣika, see, for instance, VS VI, 1, 1: *buddhipūrvā vākyakṛtiḥ vede*.

7. Cf. *India and Europe*, ch. 15.

8. See G. Chemparathy, *An Indian Rational Theology: Introduction to Udayana's Nyāyakusumāñjali*. Vienna, 1972.

9. See G. Chemparathy, *L'autorité du Veda*, 58 ff.; see also id., "Meaning and Role of the Concept of Mahājanaparigraha in the Ascertainment of the Validity of the Veda." *Philosophical Essays, Prof. A. Thakur Felicitation Vol.* Calcutta, 1987, 67–80.

10. Cf. Jayanta, NM, 243: *cāturvarṇyaṃ cāturāśramyaṃ ca yad etad āryadeśaprasiddhaṃ sa mahājana ucyate . . . vedadharmānuvarttī ca prāyeṇa sakalo janaḥ*. But see Veṅkaṭanātha, *Nyāyapariśuddhi*. Benares, 1918 (Ch SS; representing the Rāmānuja school): . . . *bahujanaparigrahādimātrasya mahājanaparigrahatvena-avivakṣitatvāt*. The following argument in Śrīdhara's *Nyāyakandalī* exhibits an undisguised conventionalism: *yatra ca sarveṣāṃ saṃvādaniyamaḥ tat pramāṇam eva, yathā pratyakṣādikam. pram-*

āṇam vedaḥ, sarveṣām avisaṃvādijñānahetutvāt, pratyakṣavat (The Bhāṣya of Praśastapāda, ed. V. V. Dvivedin. Benares, 1895, 217). Buddhists and Jainas did not fail to exploit the weaknesses of such argumentation.

11. *L'autorité du Veda,* 63 ff.; Udayana presents his interpretation of the concept of *mahājana* in several works, specifically the *Ātmatattvaviveka* and the *Kiraṇāvalī.* Jayanta, too, states that the Buddhists (unlike such radically extra-Vedic groups as the *saṃsāramocaka*) recognize certain Vedic principles; cf. NM, 243 ff.

12. Cf. Kumārila, TV, 81 (on MS I, 3, 2); TV, 113 (on I, 3, 4). See also Pashupatinath Shastri, *Introduction to the Pūrva Mīmāṃsā,* ed. Gaurinath Shastri. Benares, 1980, 140 ff.

13. See below, ch. 9.

14. Cf. NV I, 1, 33 (ed. A. Thakur, 517): *tasmād brāhmaṇena surā peyā-ity āgamavirodhaḥ.* NBh I,1,3 states that such injunctions as *agnihotraṃ juhuyāt svargakāmaḥ* are exclusively in the domain of revelation.

15. Cf. NBh I, 1, 10: *tatra-ātmā tāvat pratyakṣato na gṛhyate. sa kim āptopadeśamātrād eva pratipadyata iti. na-ity ucyate. anumānāc ca pratipattavya iti*; on *pratisandhāna,* see Uddyotakara, NV on this passage (ed. A. Thakur, 388): *āgamasya-anumānena pratisandhānārthaṃ vā, yo hy āgamena pratipanna ātmā, tasya-anumānena pratisandhānārtham.* The *Ṭīkā* and *Pariśuddhi* on this Sūtra (ed. A. Thakur, 392 f.; 398 f.) use *pratisandhāna* in a different sense. For a thorough and comprehensive philosophical analysis of the Nyāya and Vaiśeṣika arguments concerning the existence of the *ātman,* see C. Oetke, *"Ich" und das Ich. Analytische Untersuchungen zur buddhistisch-brahmanischen Ātmankontroverse.* Stuttgart, 1988.

16. Cf. NV and NVT I, 1, 33 (ed. A. Thakur, 517: *na hi vaiśeṣikeṇa śabdānityatvam āgamataḥ pratipannam, api tv anumānāt*; 523: *yady apy āgamo 'pi śabdānityatve 'sti. . . ., tathā-api . . . nityatve 'py āgamadarśanāt aniścayād anumānasya-eva-atra prāmāṇyam*). See also NBh I, 1, 3.

17. Cf. NVT I, 1, 1 (ed. A. Thakur, 59): *yady api na nyāyamātravartinī pratijñā-āgamaḥ, tathā-api prakṛtanyāyābhiprāyeṇa-etad draṣṭavyam*; what Vā-

caspati calls *prakṛtanyāya* is, of course, the "orthodox" Nyāya of Gautama and Vācaspati. On Vātsyāyana's "concordance," see also NBh I, 1, 39.

18. Cf. *Pariśuddhi* I, 1, 1 (ed. A. Thakur, 125).

19. Cf. *India and Europe*, ch. 15.

20. *Pariśuddhi*, I, 1, 1 (ed. A. Thakur, 146).

21. Cf. *India and Europe*, 275.

22. *Pariśuddhi*, I, 1, 1 (ed. A. Thakur, 146).

23. *Pariśuddhi*, 72.

24. Cf. *India and Europe*, 363; and Jayanta, NM, 5.

25. Cf. *India and Europe*, ch. 17; and below, ch. 9–10.

26. Cf. E. Frauwallner, *Kleine Schriften*, ed. G. Oberhammer and E. Steinkellner. Wiesbaden, 1982, 311–322; F. X. D'Sa, *Śabdaprāmāṇyam in Śabara and Kumārila*. Vienna, 1980, 115 ff. (on *śabdanityatva*).

27. Cf. TV, 80 (on MS I, 3, 2).

28. Cf. Medhātithi on Manu II, 6 (ed. J. H. Dave, Bombay, 1972, 163).

29. See above, n. 5 (Jayanta, NM, 4).

30. See above, n. 3.

31. Cf. F. X. D'Sa, loc. cit. (see n. 26), 199, on the role of *apauruṣeyatva* and *śabdanityatva* in Kumārila: " . . . he built a system to support these two pillars of the Mīmāṃsā." Although they are trying to establish the Mīmāṃsā as a full-fledged system of philosophy, Kumārila and other Mīmāṃsakas show a certain degree of indifference towards merely factual, as well as metaphysical, matters.

32. In particular, Kumārila is indebted to the philosophy of Bhartṛhari.

33. On Kumārila's epistemology and theory of *svataḥprāmāṇya*, see L. Schmithausen, *Maṇḍanamiśra's Vibhramavivekaḥ*. Vienna, 1965, 189 ff.

34. Among the representative works of the older Mīmāṃsā school, Maṇḍana's monographs *Bhāvanāviveka* and *Vidhiviveka* contain the most systematic discussions of the concepts of *bhāvanā* and *vidhi*. See also E. Frauwallner, *Kleine Schriften* (see n. 26), 161–201.

35. For a concise presentation of this alternative, see Rāmānujācārya, *Tantrarahasya*, ed. R. Shama Shastri. Baroda, second ed., 1956 (GOS), 57; 59. Somewhat uncautiously, Th. Stcherbatsky has associated Prabhākara's position with the Kantian notion of the "categorical imperative"; cf. "Über die Nyāyakaṇikā des Vācaspatimiśra und die indische Lehre vom kategorischen Imperativ." *Beiträge zur Literaturwissenschaft und Geistesgeschichte Indiens* (Festgabe H. Jacobi). Bonn, 1926, 369–380.

36. See K. Kunjunni Raja, *Indian Theories of Meaning*. Madras, 1963, 191, ff.; see also B. Bhattacharya, *A Study in Language and Meaning*. Calcutta, 1962, 158–187.

37. On *pramāṇsambandhayogyatā*, see Śālikanātha, *Prakaraṇapañcikā* (with *Nyāyasiddhi* by Jayapurinārāyaṇa Bhaṭṭa), ed. A. Subrahmanya Sastri. Benares, 1961, 97 ff.; see also Maṇḍana, *Brahmasiddhi*, ed. S. Kuppuswami Sastri. Madras, 1937, 85 ff. For Maṇḍana's concept of *vartamānatā* see *Vidhiviveka* (with *Nyāyakaṇikā* of Vācaspati Miśra), ed. M.L. Goswami. Benares, 1978, 44; 58; for the expression *vartamānakālasambandhitva*, see W. Halbfass, "Vyomaśiva on sattāsambandha." *Studies in Indian Culture* (S. Ramachandra Rao Felicitation Vol.). Bangalore, 1987, 65–80; ib., 79.

38. See NM, 3; with misprints; cf. also the edition by Gaurinath Sastri, Benares, 1982–1984, 8.

39. See Śālikanātha, *Prakaraṇapañcika*, ed. A. Subrahmanya Sastri. Benares, 1961, 404; Vācaspati, NVT I, 1, 1 (ed. A. Thakur, 62): *dharme pramīyamāṇe hi vedena kāraṇātmanā / itikartavyatābhāgaṃ mīmāṃsā pūrayiṣyati.*

40. See NM, 3 f. (with misprints in the verse; cf. the edition of Gaurinath Sastri, 8).

41. See NVT I, 1, 1 (ed. A. Thakur, 62); the simile of the "salt mine" (*rumā*) found in the second half of this verse occurs also in Kumārila's *Tantravārttika* I, 3, 7 (TV, ed. K. V. Abhyaṅkara and G.S. Jośī, 128: *yathā rumāyāṃ lavaṇākareṣu* . . .).

42. Cf. *Pariśuddhi* I, 1, 1 (ed. A. Thakur, 143).

43. Pāraskara, *Gṛhyasūtra* II, 6, 5.

44. Cf. the edition of Pāraskara by M.G. Bākre (with commentaries by Karka, Jayarāma, Harihara, Gadādhara and Viśvanātha). Delhi, second ed., 1982, specifically 246. See also *Yuktidīpikā*, ed. R.C. Pandeya. Delhi, 1967, 14: *vedavedāṅgatarkeṣu vedasaṃjñā nirucyate.*

45. Cf. *Vṛtti* on VP, 10.

46. Ed. K. A. Subramania Iyer. Poona, 1966, 38.

47. Cf. TV, 168 (on MS I, 3, 13); see also Vācaspati, *NVT*, in: ND, ed. A. Thakur, 62: *mīmāṃsāsaṃjñakas tarkaḥ sarvavedasamudbhavah.*

48. See below, ch. 3.

49. Cf. TV, 80 (on MS I, 3, 2): *mīmāṃsā tu lokād eva pratyakṣānumānādibhir avicchinnasampradāyapaṇḍitavyavahāraiḥ pravṛttā.*

50. Cf. Someśvara, *N Sudhā*, 1169.

51. See below, § 12.

52. See below, ch. 5.

53. Cf. BUBh I, 1, introduction (*Works* I, 608).

54. BUBh II, 5, 15 (*Works* I, 776).

55. Cf. BSBh I, 1, 5–11; II, 1, 1–11; II, 2, 1–10; and G.J. Larson, *Classical Sāṃkhya*. Santa Barbara, second ed., 1979, 209 ff. On the other hand, Śaṅkara rejects the exegetic claims of the Sāṃkhya system; cf. BSBh I, 4, 1–28.

56. Cf. BSBh II, 1, 1 (*Works* III, 182): *vedasya hi nirapekṣam svārthe prāmāṇyaṃ raver iva rūpaviṣaye*; BUBh II, 1, 20 (*Works* I, 743): *savitṛpradīpādivad*; see also Sureśvara, BUBhV II, 4, 307 (cf. S. Hino, *Sureśvara's Vārtika on Yājñavalkya Maitreyī Dialogue*. Delhi, 1982, 218): *bhānuprakāśavac chabdo nityo 'yam*. The metaphor of the sunlight appears also in Śāntarakṣita, TS, v. 2351 (*pūrvapakṣa*); v. 2807 rejects this *pūrvapakṣa* and interprets the Veda as "dense darkness." Associations of the Vedic word with "light" (*jyotis, prakāśa*) are common in Bhartṛhari; cf., e.g., VP I, 18 f.; 47 (ed. W. Rau). On the other hand, brahman itself is frequently characterized as a "sun," i.e. a universal source of light; see, for instance, the poetic imagery of the *Hastāmalaka* verses.

57. See below, ch. 5.

58. Ultimately, the Veda itself, as a linguistic entity, has to be abandoned; cf. BSBh IV, 1, 3 which cites BU IV, 3, 22 (*vedā avedāḥ*) as scriptural support for this view. According to Śaṅkara's disciple Sureśvara, the Veda teaches what is "not the meaning of a sentence," *avākyārtha*; cf. *Naiṣkarmyasiddhi* III, 9; see also IV, 37.

59. See BUBh II, 1, 20 (*Works I*, 744).

60. See above, § 9.

61. Cf. *Mahābhārata* XII, 306, 27; 33.

62. See *Pariśiṣṭa* 12 on *Nirukta* (ch. 13; ed. L. Sarup, 227); cf. L. Renou, *Le destin*, 77, n. 5; and below, n. 69 (Bhartṛhari, VP I, 151).

63. Cf. VP I, 8 (with *Vṛtti*); Cf. the form *vivartate* in VP I, 1, as well as P. Hacker, *Vivarta*, Wiesbaden, 1953 (Ak. Wiss. Lit. Mainz). See also VP I, 5 (concerning the Veda): *eko 'py anekavartmā-eva*; III/2 (*dravya*), 7–18. Referring to the process of self-manifestation, Bhartṛhari often uses such terms as *prakāś-*; cf., e.g., VP II, 30–33; III 13, 39; 87. This foreshadows the thought and terminology of Abhinavagupta and the Pratyabhijñā school.

64. Cf. VP I, 1–2:

anādinidhanaṃ brahma śabdatattvaṃ yad akṣaram,
vivartate 'rthabhāvena prakriyā jagato yatah.
ekam eva yad āmnātam bhinnaṃ śaktivyapāśrayāt,
apṛthaktve 'pi śaktibhyaḥ pṛthaktvena-iva vartate.

VP I, 4 calls this Vedic *akṣara* the "seed" (*bīja*) of the world; see also I, 124 (*śabdasya pariṇāmo 'yam . . .*).

65. Cf. VP I, 5–9, where Bhartṛhari first refers to the role of the original "seers" (*ṛṣi*; quoting Yāska, *Nirukta* I, 20), and then to the continuation and extrapolation of their work by the authors and guardians of authoritative traditions (*smṛti, āgama*). VP I, 148–153 distinguishes the authorless *śruti* or *trayī* from all subsequent traditions (*āgama*), but also presents it as their permanent "seed" (*bīja*).

66. On *anukāra*, see VP I, 5, which also describes the Veda as *prāptyupāya*.

67. Cf. VP I, 131: *anuviddham iva jñānaṃ sarvaṃ śabdena bhāsate.*

68. VP I, 153; cf. Bhartṛhari's citation of Pāraskara in his *Vṛtti* on VP I, 10.

69. Cf. VP I, 151: *vedaśāstrāvirodhinī ca tarkaś cakṣur apaśyatām.* Not only reasoning, but also "vision" and "experience" have to be grounded on the Vedic word. To be sure, Bhartṛhari cites and accepts the statement from the *Nirukta* that the Vedic "seers" have experienced or realized the *dharma (sākṣātkṛtadharmaṇ; Vṛtti* on VP I, 5) and notes that the nature and meaning of the Veda is ultimately "of the nature of vision" (*darśanātman*, ib.). But, at the same time, he transforms and reinterprets Yāska's dictum: The Vedic word itself defines and constitutes true vision; there is no true vision prior to, and independent of, the Vedic word and the tradition based upon it, nor is the Veda an expression or articulation of an underlying personal vision or experience. The seers themselves depend upon the tradition and execution of the Vedic *dharma* (cf. VP I, 29 f.). Although they "see with the (superhuman) vision of the ṛṣis" (*paśyanty ārṣeṇa cakṣuṣā*), such "vision" is nothing but a more direct and primeval presence of the Vedic word itself and quite different from the *divyacakṣus* of the Buddhists. As a matter of fact, it may be an implicit response to this Buddhist notion, and an attempt to supersede and neutralize it.

70. Cf. VP II, 484 (ed. W. Rau); *Vṛtti* on I, 30 and I, 137/129 (K.A. Subramania Iyer; I, 153 in Rau's edition). For Śaṅkara, see BSBh II, 1, 6.

71. See below, ch. 4.

72. This is as evident from Abhinavagupta's great Tantric works, especially the *Tantrāloka* and the *Tantrasāra*, as from his more "philosophically" oriented words, such as the *Īśvarapratyabhijñāvimarśinī.*

73. Cf. Śāntarakṣita, TS, v. 2807 (with *Pañjikā* by Kamalaśīla).

74. As an example of Ṛgvedic "immanence-in-transcendence," we may recall the transcendent presence of Agni in all the actual (specifically ritual) fires.

75. See below, ch. 5. We may also refer to the contrast between *śreyas* and *preyas* in the *Kaṭha Upaniṣad* II, 1, or the distinction between *parā* and *aparā vidyā* in the *Muṇḍaka Upaniṣad* I, 1, 4.

76. Cf. the beginning of Sāyaṇa's introduction to his commentary on the Ṛgveda (see P. Peterson, *Handbook to the Study of the Rigveda.* Bombay, 1892, 1 ff.; 127 ff.).

77. Cf. Muir III, 17 (the Atharvaveda as *sarvavidyā* according to *Taittirīya Brāhmaṇa* III, 10, 11, 3); see also 218 ff.; 224 ff. (on old and new hymns). The classical presentation of an instruction which encompasses and supersedes all "previous" and anticipates all "future" teaching is found in *Chāndogya Upaniṣad* VI, 1 f.

CHAPTER 3

Vedic Orthodoxy and the Plurality of Religious Traditions

Religious Plurality in Modern and Classical Hindu Thought

1. It has often been stated that Hinduism is not a well-defined, clearly identifiable *religion* in the sense of Christianity or Islam, but rather a loosely coordinated and somewhat amorphous conglomeration of "sects"[1] or similar formations. The response of modern Hinduism to this assessment has been twofold: on the one hand, Hinduism has tried to demonstrate its unity and to demarcate its identity against Christianity and other "religions" by defining its common denominators or even by producing "catechisms," etc.[2] On the other hand, the assessment that Hinduism is *not* a "religion" has been accepted, but the weakness or deficiency it suggests has been turned into an element of self-affirmation. In this view, the fact that Hinduism is not a *religion* in the ordinary sense does not imply a defect; rather, it means that it is located at a different and higher level. It is something much more comprehensive, much less divisive and sectarian than the "ordinary" religions. It is not itself a religion; i.e., it is not itself a sect. Instead, it is—according to this view—a framework, a concordance and unifying totality of sects. The "ordinary" religions, such as Christianity and Islam, should not be compared and juxtaposed to Hinduism itself, but to the sects, that is, "religions" that are contained within Hinduism. Hinduism as the *sanātanadharma* is not a religion among religions; it is said to be the "eternal religion," religion in or behind all religions, a kind of "metareligion," a structure potentially ready to comprise and reconcile within itself all the religions of the world, just as it contains and reconciles the so-called Hindu sects, such as Śaivism or Vaiṣṇavism and their subordinate "sectarian" formations.[3] A few quotes from representative Neo-Hindu authors may illustrate this.

The most famous apostle of Hinduism in the West, Vivekananda, says that "Buddhism was the first sect in India,"[4] and that, in the context of Hinduism, it was never *more* than a sect. In the world at large, it became the most successful missionary religion, spreading all over the then civilized world "from Lapland on the one side to the Philippine islands on the other. . . . But in India this gigantic child was absorbed, in the long run, by the mother that gave it birth, and today the very name of Buddha is almost unknown all over India."[5] The implicit references to Christianity can hardly be overlooked when Vivekananda and other modern Indian thinkers speak about Buddhism: Buddhism is a much older and much more universal missionary religion than Christianity; yet it is nothing more than a sect in the totality and universality of Hinduism.[6] The other religions are, or will be, ultimately included in Hinduism; Vivekananda speaks about "the infinite arms" of Vedānta, which will be able to embrace and to include all present and future developments in science, religion and philosophy.[7]

S. V. Ketkar, Vivekananda's younger contemporary, who received his Ph.D. from Cornell University and was later editor and, to a large extent, author of the great Marathi encyclopedia, denies that a "religion" in the European sense is anything more than what he calls a *sect* or a *sampradāya* in the context of Hinduism. According to Ketkar, "religion" is an "exclusively European term," which is not applicable to the comprehensive synthetic superstructure of Hinduism. "Once the entire Hindu civilization was in the process of spreading itself over the whole world," before it was "arrested" by the sectarian religions, Islam and Christianity. "The religions will take the same place in any future cosmopolitanism as the *sampradāyas* have taken under Hinduism."[8]

It sounds reminiscent of this statement when the most famous spokesman of Neo-Hinduism in this century, S. Radhakrishnan, says: "Hinduism is not limited in scope to the geographical area which is described as India. . . . There is nothing which prevents it from extending to the uttermost parts of the world."[9] A. K. Banerjee states in his *Discourses on Hindu Spiritual Culture*: "Hinduism has evolved out of itself a multitude of *religions*, each of which bears perfect analogy to Christianity and Mohammedanism, so far as the application of this term is concerned. . . . We commit an obvious logical fallacy, when we put Hinduism by the side of Christianity,

Mohammedanism, Buddhism, etc., to signify that it is one of the sectarian religions of the world."[10] The contrast between Hinduism and the other religions is thus comparable or even reducible to the contrast between Hinduism and the Hindu sects, and it is a contrast between the more comprehensive and the less comprehensive.

2. The Neo-Hindu, specifically Neo-Vedāntic references to the classical tradition that are meant to document or to illustrate the all-inclusive tolerance[11] of Hinduism and its comprehensive openness for religious plurality range from the Ṛgvedic *ekaṃ sad viprā bahudhā vadanti*[12] to many more recent texts, such as the *Prasthānabheda* of Madhusūdana Sarasvatī.[13] There is certainly no shortage of statements in which a plurality of "paths," "methods" or "names" is accepted and "tolerated" as being conducive to one and the same ultimate goal, or in which other views are presented as being compatible with, that is, contained in or preliminary to, one's own view. To refer to other ways of thinking, to articulate one's own position in terms of its relation to other positions, or by means of including and subordinating other teachings, is a genuine and essential element of classical Indian thought.[14]

Nevertheless, the contrast between the traditional inclusivistic or perspectivistic patterns and the universalistic openness claimed by Neo-Hinduism is obvious. The traditional "inclusivism" is usually coupled with or even coincides with a more or less explicit exclusivism; at any rate, it is not without formalistic and restrictive ingredients. Modern Hinduism relates its explication and justification of religious plurality to an open, universalized concept of *adhikāra*, of religious or soteriological qualification or vocation; the diversity of religious traditions in the world is seen as the correlate of a general "diversity of qualification" (*adhikārabheda*). This usage of adhikāra is characteristically different from the traditional "orthodox" understanding, which associates adhikāra with the rules of dharma and specifically with the order of castes and stages of life (*varṇāśramadharma*). In traditional Hinduism, the treatment of Buddhism etc. is usually much less conciliatory than in Neo-Hinduism. Almost invariably, non-Indian religious phenomena are disregarded or, less frequently, explicitly dismissed in the traditional schemes of harmonization or subordination. While Madhusūdana Sarasvatī states explicitly that the extra-Vedic traditions of Buddhism, etc. are not even indirectly or in a preliminary sense conducive to the goal of liberation, he simply takes it for granted that the traditions of the non-Indian "barbarians" (*mleccha*) have no soteriological relevance whatsoever.[15]

According to S. Radhakrishnan and other representatives of Neo-Hinduism, the extension and universalization of the limited traditional patterns is a simple and unproblematic adjustment to the current and wider context of knowledge: "Today the samanvaya or harmonisation has to be extended to the living faiths of mankind. . . . As the author of the Brahma Sūtra tried to reconcile the different doctrines prevalent in his time, we have to take into account the present state of our knowledge and evolve a coherent picture."[16] Referring to a verse which he erroneously ascribes to Udayana, Radhakrishnan claims that Udayana would have mentioned the Christians and Muslims in his list of religious traditions if he had known about them.[17] But Udayana could have referred to Islam if he had been interested in doing so; and Madhusūdana, who explicitly dismisses Buddhism as well as all non-Indian traditions, certainly knew about Islam and may have had personal contacts with the Mogul court.[18]

The step towards historical actualization and adjustment to the "present state" of knowledge, a simple and unproblematic step according to Radhakrishnan, has not been taken in traditional Hinduism. As a matter of fact, it would have been incompatible with the basic tendencies of traditional Hindu thought, with its ahistorical or antihistorical orientation, with its attempts to establish frameworks of legitimate religious traditions once and for all. The procedure of Madhusūdana is symptomatic. Commenting on verse 7 of the *Śivamahimnastotra*, which enumerates religious paths or "methods" (*prasthāna*), such as the Vedic path, Sāṃkhya, Yoga, Pāśupata and Vaiṣṇavism, he presents his list of the eighteen traditional "sciences" (*vidyā*) of Hinduism, and he paraphrases the religious paths as *śāstra*, "timeless" branches of learning.[19] In his view, there is no basic difference between a legitimate religious tradition, which we might call a "sectarian" tradition, and a traditional "science" or branch of learning, such as "astronomy" (*jyotiṣa*) or "etymology" (*nirukta*). Many centuries earlier, Bhāsarvajña (approximately A.D. 900) discussed the possibility of extending the shorter list of fourteen "sciences" (*vidyā, śāstra*), and he mentioned a branch of scientific learning, i.e. medicine (*vaidyaśātra*), and a "sectarian" tradition, i.e. Śaivasiddhānta, side by side as possible additions.[20]

Śaṅkara and the Limits of Religious Concordance

3. In the following, we shall discuss how Kumārila and Śaṅkara, leading exponents of the "orthodox," suprasectarian aspirations of classical Hindu thought, deal with the plurality and diversity of religious traditions.[21] In particular, we shall try to clarify how Śaṅkara understands the legitimate and authoritative "internal" differentiation of the Vedic revelation on the one hand and the merely factual "external" diversity of human opinions on the other hand.

Śaṅkara's special and most conspicuous interest is in the concordance (*samanvaya*) of the Upaniṣads, i.e. their agreement concerning the nature of brahman, which is the topic of the first adhyāya of the *Brahmasūtrabhāṣya.* It overshadows completely the wider perspective that seems to be opened by his somewhat casual observation that the one ātman is the ultimate referent of all human views and teachings, even of the most distorted ones, such as those of Buddhists or Materialists.[22]

The second adhyāya of the *Brahmasūtrabhāṣya*, especially in its first two sections (*pāda*), is a refutation of Sāṃkhya, Yoga and other traditions, which claim to be established by omniscient founders, such as Kapila, without recognizing that only the Veda can be the source of reliable and legitimate knowledge concerning dharma and ultimate reality, that is brahman. Unguided human "reasoning" (*tarka*) and "experience" (*anubhava*) are utterly insufficient to be such a source. Towards the end of the second section of the second adhyāya, Śaṅkara applies this uncompromising critique of extra-Vedic traditions to the more specifically sectarian movements of the Bhāgavatas or Pāñcarātrins:[23] Insofar as these movements claim sources of religious instruction and inspiration which are not ultimately based upon the Veda, they have to be rejected.

No plurality, no compromise concerning the knowledge of brahman can be accepted. Brahman is one, and there cannot be a variety of true teachings concerning its one identical nature; true knowledge cannot deviate from its object: *na ca-ekarūpe brahmaṇy an-ekarūpāṇi vijñānāni saṃbhavanti, na hy anyathā-artho 'nyathā jñānam.*[24]

However, a certain variety of names and concepts, of paths and approaches, of different forms of "devotion" or "meditation" (*upāsanā*), is legitimate insofar as the particularized, personified *saguṇabrahman* is concerned, that is, brahman as seen through "nescience" (*avidyā*), by those who still think and strive in terms of means and ends, of acts and rewards. The categories of "devotee," "object of devotion," etc., apply as long as brahman appears in this way; and different modes of devotion may lead to different results.[25] In other cases, the same result may be achieved by different methods; and in such a case one may choose any one among the available legitimate meditational or devotional methods, practising it with total dedication until the desired result has been obtained: *tasmād aviśiṣṭaphalānāṃ vidyānām anyatamām ādāya tatparaḥ syād yāvad upāsyaviṣayasākṣātkaraṇena tatphalaṃ prāptam iti.*[26]

All this does not imply that Śaṅkara deals with the different forms of ritual action and religious life in a universalistic or even relativistic fashion. There may be plurality and a certain degree of choice in this field; but this does not mean that there is an unrestricted variety. Even there, the Veda itself is the measure and the prototype of legitimate plurality.

4. The inclusivistic model, which presents other, competing religious and philosophical views as being ultimately included in one's own, and the idea of a didactic adjustment to different levels of qualification (*adhikārabheda*, etc.) can, of course, be used by and for very different standpoints. Several centuries after Śaṅkara, the great Naiyāyika Udayana gives one of the most impressive presentations of this model in his *Ātmatattvaviveka*,[27] arranging the other systems of thought, including Advaita Vedānta, as preliminary stages of the Nyāya system, which he calls the "ultimate Vedānta" (*caramavedānta*). In his *Nyāyakusumāñjali*, he enumerates the names of the highest principles of many religious and philosophical traditions and says that they represent in the final analysis nothing but more or less distorted ways of understanding the "Lord" (*īśvara*) of the Nyāya system.[28]

Śaṅkara is obviously aware of the relativistic dangers in using the inclusivistic model and of the potentially confusing effects of a didactic adjustment to different "levels of qualification." He accuses the Buddhists of applying such devices in an illegitimate and confusing manner, referring specifically to the Madhyamaka practice of justifying different teachings with reference to the diversity of those who have to be educated (*vineyabheda*) and of interpreting other systems of Buddhist thought as gradual preparations for the ultimate truth of Śūnyavāda.[29] Accordingly, he sees Buddhist thought as "manifold" (*bahuprakāra*) in a sense that implies disagreement and confusion: *tatra-ete trayo vādino bhavanti. kecit sarvāstitvavādinaḥ, kecit vijñānāstitvamātravādinaḥ, anye punaḥ sarvaśūnyavādina iti.*[30] Explicating the term *vineyabheda*, the commentators of the *Brahmasūtrabhāṣya* refer to the low, medium or excellent intellectual abilities (Vācaspati: *hīnamadhyamotkṛṣṭa*; Ānandagiri: *mandamadhyamottama*), to which these three types or levels of teaching correspond. Vācaspati quotes a verse from the *Bodhicittavivaraṇa*, allegedly by Nāgārjuna, which expresses the didactic adjustment of Buddhist teachings and the inclusion and ultimate concordance of all teachings in the idea of *śūnyatā*, "emptiness."[31]

Attributing these different systems to the Buddha himself, Śaṅkara accuses him of incoherent prattling (*asambaddhapralāpitva*) or even of deliberately and hatefully leading mankind into confusion by teaching such contradictory ideas: *api ca bāhyārthavijñānaśūnyavādatrayam itaretaraviruddham upadiśatā sugatena spaṣṭīkṛtam ātmano 'sambaddhapralāpitvaṃ, pradveṣo vā prajāsu viruddhārthapratipattyā vimuhyeyur imāḥ prajā iti.*[32]

On the other hand, Śaṅkara emphasizes repeatedly that the Veda itself adjusts its teachings to different levels of understanding and qualification, that it uses different methods of instruction and that it addresses different interests and capabilities. The whole "work section" (*karmakāṇḍa*) applies to those who are still in the network of "work orientation," that is, of reward-oriented nescience; but also within the "knowledge section" (*jñānakāṇḍa*), that is, the Upaniṣads, it speaks at different levels.[33] It offers various meditational and devotional methods and "symbolic" devices (*pratīka*), such as the om, to those who are of slow or mediocre understanding (*mandamadhyapratipattṝn prati*[34]). Śaṅkara is obviously convinced that such variability and didactic adjustment is legitimate and effective insofar only as it is employed, or at least sanctioned and guided, by the Veda itself, that is, insofar as it is rooted in revelation.

Just as human understanding alone is incapable of unveiling ultimate truth and reality, it is incapable of determining the various levels of eligibility or qualification for this truth and of arranging a soteriologically meaningful and effective hierarchy of teachings.

Śaṅkara rejects the idea of legitimizing the teachings of Kapila, that is, the Sāṃkhya philosophy, in this manner, of interpreting the Sāṃkhya teachings about *prakṛti/pradhāna* etc. as a legitimate aid and stage of development for those who are not qualified to receive the Vedic revelation directly, and of coordinating Sāṃkhya and Vedānta in a scheme of reconciliation.[35] No such role has been assigned to the teachings of Kapila by the Vedic revelation, and human reason alone cannot possibly ascertain it. That the Veda uses a variety of names, such as *jyotis, ākāśa,* etc., in order to refer to the one absolute ātman or brahman,[36] does not mean that the Sāṃkhya *pradhāna/avyakta*[37] or the Vāsudeva of the Bhāgavatas[38] may simply be added as other valid, though indirect indicators of ātman/brahman.

5. Of course, Śaṅkara recognizes a sense in which all systems of thought are more or less distorted references to the one absolute. Even the Materialists or the Buddhists, by postulating the "mere body" (*dehamātra*) or the "void" (*śūnya*) as ultimate reality or as the highest principle, somehow "mean" the absolute ātman.[39] As Vācaspati notes in his *Bhāmatī* on this passage, such conflicting views could not even be in conflict with one another without having the same "substratum" (*āśraya*). But such implicit unity of an "ultimate intent" remains abstract and incapable of providing the factual diversity of human opinions with a meaningful soteriological structure; Śaṅkara sees no reason to extend his search for concordance (*samanvaya*) to this open field of human views and aberrations.

Śaṅkara's approach to the problem or religious plurality is conservative and restrictive. The extent to which religious plurality, variety of approaches to ultimate reality and liberation can be accepted is limited by the *vedamūlatva* principle, as it has been developed by the Pūrvamīmāṃsā school. Accordingly, Śaṅkara follows the Pūrvamīmāṃsā also in his use of the concept of adhikāra. The Veda itself has to assign and legitimize the "qualification" and "mandate" for its revelation; and we have to accept that it excludes the Śūdras etc. from the access to Vedic teachings. Worldly capabilities alone, such as intelligence, cannot constitute adhikāra; Vedic matters require a Vedic capability and mandate: *sāmarthyam api na laukikaṃ kevalam adhikārakāraṇaṃ bhavati, śāstrīye 'rthe śāstrīyasya sāmarthyasya-apekṣitatvāt.*[40]

According to the vedamūlatva principle, the Veda is the criterion and measure of legitimacy and orthodoxy. Other teachings which appear outside the Veda or side by side with it do not have to be harmonized and reconciled with it; they have to be measured against it, and if they are incompatible, they have to be rejected. Śaṅkara's treatment of the traditions of the Bhāgavatas or Pāñcarātrins leaves no doubt in this respect: Insofar as these traditions claim to be based upon an additional, independent, extra-Vedic revelation, they are illegitimate and unacceptable.[41] This distinguishes Śaṅkara's "nonsectarian" Advaita Vedānta from the "sectarian," primarily Vaiṣṇava traditions of Vedānta, which accept additional "revelations" of equal and potentially superior authority. Yāmuna's *Āgamaprāmāṇya* (ca. A.D. 1000) is an exemplary statement concerning the authority of the so-called Pāñcarātra. According to Madhva (thirteenth century), not only the Vedas are independent sources of religious authority, but also the Mahābhārata, the "original Rāmāyaṇa" (*mūlarāmāyaṇa*), the Brahmasūtra and the Pāñcarātra which in his understanding includes the Vaiṣṇava Purāṇas.[42]

Unlike later thinkers and doxographers of the Advaita Vedānta tradition, Śaṅkara is not interested in presenting Vedānta as the culmination of an inclusivistic hierarchy of religious or philosophical teachings. In his genuine works, there is nothing comparable to the gradation of systems found in the *Sarvasiddhāntasaṃgraha* falsely attributed to him.[43] Śaṅkara is Veda-oriented not only insofar as the unity of the absolute, the truth about brahman is concerned, but also concerning the plurality of paths and stages leading to this goal. Soteriologically meaningful religious or philosophical plurality is itself a matter of Vedic revelation. There is so much room for plurality in the Veda and within the tradition based upon it, that Śaṅkara sees no reason to organize, justify or explain the general, merely man-made, extra-Vedic plurality of views and traditions. His idea of concordance (*samanvaya*) is essentially a matter of Vedic exegesis; the universalized samanvaya suggested by Radhakrishnan has no basis in Śaṅkara's own thought.[44]

Kumārila and Bhartṛhari: The Vedic Structure of Pluralism

6. Śaṅkara's application of the *vedamūlatva* principle, which accounts for the exclusivistic and restrictive implications of his access to religious and philosophical plurality, shows him in the tradition of Mīmāṃsā. The Pūrvamīmāṃsā, with which Śaṅkara disagrees on other central issues, has articulated the principles of strict, uncompromising allegiance to the Veda in its interpretation of dharma. The Veda is the ultimate source of all knowledge of dharma, of ritual and religious propriety; it is the one and only source which is self-evident and self-validating. All other sources, such as smṛti, etc., have to be measured against it and ultimately traced back to it. Any valid human orientation towards transworldly and transempirical goals must derive its legitimacy and its origin from the Veda, which is legitimately accessible to the community of the "twice-born" *āryas* only and allegiance to which, on the other hand, constitutes the identity of the "Āryan" community.[45]

In such a context of thought, the room for and interest in other traditions and in religious plurality in general can only be limited. However, it is by no means absent, nor is it restricted to merely polemical and negative interest. In the works of Kumārila, it plays a role that may appear surprising in view of the rigid "orthodoxy" of the school of which he is the most eloquent and successful advocate.[46]

Kumārila discusses the legitimacy and, although much less explicity, the origin and genesis of religious plurality, in several important sections of his *Tantravārttika*, first in connection with the meaning and status of the smṛtis, and then in his discussion of the *Kalpasūtras*, which are part of the vedāṅga literature.

In his smṛti discussion, Kumārila is faced with the problem of preventing illegitimate, unorthodox religious movements, like those of the Buddhists, from laying claim upon orthodoxy and legitimacy by postulating a "lost Veda," a forgotten branch of primeval revelation, as their original source. Since Kumārila himself works with the assumption of forgotten Vedic texts as ultimate legitimizers of traditions, which are recognized as orthodox without having a demonstrable basis in the extant Vedic texts, this is not an easy task for him. Cannot the Buddhists claim this procedure for their own teachings? Who would be able to limit the realm of application of this theory of lost texts? Could it not also be used to argue for the legitimacy of teachings which are incompatible with the directly accessible textual traditions?[47] But in this situation, the basic rule is that whatever is contradicted by a direct Vedic statement has to be rejected: *virodhe tv anapekṣyaṃ syād.*[48] And there is certainly no justification for invoking hypothetically assumed lost Vedic texts against actually accessible Vedic statements. Moreover, the Buddhists etc., unlike "orthodox" dharma teachers such as Gautama, usually do not claim any Vedic roots for their teachings: *na ca tair vedamūlatvam ucyate gautamādivat.* And finally, a "total destruction" (*uccheda*) of whole "branches" (*śākhā*) of the Vedic tradition cannot be assumed.[49]

Kumārila enumerates various types of extra-Vedic traditions, from Sāṃkhya, Yoga, Pāñcarātra etc., which have at least a certain appearance of decency and show some respect for the Vedic dharma, to those which have no regard whatsoever for this dharma and teach what would be fitting for "barbarians" (*mleccha*). These traditions are more or less "external" (*bāhya*) to the Vedic tradition, and some of them are more despicable than others. But all have to be rejected without compromise insofar as they claim an extra-Vedic legitimacy.[50]

7. The rejection of false claims of legitimacy and orthodoxy is only one side of Kumārila's procedure. The other side, although less conspicuous in his writings and generally overlooked, is at least as remarkable and relevant, that is, his assumption that even "unorthodox" Indian religious traditions, including those that reject any affiliation with the Veda, have certain actual "historical" roots in the Veda. There are certain, though distorted, Vedic elements in the teachings of the Buddhists or the Jainas. These groups are just like ungrateful and alienated children who refuse to acknowledge what they owe to their parents; that is, they do not acknowledge to what extent they are factually indebted to the Veda. The Jainas and the Buddhists use the idea of ahiṃsā as an instrument of their anti-Vedic propaganda. Yet, according to Kumārila, this very idea of ahiṃsā is actually traceable to certain Vedic rules about not killing; these have been misunderstood and falsely universalized by the Jaina or Buddhist proponents of ahiṃsā.[51] Similarly, Kumārila suggests that numerous philosophical teachings have their often unrecognized origin in the *arthavāda* sections of the Veda or in the Upaniṣads, including characteristically Buddhist teachings: *vijñānamātrakṣaṇabhaṅganairātmyādivādānām apy upaniṣadarthavādaprabhavatvam.*[52] As far as their merely theoretical dimension is concerned, i.e. insofar as they do not interfere with the injunctive core of the Vedic revelation of dharma, Kumārila shows a remarkable openness in accommodating these teachings, which he criticizes philosophically in his *Ślokavārttika*, and he seems willing to credit a wide range of different views with a certain relative and pedagogical usefulness and to find a certain basic value in the variety and confrontation of different views in general.[53] This does, of course, not mean that there is a legitimate variety of systems of religious and ritual orientation; in matters of dharma, the rigid application of the vedamūlatva principle leaves no room for variety or compromise.

The following section in the *Tantravārttika*, which deals with the Kalpasūtras, is equally significant, especially in its *pūrvapakṣa* portion. Kumārila, who considers various alternative interpretations of Mīmāṃsāsūtra I, 3, 11, introduces an objector who suggests the following: The authority of the Kalpasūtras, which prescribe ritualistic procedures in strict accordance with the Vedic texts and which are appendices of the Veda, is essentially different from that of the smṛti texts, and it never requires the assumption of lost śruti texts for its validation. This being so, should they not be regarded as parts or as authoritative "recensions" of the Veda itself rather than as mere derivations? Pursing this further into a somewhat modified interpretation, one might consider the idea that the Veda itself contains a potentially infinite internal variety, its "recensions" or "branches" (*śākhā*), including the Kalpasūtras, being of equal and equally direct authority. Could not then the Buddhists claim their share of this "infinity" and present their teachings as "branches" of the all-comprehensive Vedic revelation?[54] This implies the following important, potentially very far-reaching question: If variety or plurality has to be accepted anyway as an essential ingredient of the Vedic revelation, why should it be limited in a formalistic and artificial manner? Why should it not be extended and universalized? In his refutation of this pūrvapakṣa, Kumārila points out the basic difference between the Kalpasūtras and a Vedic "branch" or "recension" in the full sense, and he emphasizes that the vedāṅgas in general cannot be accepted as fully authoritative parts of the "superhuman," "authorless" (*apauruṣeya*) Vedic revelation.[55] In this context, he refers to the linguistic character of the Buddhist texts, and he criticizes not only the Buddhists' alleged inability to use correct Sanskrit, but also their failure to use the Prakrits properly.[56]

8. The notion of a potential "infinity of Vedic branches" (*śākhānantya*) and the attempt to use it as an argument against claims of orthodoxy and exclusivity and against the vedamūlatva principle as such are also found in the *Nyāyamañjarī* by Jayantabhaṭṭa. How can an infinitely differentiated Veda possibly function as a criterion of orthodoxy and heterodoxy? The very idea of incompatibility with the Veda does not apply because of the infinity of its lost or extant traditions: *pratyuktaṃ ca viruddhatvaṃ śākhānantyāc ca durgamam.*[57]

Jayanta (ninth century) is familiar with Kumārila's works. However, what distinguishes their approach to the Veda on the one hand and to the sectarian plurality on the other hand is the fact that Jayanta, unlike Kumārila, is a theistic philosopher who understands the Veda not as an authorless complex of meanings, but as the personal word and work of God (īśvara). The question which arises for him in this connection is: Why should the Veda as we have it today, or any part of it, be considered the only or final word of God? Why should the word of God not be present in other religious traditions as well? And why should we not accept the "validity of all traditions" (*sarvāgamaprāmāṇya*)?

Jayanta, whose presentation is richly supplemented not only by his own philosophical drama *Āgamaḍambara*, but also by the discussion in Bhāsarvajña's *Nyāyabhūṣaṇa* (ca. A.D. 900), does not subscribe to the theory of the "validity of all traditions."[58] But on the other hand, he does not rely on the vedamūlatva principle as applied by Kumārila. What he relies on in order to distinguish between legitimate and illegitimate religious traditions is the "acceptance by the great (and/or many) people" (*mahājanaparigṛhītatva*)[59]—a criterion explicitly rejected by Kumārila as potentially relativistic. Similarily, Kumārila does not recognize traditional familiarity or common acceptance (*lokaprasiddhi*) as the basis for distinguishing between dharma and adharma, between legitimate and illegitimate ways of orientation.[60] The concept of lokapraisddhi plays a more positive role in the thought of Bhartṛhari (ca. A.D. 500), with which Kumārila is thoroughly familiar. In general, Bhartṛhari's philosophy of the Vedic "word" is one of the most significant and far-reaching contributions to the theme of religious or philosophical plurality and of its relation to the unity and coherence of the Vedic tradition. The Veda is the self-differentiation of the absolute; and this fundamental internal differentiation is extended into the variety of human "views" and traditions. Whether legitimate or not, all these various "views" seem to be indebted to and originating from the inner variety of the Veda. The Vedic word, though always one, is being handed down in many different recensions; it has numerous local and other varieties and many different "forms."[61] Moreover, the arthavāda sections of the Veda and similar texts, specifically the Upaniṣads, have been open to many different—legitimate as well as illegitimate—interpretations, and on this basis, the philosophical theories of nondualists and dualists have been taught in various ways: *ekatvināṃ dvaitināṃ ca pravādā bahudhā matāḥ.*[62]

In the philosophy of Bhartṛhari, the demarcation line between the legitimate internal differentiation of the Vedic revelation and the factual variety of human opinions or ways of orientation is less clear and less significant than in the philosophy of Śaṅkara or Kumārila. Although Bhartṛhari also emphasizes the difference between thought that is guided by the sacred tradition and "dry," merely human reasoning (*śuṣkatarka, puruṣatarka*), his use of the Veda as criterion of legitimacy and "orthodoxy" is less conspicuous and overshadowed by its all-comprehensive metaphysical status.[63] Human views and interpretations somehow continue the self-differentiation of the absolute; the variety of the perspectives or approaches is internally meaningful and corresponds to the very nature of "seeing" (*darśana*). "Differentiation of seeing" (*darśana-bheda, bhinnaṃ darśanam,* etc.) has to be understood as being fully compatible with the unity and identity of its object;[64] and it has to be recognized "that insight gains distinctness by (the study of) different traditional views": *prajñā vivekaṃ labhate bhinnair āgama-darśanaiḥ.*[65];

9. In Bhartṛhari's view, the Veda is the "arranger" (*vidhātṛ*), that is, the organizing structure not only of all legitimate religious or scholarly traditions, but also of society and culture in general and ultimately of the whole world. The different branches of learning, which teach and educate mankind, proceed from the major and minor "limbs" of the Veda:

vidhātus tasya lokānām aṅgopāṅganibandhanāḥ
vidyābhedāḥ pratāyante jñānasaṃskārahetavaḥ.[66]

Bhartṛhari's autocommentary paraphrases that the Veda is both the ultimate source (*prakṛti*) and the instructor (*upadeṣṭṛ*) of the world. Accordingly, the Veda cannot be placed side by side with other religious teachings or documents. The unity of brahman (as "word" and ultimate reality), which is the source and purport of the Vedic revelation, may indeed be open or even conducive to a plurality of views and approaches. But this does not amount to perspectivistic indifference. There is an irreducible gradation or hierarchy, to be measured in terms of distance from the Vedic word; and the Veda itself assigns standpoints and conditions of legitimacy.

Bhartṛhari's understanding of religious and philosophical plurality may appear ambiguous and evasive in its combination of restrictive and universalistic implications, of inclusivism and exclusivism. At any rate Bhartṛhari, who certainly had predecessors on his way of thought, succeeded in developing an exemplary orthodox, Veda-oriented model for dealing with the problem of religious plurality, and he provided subsequent Hindu thinkers with important guidelines for meeting the challenge of extra-Vedic conceptions of religious and philosophical plurality, such as the Jaina perspectivism or the rich and complex structures of Mahāyāna Buddhist thought.

There can be no doubt that for a number of centuries Mahāyāna Buddhism has been most productive in matters of religious hermeneutics and in developing schemes and frameworks of concordance and reconciliation. The reflection on the relationship between Hīnayāna and Mahāyāna, or on the paths of the "disciples" (*śrāvaka*), the "private buddhas" (*pratyekabuddha*) and the *bodhisattvas*, has led to numerous complex and intriguing suggestions concerning the variety of approaches and expressions in relation to one ultimate goal or meaning. In particular, the Madhyamaka tradition has contributed to these developments, and it has presented Sarvāstivāda, Vijñānavāda, etc. as culminating in, and amounting to, Śūnyavāda. The different schools and levels of Buddhist teaching have been interrelated, integrated, and reconciled in various schemes of inclusion, fulfillment or gradual ascent, and the notion of one basic truth unfolding at different soteriological stages and through different layers of meaning and instruction has been expressed in many different ways. The idea of the bodhisattva and his "skill in means" (*upāyakauśalya*), the differentiation of disciples (*vine-*

yabheda) and of "lineages" (*gotra*) of aspirants, and fundamental hermeneutic distinctions between different modes of discourse and meaning (*neyārtha- nītārtha; saṃvṛti- paramārtha*, etc.) guide these remarkable efforts of thought, which have recently been dealt with in several pioneering studies by D. S. Ruegg.[67]

As an explicit program, all this remains largely an internal, intra-Buddhist affair; the various devices of interpretation and reconciliation are usually not applied to non-Buddhist teachings. But it is obvious that their usage can be easily extrapolated and universalized or adopted by other schools and for other purposes. As a matter of fact, Candrakīrti seems to observe no clear border line between Buddhist and non-Buddhist systems in his presentation and "propaedeutic" interpretation of theories that fail to recognize the principle of "voidness."[68] And another leading follower of Nāgārjuna, Bhāvaviveka (Bhavya), claims that the om/brahman of the Vedāntins is ultimately nothing but the "void" (*śūnya*) of the Madhyamaka school.[69]

The Concept of Adhikāra

10. As we have seen, Śaṅkara regards the Buddhist notions of *vineyabheda* and *upāyakauśalya* as false and illegitimate. In his view, didactic adjustments of this type, and a corresponding variety of religious and soteriological methods and levels of discourse, have to be justified and guided by the Veda. The Veda itself determines the access to its own sacred and liberating teachings concerning ultimate reality, and it assigns different kinds and levels of *adhikāra*, that is, ritual and soteriological "competence" or "vocation," to various hereditary groups of people. Śaṅkara uses his orthodox concept of adhikāra to reject and supersede the Buddhist ideas of vineyabheda, etc.; yet these ideas themselves have, in a sense, become part of his understanding of the Veda. Unlike Śaṅkara, modern Vedāntins tend to disregard the restrictive, exclusivistic implications of the concept of adhikāra. Instead they emphasize its universalistic, inclusivistic potential, and use it to explain and vindicate the plurality of religions and world-views not just in India, but in the world at large.

The concept of adhikāra is central and symptomatic in the traditional and orthodox as well as in the modern Indian approaches to religious plurality. To conclude this chapter, it seems appropriate to review the role of adhikāra in the history of Indian thought, specifically in Mīmāṃsā and Advaita Vedānta.

The *Kātyāyanaśrautasūtra* seems to be the oldest extant source dealing with adhikāra. It discusses the question which groups of living beings are qualified, eligible, or authorized to perform Vedic rituals.[70] It restricts such eligibility basically to the "twice-born" members of the three higher castes, provided they are not incapacitated by certain defects. There are, however, older occurrences of the verb *adhikṛ* that are clearly relevant for our survey. Moreover, it is helpful to recall the literal, etymological connotations of this verb: "to place above," "appoint," "authorize," "put in charge of." This meaning is present in the following passage from the *Jaiminīya Brāhmaṇa: yad āha vānaspatyam iti vanaspatibhyo hy enam adhikurvanti.*[71] Similarly, the word *adhikṛta* refers to the person who has been "put in charge" or "authorized," that is, the "superintendent" or "overseer," for instance in the *Praśna Upaniṣad: yathā saṃrāḍ eva-adhikṛtān viniyuṅkta etān grāmān etān grāmān adhitiṣṭhasva-iti.*[72] Correspondingly, adhikāra assumes such meanings as "authority," "competence," "vocation," but also "obligation," and "responsibility." It refers to "governing" functions and elements not only in nature or society, but also in texts and teachings, where it may indicate a governing rule or dominant theme.

In order to understand the kind of "authority," "governance" and "obligation" with which adhikāra is associated in its more philosophical usages, it is important to refer to its close association with the concept of dharma: Adhikāra has its place in a universe that is hierarchically structured, that has to be upheld through the performance of rituals and the observance of religious norms and social distinctions, and in which certain hereditary groups of people have a special mandate for certain types of activities. In the core areas of its orthodox usage, specifically in Mīmāṃsā, Dharmaśāstra and Advaita Vedānta, the concept of adhikāra appears as a corollary of dharma and its various interpretations, and it is inseparable from related concepts, such as *vidhi* and *niyoga.*

11. Among the presentations of the orthodox views on adhikāra, the sixth adhyāya of Jaimini's Mīmāṃsāsūtras has special significance. It resumes and continues the discussion concerning the "eligibility" for Vedic rituals that we find first documented in the Śrautasūtras; however, Jaimini and his commentators, in particular Śabara, go far beyond Kātyāyana's text. After excluding nonhuman beings from the realm of ritual adhikāra and presenting some remarkable observations on the distinction between humans and animals,[73] the Mīmāṃsā teachers examine the role of women in the rituals and finally focus on the status of the śūdras. The orthodox exclusion of the śūdras is upheld against the more liberal views of Bādari. In general, the emphasis in this section is on the restrictive and exclusivistic implications of adhikāra.[74] The most far-reaching issue in the controversy between Jaimini (who mentions Ātreya as his predecessor) and Bādari is the following one: Can the "competence" and "vocation" for the rituals be derived from natural, empirical criteria, such as intelligence and motivation, or is it based upon a scriptural "entitlement" and "authorization" that is not subject to worldly criteria of this type? Against Bādari's liberal and "naturalistic" tendencies, Jaimini and his followers articulate the orthodox legalistic view: The competence for the Vedic rituals is itself a matter of Vedic injunctions (*vidhi*); consequently, adhikāra in classical and later Mīmāṃsā is most specifically discussed under the rubric of *adhikāravidhi*.[75]

The definition of adhikāra itself is affected by this association; it varies in accordance with the different interpretations of *vidhi* and *bhāvanā*, that is, the motivating power of the Vedic word. Those followers of Kumārila who regard the Vedic "imperatives" as hypothetical, i.e. as showing the means to achieve desired ends (*iṣṭasādhanatā*), usually define adhikāra as "ownership of the results" (*phalasvāmya, phalasvāmitva*), that is, as the entitlement to reap the desired fruits of a ritual performance; *adhikāra* in this sense means primarily a "right" and an "eligibility." The followers of Prabhākara, on the other hand, view the imperative power of the Vedic injunctions as an unconditional, categorical one. The injunctions express "what ought to be done" (*kārya*), an "obligation" (*niyoga*) that cannot be reduced to a merely instrumental commitment to a desired end. The *adhikārin* who has the rightful access to the Vedic injunctions is at the same time the *niyojya*, that is, the one who is subject to the unconditional sense of obligation conveyed by the injunctions; adhikāra itself, as a virtual synonym of niyoga, means "duty" and "obligation" rather than "right" or "qualification." Obligation in turn is the very essence of dharma: *dharmo hi niyogaḥ.*[76] The "desire" (*kāma*) for the results of Vedic rituals is itself part of the niyoga or adhikāra. As such, it is no longer a natural urge, but a vocation that is integrated into an objective structure of obligation, a structure in which the actual attainment of the results is of secondary importance. The idea that there is an obligation to the work as such, regardless of its results, may remind us of Bhagavadgītā II, 47 (*karmaṇy eva-adhikāras te*) and the long series of commentaries on this famous verse.

Maṇḍana, the third great systematizer of the Mīmāṃsā and an independent and original follower of Kumārila, discusses Prabhākara's views on adhikāra, vidhi and niyoga in his *Vidhiviveka*; Vācaspati's commentary *Nyāyakaṇikā* adds much learned detail to this presentation.[77] In his later Vedānta work *Brahmasiddhi*, Maṇḍana examines the relationship between the adhikāra for ritual works and that for the knowledge of brahman.[78]

Questions concerning adhikāra are also addressed by the representatives of other systems, for instance by Udayana who excludes the śūdras from the study of the (orthodox) Nyāya.[79] The word *atha* which introduces a number of important Sūtra texts provides an opportunity for some detailed discussions concerning adhikāra both in the sense of "chapter," "leading theme," and of "eligibility," "vocation," "suitability for liberation" (*mokṣayogyatva*).[80] The inherent ambiguity of adhikāra, that is, its fluctuation between "authority," "right," and "obligation," between factual "competence" and scriptural "entitlement," and in general between the de facto and the de jure, is also reflected in its less technical, more colloquial usages in Indian literature.[81]

12. Śaṅkara adopts the Pūrvamīmāṃsā concept of adhikāra in basic accordance with its interpretation by Śabara and Kumārila.[82] His emphasis is, however, not on the adhikāra for ritual "works" (karman), but on the adhikāra for the "inquiry into brahman" (*brahmajijñāsā*) and that liberating knowledge of the self which is accessible through the Vedic-Upaniṣadic revelation. In his *Brahmasūtrabhāṣya*, he discusses the question of the eligibility of the gods for such liberating knowledge, and he argues very explicitly for the exclusion of the śūdras.[83] In doing so, he shows his commitment to the varṇāśramadharma and the hereditary interpretation of the varṇa system.

Śaṅkara recognizes the significance of intellectual, psychological and ethical prerequisites for the student of the Upaniṣads. Yet he rejects the attempt to justify the access to the knowledge of brahman merely on the basis of soteriological motivation (*arthitva*) and intellectual and other "worldly" capabilities (*śaktatva, sāmarthya*).[84] As we have noted earlier, such worldly capabilities alone cannot constitute adhikāra; Vedic matters require a competence that can only be derived from the Veda itself: *sāmarthyam api na laukikaṃ kevalam adhikārakāraṇaṃ bhavati, śāstrīye 'rthe śāstrīyasya sāmarthyasya-apekṣitatvāt.* Because the śūdras cannot undergo the *upanayana* and other Vedic ceremonies of initiation, they are excluded from the study of the Veda and, consequently, from any legitimate and effectual knowledge of brahman: *śāstrīyasya ca sāmarthyasya-adhyayananirākaraṇena nirākṛtatvāt.*[85] The problem of a potential injustice of such exclusion is, of cause, easily resolved by referring to the doctrine of karma and rebirth, which explains and justifies the current caste status and allows for a future ascent to higher stages.

The Veda "appoints," "authorizes" (*adhikaroti*) those who are eligible for its teachings;[86] it restricts the access to those "twice-born" members of the three higher castes who have undergone the upanayana ceremony and who meet the criterion of "nonexclusion" (*aparyudastatva*). It is only with reference to these hereditary groups that the Veda shows didactic flexibility and "skill in means" (*upāyakauśalya*), by addressing itself to different temperaments, types of motivation, and intelligence. The Veda itself determines the sphere of legitimate "differentiation of aspirants" or "disciples" (*vineyabheda*), and of religious plurality in general. "It is an objective, transpersonal epiphany, an authorless, yet didactically well-organized body of soteriological instruction, which distinguishes between different levels of qualification, eligibility or mandate (adhikāra). It adjusts its message, in its work and knowledge portions, accordingly. Although its ultimate message is that of the unity and identity of ātman and brahman, it carefully structures the path towards such unity through the multiplicity of appearance."[87]

Adhikāra has its place in a universe which is structured and upheld by the Vedic dharma: the "hierarchy of qualified aspirants" is based upon the "hierarchy of dharma" (*dharmatāratamyād adhi-*

kāritāratamyam).[88] More than once, Śaṅkara associates the concept of adhikāra with cosmic functions and obligations in the dharmic universe.[89] It is in reponse to this controlled "differentiation of adhikāra" (*adhikārabheda*) that "one deity evolves different names, forms, activities, attributes and powers" (*tatra ca devasya-ekasya nāmarūpakarmaguṇaśaktibhedaḥ, adhikārabhedāt*).[90] Śaṅkara's use of adhikārabheda in this passage is among the oldest traceable occurrences of the term.

Within the Vedic framework, Śaṅkara leaves much room for the "variety of personal inclinations" (*puruṣamativaicitrya*). The Veda simply reveals, in its work and knowledge portions, various relations between means and ends and leaves it to the aspirants to choose appropriate methods or approaches "in accordance with their own liking" (*yathāruci*). In doing so, it remains neutral "like a sun or a lamp": *tasmāt puruṣamativaicitryam apekṣya sādhyasādhanasambandhaviśeṣān upadiśati. tatra puruṣāḥ svayam eva yathāruci sādhanaviśeṣeṣu pravartante, śāstraṃ tu savitṛpradīpādivad upāste.*[91] The word *ruci* ("liking," "taste"), which appears in this passage, will emerge again in various later and more universalistic statements about religious plurality and the concept of adhikāra.[92]

13. Śaṅkara rejects the argument that the role of adhikāra might be fundamentally different in relation to ritual works on the one hand and the inquiry into ātman/brahman on the other hand. However, the rules of adhikāra apply only to those temporal acts and processes of studying, learning, and preparing for self-knowledge that take place within the universe of dharma and māyā. The ātman as such, with its inherent self-evidence, is not involved in these processes. It cannot have any "rights" or "obligations"; that is, it cannot be an *adhikārin*; nor can it be an object of adhikāra. It simply is what it is; and such sheer presence is incompatible with the very idea of adhikāra. It stands, as Śaṅkara says, in "opposition to adhikāra" (*adhikāravirodha*).

In his *Bhāmatī*, Śaṅkara's commentator Vācaspati explicates this as follows: "because the Upaniṣadic spirit who is not an agent and enjoyer stands in opposition to *adhikāra*. The initiator of an action, who is entitled to the enjoyment of the fruits produced by the action, is the adhikārin, i.e. 'owner,' with regard to this action. How can in this situation a non-agent be an initiator? And how can a non-enjoyer be entitled to the enjoyment of the fruits of an action?" (*aupaniṣadasya puruṣasya-akartur abhoktur adhikāravirodhāt. prayoktā hi karmaṇaḥ karmajanitaphalabhogabhāgī karmaṇy adhikārī svāmī bhavati. tatra katham akartā prayoktā? kathaṃ ca-abhoktā karmajanitaphalabhogabhāgī?*)[93]

It is, however, Śaṅkara's disciple Sureśvara who has dealt most explicitly with this issue. At the beginning of the *Sambandhavārttika*, the extensive introduction to his massive *Bṛhadāraṇyakopaniṣadbhāṣyavārttika*, Sureśvara presents his basic thesis that only a person who has completely renounced all activities, specifically ritual works (*tyaktāśeṣakriya*), is qualified for the message of the Upaniṣads.[94] He then introduces a *Pūrvamīmāṃsā* opponent who argues that final release (*mukti*), just like "prosperity" (*abhyudaya*), is brought about by ritual injunctions (*vidhi*), since without them, and without something to be done (*kārya*), the notion of somebody being "qualified" or "authorized" would not apply: *kāryaṃ vinā na-adhikārī.*[95] Sureśvara replies that the adhikāra for liberating knowledge does not imply any reference to ritual action; it simply requires readiness for, and legitimate access to, the means or prerequisites (*upāya, sādhana*) for knowledge, which include "listening" (*śravaṇa*) to the sacred texts.[96] This adhikāra is a "qualification" and "vocation" not for any kind of activity (*pravṛtti*), but for the abstention (*nivṛtti*) from all ritual and worldly acts, and ultimately from the entire realm of karma and rebirth (*saṃsāra*) itself.[97] An "agent" (*kartṛ*) who always wants to accomplish something (*siṣādhayiṣu*) can never have the vocation for the pursuit of self-knowledge.[98]

However, this does not imply that there is an adhikāra for the ātman per se, or for that ultimate knowledge (*jñāna*) which coincides with the sheer presence of the self. Sureśvara agrees with Śaṅkara: the self as such is incompatible with the idea of *adhikāra*. Its manifestation is "reality-dependent" (*vastutantra*), that is, entirely objective. An "inquiry into adhikāra" (*adhikāravicāra*) is inappropriate in this case; it applies only in the realm of means and approaches, i.e. with regard to what is *nṛtantra*, "dependent upon the person."[99]

14. Śaṅkara's orthodox, Veda-oriented concept of adhikāra, and the corresponding restrictions on the uses of *adhikārabheda/adhikāribheda* are not representative of the Hindu tradition in general. Many theistic thinkers, most conspicuously since Yāmuna (around A.D. 1000), extend the domain of genuine, didactically adjusted revelation much further; it includes not only the Vedas, but also the Purāṇas and other texts. Even within the tradition of Śaṅkara's Advaita Vedānta, the idea of *adhikārabheda* has been invoked not just to reconcile the different parts of the Veda, but also the different, apparently incompatible teachings of the orthodox philosophical systems (*darśana*). We find this approach, for instance, in the *Prasthānabheda* by Madhusūdana Sarasvatī to which we have referred earlier. In this work, Madhusūdana presents all orthodox teachers, such as Jaimini or Kapila, as omniscient proponents of the same ultimate truth, who adjusted "their teachings to the different capabilities of their disciples, trying to prepare them for the ultimate truth, and to protect them from lapsing into anti-Vedic heterodoxy (*nāstikya*)"[100] The *Prasthānabheda* presents itself as a commentary on the seventh verse of the *Śivamahimnastotra*, which states that the Vedas, Sāṃkhya, Yoga, Śaivism and Vaiṣṇavism are just different paths to the same religious goal, corresponding to a "variety of inclinations" (*rucīnāṃ vaicitryam*).

The concept of adhikāra is not always associated with the restrictions imposed by the hereditary varṇa system. In numerous devotional texts, but also in such works as the *Yogavāsiṣṭha*[101] or Abhinavagupta's *Tantrāloka*,[102] this association is more or less disregarded, if not deliberately rejected. Here, adhikāra means a kind of "soteriological competence" for which caste membership is not decisive. Yet all this falls short of those modern Indian interpretations which reduce the adhikārabheda entirely to a "distinction of natural aptitudes"[103] or a "difference in the intellecual equipments of the enquirers."[104] Such statements are symptomatic expressions of Neo-Hindu self-understanding and affiliated with the modern, "naturalistic" reinterpretations of the concepts of dharma and svadharma.

There is even less evidence in traditional Hinduism for an explicit universalization of adhikāra that would try to accommodate and reconcile all religious and philosophical traditions in the world by correlating them with different "aptitudes." This step was apparently not taken prior to the modern period of interaction with the Europeans. One of its earliest available documents is the "Preliminary Discourse" of the pandits who compiled the *Vivādārṇavasetu*, a collection of law texts which became the basis of N. B. Halhed's *A Code of Gentoo Laws* (1776):

> The truly intelligent well know, that the differences and varieties of created things are a ray of his glorious essence, and that the contrarieties of constitution are a type of his wonderful attributes. . . . He appointed to each tribe its own faith, and to every sect its own religion. . . . He views in each particular place the mode of worship respectively appointed to it; sometimes he is employed with the attendants upon the Mosque, in counting the sacred beads; sometimes he is in the temple, at the adoration of idols; the intimate of the Mussulman, and the friend of the Hindoo; the companion of the Christian, and the confidant of the Jew."[105]

Although the "Preliminary Discourse" is "absent in all manuscripts of the Sanskrit text" of the *Vivādārṇavasetu*,[106] and although there may be questions as to its genesis and authenticity, the word "appoint" obviously reflects the concept of adhikāra.

Since then, the idea of adhikārabheda has often been invoked to assert the peculiar universalism and inclusivism of the Hindu tradition against the universalistic claims of the Christian missionaries, for instance in the responses to J. Muir's *Mataparīkṣā*.[107] It has been used to vindicate religious plurality in general and to provide a basis for religious tolerance. Aurobindo Ghose has tried to combine this with modern evolutionary perspectives: "All stages of spiritual evolution are there in man and each has to be allowed or provided with its means of approach to the spirit, an approach suited to its capacity, adhikāra."[108] Yet the exclusivistic and restrictive meaning of adhikāra has by no means disappeared from its modern usages. At the beginning of the nineteenth century, we find it in the criticism which the orthodox opponents of Rammohan Roy direct against his egalitarian "market-place theology."[109] Towards the end of the nineteenth century, Vivekananda, the great spokesman of Neo-Hindu tolerance and universalism, denounces the traditional "theory of adhikārins" (*adhikārivāda*) as "the result of pure selfishness."[110]

Chapter 3: Notes

1. The historical and conceptual problems connected with the application of the term "sect" to the Indian tradition cannot be discussed in this context. At any rate, this term has had a specific affinity to the Indian religious tradition since it became known to the West; cf. R. de'Nobili, *On Indian Customs* (i.e. *Informatio de quibusdam moribus nationis Indicae*, written in 1613, ed. and trans. S. Rajamanickam. Palayamkottai, 1972), 27 ff.: "De sectis Brahmanum." The problems of finding an original Indian equivalent are illustrated by M. Monier-Williams, *A Dictionary, English and Sanskrit*. London, 1851 (reprint Delhi, 1971), s.v. "sect"; Monier-Williams suggests a wide variety of terms, including *śākhā, mārga, bhinnamārga, mata, sampradāya,* and *gaṇa.*

2. Cf. *India and Europe*, 341 ff.

3. Cf. *India and Europe*, 343 ff.; 346.

4. *Complete Works*. Calcutta, 1970–1973 (revised reprints of the Mayavati Memorial Edition), III, 536.

5. *Complete Works*, III, 511 f.

6. Already de'Nobili calls Buddhism a "sect" ("secta") of the "religion of idolaters" in his *Informatio de quibusdam moribus nationis Indicae* (see above, n. 1), 27 ff.

7. *Complete Works*, III, 251 f.; see also *India and Europe*, 408 f.

8. *An Essay on Hinduism*. London, 1911 (reprint Delhi, 1988 under the title: *Hinduism—Its Formation and Future*), 155.

9. *Religion and Society*. London, second ed., 1948, 102.

10. *Discourses on Hindu Spiritual Culture*. Delhi, 1967, 5.

11. On "tolerance" and "inclusivism", see *India and Europe*, ch. 22.

12. *Ṛgveda* I, 164, 46.

13. Madhusūdana's term *prasthānabheda*, "differentiation of approaches," refers to the words *prabhinne prasthāne* in the seventh verse of the *Śivamahimnastotra*—the one verse on which the entire *Prasthānabheda* purports to be a commentary.

14. Cf. *India and Europe*, 354 ff.

15. Referring to the teachings of the Buddhists and other heterodox groups, the *Prasthānabheda* states (ed. Gurucaraṇa Tarkadarśanatīrtha. Calcutta, 1939, 3): *vedabāhyatvāt teṣāṃ mlecchādiprasthānavat paramparayā-api puruṣārthānupayogitvād upekṣaṇīyatvam api.*

16. *The Brahma Sūtra*. London, 1960, 249.

17. *The Bhagavadgītā*. London, sixth ed.; annotations to IV, 11.

18. Cf. D.C. Bhattacaryya, "Sanskrit Scholars of Akbar's Time." *Indian Historical Quarterly* 13 (1937), 31–36; P.C. Divanji, Introduction to: *Siddhāntabindu of Madhusūdana*. Baroda,1933 (GOS), XXI.

19. Madhusūdana's eighteenfold list includes the four Vedas, six *vedaṅgas*, four *upāṅgas* (including *dharmaśāstra*, under which he subsumes "sectarian" religious traditions), and four *upavedas* (including *āyurveda*). On the timeless perspective of the traditional Indian classifications of "sciences" (*vidyā*), see *India and Europe*, ch. 19.

20. Cf. NBhūṣ, 71 (*pūrvapakṣa*): . . . *caturdaśāvadhāraṇam api na yuktam, śaivasiddhāntādīnāṃ vaidyaśāstrādīnāṃ ca bhinnaviṣayatvād iti* (implying that their separate subject-matter would require their classification as separate "sciences").

21. Cf. the role of Śaṅkara and Kumārila as defenders of the unity and identity of the "orthodox" tradition in such legendary biographies as the *Śaṅkaradigvijaya* attributed to Mādhava-Vidyāraṇya; cf. also the customary definition of the *smārta: vyavahāre bhāṭṭaḥ, paramārthe śāṅkaraḥ.*

22. BSBh I, 1, 1 (*Works* III, 6); see also Gauḍapāda, Kārikā III, 18 ff.

23. BSBh II, 2, 42 ff.

24. BSBh III, 3, 1 (*Works* III, 375).

25. Cf. BSBh I, 1, 11; accordingly, Śaṅkara, who rejects the metaphysical teachings of the Pāñcarātrins, is not opposed to their forms of worship (see II, 2, 42).

26. BSBh III, 3, 59 (*Works* III, 430); in the preceding section (III, 3, 58), the question is raised whether different procedures suggested by different Vedic "branches" (*śākhā*) should be combined; against this, Śaṅkara argues for making a choice among equally authoritative and legitimate alternatives.

27. See *Ātmatattvaviveka*, ed. Ḍhuṇḍhirāja Śāstrī. Benares, 1940 (ChSS), 448 ff.; on the plurality of approaches and the metaphor of the one city and the various travellers, cf. also *Yogavāsiṣṭha*. Utpattiprakaraṇa 96, 48 ff. (specifically v. 51). U. Mishra, *History of Indian Philosophy*, vol. 2. Allahabad, 1966, 158, suggests (apparently on the basis of the term *caramavedānta*) that Udayana sees Advaita as "the ultimate end." Similar suggestions have been made earlier, for instance by Gauḍabrahmānanda Sarasvatī (early eighteenth century) in his commentary on Madhusūdana's *Advaitasiddhi* (ed. Anantakṛṣṇa Śāstrin. Bombay, 1917, 228): *kiṃ ca-udayanācāryāṇāṃ vedāntadarśana eva mahatī śraddhā.*

28. *Nyāyakusumāñjali* I, 2 (prose section); Bhartṛhari presents the idea of the one true substance and the many words referring to it in the context of his non-dualistic metaphysics of the word (*śabdādvaita*); see VP III/2 (on *dravya*, "substance").

29. Cf. BSBh II, 2, 18 (*Works* III, 239): . . . . *pratipattibhedād vineyabhedād vā*; the expression *pratipattibheda* is ambiguous insofar as it may refer either to the Buddha's own "understanding" or to that of his disciples; the second interpretation, preferred by some of the commentators, would imply that the word *vā* does not indicate an alternative in the full sense. References to different types of disciples (*vineyajana*) and to a benevolent adjustment (*anurodha, ānurūpya*, etc.) to their different capacities are frequently found in Candrakīrti's commentary *Prasan-*

napadā on Nāgārjuna's *Madhyamakakārikā*; cf. VII, 34 (ed. L. de La Vallée Poussin, Bibl. Buddhica, p. 177); XV, 11 (p. 276); XVIII, 6 (p. 357); 8 (p.371); XXII, 10 (p.444); XXVI, 2 (p.547); on XVIII, 6 (p. 359), Candrakīrti quotes a verse attributed to Nāgārjuna himself, but not traceable in his extant works: *buddho 'vadat tathā dharmaṃ vineyānāṃ yathākṣamam.*

30. BSBh II, 2, 18 (*Works* III, 239).

31. *Bhāmatī* on BSBh II, 2, 18; Vācaspati differentiates the *sarvāstitva* view further into *vaibhāṣika* and *sautrāntika*. The expression *hīnamadhyotkṛṣṭa* is also used by Candrakīrti, *Prasannapadā* on *Madhyamakakārikā* XVIII, 6 (see above, n. 29).

32. BSBh II, 2, 32; cf. the idea of the Buddha as a deceitful incarnation of Viṣṇu.

33. Cf., e.g., BUBh V, 1, introduction.

34. On *Kaṭha Upaniṣad* I, 2, 17.

35. Cf. BSBh II, 1, 1.

36. Cf. BSBh I, 3, 40 f.

37. Cf. BSBh I, 4, 1 (reference to different *śākhās*); I, 1, 5; etc.

38. Cf. BSBh II, 2, 42 ff.

39. BSBh I, 1, 1 (*Works* III, 6); see above, n. 22.

40. BSBh II, 3, 34 (*Works* III, 236).

41. See BSBh II, 2, 42 ff.

42. Cf. Madhva, *Mahābhāratatātparyanirṇaya* I, 30 f.; see also the long series of post-Śaṅkara commentaries on BS II, 2, 42 ff. (Rāmānuja, Madhva, Nimbārka, Vallabha, etc.); and *India and Europe*, 360 ff.; 365 ff.

43. On this and other doxographies, cf. *India and Europe*, ch. 19; on the idea of an ascent from the *pariṇāmavāda* to the *vivartavāda*, see Sarvajñātman, *Saṃkṣepaśārīraka* II, 61. There is, of course, an implicit ranking in Śaṅkara's approach to the various systems; the Vaiśeṣika, the "semi-destructionist" (*ardhavaināśika*) system, is closer to Buddhism and thus "lower" than other Hindu systems, such as the Yoga; cf. BSBh II, 2, 18 (*Works* III, 239).

44. See above, n. 16. Cf. also Radhakrishnan's "Forword" to S. Kuppuswami Sastri, *Compromises in the History of Advaitic Thought*. Madras, 1946. Referring to the Hindu "spirit of comprehension" and the "master plan of Hindu thought," he says: "The revival of the spirit today will help us to take up and answer the challenge of modern times."

45. Cf. *India and Europe*, 179 ff.; 320 ff.

46. In the following, we will not deal with the intricate problems concerning the Pūrvamīmāṃsā attitude towards Vedānta, which are even more intriguing as far as the school of Kumārila's rival Prabhākara is concerned.

47. Cf. TV, 113 (on MS I, 3, 4): *ko hi śaknuyād utsannānāṃ vākyaviṣayeyattāniyamaṃ kartum?*

48. Ibid. (referring to MS I, 3, 3).

49. TV, 114 (on I, 3, 4).

50. TV, 112 (on I, 3, 4); see also Medhātithi on Manu II, 6 (ed. J. H. Dave, Bombay, 1972 ff., I, 163; 169; 171 f.; Medhātithi quotes his own *Smṛtiviveka* and criticizes the *śakhotsāda* theory).

51. See below, ch. 4.

52. TV, 81 (on I, 3, 2). ŚV, 465 (*Sambandhākṣepaparihāra*, v. 63 ff.) finds the origin of the un-Vedic and erroneous theories of the creation and dissolution of the world in literal and thus inappropriate interpretations of *stuti*, i.e. *arthavāda* passages in the Veda and such smṛti texts as the

Mahābhārata: *stutivākyakṛtaś ca-eṣa janānāṃ mativibhramaḥ*. This recalls the procedure of Bhartṛhari; cf. VP I, 8 (with Vṛtti). On *stuti/arthavāda* as motivating "commendation," see below, ch. 5, § 7.

53. Cf. TV, 81 (on I, 3, 2); however, Kumārila himself is obviously not committed to the idea of a pedagogical legitimacy of the *vijñānavāda* (which he criticizes in his TV on I, 3, 12); on the pedagogical justification of Vālmīki, Vyāsa, etc., cf. G. Jha, *Pūrva-Mīmāṃsā in Its Sources*. Benares, second ed., 1964, 109 f.

54. Cf. TV, 156 ff. (on I, 3, 11).

55. TV, 162 ff. (on I, 3, 12 ff.).

56. Cf. TV, 164 f. (on I, 3, 12).

57. Cf. NM, 245 ff.

58. On Jayanta and Bhāsarvajña, see G. Oberhammer, "Die Überlieferungsautorität im Hinduismus." *Offenbarung, geistige Realität des Menschen*, ed. G. Oberhammer. Vienna, 1974, 41–92. We may add here that Bhāsarvajña, NBhūṣ, 393, relates a theory concerning the origin of "sectarian" movements which has not yet found the attention it deserves. It suggests that the Jina and other "sectarian" teachers appealed specifically to underprivileged groups, such as the śūdras, and that their pronouncements about the end of suffering (*duḥkhakṣayopadeśa*) became subsequently attractive to other groups as well, in particular to certain brahmins who were "dull-witted" (*mandaprajña*) and "tormented by the pain of poverty" (*dāridryaduḥkhasantapta*).

59. On this concept, see G. Chemparathy, "Meaning and Role of the Concept of mahājanaparigraha in the Ascertainment of the Validity of the Veda." *Philosophical Essays, Prof. A. Thakur Felicitation Vol.* Calcutta 1987, 67–80; and above, ch. 2, § 2 (especially n. 10). Jayanta's *Āgamaḍambara* (ed. V. Raghavan and A. Thakur, Darbhanga, 1964, 96 f.) presents familiarity, continuity and decency as criteria of sectarian legitimacy.

60. Cf. TV, 113 (on I, 3, 4; on *mahājanaparigṛhītatva* and *pitrādyanugama*, "ancestral habits"); SV, 149 f. (*Autpattikasūtra*, v. 1 ff.; on *lokaprasiddhi*).

61. Cf. VP I, 5 (with Vṛtti); and I, 31 f. (*lokaprasiddhatva; prasiddhi*).

62. VP I, 8; the Vṛtti paraphrases the expression *arthavādarūpāṇi* used in the first half of the verse as an *ekaśeṣa*, comprising the meanings *arthavāda* and "what is like *arthavāda*" (*arthavādaprakāra*), and it illustrates this by citing numerous Vedic and Upaniṣadic passages. In spite of the questions raised by M. Biardeau and in accordance with the assessment by A. Aklujkar ("The Authorship of the Vākyapadīya-vṛtti," *Wiener Zeitschrift für die Kunde Südasiens* 16, 1972, 181–198), the Vṛtti deserves recognition as Bhartṛhari's own work.

63. On *śuṣkatarka* see below, ch. 5, § 6.

64. Cf. VP I, 75; 110; II; 136 (ed. W. Rau); and *India and Europe*, ch. 15 (especially 264 ff.).

65. VP II, 489; and *India and Europe*, 268 f.

66. VP I, 10.

67. See *La théorie du tathāgathagarbha et du gotra: Études sur la sotériologie et la gnoséologie du bouddhisme*. Paris, 1969 specifically 55 ff., for general observations on *nītārtha* and *neyārtha*. Several other studies supplement this monumental work, e.g. *Le traité du tathāgatagarbha de Bu ston Rin chen grub*. Paris, 1973; "The gotra, ekayāna and tathāgatagarbha Theories of the Prajñāpāramitā according to Dharmamitra and Abhayākaragupta," *Prajñāpāramitā and Related Systems. Studies in Honor of E. Conze*, ed. L. Lancaster. Berkeley, 1977, 283–312.

68. *Prasannapadā* on *Madhyamakakārikā* XV, 11 (ed. L. de La Vallée Poussin, 275 f.; quoting Nāgārjuna, *Ratnāvalī* I, 61 f.).

69. Cf. F. V. Gokhale, "Masters of Buddhism Adore the Brahman through Non-Adoration." *Indo-Iranian Journal* 5 (1961), 271–275; H. Na-

kamura, "The Vedānta as Presented by Bhavya." *Journal of the Oriental Institute* (Baroda) 14 (1964/1965), 287–296; id., "The Vedāntic Chapter of Bhavya's Madhyamakahṛdaya." *Adyar Library Bulletin* 39 (1975), 300–329; also on Bhavya as a "doxographer": C. Lindtner, "On Bhavya's Madhyamakaratnapradīpa." *Indologica Taurinensia* 12 (1987), 163–184 (distinction of correct and incorrect relative truth, *satyasaṃvṛtisatya* and *mithyāsaṃvṛtisatya*); O. Quarnström, *Hindu Philosophy in Buddhist Perspective. The Vedāntatattvaviniścaya Chapter of Bhavya's Madhyamakahṛdayākārikā.* Lund, 1989.

70. See *Kātyāyanaśrautasūtra* I, 1, 1 ff.; the historical study of the concept of *adhikāra* is now greatly facilitated by the articles on *adhikāra, adhikṛ* and related words in *An Encyclopedic Dictionary of Sanskrit on Historical Principles*, vol. 3, part 1, ed. A.M. Ghatage. Poona, 1982, 1571–1601. For some exemplary references, see also R. W. Lariviere, "Adhikāra-Right and Responsibility." *Languages and Cultures. Studies in Honor of E.C. Polomé.* Berlin, 1988, 359–364.

71. *Jaiminīya Brāhmaṇa* I, 73.

72. *Praśna Upaniṣad* III, 4.

73. See below, ch. 8.

74. See MS VI, 1, 25–38.

75. See, for instance, Laugākṣi Bhāskara, *Arthasaṃgraha*, section 48 (ed. A. B. Gajendragadkar and R.D. Karmarkar, Bombay, 1934, 39 ff.; 202 ff.; *adhikāra* as *phalasvāmya* and *phalabhoktṛtva*).

76. Cf. Śālikanātha, *Ṛjuvimalā* on Prabhākara's *Bṛhatī*, ed. A. Chinnasvāmī Śāstrī. Benares, 1929 (ChSS), 14; Prabhākara himself introduces the term *adhikāra* on p. 1 of his work); see also *Bṛhatī* and *Ṛjuvimalā* on MS VI, 1, 4 (ed. S. Subrahmanya Sastri, vol. 5, Madras, 1967, 55: the *niyojya* as *adhikārin*).

77. *Vidhiviveka* with *Nyāyakaṇikā*, ed. M.L. Goswamī. Benares, 1978, 64 ff. (see p.65, *pūrvapakṣa: adhikārahetukā ca pravṛttir iṣyate, na phalahetukā*); also 236; 240 ff.: 245; 252; 260 ff.

78. *Brahmasiddhi*, ed. S. Kuppuswami Sastri. Madras, 1937 (reprint Delhi, 1984), 26 ff.

79. Cf. *Pariśuddhi*, ed. A. Thakur, 72 ff.

80. Cf. H. N. Raghavendrachar, *Brahma-Mīmāṃsā*, vol. 1. Mysore, 1965, 107 ff.

81. Cf. *An Encyclopedic Dictionary of Sanskrit* (see above, n. 70), 1571 ff.

82. BSBh I, 3, 25 cites Jaimini's "definition of adhikāra" (*adhikāralakṣaṇa*). Apart from the controversial *Yogasūtrabhāṣyavivaraṇa* (see below, ch. 6, § 3), explicit references to or quotations from Kumārila are conspicuously absent in Śaṅkara works. Nevertheless, his acquaintance with Kumārila appears certain. It is attested by his disciple Sureśvara in his commentary on the *Taittirīyopaniṣadbhāṣya*. Sureśvara associates Śaṅkara's characterization of an unacceptable view concerning works and final liberation (*mokṣa*) with a verse from the *Ślokavārttika* (*Sambandhākṣepaparihāra*, v. 110) and calls Kumārila a "self-styled Mīmāṃsaka" (*mīmāṃsakaṃmanya*; cf. TUBhV I, 9, f.). On Śaṅkara's general expertise in Pūrvamīmāṃsā, cf. S. G. Moghe, "Śaṅkarācārya and Pūrvamīmāṃsā." *Mysore Orientalist* 4 (1971), 79–89 (reprinted in : *Studies in the Pūrva Mīmāṃsā*. Delhi, 1984, 1–13).

83. Cf. BSBh I, 3, 34 ff.; and below, ch. 10.

84. Cf. TUBh II, 1,1 (*Works* I, 287 f.); and below, ch. 8, § 8. Śaṅkara cites man's superior intelligence and his pre-eminence (*prādhānya*) among living beings in support of his special adhikāra; yet even here, he adds a reference to "non-exclusion" (*aparyudastatva*). BSBh I, 1, 1 (*Works* III, 5) mentions the four "means" (*sādhana*) of renunciation, including the "distinction between eternal and non-eternal entities" (*nityānityavastuviveka* and "desire to be liberated" (*mumukṣutva*), as prerequisites of *brahmajijñāsā*. Later Advaitins usually include these in their descriptions of the *adhikārin*; see, for instance, Sadānanda, *Vedāntasāra*.

85. BSBh I, 3, 34 (*Works* III, 136).

86. BSBh I, 3, 25 f. (*Works* III, 119 f.).

87. *India and Europe*, 388.

88. BSBh I, 1, 4 (*Works* III, 13).

89. See, for instance, BSBh III, 3, 32 (on the Sūtra *yāvadadhikāram avasthitir ādhikārikāṇām*).

90. BUBh III, 9, 9 (*Works* I, 836).

91. BUBh II, 1, 10 (*Works* I, 742 f.); see also above, § 4.

92. See, for instance, *Śivamahimnastotra*, v. 7; Nīlakaṇṭha Śāstrī Gore, *Śāstratattvavinirṇaya* VI/1, 31 (cf. R. F. Young, *Resistant Hinduism*. Vienna, 1981, 164).

93. Cf. BSBh and *Bhāmatī*, Upodghāta (ed. and trans. S.S. Suryanarayana Sastri and C. Kunhan Raja, Madras 1933, 54).

94. *Sambandhavārttika*, ed. and trans. T.M.P. Mahadevan. Madras, 1958, 7 (v. 12).

95. *Sambandhavārttika*, 11 (v. 20).

96. *Sambandhavārttika*, 116 f. (v. 227 ff.).

97. See 68 (v. 130); *mumukṣor adhikāro 'to nivṛttau sarva-karmaṇām; 130 (v. 254): nivṛttāv eva niḥśeṣasaṃsārasya . . . adhikāraḥ syād.*

98. *Sambandhavārttika*, 141 f. (v. 281 f.).

99. *Sambandhavārttika*, 117 (v. 229); see also v. 760: *adhikārapraveśitvaṃ na-ātmajñānasya yujyate.*

100. Cf. *India and Europe*, 358.

101. Cf. *Yogavāsiṣṭha*, *Utpattiprakaraṇa* 96, 48 ff.

102. Cf. Abhinavagupta, *Tantrāloka XXXV*, 35.

103. Cf. S. C. Chatterjee and D. M. Datta, *Introduction to Indian Philosophy*. Calcutta, seventh ed., 1968, 11.

104. Cf. U. Mishra, *History of Indian Philosophy*, vol. 1. Allahabad, 1957, 21.

105. *A Code of Gentoo Laws*. London, 1781, LXXIII f.

106. Cf. R. Rocher, *Orientalism, Poetry, and the Millenium: The Checkered Life of N. B. Halhed, 1751–1830*. Delhi, 1983, 66, n. 22.

107. Cf. R. F. Young, *Resistant Hinduism*. Vienna, 1981, 162 ff.; id., "Extra Vedos Nulla Salus," *Zeitschrift für Missionswissenschaft und Religionswissenschaft* 66 (1982), 81–95.

108. *The Life Divine*, vol. 2. Calcutta, 1940, 776 (as quoted by R. F. Young, *Resistant Hinduism*, 164, n. 198).

109. Cf. *India and Europe*, 210 f.

110. Cf. M.L. Burke, *Swami Vivekananda: His Second Visit to the West*. San Francisco, 1973, 11 f.-For a survey of modern Indian attitudes, see *Modern Indian Responses to Religious Pluralism*, ed. H. G. Coward. Albany, 1987.

CHAPTER 4

Vedic Apologetics, Ritual Killing, and the Foundations of Ethics

Introduction: Ahiṃsā and Dharma

1. "*Ahiṃsā* is one of the central ideas of Indian religions, and though the doctrine of 'non-violence'—literally 'non-injury (to living beings)'—is not universally followed in India, there will be only few who do not at least pay lip-service to it. In spite of its great importance for the religious attitude of the Indians, the history of the idea of ahiṃsā has rarely been investigated into, and the handbooks of Indian religions generally devote little space to it."[1] With these words, H.-P. Schmidt opens an inquiry into the origins and the early history of the doctrine of ahiṃsā. He rejects the view of L. Alsdorf,[2] that ahiṃsā is basically foreign to the Vedic tradition, and that its origins should not be sought in the teachings of the Buddha and the Jina either, but rather in non-Āryan sources. Instead, he argues that Vedic ritualism itself is its original basis and context. Schmidt does not mention that the thesis of the Vedic origin of ahiṃsā, though incompatible with the self-understanding of the anti-Vedic advocates of ahiṃsā, may be found in the argumentation of their "orthodox" opponents who tried to defend the Vedic rituals *against* the claims of ahiṃsā.

The following presentation will not investigate the origins of ahiṃsā, nor the original relationship between Vedic ritualism and ahiṃsā. Instead, it will deal with later Indian interpretations of this relationship, as well as with the role of ahiṃsā in the debates between the opponents of the Veda and its orthodox defenders, i.e., above all the Mīmāṃsakas. It will deal with the critique and defense of the bloody rituals enjoined by the Veda, as well as with other traditions associated with ritual and supposedly meritorious killing, specifically those of the Thags (*ṭhaka*) and *saṃsāramocaka*. These groups may be marginal phenomena in the history of Indian religions. Yet they represent important problems and possibilities of religious self-understanding; in the history of Indian philosophy, they have been associated with intense debates and reflections concerning the legitimacy of religious traditions and the foundations of ethics.

A history of the relations between ahiṃsā and dharma, of their affinities and tensions, of the various ways in which they have been coordinated with, or subordinated to one another, would illustrate basic trends and fundamental ambiguities of Hinduism in general. The concept of dharma is often used by the advocates and propagators of the ahiṃsā doctrine. Ahiṃsā is said to be the "supreme dharma" (*paramo dharmaḥ*), comprising and legitimizing all other, more specific, rules of conduct and orientation.[3] Together with the "Golden Rule" of not doing to others what one does not want done to oneself, it is presented as *dharmasarvasva*, as the totality and quintessence of dharma.[4] Such and similar claims are an obvious challenge to the "orthodox" understanding of dharma as a set of rules which are laid down in the sacred texts and specified according to time, place and "qualification" (*adhikāra*), which cannot be reduced to or derived from one basic principle, and which give, in fact, explicit legitimacy to certain well-defined acts of killing. The response, as documented in such texts as the *Manusmṛti*, has often been more or less apologetic; and in general, there has been a considerable variety of attempts to balance, reconcile or integrate ahiṃsā and the scriptural dharma, to reinterpret the Vedic precepts or to limit the scope of ahiṃsā.[5]

Traditionally, the animal sacrifices prescribed for certain Vedic rituals have been in the focus of debate on the relationship between ahiṃsā and dharma. They have been a main target for the anti-Vedic criticism of the Buddhists and the Jainas, and they have also been criticized by such ahiṃsā-oriented Hindu schools as Sāṃkhya and Yoga.[6] On the other hand, they are one of the central issues in orthodox Vedic apologetics. In spite of the fact that the bloody rituals were becoming more and more obsolete, and that substitutes were often used instead of living creatures, the defense of these practices against Buddhist and other detractors remained part of the orthodox self-presentation, not only in philosophical literature, but also, for instance, in the Purāṇas.[7] "Thus while the Vedic sacrificial religion was fast becoming a relic of the past, the authority of the Veda was constantly reaffirmed by Mīmāṃsakas, Smārtas, and Nyāya-Vaiśeṣikas alike".[8]

At the time of the classical systems, the Mīmāṃsā takes the lead and the most uncompromising stand in the defense of the scriptural and ritualistic dharma against the claims of ahiṃsā. Other issues which have been raised in connection with ahiṃsā, for example, capital punishment, suicide, or the fighting and killing which is part of the quasi-ritualistic caste duties of the kṣatriya, play no significant role in the context of this debate, and they may be omitted from our presentation.

Kumārila's Defense of Ritual Violence

2. In the extant Mīmāṃsā literature preceding Kumārila, that is, in the *Mīmāṃsāsūtra* and in Śabara's *Bhāṣya*, the attention paid to the problem of sacrificial *hiṃsā* and to the relationship between ahiṃsā and dharma, remains somewhat marginal. Śabara refers to the notion of hiṃsā in his commentary on Mīmāṃsāsūtra I, 1, 2, discussing the implications of the word *artha* in Jaimini's definition of dharma. Such rituals as the *śyena* sacrifice, meant to lead to the destruction of enemies, other human beings, cannot be considered acts of dharma since they lack the criterion of artha. According to Śabara, they are only described, but not enjoined by the sacred texts; the Veda teaches them as means, not giving any legitimacy to the ends to which they are supposed to be conducive; *hiṃsā hi sā, sā ca pratiṣiddhā. kathaṃ punar anarthaḥ kartavyatayā-upadiśyate? ucyate, na-eva śyenādayaḥ kartavyatayā vijñāyante. yo hi hiṃsitum icchet, tasya-ayam abhyupāya iti hi teṣām upadeśaḥ* ("This is violence, and it is forbidden. Why then is a harmful act taught as something that ought to be done? The answer is: Such rituals as the *śyena* sacrifice are not put forth as something that ought to be done. They are taught only in the following sense: 'If someone wants to hurt, then this is an effective method'.")[9] The issue in this discussion is an act of violence and destruction which is external to the sacrificial act itself, that is, not taking place during the ritual but supposed to result from it. The question of how to judge the killing of the sacrificial animal which takes place as an integral part of the śyena ritual itself is not discussed by Śabara, and, in general, he does not pay explicit attention to the issue of internal sacrificial hiṃsā or to other basic problems implied in the relationship between dharma and ahiṃsā. This is done by his great commentator Kumārila.

In the *Codanāsūtra* section of his *Ślokavārttika*, Kumārila places the explication of the Vedic dharma and of the bloody rituals which it implies in a much wider context than Jaimini or Śabara. He defends its uniqueness and irreducibility much more explicitly and vigorously, and takes special care to deny any independent, extra-scriptural authority to the principle of ahiṃsā.[10]

Kumārila rejects the idea of a universal cosmic causality, a general law of retribution that would cause the pain or injury inflicted upon a living creature to fall back upon its originator. This magico-ritualistic notion of cosmic retribution, which is based upon the presupposition of universal balance and reciprocity, is obsolete for Kumārila. He tries to give a "rational" refutation of such a notion, which seems to play a considerable role in the texts quoted by Schmidt, which has been preserved and developed in the traditions of Sāṃkhya and Yoga, and which, closer to Kumārila's own time, is well documented in Vyāsa's *Bhāṣya* on Patañjali's *Yogasūtra*.[11] There is not only no scriptural, but also no perceptual or inferential evidence for the idea that somebody who causes pain or injury during a sacrificial performance is liable to a corresponding retributive suffering. Trying to infer suffering for the actor (*kartur duḥkhānumānam*) from the fact that the sacrificial victim has to suffer (*hiṃsyamānasya duḥkhitvam*) is nothing but a logical fallacy, based upon false analogies.[12]

If reciprocity were indeed the foundation of dharma and adharma, of reward and punishment, how could this apply to such obvious, though "victimless," violations of the norm as illicit drinking?[13] And if benevolence and the production of well-being or pleasure were dharma, would a sexual act with the wife of one's guru, a mortal sin (*mahāpātaka*) according to the *dharmaśāstra* rules, not be an act of dharma?[14] One should leave aside the criteria of pleasure and pain in trying to determine what is right and wrong in the sense of dharma and adharma. The only source that can teach us about dharma and adharma are the injunctions and prohibitions (*vidhi, pratiṣedha*) of the Vedic "revelation."[15] They are specified according to the occasion of the act and the qualification of the actor, and they cannot be translated into or reduced to general, commonsensically "reasonable" rules and principles concerning pleasure and pain, violence or non-violence.

In this sense and on this basis Kumārila deals with another objection: Doesn't the Veda itself prohibit killing and injuring? How then can sacrificial killing be legitimate? Does the Veda contradict itself?[16] Indeed, the Veda contains some very specific prohibitions about killing; in particular, the killing of a brahmin is one of the "mortal sins" (*mahāpātaka*). But according to Kumārila, generalizing and universalizing such prohibitions indicates a basic misunderstanding of the Vedic dharma, which relates all acts to a specific frame of reference. Just as the identity of the *vaiśyastoma* ritual depends on its being performed by a *vaiśya*, and the identity of the *agnihotra* depends on its being performed at the right time of day, so acts of violence are specified by their dharmic situation.[17] Killing that is an integral part of a positively enjoined, legitimate ritual such as the *jyotiṣṭoma* can certainly not have any negative value or effect. Although there may be no visible "difference in the form of killing etc.," it makes an essential difference whether or not such an act is a subsidiary part (*aṅga*) of a ritual: *rūpābhede 'pi hiṃsāder bhedo 'ṅgānaṅgakāritaḥ.*[18] Should the opponent nevertheless maintain that acts of hiṃsā, insofar as they are hiṃsā, have the same negative character and lead to the same result then one could say the same about all activities, insofar as they are activities; there would be a total collapse of distinctions (*sarvasaṅkara*), and all sacrifices, such as the *citrā* etc., would have the same result.[19]

Kumārila applies the demarcation of "internal," sacrificial hiṃsā and "external," non-sacrificial hiṃsā also to the *śyena* sacrifice which may be used for destructive and harmful purposes. Even in this case, the internal hiṃsā as such is not to be considered as demerit or evil, being comparable to a sword, which can, but need not be an instrument of adharma.[20] If the act turns out to be an evil one, and if demerit accrues to its performer, it is because of its being used for an evil external purpose of violence and destruction.[21]

Concluding this discussion, Kumārila emphasizes that anybody who denies the special status of sacrificial hiṃsā and claims that it is conducive to evil because of the common denominator of being hiṃsā (*hiṃsātvasādharmya*) is guilty of contradicting the sacred tradition (*āgamabādhana*).[22]

3. It is evident from our brief presentation of Kumārila's discussion that it goes far beyond the text it explicates, that is, Śabara's statements on the *śyena* sacrifice in his commentary on *Mīmāṃsāsūtra* I, 1, 2. His contribution to the issue of hiṃsā and dharma is remarkable not only in terms of its peculiar style and intensity, but also in terms of its philosophical scope and context. Yet it would be quite inappropriate to say that Kumārila initiated this kind of discussion concerning the legitimacy of ritual hiṃsā. There is clear evidence that by this time the issue had already been debated for a number of centuries in the schools of Vedic exegesis.

One of the contexts in which it appears is the exegesis of the doctrine of the "two ways," i.e. the "way of the fathers" (*pitṛyāna*) and the "way of the gods" (*devayāna*), which is found in such texts as the *Jaiminīya Brāhmaṇa* and, above all, in two closely related sections of the *Bṛhadāraṇyaka* and the *Chāndogya Upaniṣad*.[23] The "way of the gods" is the way of those who, because of their knowledge and faith, reach the "world of brahman" beyond the sun, and liberation from earthly existence. The "way of the fathers," on the other hand, is the way of those who have relied on rituals and similar works and have enjoyed the reward resulting from these deeds, i.e. the sacrificial merit, in heaven, but have ultimately been unable to avoid returning to an earthly existence.[24] In accordance with its basically Upaniṣadic character, this doctrine, together with the "five-fire-doctrine" (*pañcāgnividyā*), has traditionally been commented upon not in the literature of Pūrvamīmāṃsā, but of Uttaramīmāṃsā.

One of the questions discussed is why those who enter upon the "way of the fathers" have to return to earth, and in many cases into a low and unpleasant earthly existence. Among the proposed answers, the suggestion is made that this is due to the "impurity" of the acts of killing that are part of the rituals, that is, to an element of demerit accompanying the sacrificial merit. Many centuries before Kumārila, this suggestion was already rejected by Bādarāyaṇa in his *Brahmasūtra* III, 1, 25; what is enjoined by the sacred word cannot be impure: *aśuddham iti cen, na, śabdāt*. In discussing this issue, Bādarāyaṇa—or whoever the compiler of the *Brahmasūtra* may have been—obviously had predecessors, such as Kārṣṇājini or Bādari.[25]

The oldest extant commentary, Śaṅkara's *Brahmasūtrabhāṣya*, is quite explicit and precise in dealing with the problem: Since dharma and adharma are specified according to "place, time, and occasion" (*deśa, kāla, nimitta*), only the sacred texts can tell us what they are. If they tell us that the *jyotiṣṭoma* ritual, which includes the killing of animals, is an act of dharma, this has to be accepted. The fact that elsewhere the texts prohibit the killing of living creatures does not constitute a contradiction. The specific injunction to kill an animal for the *agnīṣomīya* offering that is part of the *jyotiṣṭoma*—*agnīṣomīyaṃ paśum ālabheta*—is an "exception" (*apavāda*) which is stronger than the general rule (*utsarga*); an act enjoined in this manner cannot imply adharma.[26]

Although Śaṅkara was probably familiar with the work of Kumārila, the present passage need not be taken as reflecting such familiarity and indebtedness; it may rather correspond to a tradition already well-established in Uttaramīmāṃsā itself. Śaṅkara discusses the issue of sacrificial hiṃsā also at various other places, for example, in his commentary on the *Chāndogya Upaniṣad*.[27]

Further Arguments on Ahiṃsā and Dharma

4. It is not necessary to present further textual references concerning this matter. There is, however, one other text that deserves special attention: the *Yuktidīpikā*, the anonymous, but highly informative commentary on Īśvarakṛṣṇa's *Sāṃkhyakārikā* which E. Frauwallner has assigned to the sixth century A.D. The *pūrvapakṣa* presented in the commentary section on verse 2, which deals with Vedic rituals, comes surprisingly close to Kumārila's own argumentation. Just as the *Ślokavārttika* passage summarized earlier, it rejects the attempt to employ "helping" (*anugraha*) and "harming" (*upaghāta*) or the production of pleasure and pain as criteria of dharma and adharma; moreover, it states that, if this hypothesis were accepted, an act of cohabitation with one's teacher's wife could be associated with merit because of its potential of "helping" another being. The Mīmāṃsā rule concerning *apavāda* and *utsarga*, which we found being used by Śaṅkara, is also referred to. Responding to this, the *uttarapakṣa* states that, although the Vedic sacrifices may lead their performer to the desired results, this gain is possible only at the expense of other beings, that is, the sacrificial victims; and it involves a violation of one's sense of compassion (*kāruṇya*) and of the "Golden Rule" (*na tat parasya sandadhyāt pratikūlaṃ yad ātmanaḥ*) which in itself constitutes an imperfection and an impurity.[28] The date of the *Yuktidīpikā* remains uncertain; moreover, the work may comprise different layers. There is no conclusive evidence for Frauwallner's suggestion that the work was composed around A.D. 550.[29] As a matter of fact, the passage just cited and discussed seems to be a response to the *Ślokavārttika*.

In the same context, the so-called *Sāṃkhyasaptativṛtti*, another anonymous commentary on the *Sāṃkhyakārikā*, raises the issue of human sacrifices, which it associates with the royal *aśvamedha* ceremony and the injunction in *Taittirīya Brāhmaṇa* III, 4, 11 that "one should sacrifice a brahmin to *brahman*" (*brahmaṇe brāhmaṇam ālabheta*), etc. The *Yuktidīpikā* alludes more casually to this same text.[30] Human sacrifices, specifically the sacrificial killing of brahmins, are also referred to in Buddhism and, most conspicuously, in the Jaina polemics against the Vedic tradition. The notorious phrase *brahmaṇe brāhmaṇam ālabheta* appears, for instance, in Bhavya's *Tarkajvālā* [31] and, in Jainism, in Somadeva's *Yaśastilaka* and Bhāvasena's *Viśvatattvaprakāśa*.[32] Other Jaina sources refer to such allegedly Vedic practices as the ritual slaughter of one's own mother and father (*mātṛmedha, pitṛmedha*).[33] There is, however, no evidence that ceremonies of this kind ever took place, or that other human sacrifices played an actual role in the Vedic ritual tradition.[34] In general, the statements of the Jainas concerning Vedic ritualism contain major distortions, and they are not based upon a study of the original Vedic sources. Their references to the ritual killing of one's parents may be nothing more than a more or less deliberate distortion of an old argument attributed to the Cārvāka materialists and rationalists: A person who believes that ritual killing is not only meritorious for the sacrificer, but also beneficial for the sacrificial victim, should not hesitate to slaughter his own father.

At this point, it may be appropriate to add some observations concerning Prabhākara, Kumārila's great rival in the history of Pūrvamīmāṃsā and quite possibly his contemporary. As usual, Prabhākara's treatment in his *Bṛhatī* is much shorter and stays closer to Śabara's Bhāṣya. He explains the prohibition referred to by Śabara in the statement *hiṃsā hi sā, sā ca pratiṣiddhā* as a prohibition relating to the qualification of the sacrificer (*adhikāragata*) and not to the employment of any sacrificial techniques. It has to be understood as being *puruṣārtha*, "for the sake of the person," that is, relating to the motivation of the sacrificer, and not as *kratvartha*, "for the sake of the sacrifice," that is, relating to the internal structure and the completion of the ritual. Therefore, the prohibition of hiṃsā indicates only the illegitimacy of acts of "magic" rooted in evil, destructive intentions, but not of an act like the *agnīṣomīya* killing, which is only done for the sake of completing the ritual: *tasmād abhicārasya-anarthatāṃ pratipādayituṃ kṣamo na-agnīṣomīyadeḥ, kratvarthatvāt.*[35]

The implications of this become clearer in Śālikanāthamiśra's *Ṛjuvimalā*: The prohibition of killing restricts man only in his pursuit of such actions as are motivated by his natural, spontaneous desire for results (*phale hi svataḥ pravṛttiḥ*); it certainly prohibits any killing motivated by a desire to kill. It does, however, not limit him at all in executing what is part of his ritual duty (*kārya*), in doing what he does only because the Veda tells him to do it. The "obligation" and "mandate" (*niyoga, adhikāra*) derived from the Vedic injunctions is unconditional and incontestable.[36]

5. We have already noticed that Kumārila denies any independent, extra-scriptural authority to the principle of ahiṃsā. In his view, there is no rational or perceptual basis for finding faults or defects (*doṣa*) in an act of killing. Even in the case of nonritual hiṃsā, we do not actually *see* any "defects"; our uncertainty or uneasiness (*vicikitsā*) in this case is itself based upon the teachings of the sacred texts: *na hi hiṃsādyanuṣṭhāne tadānīṃ doṣadarśanam/bāhye'pi, vicikitsā tu śāstrād eva-upajāyate.*[37]

Ahiṃsā is not a rule that in itself would be "rationally" or "morally" self-evident; it is valid only insofar as it is scripturally enjoined. Even in this sense and on this basis, Kumārila does not like to present it as universal, *prima facie* valid rule that would be modified only by a specific clause such as the traditional *anyatra tīrthebhyaḥ*, "elsewhere than at sacred places," i.e. "if not during rituals."[38] Just as certain acts of killing are specifically enjoined, other acts of killing are specifically prohibited; among these, the killing of a brahmin is the most grave.[39]

In this as well as in other cases, "morality" is derived from "legality." The moral claims of ahiṃsā are rooted in scriptural prohibitions. Such heretics as the Buddhists and Jainas, who advocate ahiṃsā against the Vedic ritual injunctions, owe the basis and starting point of such anti-Vedic teachings to the Veda itself. Only, they have misused or misunderstood the Veda, have falsely universalized its prohibitions and have disregarded the internal differentiation of its dharma. In his *Tantravārttika*, Kumārila suggests that this has to do with a predilection for "dialectics" (*hetūkti*), the influence of the Kali age (*kalikālavaśa*), etc. Just like bad children who hate their parents, the Buddhists and others who teach ahiṃsā are no longer willing or able to admit the Vedic roots of their teachings.[40] Statements in the *śruti* and *smṛti* texts themselves which seem to criticize or discredit sacrificial hiṃsā have, of course, to be reinterpreted according to Mīmāṃsā rules concerning the concordance of the sacred tradition, and they are to be relegated to the level of "descriptive statements" (*arthavāda*), which by definition can never contradict a direct injunction (*vidhi*).[41]

To conclude that ritual hiṃsā entails adharma just because it is hiṃsā is a false application of an "analogical" (*sāmānyato dṛṣṭa*) inference, which is built upon the merely abstract and external similarity of intrinsically and essentially different types of actions.[42] Ultimately, this anti-Vedic analogical reasoning is nothing but a misuse of, and illegitimate extrapolation from, a Vedic premise, i.e., the forbiddenness of certain types of hiṃsā. Similarly, to invoke the "voice of conscience" against the Vedic hiṃsā is nothing more than misusing an indicator which owes its legitimacy and its very existence to the Veda by turning it against its own source. According to Kumārila, the "inner consent" (*ātmatuṣṭi* etc.), next to śruti, smṛti and the "conduct of the good" (*sadācāra*), one of the four sources for the knowledge of dharma, can indeed have a legitimate function, but only in strict alliance with and subordination to the Veda.[43] This "inner consent" or its negative counterpart, the "outcry of the heart" (*hṛdayakrośana*),[44] the warning and censuring voice of conscience, is de facto and de jure based upon the Veda. To claim any independent authority for it amounts to heresy. The *mleccha*, by the way, who has never had any access to the Veda or the Vedic tradition, is not credited with any "voice of conscience" or inner "affliction" at all.[45]

Merely as such, the "voice of conscience" is a fickle, unreliable guide. Accordingly, Kumārila can agree with the position stated in a pūrvapakṣa section of his *Tantravārttika*: While the "twice-born" Āryans are pleased when they see animals being killed for a ritual, such acts cause inner pain to the Buddhists.[46]

The rule of ahiṃsā, together with other general ethical ingredients in the teachings of the heretics, may indeed represent certain traces of Vedic dharma; but they are completely interwoven with their heterodox context and overshadowed by what is a mere "appearance of dharma" (*dharmābhāsa*).[47] In this context, the ideas of ahiṃsā etc., although originating from a good source, are "like milk put into a dog's bladder."[48] Accordingly, the teachings of the Buddhists or Jainas should be distrusted even when they seem to be in accordance with the Veda. Udayana, the great Naiyāyika and champion of "orthodoxy" around A.D. 1000, presents the teachings of such heretics as the Buddhists on ahiṃsā etc. as a kind of fraudulent, hypocritical use of Vedic ideas, destined to produce faith in their heretical teachings (*śraddhāpādanāya*).[49]

Other Naiyāyikas have cited the inferential argument against Vedic hiṃsā, which Kumārila rejected, as a familiar case of false or questionable inference (*anumāna*). The *Tarkabhāṣā* by Keśavamiśra (thirteenth century), one of the most popular introductory surveys of the Nyāya system, refers to it three times in order to exemplify problems and defects of inferential reasoning, such as the role of the "additional qualifier" (*upādhi*) or the "pseudo-reason" (*hetvābhāsa*) known as *vyāpyatvāsiddha*.[50]

The "Liberators from Saṃsāra" (*saṃsāramocaka*)

6. The relationship between dharma, ahiṃsā, and hiṃsā is again discussed in the introductory verses of the first *Autpattikasūtra* section of Kumārila's *Ślokavārttika*. Again, the question is raised whether the distinction between dharma and adharma does not ultimately amount to the distinction between "helping" (*anugraha*) and "harming" (*pīḍā*). Even if sense-perception and inference fail to establish this correlation, isn't it simply a matter of universal recognition, of traditional, habitual familiarity (*lokaprasiddhi*)?

Kumārila, who seems to be alluding to Bhartṛhari's remarks on *lokaprasiddhi*, replies that *lokaprasiddhi* requires a foundation, and that one has to search for this foundation. For the *saṃsāramocaka*, etc., hiṃsā, the very opposite of what the opponent presents as being established by *lokaprasiddhi*, means merit; others feel that penance—causing pain to oneself—cannot be meritorious. Since Āryans and barbarians (*ārya* and *mleccha*) disagree in such a manner, one cannot say that dharma is established by virtue of its traditional familiarity and common acceptance.[51] Only the absolutely authoritative śāstra which is the genuine and unique heritage of the ārya can establish dharma; and the ārya can maintain his uniqueness only insofar as he relies on this *śāstra: na ca-āryāṇāṃ viśeso 'sti yāvac chāstram anāśritam.*[52]

Kumārila does not give any further information on the teachings of the *saṃsāramocaka*, these so-called "liberators from saṃsāra," and apart from his subsequent reference to the disagreement between Āryans and non-Indian barbarians, he does not give us any clues as to their historical identity. His commentators do not provide any help either. Sucaritamiśra tells us that the "liberators from saṃsāra" are heretics who teach that "external hiṃsā" is meritorious (*saṃsāramocakā nāma nāstikā bāhyahiṃsām eva dharmam āhuḥ*).[53] What exactly this "external," i.e. extra-ritual hiṃsā amounts to is not made clear, and it was obviously unknown to Sucaritamiśra himself. Various philosophical writers after Kumārila refer to the saṃsāramocaka, but again without providing any concrete details. The most significant among these references, insofar as the Hindu sources are concerned, is found in Jayanta's *Nyāyamañjarī* (ninth century). A. Wezler has dealt with this passage, noticing that the saṃsāramocaka so far seem to have been overlooked by the historians of Indian religions. We may add that the term itself has often been misunderstood by Western scholars as well as modern Indian pandits.[54]

Jayanta mentions the saṃsāramocaka, whom he characterizes as "devoted to the killing of living creatures" (*prāṇihiṃsāparāyaṇa*) and as "acting from delusion" (*mohapravṛtta*), side by side with the Buddhists.[55] Whatever their distinguishing features may be, both have in common that their traditions are outside the Veda (*vedabāhya*) and nothing but a fraud (*vañcanā*). Of course, the Buddhists are more adjusted to the Vedic norms, including the norms of purity; Jayanta notes that even they avoid contact with the saṃsāramocaka. In a somewhat dubious paraphrase, Cakradhara's *Nyāyamañjarīgranthibhaṅga* seems to associate Jayanta's reference with the equally mysterious "pot-breakers" (*ghaṭacaṭaka*) or *khārapaṭika*. According to Amṛtacandra, a Jaina author of the twelfth century, this group taught "immediate liberation through breaking the pot" (*jhaṭiti ghaṭacaṭakamokṣaḥ*), implying that the body is a kind of container from which an imprisoned soul ought to be liberated.[56] The theme of ritual hiṃsā is referred to in the subsequent section of the *Nyāyamañjarī* where Jayanta presents a survey of the *sarvāgamaprāmāṇya* theory. This theory explains all well-established traditions as being revealed by God; it also advocates a certain level of tolerance in the realm of ritual practice. Just as the Vedic practice of animal sacrifices, although it may be repugnant to "compassionate people" (*kāruṇiko lokaḥ*), is not considered to be discrediting to the validity and reputation of the Veda, so should other and comparable religious habits be respected.[57]

Vācaspati's *Sāṃkhyatattvakaumudī*, commenting on *Sāṃkhyakārikā* 5, mentions the "pseudo-traditions of Buddhists, Jainas, saṃsāramocaka etc." (*śākyabhikṣunirgranthakasaṃsāramocakādīnām āgamābhāsāḥ*). The modern pandit Balarama Udāsīna gives an obviously problematic explanation, when he refers in this connection to a "special branch of materialists" who advocate hiṃsā on the basis of the assumption that "final release" takes place when the body is destroyed, coinciding with the destruction of the "soul" contained in it.[58] In a similar context, also side by side with the Buddhists, the saṃsāramocaka appear again in Śrīdhara's *Nyāyakandalī* and in Udayana's *Ātmatattvaviveka*.[59] In the so-called *Yogasūtrabhāṣyavivaraṇa* and Vācaspati's *Tattvavaiśāradī* on *Yogasūtra/Yogabhāṣya* II, 5, they exemplify an attitude which confuses merit with demerit.[60] A further text mentioning them is Medhātithi's commentary on *Manusmṛti* II, 6, in its introductory section. Of course, when Buddhist texts present the Buddha himself as "liberator from saṃsāra," this has an entirely different meaning.

7. Further statements about alleged teachings of the *saṃsāramocaka* (Ardhamāgadhī: *saṃsāramoyaga*) are found in Jaina literature, beginning with Haribhadra's *Śāstravārttāsamuccaya* (eighth century).[61] Malayagiri's commentary on the *Nandīsūtra* (around A.D. 1200) is by far the most explicit source. According to Malayagiri, the "liberators from saṃsāra" argue that killing and even torturing can be a genuinely meritorious activity, motivated by compassion and altruism and guided by therapeutic skills. Inflicting pain and death upon living creatures can be a cure, a method of purification, a selfless way of helping others (*paropakāra*). It can serve as a means of liberating them from the power of the bad karma that keeps them attached to the miseries of the "ocean of saṃsāra."[62] Around the same period, Abhayadevasūri mentions the hiṃsā of the saṃsāramocaka side by side with that of the "barbarians" (*mleccha*) and the Vedic ritualists.[63]

Kumārila's *Ślokavārttika* is older than any other Hindu or Jaina source we have consulted so far. There are, however, some occurrences of *saṃsāramocaka* in Buddhist literature which clearly predate Kumārila. In the sixth century, the *Madhyamakahṛdayakārikā* by Bhāvaviveka/Bhavya uses the term. The commentary *Tarkajvālā* which the Tibetan tradition attributes to the same author but which may have been composed approximately two centuries later explains that the adherents of this tradition (Tibetan: *'khor ba sgrol byed pa*) visit desolate, barbarous border regions in order to kill large numbers of beetles, ants, and other small and low creatures (*kīṭa, pipīlika, pataṅga*).[64] Even earlier, i.e., around A.D. 500, we find the "liberators from saṃsāra" in Dhammapāla's commentary on the *Petavatthu*. Here, too, they are "adherents of false views" (*micchādiṭṭhika*) who practice the systematic and apparently ritual killing of beetles and similar creatures (*kīṭapaṭaṅga*).[65]

Apart from the use of the word *saṃsāramocaka*, is there a common denominator in these references from different periods and traditions? All texts seem to agree that the saṃsāramocaka practice the killing or harming of living beings (*prāṇin*), and that they believe that this constitutes "merit" (*dharma*). Some texts mention specifically the killing of insects and other "little creatures,"[66] others extend this to the level of human beings. The term itself seems to imply the claim that such practices amount to compassionate acts of "liberation." Malayagiri's presentation expands this into a full-fledged rationalization of violence. Here, the saṃsāramocaka poses as a benevolent doctor in the wider context of karma and rebirth. His victims are patients; being an expert physician, he knows that he may have to administer a harsh medicine in order to bring about a change for the better (*pariṇāmasundara*).[67] This would seem to be basically compatible with Kumārila's brief and cryptic reference. First of all, it illustrates the failure of *lokaprasiddhi*, "common acquaintance," to provide reliable criteria for the distinction between right and wrong in ethics and religion. Beyond this, it reflects Kumārila's conviction that dharma cannot be defined in terms of utilitarianism or altruism.[68] "Helping" (*upakāra*) and "harming" (*pīḍā*) are ambiguous. What appears to be *pīḍā* can be interpreted as *upakāra* in the context of saṃsāra. The saṃsāramocaka may present himself as the ultimate altruist and utilitarian.

In Malayagiri's perspective, the "liberators from saṃsāra" are, of course, not really good and compassionate doctors. Their "altruism" is a travesty. Their "therapeutic" measures can only be counterproductive. Instead of delivering the victims from their bad karma, they will intensify their "afflictions" (*kleśa*) and thus keep them in the bondage of karma and saṃsāra. In general, the Jainas (for instance, Amṛtacandra in his *Puruṣārthasiddhyupāya*) reject the ideas of benevolent killing and euthanasia.

8. Who were the saṃsāramocaka? Is there reliable evidence for the existence of a group actually practicing or propagating what is ascribed to the "liberators from saṃsāra"? Do we have any documents produced by such a group? Are there schools of thought and ritual practice in India which provide significant parallels and similarities? Is there anything more tangible than the obscure and elusive references to the "pot-breakers" or *khārapaṭika*?

Perhaps the most obvious association would be with certain Śaivite texts, in which bloody rituals are described and explained, and in which the killing of living beings, including humans, has a religious function and value. Among the older texts of this kind, the *Netratantra* deserves special attention. Chapter 20 of this text, which—though not one of the most ancient Tantras—has been repeatedly referred to by Abhinavagupta and commented upon by his disciple Kṣemarāja, exemplifies in a somewhat cryptic manner this idea of ritual killing (attributed to the so-called Yoginīs), which is motivated by a desire of "helping" (*anugraha*) the victims, of liberating living creatures from their "sins" (*pāpa*) and from the "fetters" (*pāśa*) and "stains" (*mala*) of their worldly existence. Ritual killing in this context and perspective is quite different from any act of "putting to death" (*māraṇa*) in the ordinary sense; it is an act of "liberation" (*mokṣaṇa*) or, as Abhinavagupta says in a passage of his *Tantrāloka* which paraphrases this section of the *Netratantra*, of "miraculous initiation" (*dīkṣā citrarūpiṇī*). The necessity of the right qualification of the sacrificer, of being without greed, delusion, etc., is explicitly emphasized.[69]

These Śaivite teachings are based upon a strict separation of ritual and worldly killing. Their proponents obviously would have rejected the characterization as "external" (*bāhya*), i.e., nonritual killing that authors like Sucaritamiśra apply to the practices of the saṃsāramocaka; and they are certainly far from propagating the meritorious character of hiṃsā per se. As a matter of fact, the general validity of ahiṃsā is accepted, and the presentation of the extraordinary case of ritual hiṃsā is often apologetic, for example, in Jayaratha's commentary on Abhinavagupta's *Tantrāloka* (chapter 16), which follows the "orthodox" Vedic justification of ritual violence.

The idea of benevolent and meritorious killing, which should be motivated by a desire to "liberate" the victim from his evil and ominous karmic tendencies, occurs also in Buddhist Tantrism. In the Tibetan Vajrayāna tradition, it was known as *sbyor sgrol*, ritual liberation. The assassination of King Glan dar ma, the notorious persecutor of Buddhism, has been associated with this idea. The minister who committed this act in 842 "had first to engender special compassion (*snin rje khyad par can*) for the king who needed to be liberated from his evil deeds and his wicked state of existence."[70]

However, such Tantric associations would seem to be rather far-fetched insofar as our oldest sources are concerned, that is, Dhammapāla, Bhavya and Kumārila. The context suggests other possible connections. Immediately following his citation of the saṃsāramocaka, Kumārila refers to the "disagreement" (*vigāna*) between Āryans and non-Indian barbarians concerning the nature of dharma. Bhavya/Bhāvaviveka associates their eccentric activities with remote border areas, although he never identifies or even affiliates the "liberators from saṃsāra" and the Iranian *maga* or *pārasīka*.

Should we consider the possibility that the traditions about the saṃsāramocaka could have extra-Indian origins? Before we pursue this question further, it seems appropriate to refer to another Indian tradition commonly associated with the idea of meritorious, religiously motivated killing: the notorious sect of the Thags (*ṭhaka*).

The Thags in Classical and Colonial India

9. First of all, we have to mention the *Nyāyabhūṣaṇa* by Bhāsarvajña, whose lifetime may be very close to that of Jayantabhaṭṭa. In a discussion concerning the validity of sacred texts and traditions (*śāstra, āgama*) Bhāsarvajña presents the following *pūr-*

vapakṣa: The Veda is not fundamentally different from texts and traditions produced by other authors, including those "who say that the killing of brahmins and so forth is a means of attaining heaven or final liberation" (*ye brāhmaṇādivadhaṃ svargasya mokṣasya vā sādhanaṃ vadanti*). Immediately thereafter, we hear about the "traditions of the Jina, the Buddha, etc." (*jinabuddhādyāgama*).[71]

In his refutation of this pūrvapakṣa, Bhāsarvajña paraphrases the opponent's remark about the "killing of brahmins and so forth" by referring to the "sacred texts of the Thags" (*ṭhakaśāstra*); this statement seems to be the oldest extant reference in Sanskrit to this sect of assassins.[72] There is no authority in the texts of the Thags and similar groups. They are "produced for a visible purpose by somebody stricken with passion and other afflictions" (*rāgādyupahatena-eva dṛṣṭārthaṃ ṭhakaśāstrādi praṇītam*). They are as invalid and illegitimate as the abominable *Ḍākinītantras* mentioned a little later,[73] and they illustrate the dangers of not being under the guidance of the true source, i.e., the Veda.

We may question the authenticity of Bhāsarvajña's pūrvapakṣa. Nevertheless, it seems reasonable to assume that he did not invent the reference to the Thags, and that they had indeed been cited by earlier antagonists of the authority of the Veda, although clear and explicit statements of this kind may no longer be extant today. There is, however, a passage in Bhavya's *Tarkajvālā* (available only in a Tibetan translation), which might be interpreted as a reference to the Thags. It mentions a tradition of "deceivers" (*slu byed pa*) who practice ritual killing. Some time after Bhāsarvajña, the Thags, as well as their practices and even their "sacred traditions" (*ṭhakāgama*), appear again in several Jaina works such as Anantavīrya's *Siddhiviniścayaṭīkā*, and specifically in Prabhācandra's *Nyāyakumudacandra* (probably eleventh century).[74] Prabhācandra illustrates his reference to the teachings of the Thags by citing the maxim that somebody who wants to get rich ought to slay a wealthy brahmin (*sadhanaṃ brāhmaṇaṃ hanyād bhūtikāmaḥ*). He associates this maxim with such Vedic injunctions as the killing of a white goat (*śvetam ajam ālabheta*). Prabhācandra's argument is included in his discussion concerning the definition and the status of the Apabhraṃśa languages.[75] In this context, it serves to ridicule the obsession of the brahmins with the purity and sanctity of the Sanskrit language, and their blind and "orthodox" allegiance to the Veda. For Bhāsarvajña, on the other hand, the *ṭhaka* exemplify the risks involved in disregarding the authority of the Veda, and in giving human emotions and personal interests a role in the establishment of religious traditions.

10. Unlike the *saṃsāramocaka*, the Thags have not been overlooked and forgotten by later generations; nor can it be questioned that there were real, "practicing" Thags in India. Their actual role in Indian religious history, and the extent of their activities, is of course open to questions. In the nineteenth century, the Thags (*ṭhaka, ṭhaga*) became part of a popular Gothic-Romantic image of India; and as "Thugs," they found their way into the English language. The publicity they received was certainly exaggerated. The phenomenon of "Thuggee" appealed not only to ordinary sensationalism, but also to the British sense of destiny in India, and it was used to propagate the legitimacy of colonial rule.

In 1836, W.H. Sleeman wrote that "India is emphatically the land of superstition" and that "in this land the system of Thuggee . . . had found a congenial soil";[76] a few years later, he expressed his confidence that the eradication of this "far-spread evil" would "greatly tend to immortalize British rule in the East."[77] Yet in spite of all political and ideological associations, and in spite of their solid commitment to British colonial rule, the reports of Sleeman and his collaborators, in particular J. Paton, seem to be basically authentic.[78]

The British accounts of the nineteenth century are supplemented by earlier European references, beginning with J. de Thévenot in the seventeenth century, as well as reports in Muslim literature, and perhaps even by Hsüan-tsang's travel book from the seventh century. Although some efforts have been made to collect and analyze the available evidence, the background and early history of Thagism have remained obscure; even the explanation of the word "Thag" (*ṭhaka*) continues to be controversial. The references in the works of Bhāsarvajña, Anantavīrya and Prabhācandra have neither been noticed by the historians of religion, nor by the lexicographers who have tried to trace the history of the word.

Following H. Jacobi, modern historians of Thagism, such as R. Garbe and G. Pfirrmann, have referred to a twelfth-century text from Kashmir, the *Śrīkaṇṭhacarita* by the poet, lexicographer and politician Maṅkha (also known as Maṅkhuka or Maṅkaka), as the oldest traceable evidence for the word *ṭhaka*. However, Maṅkha does not say anything about Thag practices; for this, the history of the Sultanate of Firōz Shāh Tughlug by Ḍiyā ad-Dīn Baranī has been proposed as the oldest available source.[79]

Concerning the word *ṭhaka* and its variants, two other twelfth-century authors, Hemacandra and Puruṣottamadeva, provide additional information. In the Jaina Prakrit work *Kumārapālacarita* by Hemacandra (1145–1229), we have an early occurrence of the form *ṭhaga*, which has become common in Hindi and other modern Indian languages.[80] The Sanskrit commentary by Pūrṇakalaśagaṇi paraphrases this as *ṭhaka*. In his Prakrit dictionary *Deśīnāmamālā*, Hemacandra uses *ṭhaka* to paraphrase *dhūrta*, "rogue," "deceiver," which in turn explains the Prakrit word *kālaya*.[81] Puruṣottamadeva, who may have been Hemacandra's older contemporary, gives *sthaga* as a synonym of *dhūrta* in his Sanskrit dictionary *Trikāṇḍaśeṣa*.[82] This may be a Sanskritization of *ṭhaga/ṭhaka*. The etymological connection of *ṭhaka* with the Sanskrit root *sthag*, "to cover," "conceal," which has been accepted by scholars such as Garbe, as well as numerous lexicographers, may still be valid,[83] but should certainly not be taken for granted. The possibility of other derivations, and perhaps an original association with a tribal deity, cannot be excluded.[84] Muslim writers such as Maqdisī (tenth century), Marvazī (eleventh century) and Shahrastānī (twelfth century) refer to practitioners of human sacrifices whom they call Tahkiniyya, Dahkīnīya, etc. Whether there is any connection with the Thags remains to be seen. That there are no references to strangling in their accounts would not be relevant in this case.[85] This method of assassination, which was commonly associated with the Thags of the nineteenth century (and first mentioned in Western literature by Thévenot) seems to be of relatively recent origin. Among the devices employed by the "throttling Thags," the strap was allegedly introduced under Western influence.[86]

11. The comments of Bhāsarvajña and Prabhācandra, together with other pieces of evidence, leave little doubt that the traditions of the Thags date back to the pre-Muslim era in India, although later on Muslims were also involved in their activities. However, unlike these early sources, the later accounts, in particular Sleeman's detailed reports, do not contain any specific reference to the killing of brahmins. The "blood chapter" (*rudhirādhyāya*) of the *Kālikāpurāṇa*, which has been suggested as a possible source of inspiration for the Thags, expressly prohibits the killing of brahmins as well as women.[87] It would certainly be very uncautious to assume that Bhāsarvajña and Prabhācandra derived their information from an actual Sanskrit canon of the Thags; the polemical irony in Prabhācandra's "quote" is hard to overlook. Nevertheless, the reference to the killing of brahmins may not be entirely baseless.

The British administrators in India, as well as European Indologists such as R. Garbe, have tended to interpret Thagism as a symptomatic product of the Indian religious environment, or even as a reflection of the essence of Hinduism. Sleeman called India the "congenial soil" for Thagism.[88] In his view, it was India and the general atmosphere of Hinduism that allowed the Thags to develop their perverted sense of self-respect and lack of remorse. Others added that the Thags were respected, even admired by their countrymen. "The Thugs and Dacoits thought none the worse of their profession, and were regarded by their countrymen with an awe which in India at that time could hardly be distinguished from veneration."[89] To the British, Thagism was bound to flourish in India, its natural habitat, as long as the country was not ready to accept the blessings of the Christian religion and of British colonial administration. "Such, under the rule of Satan, is human nature."[90]

J. N. Farquhar, otherwise a sympathetic observer of the Indian scene, emphasized the easy combination of criminal and religious elements in the Indian context: "These facts enable one to realize that, in medieval India, there might readily appear a community organized on the basis of the worship of the goddess and the practice of murder and robbery . . . to pass from participation in human sacrifice before the altar of the goddess to the search for victims for her on the high roads would be no violent change."[91]

Implicitly or explicitly, the Thags were associated with what was seen as the all-pervasive spirit of the caste system in India, with an alleged subordination of all universal ethics to hereditary forms of behavior, and with the entire social and ritual system represented and guarded by the brahmins. R. Garbe even suggests that brahmins were the majority as well as the actual leaders among the Hindu Thags, and that it was their influence to which Thagism owed "its religious character and its organization."[92] Garbe's assessment was based on the memoirs of John Malcolm. It does not find support in most of the other sources, specifically in the records kept by James Paton. But whatever the image of the Thags in nineteenth-century Europe may have been, we now have to return to their role in the ethical and religious debates of the classical period—a role of which the European scholars and administrators were entirely unaware.

Both the ṭhaka and the saṃsāramocaka illustrate an ethical and religious aberration. They exemplify the potential perversions to which human nature is subject if it abandons the guidance of the Veda (according to Hindu orthodoxy) or of the universal principle of ahiṃsā (according to the Buddhist and Jaina critics of the Veda). But apart from this, there is nothing to suggest an actual linkage, not to mention identity, between the two groups. This brings us back to our earlier questions concerning the historical identity of the saṃsāramocaka and their alleged teachings, and whether we should consider the possibility of an extra-Indian, "barbarian" (*mleccha*) affiliation.

Iranian Traditions and the Origin of the Saṃsāramocaka

12. In general, the Mlecchas, as exemplified by such "barbarian" invaders as the "Huns" and "Turks" (*hūṇa, turuṣka*),[93] are associated with the ideas of violence and indiscriminate killing, of not respecting life, that is, with a fundamental lack of dharma. Most of this is rather vague and stereotyped. There are, however, more specific references to the practices of certain Iranian groups. The *Bhūridatta Jātaka* says about the East Iranian Kambojakas, that they commit acts of killing for the sake of religious merit. They believe that it is purifying to kill beetles and other insects, snakes, frogs, worms, and flies.[94] This statement is supplemented by references to "Iranian" habits in numerous other texts.

S. Kawasaki and, more recently, Chr. Lindtner have drawn attention to the remarkable references to the Zoroastrian Magi (*maga*) and "Persians" (*pārasīka*; Tibetan *par sig*) in the *Tarkajvālā*. As indicated earlier, the Tibetan tradition treats this work as Bhavya's/Bhāvaviveka's autocommentary to his *Madhyamakahṛdayakārikā* (sixth century and one of our earliest sources for the saṃsāramocaka), although it may be the work of another, somewhat later author by the name Bhavya.[95]

Among the "perverted beliefs" of these people "who live in the land of the barbarians (*mleccha*)," Bhavya mentions specifically their traditions of incest and of killing or harming living creatures, such as ants and other small creatures, but also, for instance, bulls. He notes that those perverted views and practices correspond to Vedic injunctions concerning animal sacrifices and ritual incest. He concludes that, because of such similarities, the Veda cannot be an appropriate source for the study of dharma.[96]

In addition, Lindtner has referred to another section of the work which associates ritual killing and incest with the teachings of a certain Yonākadeva.[97]

As noticed by Kawasaki and Lindtner, Bhavya was not the first Buddhist author to refer to such and similar practices. Before him, Vasubandhu, author of the *Abhidharmakośa* and its *Bhāṣya*, mentioned the "Persian" practices of hiṃsā and of incest, and in particular the tradition of killing one's own parents when they are old, weak and sick.[98] According to Vasubandhu, the habits of the Persians (*pārasīka*) illustrate *moha*, "delusion" (concerning dharma and adharma), as a cause for destroying lives (*prāṇātipāta*), "greed" (*lobha*) and "hate" (*dveṣa*) being the other causes. The practices of the Vedic ritualists (*yājñika*) and the actions of rulers who, following the "authority of the dharma-specialists" (*dharmapāṭhakaprāmāṇya*), seek merit by punishing offenders, are mentioned as additional cases of killing "caused by delusion" (*mohaja*); other sources, including the so-called *Yogasūtrabhāṣyavivaraṇa*, describe the "demerit" of the *saṃsāramocaka* as *mohaprabhava*.[99] Even earlier than the *Abhidharmakośabhāṣya*, the *Mahāvibhāṣā*, a massive Sarvāstivāda compendium from Kashmir (second century A.D.), refers to the Persian practices of killing and incest. It may have served as a source for both Vasubandhu and Bhavya.[100]

The "barbarian" traditions of the "Persians" (*pārasīka, maga*) appear again in numerous Buddhist texts after Bhavya; the authors include Dharmakīrti, Prajñākaragupta, Durvekamiśra, Śāntarakṣita and Kamalaśīla.[101] We find them also in Jaina literature, where they are usually ascribed to the "barbarians" (*mleccha*) in general.[102] They are less conspicuous, though not entirely absent, in Hindu literature.[103]

The question to what extent the Buddhist statements about the *maga* and *pārasīka* correspond to historical reality need not concern us here. A few brief notes may suffice. Directives concerning the killing of certain "noxious animals" are indeed familiar in Zoroastrianism. The most conspicuous Avestan passage prescribing such "purificatory" killing is Vendīdād (Vidēvdād) XIV, 5–6. Moreover, the testimony of Greek and Latin writers, beginning with Herodotus, seems to corroborate the information provided by the Buddhist texts.[104] The references to incest are also supported by other sources.[105]

13. Could there be a connection between the reports about the "Persians" (*pārasīka, maga, kamboja*) and the traditions relating to the *saṃsāramocaka*? The parallels in the oldest relevant sources are obvious. Dhammapāla describes the saṃsāramocaka as killers of beetles and other insects (*kīṭapaṭaṅga*); the same words appear in the list of creatures killed by the East Iranian *kambojaka* according to the *Bhūridatta Jātaka*. Other texts about the saṃsāramocaka, such as Malayagiri's commentary on the *Nandīsūtra*, also mention insects and other "little creatures."[106] Admittedly, the Hindu sources refer only in a general fashion to violence towards living beings (*hiṃsā, prāṇihiṃsā*). But as we noticed earlier, Kumārila's citation of the saṃsāramocaka is followed by a reference to the disagreement between "Āryans" and "barbarians" (*mleccha*). On the Buddhist side, Bhavya's use of the term *saṃsāramocaka* (*'khor ba sgrol byed pa*) occurs in the same section as his Iranian references, though without any explicit connection. However, he has the "liberators from saṃsāra" pursue their ritual activities in remote border regions.[107]

On the other hand, the idea of a "liberation from saṃsāra," and even the notion of saṃsāra itself, would seem to be out of place in the Iranian, Zoroastrian context. It certainly does not find any support in the relevant sections of the Vendīdād or in the Greek reports. How then can we account for the ideology of compassionate, soteriologically meaningful killing which some later Indian sources ascribe more or less explicitly to the saṃsāramocaka? At this point, Bhavya's curious references to "Yonākadeva" (Yonakadeva?) may provide a clue; unfortunately, Lindtner's translation misunderstands the Tibetan text at a crucial point. According to the *Tarkajvālā*, the adherents of "Yonākadeva" hold the following view: "When an ant has been killed in a golden vessel, being pierced with a golden needle, it is liberated from saṃsāra; and he, too, who kills it is supposed to have accumulated the seeds of liberation."[108] Whatever the identity and the historical origin of "Yonākadeva" may be, the "Western," "Persian" connections (the *yona/yonaka* are frequently associated with the *kamboja/kambojaka*) are obvious. In accordance with a suggestion by W. Sundermann, we may identify this deity (Tibetan: *nam mkhaʿi lha*, "god of the sky") as Ahura Mazdā, whom the Sogdian Buddhists, potential mediators in this case, used to call Indra.[109] On the other hand, the terminology of "liberation from saṃsāra" in the *yonākadeva/nam mkhaʿi lha* passage leaves no doubt about connections with the saṃsāramocaka.

Yet the association of the killing of the ant with the notions of saṃsāra, and liberation from saṃsāra, does not seem to be Persian at all. May we assume that it was proposed by a *maga/pārasīka* in India, who tried to explain and justify Zoroastrian practices in accordance with Indian ways of thinking? Or should we assume that it was an indigenous Indian interpretation or reinterpretation of such practices? Could it be that an Indian, or Indianizing, interpretation of this kind provides the missing link between the reports about the Persians and the later traditions concerning the "liberators from saṃsāra"? According to the *Mahāvibhāṣā*, the "Western barbarians" or Magi (*maga*, "mou-kia") considered the killing of one's own parents as an act of liberation from pain and decomposition.[110] Could it be that the ideas which later Indian authors ascribed to the "liberators from saṃsāra" were extrapolations and generalizations of this special concept of euthanasia?

All this is undeniably speculative. Nevertheless, the following hypothesis seems to be suited to our preceding observations: The traditions relating to the saṃsāramocaka preserve certain reminiscences of Iranian, Zoroastrian practices. These, however, merged with original Indian ideas concerning liberation from saṃsāra and, more specifically, with speculations about benevolent and meritorious killing, which would help other creatures, humans as well as nonhumans, to escape from bad karmic circumstances and, ideally, from saṃsāra altogether. This may have included such obscure and marginal phenomena as the "pot-breakers" or *khārapaṭika*. In the process, Buddhists, Jainas, and Hindus added their own peculiar perspectives to these traditions; and their Iranian origin was eventually forgotten.

At any rate, we have no evidence for the existence of an organized sect of saṃsāramocaka who would have practiced the benevolent killing of humans or animals on a regular basis comparable to the activities of the Thags. The saṃsāramocaka, as he appears in classical Indian philosophical literature, represents primarily a certain theoretical possibility of ethical and religious orientation and perversion, instead of an actual historical and social phenomenon.

Ethical Relativism and the Vedic Derivation of Ahiṃsā

14. We may assume that the opponents of the Vedic tradition first introduced the Persians, the saṃsāramocaka and the Thags into the debate. All these groups were meant to discredit the authority of the Veda by association. The "orthodox" advocates of the Veda tried to turn the argumentation around. Kumārila and many others invoked the saṃsāramocaka against the Buddhists, Jainas and other ahiṃsā-oriented movements. Bhāsarvajña did the same with the *ṭhaka*. In the orthodox perspective, the *ṭhaka* and *saṃsāramocaka* typify the relativism and the potential of aberration inherent in all extra-Vedic traditions.

Kumārila is aware of the possibilities of rationalizing hiṃsā as well as ahiṃsā. He knows about the temptation to justify a tradition in terms of its common familiarity (*lokaprasiddhi*), its acceptance by "important" (or numerous) people (*mahājanaparigṛhītatva*), its accordance with ancestral habits (*pitrādyanugama*). But he also knows that others can claim these same criteria, related to other "continents," areas outside India, in support of their own views: *mahājanaparigṛhītatvaṃ pitrādyanugamādi ca/te 'py dvīpāntarāpekṣaṃ vadanty eva svadarśane*. To defend the Vedic dharma, including its animal sacrifices, just in these terms would amount to abandoning it. It has to be accepted in its own right, without relying on external, merely human and potentially relative standards. Only the Veda itself can uphold the authority and identity of its dharma. Only the Vedic injunctions (*codanā, vidhi*) can save dharma and adharma from the "jaws of non-being" (*abhāvavaktra*).[111]

Although the Mīmāṃsakas defend and invoke the Vedic rituals as the basis of the Āryan dharma, they are no longer at home in the world in which these rituals were originally developed and enacted. The historical conditions have changed; their world is different from the old magico-ritualistic universe of the Veda. We have noticed earlier that Kumārila rejects the idea of a cosmic reciprocity which would imply that any act of hurting falls back upon its perpetrator; in so doing, he rejects an idea which is a serious concern to the Vedic ritualists themselves and which is still important in such Hindu systems as Sāṃkhya and Yoga.[112] Kumārila has to reject it because he cannot accept a universal cosmic causality that could interfere with or even supersede the specific, scripturally determined causality of the ritual. Even if there is hiṃsā present in it, a positively enjoined ritual cannot have negative side-effects, that is, an ambiguous two-fold causality (*ubhayahetutva*).[113]

The Vedic rituals, if performed accurately by those who are qualified to perform them, produce *apūrva*, a "new" potential not subject to ordinary worldly causality and to what other schools may present as a more general mechanism of cosmic retributive causality.[114] The *apūrva* is inseparable from the Vedic dharma; and this dharma, as interpreted by the Mīmāṃsakas, is altogether different from a universal ethical code. It has as its center the Vedic ritual injunctions (*vidhi, codanā*), rules which apply only to those who are within the Āryan order of castes (*varṇa*) and "stages of life" (*āśrama*) and which are by definition transempirical and not susceptible to rationalization and universalization. Within the ritualistic context of the Vedic dharma, the special injunctions concerning the killing of specific animals for ritual purposes are stronger than rules concerning life in general. In Mīmāṃsā as well as in grammar, the exception (*apavāda*) is stronger than the general rule (*utsarga*). And the apūrva, the special result of the special ritual, is by definition stronger than any general retributive causality or the "common karma" (*sāmānyādṛṣṭa*) referred to by Jayanta.[115] If the apūrvic value of a sacrificial performance is a positive one, all the parts of the ritual can only be seen as contributing to this positive outcome, and none of them can produce any independent and negative side-effects.[116]

15. In accordance with his understanding of dharma, vidhi and apūrva, Kumārila does not consider it necessary to commit himself to the apologetic and conciliatory style found in numerous other texts, such as the eighth chapter of the *Manusmṛti*. He does not try to explain away the ritual slaughter of animals (*paśuhiṃsā*), or to justify it by reconciling it with the ideal of ahiṃsā. He does not rely on the old argument that the sacrificial animal itself benefits from its role, and that its ritual death secures its residence in heaven. By the time of Kumārila, this argument was widely discredited; it had been ridiculed by the Cārvāka materialists and other opponents of the Vedic tradition.[117]

In reality, there is no need for apologies or acts of appeasing (*śānti*). In his commentary on the *Ślokavārttika*, Pārthasārathi quotes a Vedic prayer to Agni, asking for release from the sin (*enas*) incurred because of ritual hiṃsā, and he emphasizes that according to Kumārila this can only be an *arthavāda* which should not be taken literally.[118] There is in reality no such "sin" in the sacrifice from which Agni would have to liberate us. It is symptomatic that a Jaina text of the thirteenth century, refuting the Mīmāṃsā defense of ritual hiṃsā, utilizes this same prayer to Agni as an expression of support for the idea of ahiṃsā and as Vedic evidence against the Mīmāṃsā.[119]

"The ritualists were . . . deeply concerned with the killing and injuring of animate beings which occurs in the sacrifice itself."[120] H. P. Schmidt's article on the "origin of ahiṃsā," the starting-point of our investigations, provides ample evidence for the accuracy of this statement. The fear of committing hiṃsā was clearly present with the "ritualists." But does this mean that the origin of ahiṃsā has been identified, and that the Vedic ritualistic world-view itself constitutes the one true source of ahiṃsā? Was there really a "ritual ahiṃsā-theory"? And in what sense can we say that this "ritual ahiṃsā-theory is the ultimate source of the later renunciatory ahiṃsā-doctrine"?[121] Does it not seem more likely that external factors contributed to these developments which subsequently led to a sharp antagonism between Vedic ritualism and ahiṃsā as two basically different forms of religious orientation?

However deeply the ritualists may have been concerned about the harming and killing that occurred during the ritual, we cannot say that such concern was intrinsic to, or inseparable from, their ritualism; we cannot derive it from their ritualism as such. They may have been concerned that certain means employed in the rituals might violate rules that were not those of the rituals themselves, and unleash forces that might turn against the ritualists. We do not know the nature and origin of such fears. We can only say that their system tried to accommodate both ritual slaughter and a certain respect for the life of the sacrificial victims. There was a place for hiṃsā and for ahiṃsā, just as there was a place for vegetarianism and for meat-eating within the complex patterns of ritual behavior.[122] The transition from such premises to the universalized ethics of ahiṃsā was certainly not a simple, natural, immediately obvious process.

Whatever the origin of ahiṃsā may have been, the tension and conflict between Vedic ritualism and ahiṃsā is a characteristic phenomenon of later religious thought in India.[123] Hindu "orthodoxy," as represented by the Mīmāṃsā, sees the universalization of the ahiṃsā doctrine as a threat to the Vedic dharma and the Āryan tradition. It tries to establish the full legitimacy of the bloody Vedic rituals against the claims of ahiṃsā. At the same time, however, it tries to demonstrate that the true origins of this false anti-Vedic ahiṃsā can be traced to the Veda itself, and that even in their criticism and opposition, the opponents of the Veda are ultimately indebted to the Veda.[124]

Chapter 4: Notes

1. H.-P. Schmidt, "The Origin of *ahiṃsā*." *Mélanges d'Indianisme à la mémoire de L. Renou*." Paris, 1968, 625–655; ib., 625.

2. Cf. *Beiträge zur Geschichte von Vegetarismus und Rinderverehrung in Indien*. Wiesbaden, 1962 (Ak. Wiss. Lit. Mainz). Further contributions to the study of ahiṃsā are found in: C. della Casa, "Ahiṃsā: Significato e ambito originari della non-violenza." *Indologica Taurinensia* 3/4 (1975/76), 187–196; U. Tähtinen, *Ahiṃsā*. London, 1976; P. Schreiner, "Gewaltlosigkeit und Tötungsverbot im Hinduismus." *Angst und Gewalt*, ed. H. von Stietencron. Düsseldorf, 1979, 287–308; D. S. Ruegg, "Ahiṃsā and Vegetarianism in the History of Buddhism." *Buddhist Studies in Honour of W. Rahula*. London, 1980, 234–241; G. Spera, *Notes on ahiṃsā*. Turin, 1982 (Pubblicazioni di "Indol. Taur."). J. C. Heesterman, "Non-Violence and Sacrifice." *Indologica Taurinensia* 12 (1984), 119–127. On the word *ahiṃsā*, cf. J. Gonda, *Four Studies in the Language of the Veda*. The Hague, 1959, 95–117.

3. Cf. *India and Europe*, ch. 17, especially 330f.; see also Mahābhārata XII, 237, 18 f.: all other dharmas disappear in ahiṃsā just as the foot-prints of all other animals disappear in those of the elephant.

4. Cf. *India and Europe*, 330; 333.

5. Cf. L. Alsdorf, *Beiträge* (see above, n. 2), 18 ff.; see also the compilations of texts in: Mitramiśra, *Vīramitrodaya*, ed. Nityānanda Śarmā, vol. 2. Benares, 1913 (ChSS), 526 ff. (*māṃsabhakṣyābhakṣyanirṇayaḥ*), and 537 ff. (*paśuhiṃsāvidhipratiṣedhau*); Santaśaraṇa, *Saddharma ahiṃsāprakāśa*. Kathmandu, 1974. The *Vaiśeṣikasūtra* pays special attention to the legitimacy of killing in self-defense (VI, 1, 10 ff.; ed. Jambuvijaya), thus illustrating another aspect of the limitation of ahiṃsā; the text uses the euphemism *tyāga*, also referring to suicide as *ātmatyāga*. Concerning self-defense, see also Medhātithi on Manu VIII, 350; IV, 162.

6. Cf. SK 2, together with its commentaries; YBh on YS II, 29 ff.; and especially II, 34.

7. See, for instance, *Viṣṇupurāṇa* III, 18.

8. K. K. Handiqui, *Yaśastilaka and Indian Culture*. Sholapur, 1949, 390.

9. Cf. E. Frauwallner, *Materialien zur ältesten Erkenntnislehre der Karmamīmāṃsā*. Vienna, 1968, 20 f.

10. ŚV, 79 ff. (v. 201 ff.).

11. See YBh II, 34; from a much later period, cf. *Sāṃkhyasūtra* I, 84 with Aniruddha's commentary. Sāṃkhya ideas seem to be the main target of Kumārila's argumentation in this section. See also the reciprocity of "eater" and "food" in the *Śatapatha Brāhmaṇa* XII, 9, 1, 1; and the "etymology" of *māṃsa* in Manu V, 55.

12. ŚV, 86 (v. 234 f.); it seems to be this type of false reasoning about *hiṃsā* which Kumārila refers to as *karmānurūpya*, "conformity to the act," in TV, 124; Someśvara explains: *parapīḍātmakāt karmaṇas tadanurūpam ātmanaḥ pīḍātmakaṃ phalam bhavati-iti karmānurūpyopamānam* (NSudhā, 184).

13. ŚV, 87 (v. 236 f.).

14. ŚV, 88 (v. 244 f.); also 87 (v. 236); cf. YD, 15 (see below, n. 28).

15. ŚV, 88 (v. 242 f.):

> *vihitapratiṣiddhatve muktvā-anyan na ca kāraṇam*
> *dharmādharmāvabodhasya, tena-ayuktā-anumānagīḥ.*

16. Cf. ŚV, 89 (v. 249 ff.). The commentator Umbeka (ed. S. K. Ramanatha Sastri. Madras, 1971, 112) attributes this to the Sāṃkhya author Mādhava, who is often referred to as "destroyer of Sāṃkhya" (*sāṃkhyanāśaka*; this seems to be the correct reading instead of the *-nāyaka* in the printed text); see also V. Raghavan, "Mādhava, an Early Unfaithful Exponent of the Sāṅkhya." *Sarūpa Bhāratī* (Lakshman Sarup Memorial Vol.). Hoshiarpur, 1954, 162–164.

17. ŚV, 89 (v. 252 ff.).

18. ŚV, 90 (v. 258).

19. ŚV, 90 (v. 259):

> *tathāpy ekaphalatvaṃ cet, kriyātvāt sarvasaṅkaraḥ*
> *yajitvādyaviśeṣāc ca citrādiphalatulyatā.*

20. ŚV, 80 (v. 205): *śyenas tatra-asivat pṛthak*; cf. also 84 v. 223 ff.); Pārthasārathi, *Śāstradīpikā*, ed. Laxman Shastri Dravid. Benares, 1916, 93: *śyenaphalaṃ ca hiṃsā, na śyenaḥ*.

21. It is *anartha* because of "another action" (*kriyāntara*) to be accomplished by the ritual itself; cf. ŚV, 92 (v. 268).

22. ŚV, 92 (v. 273 f.). Cf. Medhātithi on Manu II, 10: *rāgalakṣaṇā laukikī hiṃsā, vidhilakṣaṇā-alaukikī hiṃsā*; also on II, 6 (ed. J. H. Dave, I, 167 f.).

23. Cf. *Jaiminīya Brāhmaṇa* I, 18, 45 ff.; *Bṛhadāraṇyaka Upaniṣad* VI, 2 (i.e. *Śatapatha Brāhmaṇa* XIV, 9, 1); *Chāndogya Upaniṣad* V, 3–10.

24. *Chāndogya Upaniṣad* V, 10, 3: *ya ime grāma iṣṭāpurte dattam ity upāsate; Bṛhadāraṇyaka Upaniṣad* VI, 2, 16: *ye yajñena dānena tapasā lokāñ jayanti.*

25. Kārṣṇājini is mentioned in BS III, 1, 9, Bādari in III, 1, 11; see also the reference to Pañcaśikha in Vācaspati's *Tattvakaumudī* on SK 2.

26. Cf. Śaṅkara on BS II, 1, 25. See also YD, 15 (*pūrvapakṣa*): *sāmānye hi śāstram ahiṃsām utsṛjya viśeṣe kratulakṣaṇe 'pavādam śāsti, sāmānyavihitaṃ ca viśeṣavihitena bādhyate . . . tasmād utsargāpavādayor viṣayabhedān na-asti śāstravirodha iti.* The Sāṃkhya reply is to reject the applicability of the *utsarga/apavāda* rule and to claim that the limited and merely instrumental validity of the sacrificial injunctions and the basic norm of ahiṃsā exist side by side; cf. in particular Vācaspati, *Tattvakaumudī* on SK 2; also YD, 16. The rule has its origin in grammar; cf. *Mahābhāṣya* on Pāṇini III, 1, 94.

27. Especially on V, 10, 6.

28. YD, 15: *evam hi parikalpyamāne gurubhāryāgamane 'pi sattvāntarānugrahasāmarthyād iṣṭaphalasambandhaḥ syāt*; see also YD, 16.

29. Cf. E. Frauwallner, *Geschichte der indischen Philosophie*, vol. 1. Salzburg, 1953, 287 (*History of Indian Philosophy*, trans. V. M. Bedekar, vol. 1. Delhi, 1973, 226). The cautious formulation in the original that the *Yuktidīpikā* "might have originated around A.D. 550" ("entstanden sein dürfte") appears as "*must* have originated" in the English version. Bedekar's translation often distorts the original.

30. *Sāṃkhyasaptativṛtti* (V1), ed. E. A. Solomon. Ahmedabad, 1973, 7: [*agniṣṭome*] *tāvat paśuvadho 'śvamedhe mānuṣavadho 'pi*. On this text and the *Sāṃkhyavṛtti*, also edited by E. A. Solomon, see my review, *Journal of the American Oriental Society* 96 (1976), 144 f. Cf. also YD, 14: *brahmaṇe* (instead of *brāhmaṇe* in the printed text) *brāhmaṇam ālabheta-ityadi*.

31. Cf. S. Kawasaki, "Quotations in the Mīmāṃsā Chapter of Bhavya's *Madhyamaka-hṛdaya-kārikā*." *Journal of Indian and Buddhist Studies* (Tokyo) 22/2 (1974), 1127–1120 (i.e., 1–7); ib., 5).

32. Cf. K. K. Handiqui, *Yaśastilaka and Indian Culture*. Sholapur, 1949, 382; Bhāvasena, *Viśvatattvaprakāśa*, ed. V. P. Johrapurkar. Sholapur, 1964, 98; Bhāvasena likens such Vedic teachings to those of the "authoritative texts of the Turks" (*turuṣkaśāstra*).

33. Cf. K. K. Handiqui, 386 f.

34. For a critical review of the available evidence and its interpretations, see D. Schlingloff, "Menschenopfer in Kauśambī?" *Indo-Iranian Journal* 11 (1968/69), 175–189.

35. Cf. Prabhākara, *Bṛhatī* with *Ṛjuvimalā* of Śālikanātha Miśra, ed. A. Chinnasvāmī Śāstrī, fasc. 1. Benares, 1929 (Ch SS), 31; on the definition of *puruṣārtha* and *kratvartha*, see Śabara on MS IV, 1, 2.

36. Ibid. See also Padmapāda, *Pañcapādikā*, ed. Rāmaśāstrī Bhāgavatācārya. Benares, 1891 (Vizianagram Sanskrit Series), 91 f. (non-injury either as a prohibition or as a positive mental act, *mānasī saṃkalpakriyā*). On *kratvarthā hiṃsā*, cf. YSBhV, 323 (on IV, 7).

37. ŚV, 86 (v. 233 f.); cf. 89 (v. 255 f.): *pratiṣedhajaṃ pratyavāyārthatājñānam*.

38. Cf. *Chāndogya Upaniṣad* VIII, 15.

39. Cf. TV, 135 ff. (on I, 3, 7; concerning the killing of female members of the brahmin caste); and the quote in Someśvara, NSudha, 201: *antaraṃ yādṛśaṃ loke brahmahatyāśvamedhayor*. See also Śaṅkara, BUBh III, 3, 1: *bhrūṇahatyāśvamedhābhyāṃ na paraṃ puṇyapāpayor iti smaranti*. The *aśvamedha*, this "most meritorious" of all rituals, is, of course, traditionally associated with killing.

40. TV, 113 (on I, 3, 4): *vedamūlatvaṃ punas te . . . mātāpitṛdveṣiduṣṭaputravan na-abhyupagacchanti*; cf. also 162 (on I, 3, 12): *ahiṃsādy apy atatpūrvam ity āhus tarkamāninaḥ* (concerning the Buddhists etc., who do not accept the Vedic origin of *ahiṃsā*).

41. Cf. ŚV, 93 (v. 275 f.):

> *gītāmantrārthavādair yā kalpyate 'narthahetutā*
> *pratyakṣaśrutibādhyatvāt sā-anyārthatvena nīyate.*

42. Cf. TV, 124 (on I, 3, 7); Someśvara, NSudhā, 184, explains this inference as: *vaidiky api hiṃsā laukikīvad adharma iti*. In Bhartṛhari's terminology, this would be a case of "dry reasoning" (*śuṣkatarka*), based upon external and deceptive "similarities and dissimilarities" (*sādharmyavaidharmya*); cf. Vṛtti on VP I, 137/129 (i.e. I, 153, ed. W. Rau).

43. Cf. Manu II, 6; 12; *India and Europe*, 324 ff.

44. ŚV, 88 (v. 246; also 244: *krośatā hṛdayena*); cf. the reference to *paritāpa*, the "anguish" of compassion, YD, 16.

45. ŚV, 88 (v. 247): *aśāstrajño mleccho na-udvijate kvacit*; in his commentary on this verse, Pārthasārathi mentions the "absence of the voice of the heart" (*hṛdayakrośābhāva*) in the mleccha.

46. TV, 125 (on I, 3, 7):

> *paśuhiṃsādisambandhe yajñe tuṣyanti hi dvijāḥ,*
> *tebhya eva hi yajñebhyah śākyāḥ krudhyanti pīḍitāh.*

47. TV, 124 (on I, 3, 7).

48. Loc. cit.: *sanmūlam apy ahiṃsādi śvadṛtinikṣiptakṣīravad.*

49. Cf. Udayana, *Ātmatattvaviveka*, ed. Ḍhuṇḍhirāja Śāstrī. Benares, 1940 (Ch SS), 418; Udayana uses the term *biḍālavratanyāya* to refer to the "hypocritical" behavior of the heretics.

50. Keśavamiśra, *Tarkabhāṣā*, ed. Rudradhara Jhā. Benares, 1952, 8; 13; 37.

51. ŚV, 150 (v. 5 f.):

saṃsāramocakādeś ca hiṃsā puṇyatvasammatā.
na paścāt puṇyam icchanti kecid, evaṃ vigānataḥ.
mlecchāryāṇāṃ prasiddhatvaṃ na dharmasya-upapadyate.

On Bhartṛhari's use of *lokaprasiddhi, lokaprasiddhatva* etc., which also affects his understanding of *āgama*, cf. VP I, 30 ff. In v. 3 of the *Autpattikasūtra* section (ŚV, 149), Kumārila quotes a verse which is identical with VP I, 40:

idaṃ puṇyam idaṃ pāpam ity etasmin padadvaye
ācaṇḍāla(ṃ)manuṣyāṇām alpaṃ śāstraprayojanam.

However, Kumārila attributes this verse, which is also quoted by Jayanta (NM, 230) as a statement by "Vyāsa," to Pārāśarya (i.e. Vyāsa); Jayanta defines *lokaprasiddhi* as *laukikānām avicchinnā smṛtiḥ*, which implies that it has no independent authority, but depends on *śruti* as its "root" (*mūla*).

52. ŚV, *Autpattikasūtra*, v. 7.

53. *Mīmāṃsāślokavārttika* with the commentary *Kāśikā* of Sucaritamiśra, ed. K. Sāmbaśiva Śāstrī, pt. 2. Trivandrum, 1929, 3.

54. A. Wezler, "Zur Proklamation religiös-weltanschaulicher Toleranz bei dem indischen Philosophen Jayantabhaṭṭa." *Saeculum* 27 (1976), 329–348; ib. 335. For characteristic misinterpretations of the term, see, for instance, R. Garbe's German translation of Vācaspati's *Tattvakaumudī* (Digambara Jainas) or, more recently, *Elucidation of the Intrinsic Meaning* (*Paramatthadīpanī* by Dhammapāla), trans. U Ba Kyaw; ed. P. Mase-

field. London, 1980, 82, n. 1 (Ājīvikas); on the modern pandit Balarāma Udāsīna, see below, n. 58.

55. NM, 242f.

56. See Amṛtacandra, *Puruṣārthasiddhyupāya*, ed. and trans. Ajit Prasada. Lucknow, 1933 (Sacred Books of the Jainas), 43 (v. 88). Cakradhara, *Nyāyamañjarīgranthibhaṅga*, ed. N. J. Shah. Ahmedabad, 1972, 113, reads (repeated in the edition of NM by Gaurinath Sastri, Benares, 1982–1984): *ghūkacaṭakanyāyena prāṇivadhaṃ dharmam icchanti*. On p. 100, Cakradhara uses the same term to illustrate Jayanta's rejection of *lokaprasiddhi* as a source for the knowledge of dharma. In both cases, the reading *ghūkacaṭakanyāya* ("maxim of the owl and the sparrow") seems unacceptable and may be based upon a scribal error or an inappropriate emendation. In accordance with Amṛtacandra's *ghaṭacaṭakamokṣa*, we suggest *ghaṭacaṭakanyāya*. Subsequently, Cakradhara (possibly twelfth century) also refers to a *Bhairavatantra*.

57. NM, 245; Jayanta mentions the *agnīṣomīya* offering and the *śyena* sacrifice.

58. Balarāma Udāsīna is quoted by G. Jha, *The Tattva-Kaumudī, trans. into English*. Poona, third ed., 1965, notes, p. 9: *dehabhaṅge tadantargatajīvabhaṅga eva mokṣa ity evaṃ bruvāṇāś cārvākaviśeṣāḥ*.

59. Cf. NK, 179 f. (in: PB, ed. V. P. Dvivedin); *Ātmatattvaviveka* (see above, n. 49), 419: *saṃsāramocakāgama*; cf. 420: *sugatādyāgama*.

60. YSBhV, 134: *etena-apuṇye puṇyapratyayaḥ*; *Tattvavaiśāradī*, ed. Nārāyaṇamiśra. Benares, 1971, 148: *apuṇye hiṃsādau saṃsāramocakādīnāṃ puṇyapratyayaḥ*; cf. also YSBhV, 144 (on II, 12).

61. Cf. Haribhadra, *Śāstravārttāsamuccaya*, v. 150: *saṃsāramocakasya-api, hiṃsā yad dharmasādhanam*; v. 157 refers to the *hiṃsā* which is "enjoined by the Veda" (*vedavihita*).

62. Cf. *Nandīsūtra* with *Vṛtti* by Malayagiri (*Srimanmalayagiryācāryapraṇītavṛttiyutam . . . śrīmannandīsūtram*), ed. Veṇīcanda Suracanda. Bombay, 1924, fol. 13 a f. (cf. also the extensive excerpt given by Vijayarājendra

Sūri in his encyclopedia *Abhidhānarājendra*. Ratlam, 1913–1925, vol. 7, 252 f.; s.v. *saṃsāramoyaga/saṃsāramocaka): tatas te 'vaśyam tatpāpakśapaṇāya paropakārakaraṇaikarasikamānasena vyāpādanīyāḥ . . . tīvraduḥkhavedanābhibhavavaśāc ca prāg baddhaṃ pāpakarma-udīrya-udīrya-anubhavantaḥ pratikṣipanti.* Human as well as non-human creatures are mentioned. Another, shorter reference is found in the *Syādvādaratnākara* by Vādideva Sūri (ca. 1100), as indicated by N. J. Shah in his edition of the *Nyāyamañjarīgranthibhaṅga* (see above, n. 56), 113, n. 1.

63. Cf. Siddhasena Divākara, *Sanmatitarka* with Abhayadeva Sūri's *Tattvabodhavidhāyinī*, ed. Sukhlāl Sanghvī and Becardās Dośī. Ahmedabad 1924–1931 (reprint Kyoto, 1984), 731.

64. Cf. S. Kawasaki (ed.), "The Mīmāṃsā Chapter of Bhavya's *Madhyamaka-hṛdaya-kārikā*. Sanskrit and Tibetan Texts. 2: Uttara-pakṣa." *Tetsugaku shisō ronshū* (Department of Philosophy, Tsukuba University) 12 (March 28, 62; i.e. 1987), 1–23; ib. v. 35. For the *Tarkajvālā*, see the Peking edition of the Tanjur, No. 5256, 322a (reprint Tokyo, vol. 96, p. 131). I thank Dr. Karin Preisendanz (Berlin) for her advice on this passage.

65. Cf. *Paramattha-Dīpanī*, part 3 (commentary on *Petavatthu*), ed. E. Hardy. London, 1894 (PTS), 67 (i.e. II, 1); for an English translation, see above, n. 54.

66. The idea that the existence of such creatures is a miserable one is, of course, an old and familiar one; cf. Mahābhārata XIII, 118, 14 f. (a passage mentioned to me by A. Wezler), where a *kīṭa* (beetle or worm) is told that it should consider death as a relief (*maraṇaṃ te sukhaṃ manye*). However, the animal declines the offer of euthanasia.

67. Cf. Malayagiri, *Vṛtti* (see above, n. 62), fol. 13a: *yat pariṇāmasundaraṃ tad āpātakaṭukam api pareṣām ādheyam, yathā rogopaśamanam auṣadham.* The term *pariṇāmasundara* is also used by Jineśvara, *Pañcalingī*, v. 60 (as quoted by Malliṣeṇa, *Syādvādamañjarī*, ed. A. B. Dhruva. Bombay 1933, 64). On medical metaphors and the therapeutic paradigm in general, see below, ch. 7.

68. Cf. TV, 114 (on I, 3, 4), where the extreme altruism expressed in the bodhisattva's vow to take all suffering upon himself is presented as a case of self-deception and transgression (*vyatikrama*) of dharma.

69. Cf. *Netratantra* with comm. by Kṣemarāja, ed. M. Kaul Shastri. Bombay 1926–1939 (Kashmir Series of Texts and Studies), 216 ff.; 222 f. (ch. 20, v. 4 ff.; 18 ff.). See specifically v. 8:

    eṣām anugrahārthāya paśūnāṃ tu, varānane,
    mocayanti ca pāpebhyaḥ pāpaughāṃs chedayanti tān.

    Kṣemarāja paraphrases *anugraha* as *mukti*. Cf. also v. 20:

    troṭayanti paśoḥ pāśāñ charīraṃ yena naśyati,
    śarireṇa pranaṣṭena mokṣaṇam, na hi māraṇam.

    On the contents, character and date of the *Netratantra*, cf. H. Brunner, "Un Tantra du Nord: Le Netra Tantra." *Bulletin de l'École Française d'Extrême-Orient* 61 (1974), 125–197; on ch. 20, see 183 ff. Abhinavagupta discusses the topic of ritual hiṃsā in ch. 16 of his *Tantrāloka*; in his commentary on v. 58–62, Jayaratha quotes *Netratantra* 20, 8; 18–21; cf. *Tantrāloka* with comm. by Rājānaka Jayaratha, ed. M. Kaul Shastri (vol. 1: Mukund Ram Shastri). Bombay (vol. 1: Allahabad), 1918–1938 (Kashmir Series of Texts and Studies), vol. 10, 23 ff. (enlarged reprint in 8 vols., ed. R. C. Dwivedi and N. Rastogi. Delhi, 1987).

70. Cf. D. S. Ruegg, "Problems in the Transmission of Vajrayāna Buddhism in the Western Himālaya about the Year 1000." *Acta Indologica* (Naritasan Shinshoji) 6 (1984; "Mysticism"), 369–381; especially 377 f.

71. NBhūṣ, 391; cf. also 403: *purīṣādibhakṣaṇaṃ brāhmaṇādivadhaṃ ca kuryāt svargakāmaḥ.*

72. Cf. NBhūṣ, 392.

73. Cf. NBhūṣ, 395; these texts teaching despicable practices are also referred to by Dharmakīrti in his autocommentary on *Pramāṇavārttika* I, 308 (ed. R. Gnoli. Rome, 1960, 163).

74. Cf. Prabhācandra, *Nyāyakumudacandra*, ed. Mahendra Kumar. Bombay, 1941, 763; Anantavīrya, *Siddhiviniścayaṭīkā* (commentary on Akalaṅka's *Siddhiviniścaya* and *Vṛtti*), ed. Mahendra Kumar. Benares, 1959, 335 ff., mentions *ṭhaka* and *ṭhakaprayoga* in connection with procedures of debate. I owe the reference to the *slu* (instead of *slus*) *byed pa* (Peking edition, No. 5256, 321a; vol. 96, p. 130) to Dr. Karin Preisendanz.

75. See Prabhācandra, *Nyāyakumudacandra*, 763; cf. 765, on *sādhutva and mlecchavyavahāra*.

76. *Ramaseeana or a Vocabulary of the Peculiar Language of the Thugs*. Calcutta, 1836, 13.

77. *Report on the Depredations Committed by the Thug Gangs of Upper and Central India*. Calcutta, 1840, VI (preface).

78. On J. Paton, see G. Pfirrmann, *Religiöser Charakter und Organisation der Thag-Brüderschaften*. Diss. Tübingen, 1970, 27 f.; 127 ff.

79. Cf. R. Garbe, *Beiträge zur indischen Kulturgeschichte*. Berlin, 1903, 185–198; G. Pfirrmann, 6 ff.; 30 f. (on Hsüan-tsang).

80. Cf. *Kumārapālacarita* III, 59 (ed. S. Pandurang Pandit. Bombay, 1900, 100).

81. Cf. *Deśīnāmamālā* II, 28 (ed. R. Pischel and P. V. Ramanujaswami. Bombay, second ed., 1938, 92).

82. *Trikāṇḍaśeṣa* III, 1, 14; cf. Th. Zachariae, "Prākṛtwörter in Purushottama's Trikāṇḍaçesha" (1886). *Opera minora*, ed. C. Vogel. Wiesbaden, 1977, 153.

83. Cf. also Pali *thaketi*.—For a similar semantic development, G. I. Ascoli, *Kritische Studien zur Sprachwissenschaft*. Weimar, 1878, 257, n. 39, refers to *chadman* ("deceit," "fraud"; from *chad*, "to cover").

84. E. W. Hopkins, *The Religions of India*. Boston, 1895, 535, refers to the tribal goddess Thākurānī: "She was doubtless the first patroness of the

throttling Thugs (*ṭhags* are *ṭhaks*, assassins), and the prototype of their Hindu Kālī." Cf. also 493 f. The names of some of the sixty-four Yoginīs (Ṭhakinī, Ḍākinī) are also suggestive. G. Pfirrmann, *Religiöser Charakter* (see ab ove, n. 78), 108 f., tries to trace Thagism to the "theology of aboriginal tribes."

85. Cf. B. B. Lawrence, *Shahrastānī on the Indian Religions*. The Hague, 1976, 226–237; especially 235 f. Both Marvazī and Shahrastānī emphasize the treachery and deceit in the methods of these groups.

86. R. J. Blackham, *Incomparable India*. London, 1933, 172, refers to "an Irish soldier named Creagh." W. H. Sleeman, *Ramaseeana* (see above, n. 76), 9 f., suggests a Near Eastern origin of the practice of strangling; cf. also A. S. Tritton, "Muslim Thugs." *Journal of Indian History* 8 (1929), 41–44.

87. Cf. *Kālikāpurāṇa*, ch. 71; for an early English translation of this chapter, see W. C. Blaquiere, *Asiatic Researches* 5 (1799; reprint 1801), 369 ff.; especially 381 ff. W. Crooke's claim that "in the Ellora cave temple, which was constructed about 760 A.D., we have a Thug represented strangling a Brahman" (*Things Indian*. London, 1906, 474) cannot be substantiated and may be based upon a misinterpretation. However, the Thags themselves used to refer to the Ellora caves; cf. G. Pfirrmann, *Religiöser Charakter*, 76 ff.

88. See above, n. 76.

89. Cf. G. Pfirrmann, 45 (quotation from W. W. Hunter, *The Annals of Rural Bengal*. London, 1868, 72).

90. G. Pfirrmann, 45 (from W. Tayler, *Thirty-Eight Years in India*, vol. 1. London, 1881, 194).

91. Cf. J. N. Farquhar, art. "Thags." *Encyclopaedia of Religion and Ethics*, ed. J. Hastings. Edinburgh, 1908–1926; reprint New York 1955), vol. 12, 259 ff.

92. Cf. R. Garbe, *Beiträge* (see above, n. 79), 186; and G. Pfirrmann, *Religiöser Charakter*, 113.

93. On the *turuṣka*, see above, n. 32; the term *hūṇa* was also occasionally applied to the Europeans; cf. *India and Europe*, 194.

94. Jātaka, ed. V. Fausboll. London, 1877–1897, vol. 6, 208:

kīṭā paṭaṅgā uragā ca bhekā
hantvā kimiṃ sujjhati makkhikā ca . . .

95. Cf. S. Kawasaki, "A Reference to Maga in the Tibetan Translation of the *Tarkajvālā*." *Journal of Indian and Buddhist Studies* (Tokyo) 23/2 (1975), 1103–1097 (i.e., 14–20); Chr. Lindtner, "Buddhist References to Old Iranian Religion." *A Green Leaf. Papers in Honour of Prof. J. P. Asmussen*. Leiden, 1988, 433–444. On the authenticity of the *Tarkajvālā*, cf. the arguments of Y. Ejima, as presented by Chr. Lindtner: "Adversaria Buddhica." *Wiener Zeitschrift für die Kunde Südasiens* 26 (1982), 167–194; ib. 182 f. Lindtner's rejection of these arguments is not convincing; see also D. S. Ruegg, *The Literature of the Madhyamaka School of Philosophy in India*. Wiesbaden, 1981, 66 f. (especially n. 214).

96. S. Kawasaki, "A Reference," 14; cf. Chr. Lindtner, "Buddhist References," 439. The reference to bulls may remind us of the Greek "sacrifice of a hundred oxen" (*hekatombe*).

97. Cf. Lindtner, 435.

98. Cf. Lindtner, 439 ff.; Kawasaki, 18 ff. See also *Abhidharmadīpa with Vibhāṣāprabhāvṛtti*, ed. P. S. Jaini. Patna, second ed., 1977, 154.

99. Cf. Vasubandhu, *Abhidharmakośabhāṣya*, ed. P. Pradhan. Patna 1967, 240; YSBhV, 144 (on II, 12); cf. also YS II, 34: *lobha, krodha* and *moha* as causes of hiṃsā.

100. Cf. Lindtner, 440 f.; this text has survived in a Chinese translation.

101. Cf. Dharmakīrti, *Pramāṇavārttika* I, 321 (autocommentary; ed. R. Gnoli. Rome, 1960, 170): *pārasīkamātṛmithyācāravat*; and the commentary literature following Dharmakīrti, especially Prajñākaragupta, *Pramāṇavārttikabhāṣya*, ed. R. Sāṅkṛtyāyana. Patna, 1953, 329 (v. 565);

Durvekamiśra, *Dharmottarapradīpa*, ed. D. Malvania. Patna, third ed., 1971, 14 f. (*pārasīkaśāstra*). Several references are found in Śāntarakṣita's *Tattvasaṃgraha* and its commentary by Kamalaśīla; cf. v. 2446 f.; 2796 f.; 2806 f.

102. Cf. Abhayadeva (as cited above, n. 63); Prabhācandra (see above, n. 74 f.); on Bhāvasena's reference to the *turuṣka*, see above, n. 32.

103. Cf. Bhāsarvajña, BNhūṣ, 406 (*mātṛvivāha*); see also P. V. Kane, *History of Dharmaśāstra*, vol. 3. Poona, 1946, 859, n. 1665.

104. Cf. G. Widengren, *Die Religionen Irans*. Stuttgart, 1965, 133 ff.; for a collection of the Greek and Latin references, see C. Clemen, *Fontes historiae religionis Persicae*. Bonn, 1920.

105. Cf. G. Widengren, *Religionen Irans*, 288 ff.; see also S. K. Hodivala, *Parsis of Ancient India*. Bombay, 1920, 126 ff.; also 55 (on a "Pahlavi Nirang to kill noxious animals" from Gujarat).

106. See above, n. 65; 94; 62.

107. See above, n. 64.

108. Cf. Lindtner, "Buddhist References" (see above, n. 95), 434, n. 5, for the Tibetan text: *gser gyi snod* (instead of Lindtner's *snon*) *du gser gyi khab kyis grog ma phug nas bsad na 'khor ba las grol bar 'gyur la. de gsod pa po yaṅ thar pa'i sa bon bsags par 'dod pa daṅ.* Lindtner translates as follows: "When one kills an ant in a golden vessel by piercing it with a gold needle one is liberated from *saṃsāra*, and the one who kills it accumulates the seeds of liberation." This disregards the word *yaṅ* ("too"), which indicates a second subject. I thank my friend and colleague Ernst Steinkellner, who has helped me analyze and clarify this passage.

109. Cf. Lindtner, 435 f.; 441 ff. Lindtner does not accept Sundermann's suggestion.

110. Cf. *L'Abhidharmakośa de Vasubandhu*, traduit et annoté par L. de La Vallée Poussin, vol. 3 (chap. 4). Paris/Louvain, 1924, 145, n. 2; Lindtner, 440. This idea is echoed by Vasubandhu.

111. Cf. TV, 113, (on I, 3, 4); SV, 150 (v. 8).

112. See above, n. 11; also Vācaspati, *Tattvakaumudī* on SK 2.

113. Cf. Śaṅkara, who usually follows the Pūrvamīmāṃsā in such matters, on *Chāndogya Upaniṣad* V, 10, 6: *na ca vaidikānāṃ karmaṇām hiṃsāyuktatvena-ubhayahetutvaṃ śakyam anumātum, hiṃsāyāḥ śāstracoditatvāt*; but see also YSBhV, 323 (on IV, 7).

114. Cf. TV, 242 (on I, 3, 30): *yāgānuṣṭhānāt pūrvam abhūtam anuṣṭhānottarakālaṃ ca-apūrvam jāyata iti yaugikatvād eva-apūrvaśabdābhidhānaṃ sarvatra labhyate*. On the concept of *apūrva*, see below, ch. 9.

115. Cf. NM, 253 f.; the problem is how the specific results of the "rain-producing" *kārīrī* ceremony relate to the pleasure or pain produced by "ordinary" merit or demerit; cf. also the expression *sāmānyasukhasādhanādṛṣṭa* (254).

116. Such side-effects are often suggested by Yoga and Sāṃkhya authors; cf. Vācaspati, *Tattvavaiśāradī* on YS II, 13; *Tattvakaumudī* on SK 2: This is sometimes associated with the name of the old Sāṃkhya teacher Pañcaśikha.

117. See, for instance, the Cārvāka chapter in Mādhava-Vidyāraṇya's *Sarvadarśanasaṃgraha*; cf. also L. Alsdorf, *Beiträge* (see above, n. 2), 35 f.

118. Cf. ŚV, 93 (commentary on v. 275 f.): *agnir mā tasmād enaso viśvān muñcatv aṃhasaḥ*.

119. Cf. Malliṣeṇa, *Syādvādamañjarī*, ed. A. B. Dhruva. Bombay, 1933, *66: agnir mām etasmād dhiṃsākṛtād enaso muñcatu*.

120. H.-P. Schmidt, "The Origin" (see above, n. 1) 645.

121. H.-P. Schmidt, 650.

122. Cf. J. C. Heesterman, "Non-Violence and Sacrifice." *Indologica Taurinensia* 12 (1984), 119–127; especially 123.

123. On various ways in which this tension has been articulated, and on attempts to resolve and reconcile it, cf. L. Alsdorf, *Beiträge* (see above, n. 2).

124. On the other hand, Kumārila and his successors do not try to affiliate Śaivite and other extra-Vedic bloody rituals with the Veda. However, Śaivite Tantric authors themselves, such as Jayaratha in his commentary on Abhinavagupta's *Tantrāloka* (ch. 16), have referred to the Veda, and they have used and extrapolated arguments found in Mīmāṃsā and Dharmaśāstra.

CHAPTER 5

Human Reason and Vedic Revelation in Advaita Vedānta

Introduction to the Problem

1. The role of reason in the teachings of Śaṅkara has often been discussed; and some basic patterns and problems of the philosophical encounter between India and the West, of Western self-understanding and of the Indian response to the Western challenge have been reflected in these discussions. Śaṅkara's thought has been questioned, criticized, and defended in terms of the relationship between reason and revelation, autonomous thinking, and sacred tradition. On the Indian side, in Neo-Hinduism or Neo-Vedānta, the approach is often apologetic. Śaṅkara is defended against the claims of Western "rationality," either in the name of reason itself or in the name of a transrational "experience," which includes and fulfills, but does not contradict, the aspirations of human reasoning.

Already Rammohan Roy (1772–1833), who has been called the "father of modern Indian thought" and who has in fact initiated important modernistic developments in Hinduism, claims that the Upaniṣads, as well as their interpretation by Śaṅkara, if rediscovered and understood in their genuine meaning, are fully compatible with Western rational and scientific thought, and that they contain all the potential of a true "religion of reason." "Reason," correlated to the Sanskrit term *yukti,* is a key concept in Rammohan's thought.[1] In the writings of Rammohan's successors, who are less directly exposed to the ideas of the European age of enlightenment, the appeal to reason and common sense is less conspicuous. It is frequently overshadowed by or even replaced with the notion of a suprarational, but not antirational "experience" or "intuition," which is associated with such Sanskrit terms as *darśana* and presented as the central and guiding principle of the Indian philosophical tradition and of Śaṅkara's philosophy in particular.[2]

Yet the defense of Advaita Vedānta in the name of reason or rationality has remained an important concern of modern Indian thought, and it is one of the characteristic features of Neo-Vedānta. Numerous authors have argued for "the rational basis of Advaitism,"[3] and they have presented the teachings of *śruti,* the Vedic-Upaniṣadic "revelation," as "rational truth." In their interpretation, Advaita Vedānta is a religion that "reconciles revelation with reason," or a philosophy that "reconciles the claims of reason with those of religious faith";[4] it appears as a system in which there is no room for the Western dichotomy and antagonism of reason and faith. Again and again, it is emphasized that Śaṅkara is not a dogmatic in the sense of blindly following his sacred tradition, and that his allegiance to the Veda "is not only founded on reason, but also ever remains open to it."[5] Moreover: "Though Śaṅkara accepts the authority of the Vedas so earnestly, yet he is not in the least reluctant to shake off its authority absolutely and without reservation when reason demands it."[6]

Such presentations should not primarily be seen as contributions to historical and philological research. They may be respectable attempts to rethink or reinterpret Advaita Vedānta in the context of the modern world; but their apologetic goal often overshadows the requirements of philological accuracy and conceptual precision. Other contributions are more cautious and closer to Śaṅkara's own words. N. K. Devaraja finds "inconsistent, even contradictory, statements" about the role of reason (*tarka*) in Śaṅkara's writings, and he tries to trace this "inconsistency" to a "confusion between two very different meanings or conceptions of reasoning," that is, between tarka as "hypothetical argument" and as "valid inference."[7] The critical and differentiated treatment of the topic in K. S. Murty's book *Revelation and Reason in Advaita Vedanta* (1959; second ed., 1974), which emphasizes the subordination of reason and argumentation (yukti, tarka) to the authority of the Vedic revelation, is particularly remarkable and a somewhat unusual contribution from the Indian side.[8]

In Western literature on Śaṅkara, the question of the relationship between reason and the authority of the sacred texts plays a less conspicuous, but by no means negligible role. P. Deussen, certainly one of the most dedicated Western students of Śaṅkara and exemplifying an approach which is both scholarly and sympathetic, has paid special attention to this question; he emphasizes the extent to which autonomous philosophical reflection actually occurs in Śaṅkara's thought and argumentation, in spite of the programmatic relegation of reasoning to a subordinate, merely auxiliary function: "Of the possibility here suggested, of bringing in reflection as an aid, our author makes a far more extensive use than might appear from these expressions. Since this side of Śaṅkara's work has for us the chief interest, we will, as far as possible, pass over his endless quotations from the Veda, but, on the other hand, bend our whole attention to the philosophic reflection."[9] Of course, Deussen was writing at a time when most European historians of philosophy disregarded or denounced Indian thought, just as Oriental thought in general, as not being truly philosophical, and as amounting to myths, dogmas, and mere exegesis without autonomy of reason.[10] More recent authors, to whom the existence of genuine philosophy in the Indian tradition is no longer a matter of debate, still tend to dismiss the exegetical dimension of Śaṅkara's thought as philosophically irrelevant: "The exegetical dimension of Vedānta is of great interest to students of linguistics and Indian cultural history (and naturally Indian scholars themselves), but it is of very little interest to Western students of philosophy."[11]

Although from Japan, H. Nakamura, one of the leading Vedānta scholars of our time, echoes the traditional attitudes of Western thought and scholarship when he sees an unreconciled "conflict between traditionalism and rationalism" in Śaṅkara's thought; accordingly, he finds Śaṅkara's "philosophical standpoint" lacking in "thoroughness (or consistency)."[12] In this view, Śaṅkara appears as a philosopher in spite of himself, a serious and creative thinker insofar as his own reason and originality are able to stand up against his exegetic and traditionalistic preconceptions. S. Mayeda, H. Nakamura's successor and himself one of the most dedicated Śaṅkara specialists, states: "However, Śaṅkara is endowed with too much creativity and reasoning power to remain a simple traditionalist."[13]

2. To what extent does the problem of "reason" and "revelation," "rationalism" and "traditionalism" really apply to Śaṅkara himself and to the classical Indian tradition? To what extent have

European problems and perspectives, specifically of the nineteenth century, been projected and superimposed upon Śaṅkara and the Indian situation? The manner in which it was understood by the nineteenth-century Western historians of philosophy is certainly not the only way of understanding the nature of philosophical reflection and the relationship and tension between "reason" and "revelation." There is nothing like the classical Greek or Cartesian self-proclamation of human reason in the Indian tradition. The separation and confrontation of "reason" and "revelation," autonomous thought and sacred tradition is often rather evasive and ambiguous and generally less radical and conspicuous than in the European tradition. The Indian tradition and Advaita Vedānta in particular have developed their own ways of contrasting, interrelating, or reconciling these two dimensions of human thought and orientation, and we have to be ready to question and to readjust our Western conceptual patterns while using them as tools of interpretation.[14]

The following Sanskrit terms, used by Śaṅkara himself as well as by other Indian thinkers, relate to the problems of "reason" and "revelation": On the one side (i.e., on the side of "reason,") we have *yukti, tarka, upapatti, puruṣabuddhi,* but also *anumāna* ("inference") and other terms referring to "worldly" methods of knowledge.[15] On the other side, we find, in addition to *veda* and *śruti,* such terms as *āgama, śāstra, upadeśa, śabda, vākya,* which have the connotation of authoritative "testimony" and "instruction," of something to be listened to, received and respected.

On the side of "reason," yukti and tarka are the most conspicuous and significant terms. Śaṅkara does not formally define these terms, nor does he use them in a strictly technical sense. He alludes to, but does not commit himself to, the technical meanings which the terms, in particular tarka, may have in other systems. In Nyāya, tarka, if used in a technical sense,[16] is not a "means of knowledge" (*pramāṇa*) in the full sense, but rather an auxiliary method of hypothetical or circumstantial reasoning which is supposed to contribute to the elimination of doubt and to bring about some kind of conditional certainty. The definition given in *Nyāyasūtra* I, 1, 40 (*avijñātatattve 'rthe kāraṇopapattitas tattvajñānārtham ūhas tarkaḥ*) has been open to a variety of interpretations that often emphasize the negative, reductive functions of tarka, consisting in the elimination of false views rather than the establishment of truth.[17] Although Śaṅkara must have been familiar with the Nyāya definition of tarka,[18] other less technical uses were probably more significant to him. The word is already used, indicating various degrees of human "independence" or even of opposition to the sacred texts, in the Upaniṣads, the Mahābhārata, and other ancient texts.[19] More specifically, Bhartṛhari's usage of tarka (including the compounds *śuṣkatarka* and *puruṣatarka*) seems to have had its impact upon Śaṅkara.[20]

Yukti, etc. are often used as synonyms of tarka, but less frequently with a pejorative connotation. Yukti, nyāya, etc. may express, in a general sense, the claim of sound argumentation, of intelligibility and concordance with established rules and criteria, as opposed to blind "faith" (*śraddhā*) and uncritical traditionalism. In a famous, frequently quoted or adapted verse, Kumārila claims that he is "without faith" (*aśraddadhāna*) and demands sound argumentation (yukti[21]). In another verse, Śaṅkara's Jaina contemporary Haribhadra says that he is not biased in favor of his own or against other traditions, and that one should follow the teacher whose teaching is "reasonable" (*yuktimat*[22]). Yet yukti is also seen as potentially destructive, isolating human thought in itself and its own speculations.

One very significant field of application of yukti and upapatti and the corresponding verb forms (*yujyate, upapadyate*) is primarily negative and dialectical (i.e., related to refutations and reductio ad absurdum); this is best exemplified by the *Madhyamakakārikā* of Nāgārjuna, which has had an undeniable impact upon the methodology of Advaita Vedānta.[23]

Śaṅkara is obviously aware of the different connotations and more or less negativistic implications of tarka, yukti, etc. But N. K. Devaraja's suggestion that there is one meaning of tarka in which it is rejected by Śaṅkara and another one in which it is accepted as a fully authoritative source of knowledge[24] is not very helpful and misses the basic issue: even if tarka amounts to "valid inference," it is still on the side of merely worldly "human cognition" (*puruṣabuddhi*[25]), and it cannot claim any authority which would be independent from or equal to that of the Veda.[26]

If there is a wide variety of implications, ambiguity and complexity on the side of "reason," the same can certainly be said about the other side, that is, "revelation" or the Veda. It need not be emphasized that the Veda is not a well-defined body of clearly recognizable teachings. Śaṅkara's own thinking about the Veda is preceded by many centuries of Vedic exegesis, of debates over its extent and content, of epistemological and linguistic controversies concerning its status, structure and authority.[27] The Veda is not just a set of traditionally received and accepted texts or doctrines, but itself the mirror, if not projection, of highly complex and varying philosophical aspirations. The subordination of reason to the Veda, as found in Mīmāṃsā and Vedānta, is not just a matter of habit or custom, but also of intense reflection and argumentation.

Our following presentation will show in detail how Śaṅkara sees the Veda as a complex, differentiated structure of discourse, speaking at different levels and with different voices. The Veda not only teaches or enunciates the supreme and liberating truth concerning ātman and brahman; it also paraphrases itself, appeals to the capabilities of those who rely on it, relates itself to the world of appearance from which liberation is sought. It is not only the source of those supreme teachings themselves, but also of the human possibilities of understanding and clarifying them, of legitimately reasoning and arguing about them. It speaks not only the language of authoritative testimony and instruction, but also of explication, persuasion, and reasoning.[28] This is crucial for our topic, and it seems to be crucial for Śaṅkara's own self-understanding. Yet it has rarely been taken seriously in the discussions about Śaṅkara's approach to "reason" and "revelation"; and in general, few serious and philologically conscientious attempts have been made to explore and to clarify this theme in the horizon of Śaṅkara's self-understanding.

Reason and Revelation in Śaṅkara: Some Recent Interpretations

3. It is now widely recognized that the study of Śaṅkara received a new impetus and direction from the investigations of P. Hacker, which provide examples of thoroughly philological, yet philosophically focused and committed research.[29] In 1979, the year of Hacker's death, three works were published which all reflect and acknowledge the influence of Hacker's works and which have also, directly or indirectly and more or less explicitly, a bearing on our theme of "reason" and "revelation":

1. *A Thousand Teachings. The Upadeśasāhasrī of Śaṅkara.* Translated with introduction and notes by S. Mayeda. Tokyo, 1979.
2. H. Brückner, *Zum Beweisverfahren Śaṃkaras. Eine Untersuchung der Form und Funktion von dṛṣṭāntas im Bṛhadaraṇyakopaniṣadbhāṣya und im Chāndogyopaniṣadbhāṣya des Śaṃkara Bhagavatpāda.* Berlin, 1979 (Diss. Marburg).
3. T. Vetter, *Studien zur Lehre und Entwicklung Śaṅkaras.* Vienna, 1979.

Although it does not thematically focus on the problems of "reason" and "revelation," T. Vetter's book is clearly the most pertinent of these three works published in 1979. It contains numerous stimulating observations and suggestions concerning the uses of yukti and tarka and their relation to the testimony of the Veda, and it will be extensively referred to and discussed in our following presentation.[30] S. Mayeda's translation of the *Upadeśasāhasrī* follows his exemplary critical edition of this text which is perhaps the only authentic noncommentarial work among the numerous writings attributed to Śaṅkara. Its direct thematic bearing on our topic may be rather limited; however, Mayeda's interpretation of Śaṅkara's use of *anvayavyatireka*, "positive and negative concomitance," will have to be discussed later.[31]

The title of H. Brückner's dissertation seems to refer to an explicit thematic treatment of our topic. However, it turns out that Brückner disregards almost completely the complex and problematic implications and ramifications which her notion of "Beweisverfahren" ("method of proof") has in the context of Śaṅkara's thought. And apart from being a useful collection of textual passages, her study is challenging by virtue of its curious and consistent manner of *not* addressing the basic issue of "reason" and "Vedic authority" or "revelation."

As the subtitle of her dissertation indicates, H. Brückner wants to investigate Śaṅkara's use of "examples" in two of his major Upaniṣad commentaries. She insists that in Śaṅkara's writings the "examples" are part of a procedure of "proof" or "demonstration" in the full and strict sense, in accordance with the role which the *dṛṣṭānta* or *udāharaṇa* plays in the Nyāya theory of inference (*anumāna*); she emphasizes the central importance of this "demonstrative function" ("Beweisfunktion") against all connotations of mere "illustration" or "persuasion," as well as against the conclusions presented in a dissertation by R. Brooks.[32] According to Brückner, Śaṅkara actually describes his own procedure when he says that in the Upaniṣads unity or identity is first presented as a mere thesis and then again as a conclusion which has been established by means of examples and reasons (i.e., that a basically "syllogistic" or inferential scheme is applied).[33] The implication is that Śaṅkara himself tries to prove or validate what he finds in the sacred texts as an authoritative, yet unproven thesis (*pratijñā*) and that he tries to subject the statement of śruti to the "categories of scientific logic."[34] The question what such a "procedure of proof" would imply in Śaṅkara's own context of thought, how it would relate to his understanding of the Veda and how, if at all, it might be reconciled with his numerous statements about the inadequacy of anumāna and of all worldly reasoning is never asked in Brückner's study.[35]

If this were actually his procedure, how could he, without compromising himself, criticize or attack the "reasoners" (*tārkika, haituka*)? It is hard to imagine that he should not have noticed an inconsistency of this kind.[36] Would there be any basic difference between the procedure described by Brückner and what Śaṅkara finds unacceptable in the methods of the "reasoners"? Of course, Brückner notes that Śaṅkara's "Beweisverfahren" is supposed to acknowledge Vedic "premises" and to proceed in such a way that it does not question or contradict the basic truths of the sacred tradition.[37] But does Śaṅkara criticize those "reasoners" only who, like the Buddhists, reject the authority of the Veda and who use reason and inference regardless of or even against the Vedic teachings? He is no less concerned about those who claim to use inference etc. as independent means of demonstrating or validating such Vedic truths as the existence of the self etc. and who credit these worldly instruments of cognition with an epistemic authority that belongs to the Veda alone.[38] Not only the anti-Vedic application of human reason, but any attempt to use it as an independent, potentially competing way to supreme truth has to be rejected.

Śaṅkara's statements about "demonstrative" procedures in the Upaniṣads have to be taken literally and not as vicarious statements about his own claims and methods. To find the language of "demonstration" and "proof" in the sacred texts is essentially different from crediting one's own human reasoning with the ability to supply such proofs or demonstrations.

4. As noticed earlier, T. Vetter's *Studien zur Lehre und Entwicklung Śaṅkaras* is highly relevant for our discussion, without thematically focusing on "reason" and "revelation." In this book[39] Vetter elaborates ideas and observations first presented at a symposium in Vienna in 1977.[40] Focusing on the "method of gaining release" ("Methode der Erringung des Heils"), he tries to utilize its varying constellations and formulations as a basis for establishing the chronological order of Śaṅkara's writings. In this attempt, he builds upon the investigations and hypotheses of P. Hacker. He accepts the *Yogasūtrabhāṣyavivaraṇa* as an early work of Śaṅkara, dating back to a period when he was still affiliated with the tradition of Yoga. Just like Hacker, he sees the commentary on the *Māṇḍūkya Upaniṣad* and on Gauḍapāda's *Kārikās* as the earliest document of Śaṅkara's transition to Advaita Vedānta. Concerning Śaṅkara's other works, in particular the *Upadeśasāhasrī*, Vetter further differentiates and occasionally modifies Hacker's views. Specifically, his book deals with the following texts or portions of texts:

1. Yogasūtrabhāṣyavivaraṇa.
2. Māṇḍūkya-Upaniṣad-Bhāṣya with Gauḍapādīya-Kārikā-Bhāṣya.[41]
3. Upadeśasāhasrī, Gadyabandha II.
4. Upadeśasāhasrī, Padyabandha XVIII, 90–101; 169–95; 198–204.
5. Brahmasūtrabhāṣya IV, 1, 2 (also I, 1, 1–4).
6. Upadeśasāhasrī, Gadyabandha I.

The guiding theme of Vetter's painstaking textual research is the "method of liberation." But although the relation between reason and Vedic revelation is not the thematic focus, it turns out to be a very important, even crucial issue, accounting for a good deal of what is particularly noteworthy, stimulating, and perhaps questionable in Vetter's presentation.[42] As a matter of fact, it is a theme that plays a peculiar and conspicuous role in the text that is the subject-matter of Vetter's longest chapter, that is, in Śaṅkara's Gauḍapāda commentary, supposedly his earliest Advaita work. Śaṅkara himself sees a scheme of "reason" and "revelation" (or "authoritative tradition") in the structure of Gauḍapāda's text; in his introduction,[43] he characterizes its four chapters as follows: The first chapter, devoted to the clarification of the *om*, is "dominated by authoritative tradition" (*āgamapradhāna*) while serving as an "aid to the understanding of the nature of the self" (*ātmatattvapratipattyupāya*). The second chapter is designed to teach "with reasons" (*hetutas*) the "falsity" or "emptiness" (*vaitathya*) of the world of plurality. The third chapter is supposed to teach, in an "argumentative," "rational" manner (*yuktitas*), the positive nature (*tathātva*, as opposed to *vaitathya*) of nonduality (*advaita*), since otherwise this nonduality, too, might be reduced to "emptiness" in the process of reasoning. The fourth chapter is designed to refute those un-Vedic teachings which are "opposed to the understanding of the true, positive nature" (*tathātvapratipattivipakṣa*) of nonduality, by using their own arguments (*upapatti*) and insofar as their falsity follows from the fact that they are mutually contradictory (*anyonyavirodhitva*).

Śaṅkara refers again to this scheme when he introduces chapters II, III, and IV,[44] stating that both the falsity of plurality and the truth of nonduality are first presented through authoritative tradition alone (*āgamamātra*) or as a "mere thesis" (*pratijñāmātra*) and subsequently supported by "examples," "reasons," "logical reflection" (*dṛṣṭānta, hetu, tarka*), so that they are finally established "by scripture and reason" (*śāstrayuktibhyām*[45]).

It is obvious that these statements, which go far beyond anything said by Gauḍapāda himself,[46] are very significant, insofar as the relationship between reason and revelation is concerned, and they are suggestive also with reference to Śaṅkara's later approach to this matter. However, it may be necessary to differentiate between the statements in this supposedly earliest and perhaps still transitional Advaita work and those in his later writings, which reflect his mature and definitive understanding of the nature and necessity of Vedic revelation. It should also be noted that Śaṅkara considers neither Gauḍapāda's verses nor the prose of the Māṇḍūkya "Upaniṣad" as śruti.[47] However, subsequent sections of our presentation will show to what extent Śaṅkara's observations on Gauḍapāda correspond to his statements about the didactic structure of śruti itself, as we find them in his supposedly later works, most conspicuously in his commentary on the Bṛhadāraṇyaka Upaniṣad.[48] To conclude this digression from our survey of Vetter's book, we may consider the possibility that what Śaṅkara first noticed about Gauḍapāda was subsequently included in and adapted to his understanding of śruti itself.

In general, Vetter says about the relationship between śruti and "rational argumentation" in Śaṅkara's works: "Das Gewicht dieser Quellen und ihr mögliches Nacheinander auf dem Erlösungsweg ist aber nicht in allen Texten gleich. Damit verbunden kann die Art des erlösenden Wissens mehr positiv oder mehr negativ sein; wo rationale Argumentation überwiegt, darf man ein mehr abstrakt negatives Wissen erwarten. Śruti-stellen hingegen können sowohl negative als positive Inhalte übermitteln."[49] More specifically, Vetter deals with the meaning and function of yukti/tarka according to Śaṅkara's interpretation of Gauḍapāda's third chapter. He states a "vage Bedeutung des Überlegens, Nachdenkens, Räsonierens und indirekt Beweisens" and suggests: "*yukti* und *tarka* sind 'Überlegung' der Möglichkeit und (vor allem) Unmöglichkeit einer Sache oder Lehre."[50] In a later passage, he summarizes his observations on the role of reasoning in the *Gauḍapādīya-Kārikā-Bhāṣya*: "Rationales Erwägen kann mittels Schlußfolgerung die Irrealität der Vielheit beweisen (3.32), mittels Überlegung (yukti/tarka) erreicht es das Selbst als das, was dem Irrtum der Vielheit zugrunde liegen muß (3.33); Überlegung ist insofern nicht unabhängig von Überlieferung, als sie zeigt, daß die Welt ohne die von der Überlieferung verkündete höchste Entität nicht erscheinen könnte (vgl. auch 4.121)."[51]

The question of "reason" and "revelation," of the sources of supreme, liberating knowledge is again discussed in Vetter's analysis of selected passages of the *Upadeśasāhasrī* and of the *Brahmasūtrabhāṣya*. Concerning the second prose chapter of the *Upadeśasāhasrī*, Vetter maintains that it presents liberating knowledge as the result of yukti, of (human) thought and observation alone: "Wo kommt der Inhalt der erlösenden Wissens her? Śruti und Smṛti werden nirgends erwähnt, er wird als das Resultat von Denken und Beobachtung präsentiert."[52] Already P. Hacker characterizes this chapter, which according to Vetter may be Śaṅkara's most significant philosophical endeavor,[53] as "purely argumentative."[54]

Further references to our theme are found in Vetter's discussion of exemplary passages in the longest and most intricate chapter of the *Upadeśasāhasrī*, its verse-chapter XVIII. Concerning liberating knowledge, Vetter finds a cooperation and mutual supplementation of reasoning or deliberation (yukti, etc.) and the authority of the "great sayings" such as the *tat tvam asi.* He sees it as the peculiar and in a sense independent accomplishment of yukti to lead us to the true meaning of the word "I" (i.e., of the *tvam*, "you," in the *tat tvam asi*) and thus to the metaphysical "core of the individual."[55] The method by which yukti is supposed to achieve this goal is the method of "positive and negative concomitance" (*anvayavyatireka*), which Vetter discusses in an extensive, yet somewhat indecisive, note.[56]

While Vetter still sees a certain ambiguity in the relationship between yukti/tarka and śruti/śāstra in most of the passages under discussion, he finds a definite and precise "division of responsibilities" ("Verteilung der Aufgaben") between these sources of knowledge in Śaṅkara's commentary on *Brahmasūtra* IV, 1, 2: Yukti alone is credited with making accessible the meaning of the "you" (*tvam*), i.e., the "core of the person" ("Kern der Person"[57]), while śruti is said to reveal the meaning of the "that" (*tad*). In Vetter's interpretation, this appears as the implicit goal and conclusion of Śaṅkara's other, less definite, statements on the relation between "reason" and "revelation," although not as his final word in a chronological sense.[58]

5. Vetter finds contradictions in Śaṅkara's works, but at the same time one "common intent." In the area of merely theoretical matters, Śaṅkara is, according to Vetter, not seriously concerned about systematic consistency and the avoidance of contradictions. However, unity and consistency are essential to him when he is dealing with the "attainment of salvation" ("Gewinnung des Heils").[59] If there are inconsistencies in this area, they cannot be relegated to a lack of concern about consistency, but have to be taken as indicating different stages in his development: Insofar as the "more practical instructions" are concerned, Śaṅkara is said to be more serious and conscientious about unity than in the "more theoretical passages."[60] Unfortunately, Vetter never tells us in unambiguous terms what he means by "theory" and "practice" and how these two relate to what he calls "method of attaining liberation," which, one might assume, has in itself an aspect of theory as well as of practice and cannot simply be equated with the side of "practice."[61] Vetter's index has seven entries under "Theorie und Praxis," but none of these refers to a clear definition or sufficiently explicit discussion. One implication seems to be that "theory" has to do with exegesis and polemics against other schools.[62] But may exegesis and polemics not relate to "practice" as well as to "theory"?

In his application of the concepts of theory and practice Vetter goes so far as to suggest that Śaṅkara may use the *theory* of Advaita, "nondualism," as a convenient device for exegesis and polemics, while his actual soteriological path, which is a matter of more serious concern to him, is based upon or implies a dualistic worldview.[63] Vetter's treatment of the relationship between yukti and śruti is part of his presentation of the practical-soteriological dimension of Śaṅkara's thought, from which he takes his clues for a "construction of Śaṅkara's development"[64] and for his attempted establishment of a relative chronology of his writings.

Vetter admits that in Śaṅkara's works theory and practice "occasionally merge with one another" and, moreover, that this whole distinction is extraneous to Śaṅkara's own thought and would be unacceptable to him.[65] Nevertheless, he takes it for granted as a basic premise of his textual and chronological analysis. When Vetter notes in this context that Śaṅkara, while interpreting an Upaniṣadic passage or polemicizing against the Buddhists, also "guides souls to salvation" ("führt Seelen zum Heil"), he uses expressions with potentially misleading connotations. Śaṅkara may not be a theorizing metaphysician; but even less is he a soteriological practitioner. There is no temporal or eschatological urge to "save souls" in his thought. He teaches what he sees as the ultimate truth, a truth, however, that happens to be the truth of liberation and itself liberating truth. In addition, he explores and teaches what he regards as the conditions of understanding and realizing this truth, which means to understand and to realize it as being beyond all contexts of result-oriented physical or mental activities and techniques.[66] The "theoretical" statements of truth and fact in the Upaniṣads have to be accepted as such; one of the main targets of Śaṅkara's argumentation against the Pūrvamīmāṃsā is its tendency to relegate such statements to subordinate functions in "practical" contexts, i.e., in the context of goal-oriented methods and paths.

On the other hand, if one emphasizes the practical and soteriological orientation in Śaṅkara's thought, it seems hardly appropriate to separate it from the pedagogical dimension[67] which is its indispensable supplement and an essential ingredient of any soteriology which is not just a theory of liberation. According to Śaṅkara's own explicit statements, it is the "pedagogical" side (of methods of instruction and preparation for liberating knowledge) which leaves room for flexibility and variability, while there can be no compromise or variation as far as the nature of ultimate reality is concerned.[68]

We cannot and need not discuss here in further detail the problems and prospects raised by Vetter's approach. It is important to keep in mind that his construction of Śaṅkara's development remains inevitably hypothetical.[69] We have no factual biographical framework to which we could relate doctrinal variations; the framework itself has to be construed out of such variations. This is further complicated by the fact that Śaṅkara's writings do not simply present us with "doctrines," but also with complex and ambiguous patterns of relating one basic teaching or intent to a great variety of approaches and expressions. Their commentarial, dialectical, and pedagogical dimensions imply such a wide range of immanent, legitimate flexibility and variability that it requires extreme caution to identify "inconsistencies" and "contradictions" that would be illegitimate in Śaṅkara's own horizon and that would provide reliable, unambiguous clues for actual *changes* in his thought and for a development from earlier to later positions.

Without questioning the merits of Vetter's meticulous textual analysis, we shall proceed on the basis of the assumption that there can be a meaningful and conscientious study of the texts that pays much less attention to differences and inconsistencies.[70] Instead, it may be oriented towards understanding that horizon or context of thought within which such real or alleged inconsistencies are perhaps less relevant than they appear to the modern philological interpreter, for instance insofar as the relationship between "reason" and "revelation" (yukti and śruti) is concerned. Our discussion of this issue on the basis of those texts which both Hacker and Vetter accept as genuine works by Śaṅkara will find much less significant variety and inconsistency than Vetter's *Studien*.[71] However, certain specific problems are posed by Śaṅkara's commentary on the *Māṇḍūkya Upaniṣad* and on Gauḍapāda's *Kārikās*, which seem to require a developmental explanation. It can hardly be denied that Hacker's interpretation of this text as Śaṅkara's first Advaita work, marking the transition from Yoga to Advaita Vedānta and to a more Upaniṣadic, scriptural orientation,[72] appears attractive in the context of our presentation, although it should certainly not be taken for granted. In general, it is not our intention to confirm or to refute this or other chronological hypotheses; at any rate, the exemplary value of Hacker's and Vetter's investigations, the challenge and stimulus they will provide for our further discussions, does not depend on the correctness of their chronological assumptions.

Reason and Revelation: Conflict and Concordance

6. There is no systematic and comprehensive discussion of the relationship between reason and revelation in Śaṅkara's works; but there are many explicit statements, as well as casual remarks and symptomatic phrases. These statements can be easily divided into several different and apparently divergent groups.

Quite frequently, Śaṅkara emphasizes the supreme or exclusive authority of the Vedic "revelation" in matters of metaphysical and soteriological relevance, that is, concerning the ultimate, liberating truth of *ātman/brahman*. Reasoning which is opposed to the Veda is to be rejected. Accordingly, Śaṅkara denounces the idea of an independent, extra-Vedic authority and usage of human reasoning and of the worldly means of cognition, and he criticizes and attacks the "reasoners" (*tārkika*[73]). Human reasoning as such is said to be groundless, restless, and helpless without the light and guidance of the Veda.[74]

On the other hand, there are numerous more favorable references, which indicate a concordance and cooperation of reason and Vedic revelation. "Reason" and "scripture" appear side by side, often in *dvandva* compounds, such as *śāstrayukti, śāstranyāya, śāstrānumāna, śāstratarka, āgamopapatti, śrutiyukti, tarkāgama, śrutyupapatti*[75] or, with the addition of smṛti, in *śrutismṛtinyāya*, etc.[76] In Śaṅkara's commentary on the *Taittirīya Upaniṣad*, a statement against the "science of reasoning" (*tarkaśāstra*) in Sāṃkhya and Vaiśeṣika is immediately followed by a remark which joins śruti and upapatti in a dvandva compound and implies their agreement.[77]

However, the exact meaning of the concordance of reason and

revelation expressed in such compounds or juxtapositions may be ambiguous and is certainly not identical in all cases. It may refer to a relationship in which the function of reason is primarily exegetic, in accordance with the programmatic formula *vedāntavākyamīmāṃsā tadavirodhitarkopakaraṇā.*[78] But these compounds may also suggest mutual supplementation or parallelism rather than strict subordination of reason. In many cases, reason and Vedic revelation are joined together against a common target of refutation and in a common negative function, e.g., in such expressions as *śāstrayuktivirodha* or *śāstrayuktivivarjita.*[79] Insofar as the negative or reductive function of reason is concerned, Śaṅkara acknowledges that it may be "autonomous" (*svatantra*) and without the support of scriptural statements (*vākyanirapekṣa*[80]).

There are other types of references to the relationship between reason and revelation that may be less conspicuous, but that are nevertheless essential for understanding this issue in the context of Śaṅkara's own thought. Among these, the statements relating to the manner in which the Veda itself employs, exemplifies and "originates" valid and legitimate reasoning are most central and significant.[81]

But first of all, we have to return to those statements that criticize and denounce the independent, unrestrained use of reason and argumentation and the attempts to gain an extra-Vedic, worldly access to that truth and reality that only the Veda can reveal. Unguided reasoning is "dried up" (*śuṣka*), i.e., fruitless and groundless.[82] Ultimate truth is not accessible to "mere tarka" or "mere reasonings."[83] Without the authority of the sacred tradition, the tārkika entangles himself in the figments of his own mind: *tārkiko hy anāgamajñaḥ svabuddhiparikalpitaṃ yatkiṃcid eva kalpayati.*[84] Mere argumentation inevitably leads to conflicting statements and viewpoints, to confusion and frustration, specifically insofar as the crucial theme of the self (ātman) is concerned.[85] Reasoning, worldly inference alone, is never definitive, has no final basis and conclusion (*niṣṭhā*[86]). It is the very essence of human reason to refute itself, to supersede itself, to be unstable and unfounded: *puruṣotprekṣāmātranibandhanās tarkā apratiṣṭhitā bhavanti . . . kaiścid abhiyuktair yatnena-utprekṣitās tarkā abhiyuktatarair anyair ābhāsyamānā dṛśyante. tair apy utprekṣitāḥ santas tato anyair ābhāsyanta iti na pratiṣṭhitatvaṃ tarkāṇāṃ śakyam āśrayituṃ, puruṣamativairūpyāt.* ("Conclusions which are based upon human reflection alone are unfounded. . . . Conclusions at which expert reasoners have arrived with great effort of reflection are viewed as spurious by others, even more expert ones. And the conclusions to which they have come are subsequently shown to be spurious by others. In this way, it is impossible to find a foundation for the conclusions of reasoning, because of the variety of human ways of understanding.")[87] In this same section of his *Brahmasūtrabhāṣya*, Śaṅkara refers to and dismisses a *pūrvapakṣa* view according to which the very insight into the "instability" (*apratiṣṭhitatva*) of reason should be seen as an achievement of reason and this "instability" itself should be recognized as a positive distinction (*alaṃkāra*) of reason, insofar as it implies openness for correction and improvement.[88]

Already Bādarāyaṇa's *Brahmasūtra* II, 1, 11, on which Śaṅkara comments, contains the word *tarkāpratiṣṭhāna*. Moreover, Śaṅkara's statements seem to be influenced by formulations in Bhartṛhari's *Vākyapadīya*, e.g., I, 34: *yatnena-anumito 'py arthaḥ kuśalair anumātṛbhiḥ abhiyuktatarair anyair anyathā-eva-upapādyate*. ("Even something that has been deduced with great effort by skilled reasoners is explained differently by others, even more expert ones.") Bhartṛhari also uses the words *śuṣkatarka* and *puruṣatarka*.[89] *Śuṣkatarka* becomes generally familiar as a pejorative expression.[90]

More specifically, Śaṅkara criticizes various philosophical traditions because they give too much weight and authority to human reasoning and experience. In this context, Sāṃkhya and Vaiśeṣika are frequently referred to;[91] but also Pūrvamīmāṃsā is seen as a school which misuses reason in its attempts to establish the existence and nature of the soul in an inferential manner.[92]

In Śaṅkara's thought, the problem of the relation between revelation and reason is obviously connected with his understanding of the relationship between śruti and smṛti and with the postulate that the authority of smṛti is subordinate to that of śruti; this is specifically significant in Śaṅkara's extensive criticism of the Sāṃkhya philosophy.[93] Traditionally, the Sāṃkhya smṛti has been associated with reasoning and inference, to the extent that already Bādarāyaṇa (as interpreted by Śaṅkara) may refer to the Sāṃkhya *prakṛti* or *pradhāna*, i.e., its ultimate "nature" or "matter," by such terms as *ānumānika* or *anumāna*.[94] The variety of extra-Vedic philosophical traditions (*smṛti*, etc.) corresponds to the inevitably divergent attempts of unguided human reasoning to find its own ways and goals. Traditional teachings based upon mere reasoning have to be rejected; they are acceptable only insofar as they serve the goal of understanding the truth revealed by the Veda: *etena sarvāṇi tarkasmaraṇāni prativaktavyāni. tāny api tarkopapattibhyāṃ tattvajñānāya-upakurvanti-iti ced. upakurvantu nāma, tattvajñānaṃ tu vedāntavākyebhya eva bhavati.* ("Thus all traditions of reasoning must be contested. If you say that they, too, contribute, by virtue of reasoning and argumentation, to the knowledge of truth, then we respond: They may well contribute; yet the knowledge of truth results only from the statements of the Upaniṣads.")[95] "Traditions of reasoning," such as Kapila's Sāṃkhya, are just as much subject to the authority of the Veda as any other "tradition" (smṛti).[96]

Only the Veda has unconditional validity and authority; the smṛtis depend on it, just as, in the realm of worldly cognition, inference (anumāna) depends on perception (pratyakṣa[97]). Already the *Brahmasūtra* text itself uses the word *pratyakṣa* in the sense of *śruti* and *anumāna* in the sense of *smṛti*.[98]

7. In his treatment of the unconditional authority of the Veda, Śaṅkara is obviously indebted to the *vedamūlatva* principle, as used and systematized in Pūrvamīmāṃsā. Yet, he is in fundamental disagreement with the Pūrvamīmāṃsā understanding of the relationship between reason and revelation and with its assumption that the Veda teaches primarily what has to be done, i.e., that its authority is in the area of ritualistic duty (dharma) and expressed in the form of injunctions (*vidhi*). He criticizes the Mīmāṃsakas for giving too much weight and authority to reason and inference insofar as such "factual" matters as the existence and nature of the soul (ātman) are concerned: In this respect, they appear side by side with the "reasoners" (tārkika) of the Sāṃkhya or Vaiśeṣika schools.[99] Obviously, their misuses of reason are seen as a reflection of the fact that they do not properly understand the nature and domain of the Vedic revelation and its relation to the worldly sources of knowledge.

The Mīmāṃsakas, just as the Naiyāyikas and Vaiśeṣikas, claim to be able to demonstrate the existence of a non-corporeal permanent self by using inference or other worldly means of knowledge. But their claims are unfounded. Such worldly indicators (*laukika-*

liṅga) as the ego-consciousness (*ahaṃpratyaya*), which they regard as their own intellectual accomplishments, are valid inferential reasons for the existence of the ātman only insofar as they have been put forth as such by the Veda itself: *āgamena tv ātmāstitve 'vagate vedapradarśitalaukikaliṅgaviśeṣaiś ca tadanusāriṇo mīmāṃsakās tārkikāś ca-ahaṃpratyayaliṅgāni ca vaidikāny eva svamatiprabhavāni-iti kalpayanto vadanti pratyakṣaś ca-anumeyaś ca-ātmā-iti.* ("Once the existence of the self has been grasped by means of the Veda and of certain worldly indicators mentioned by it, the Mīmāṃsakas and the dialecticians who follow this lead imagine that such Vedic indicators as the ego-consciousness derive from their own intelligence, and they assert that the self is knowable by means of perception and inference.")[100] Moreover, they are indebted to what Bādarāyaṇa has extracted from the Upaniṣads; Jaimini's Mīmāṃsāsūtras do not contain a proof for the existence of the self; what the commentator Śabara introduces is, in Śaṅkara's view, borrowed from Bādarāyaṇa's Brahmasūtras.[101] Since the Mīmāṃsakas do not recognize the true, i.e., Vedic source of their own proofs for the ātman, nor the nature and extent of its authority, they fail to recognize the true nature of the self and even argue against it.[102]

As a root of this misuse of reason, Śaṅkara sees the Mīmāṃsā interpretation of the Veda as a revelation of dharma only. They understand the central message of the Veda as a message of injunctions or commandments (*vidhi, codanā*) concerning what has to be done or accomplished (*kārya, sādhya*), while the noninjunctive statements found in the Veda, specifically the so-called arthavādas, have a secondary, less directly authoritative status. The arthavādas are supplementary, auxiliary, factual or quasi-factual statements, designed to motivate man for those actions which are enjoined by the vidhis, to explicate and exemplify their meaning and importance and to provide reasons and incentives that are intelligible and attractive to the human mind. The concept of arthavāda, which has its roots in the ritual Sūtras,[103] adds a pedagogical, didactic dimension to the impersonal, superhuman authority of the Veda. Here, the Veda not only enjoins or commands, but it also appeals to its students to follow and execute its commands. Being a "pedagogical," motivating device, an arthavāda does not commit the reader or listener to its literal truth, and it gives him the freedom of indirect, metaphorical interpretation. Concerning the details of how the arthavāda sections of the Veda should be treated, there is considerable debate and disagreement among the schools of Pūrvamīmāṃsā; moreover, there are various subdivisions of the arthavādas (*guṇavāda*, etc.). A further discussion of these problems is beyond the scope of this presentation.

However, a question which is of immediate interest as far as Śaṅkara's relation to Pūrvamīmāṃsā and his understanding of the role of reason are concerned, is the place of the Upaniṣads in the framework of vidhi and arthavāda. Quite frequently, the Upaniṣads are more or less explicitly associated with the arthavādas. Before the time of the classical Mīmāṃsā philosophers, this is already done by Bhartṛhari.[104] Kumārila mentions the Upaniṣads side by side with the arthavādas, and he tends to see the Upaniṣadic teachings about the self as being auxiliary to dharma, that is, to the performance of ritual actions, insofar as the notion of a noncorporeal permanent self is a condition and incentive for performing such acts which are supposed to bear fruit in another life or world.[105] Maṇḍanamiśra, a Mīmāṃsaka as well as a Vedāntin and possibly Śaṅkara's contemporary, uses the phrase *mantrārthavādāḥ sopaniṣatkāḥ* in his Mīmāṃsā work *Vidhiviveka* as well as in his later Vedānta work *Brahmasiddhi*.[106] On the other hand, and by no means in a mutually exclusive manner, the Mīmāṃsakas interpret the central message of the Upaniṣads in terms of "meditative injunctions" (*upāsanāvidhi*) relating to mental acts of concentration or worship which are internalized quasi-rituals; or they present the exploration and understanding of the ātman itself as a duty which has to be performed.[107]

Śaṅkara himself uses the term *arthavāda* as a familiar device of exegesis.[108] But he insists that even an arthavāda can be the vehicle of genuine, fully authoritative revelation, provided that it is a *vidyamānārthavāda*, that is, neither a mere repetition (*anuvāda*) of what is already known otherwise, nor a *guṇavāda*, which has to be explained metaphorically, since its literal interpretation would contradict obvious facts.[109] In general, however, Śaṅkara leaves no doubt that in his view the concept of arthavāda cannot do justice to the Upaniṣads, this "culmination of the Veda" (*vedānta*). On the other hand, the central statements of the Upaniṣads cannot be interpreted in terms of cognitive or meditational injunctions; the truth concerning ātman/brahman is nothing "to be done" or "enacted" (*kārya*[110]).

Just insofar as they teach what truly *is* and has always been, the Upaniṣads are revelation in the fullest possible sense.

But although Śaṅkara does not agree with the Mīmāṃsā, its way of seeing the Veda as a complex, highly differentiated structure of discourse provides the indispensable background for understanding his own approach to the Veda. The notion of arthavāda is an important model for his own interpretation of the Veda as paraphrasing itself by means of examples and argumentation (*yukti*), as explicating its central statements for the sake of human comprehension.[111] His disciple Padmapāda occasionally uses the term *yuktyarthavāda*.[112]

Worldly Knowledge and the Domain of Vedic Revelation

8. Insofar as they teach the truth of nondualism, the Upaniṣads reveal what cannot be known otherwise: The worldly means of knowledge (pramāṇa) do not apply to the absolute unity of brahman. They are inherently related to the realm of "name and form," that is, to particularity and plurality; they function properly in the context of *vyavahāra*, accompanying and guiding such ordinary worldly activities as eating and drinking.[113] But in the case of brahman, there is no "mark" (*liṅga*) that would make it accessible to inference. Absolute unity escapes the worldly means of knowledge, since it is incompatible with their underlying conditions; these means alone can neither prove nor disprove it.[114]

Does this imply that there is no direct confrontation between śruti and the worldly means of knowledge (pratyakṣa, anumāna, etc.)? They do not function in the same horizon or at the same level; and since śruti deals with what can never be the object of perception, etc., it seems that there can be no mutual contradiction. Indeed, Śaṅkara states that the Veda does not try to tell us that fire is cold and makes things wet.[115] It does not try to establish specific worldly facts *against* the data of our worldly experience. Yet, there is no such consistent "separation of domains" as we find it in Pūrvamīmāṃsā. In fact, Śaṅkara argues explicitly against the attempt to restrict the authority of śruti to its own specific domain (*svaviṣaya*) and to leave what is not within this domain to the claims of human reasoning; it is unacceptable for him to say: *yady api śrutiḥ pramāṇaṃ svaviṣaye bhavati, tathā-api pramāṇāntareṇa viṣayāpahare 'nyaparā bhavitum arhati.* ("Even if the Veda is authoritative with reference to its own proper domain, it may still be subject to another criterion, if a domain has been taken over by another means of knowledge.")[116] There is no self-sufficient "domain" in which human cognition could have a sovereignty and authority equal to the unconditional authority of the Veda; and the Veda does not simply leave this world to the "worldly" means of knowledge. On the other hand, the Pūrvamīmāṃsakas use the principle of the separation of domains against Advaita Vedānta. They claim that it would be factually and psychologically impossible for the Veda to remove that conviction concerning the reality and plurality of worldly existence that is upheld by the more immediate testimony of sense perception, and that the human mind has the necessary freedom of responding to verbal revelation only in the area of dharma, which is inaccessible to worldly ascertainment.[117]

In Śaṅkara's view, the Vedic revelation negates the ultimate truth of plurality, the framework in which it appears and in which its worldly ascertainment is possible.[118] But this does not mean that it concerns only the ultimate metaphysical status of the world of plurality, without affecting its own internal conditions. Insofar as it speaks about transcendence, the Veda also speaks about what has to be transcended. There are no strict borderlines. The Veda "reveals" reality as well as appearance in its soteriologically relevant details; and it precludes a systematic and unrestricted usage and development of the worldly means of knowledge even within this world.

Śaṅkara sees this world as a constellation of "place, time and causality" (*deśakālanimitta*) or a network of "ends and means" (*sādhyasādhanabhāva*[119]). But this does not mean that it is a structure of empirically verifiable or falsifiable regularities. It is not at all a Kantian "context of experience," a realm of empirical inquiry and of progressive discovery of order and regularity. Instead, it is the realm of saṃsāra, of transmigration and of retributive causality, and it is governed by factors (such as adhikāra, adṛṣṭa/apūrva, etc.) that are themselves not amenable to worldly ascertainment and explanation. "Śaṅkara emphasizes that only śruti is a really authoritative source for our knowledge and understanding of the processes of karma and transmigration: attempts to explain this matter in terms of assumptions produced by human thought alone (*puruṣamatiprabhavāḥ kalpanāḥ*) are inevitably futile; the various theories and conceptualizations presented by the Sāṃkhya or the Vaiśeṣika, by the Buddhists or the Jainas, are contradicted by one another as well as by śruti."[120]

Śaṅkara agrees with the Mīmāṃsā that the Veda is the authoritative source of the knowledge of dharma; and he does not question the validity of the Vedic injunctions which constitute the center of dharma. But he does not understand this dharma in terms of a nonfactual "ought." The "work portion" of the Veda "enjoins" only insofar as it describes the network of *sādhyasādhanabhāva*; it reveals the relationship between acts and results, means and ends, and it leaves it to man to pursue such ends or not.[121] In this sense, Śaṅkara may be called the most radical advocate of the *iṣṭasādhanatā* interpretation of the Vedic injunctions.

The "certainty" of anumāna is derived from the regularity of natural phenomena; but the world is such that the possibility of exceptions or irregularities can never be excluded. Because of the "variety of place, time and occasion" (*deśakālanimittavaicitrya*), the same causal factor may produce completely different effects—in a manner which cannot be ascertained "by mere reasoning" (*kevalena tarkeṇa*[122]). Even the most familiar case of anumāna, the inference of fire from smoke, may be used to illustrate the unreliability of inference: *udvāpite 'py agnau gopālaghuṭikādidhāritasya dhūmasya dṛśyamānatvāt* ("because the smoke which is, for instance, kept in the containers of cowherds, is still seen even after the fire has been extinguished").[123]

"Examples" (dṛṣṭānta, udāharaṇa) cannot exclude the possibility of such exceptions, and they cannot establish the "*invariable* concomitance" of such phenomena as fire and smoke, and they would certainly not be sufficient to establish brahman as the cause of the world (i.e., to justify a "cosmological proof").[124] There are no worldly "examples" which could add such proof or validation to the Upaniṣadic teachings about brahman.

It is a fundamental advantage which the Vedāntic teacher has over his opponent, the "logician," that he does *not* have to rely on "examples" and on the patterns of worldly experience, and that his teachings do *not* always have to be "in accordance with experience" (*yathādṛṣṭam*[125]). In various commentarial contexts, references to such "examples" or data of experience are dismissed as irrelevant, and the need to adjust the teachings of Vedānta to worldly experience is denied.[126] Of course, Śaṅkara himself uses many "examples," and he leaves no doubt that in his view they work at least as well for the teaching of Vedānta as they work for any other teaching; but unlike other teachings Vedānta is not built upon worldly "examples."[127]

9. Reason (yukti, tarka) as such cannot produce parallel, equally authoritative demonstrations of the truth of the Upaniṣadic "great sayings." It has its legitimate role under the guidance of and in cooperation with śruti. But this in itself has far-reaching implications and ramifications.

First of all, it requires according to Śaṅkara, that śruti should be interpreted consistently, that is as teaching one identical truth and as not contradicting itself: There cannot be different and conflicting doctrines concerning the one identical brahman. Variety may be found in the methods of preparation, the meditational or devotional approaches to what has not yet been properly understood as ultimate reality; but there can only be one true "science" concerning this reality: *na ca-ekarūpe brahmaṇy anekarūpāṇi vijñānāni sambhavanti. na hy anyathā-artho 'nyathā jñānam ity abhrāntaṃ bhavati. yadi punar ekasmin brahmaṇi bahūni vijñānāni vedāntāntareṣu pratipipādayiṣitāni, teṣām ekam abhrāntaṃ, bhrāntāni-itarāṇi-ity anāśvāsaprasaṅgo vedānteṣu.* ("There cannot be different cognitions relating to the one identical brahman, since it cannot be true that knowledge and its object are at variance. If, however, many different cognitions concerning the one brahman were being proposed in different Upaniṣads, then only one of these could be true, and the others would be erroneous. As a result, there would be a loss of confidence in the Upaniṣads.")[128] Ultimately, the one Vedic message concerning the one identical brahman is conveyed by one single sentence (of the type of the *tat tvam asi*): *jñānaikārthaparatvāt taṃ vākyam ekaṃ tato viduḥ.*[129]

The interpretation of śruti has to be committed to the postulate that it teaches the same truth about the same subject-matter, ātman/brahman, which may be referred to by a great variety of names. Within śruti, i.e., the Vedic-Upaniṣadic texts themselves, full reconciliation or concordance (samanvaya) has to be the goal of exegesis; in order to achieve this goal, Śaṅkara applies various exegetic devices, which we do not have to discuss in detail. His basic perspective is the distinction of "levels" of truth or rather of discourse, adjusted to different levels of understanding.[130] Concerning the relation of śruti to smṛti, purāṇa, etc., it is not seen in terms of strict samanvaya, but according to the vedamūlatva principle, which implies a subordination of all other sources to the authority of the Veda and their partial and conditional recognition only. While Śaṅkara is indebted to the Pūrvamīmāṃsā view of the relation between śruti and smṛti, his view of the relation between śruti and reason is, as we have seen, quite different.[131]

This difference follows from the fundamental difference between the subject-matters of Pūrva- and Uttaramīmāṃsā, that is, dharma and ātman/brahman. In the case of dharma, reason or secular human knowledge has a strictly and exclusively exegetic role in that it can only be applied to the sacred texts dealing with dharma, never to dharma as such and per se. In the case of brahman, on the other hand, there is an applicability, though governed and controlled by the sacred texts dealing with this subject-matter, not just to these texts, but also to their subject-matter itself and as such. After emphasizing that the understanding of brahman (*brahmāvagati*) is only achieved through thinking about and clarifying the meaning of the sacred words (*vākyārthavicāraṇādhyavasāna*), not by using such worldly means of knowledge as anumāna, Śaṅkara states: *satsu tu vedāntavākyeṣu jagato janmādikāraṇavādiṣu tadarthagrahaṇadārḍhyāya-anumānam api vedāntavākyāvirodhi pramāṇaṃ bhavan na nivāryate, śrutyā-eva ca sahāyatvena tarkasya-abhyupetatvāt.* Referring to Bṛhadāraṇyaka Upaniṣad II, 4, 5 and Chāndogya Upaniṣad VI, 14, 2, he adds: *iti ca puruṣabuddhisāhāyyam ātmano darśayati. na dharmajijñāsāyām iva śrutyādaya eva pramāṇaṃ brahmajijñāsāyāṃ, kiṃtu śrutyādayo 'nubhavādayaś ca yathāsambhavam iha pramāṇam anubhavāasānatvād bhūtavastuviṣayatvāc ca brahmajñānasya.* ("Once there are such Upaniṣadic statements which tell the cause of the world etc., then also inference, insofar as it is a means of knowledge not opposed to the Upaniṣadic texts, is not ruled out in order to strengthen the understanding of the meaning of those statements, for it is revelation itself which admits reasoning as a supporting factor. . . . With these words, the Vedic revelation shows its alliance with the human intellect. Concerning the inquiry into brahman, the Veda and other authoritative texts are not, as is the case with the inquiry into dharma, the only authority; here, the Veda and, as far as appropriate, perceptual experience and so forth are authoritative means of knowledge, since the knowledge of brahman amounts ultimately to experience, and has as its object something that is really there.")[132]

This important programmatic statement has to be supplemented by cautionary remarks in later sections of the Brahmasūtrabhāṣya. In the commentary on Sūtra II, 1, 4, a *pūrvapakṣin* is presented who tries to utilize what has been said in the commentary on I, 1, 2 as an argument for the independent authority of reason. Śaṅkara responds to this in his commentary on II, 1, 6, trying to make sure that his own previous statements are not used for propagating independent reasoning under the pretext of scriptural exegesis: *na-anena miṣeṇa śuṣkatarkasya-ātmalābhaḥ sambhavati. śrutyanugṛhīta eva hy atra tarko 'nubhavāṅgatvena-āśrīyate.* ("In such a spurious fashion, dry reasoning cannot be established, since only such reasoning which is approved by the Veda is here referred to as being conducive to true experience.")[133] This corresponds to the formula used in the concluding commentarial statement on Sūtra I, 1, 1: *vedāntavākyamīmāṃsā tadavirodhitarkopakaraṇā.*

The statement on Brahmasūtra I, 1, 2 is not only an important indication of how Śaṅkara's references to an alliance between reason and Vedic revelation should be understood. It may also provide a key for interpreting his other, at times apparently conflicting, statements in this matter. The Veda itself indicates its alliance with worldly, human insight, legitimizing, guiding, limiting its use: This is a framework and context that includes and covers most of Śaṅkara's different and allegedly divergent statements, a framework that accounts for a certain flexibility and variability in approaching the theme of reason and revelation and that provides the background for a basically coherent and consistent inerpretation. On the one hand, Śaṅkara's way of finding reason and argumentation in the Upaniṣads themselves, in particular in the Bṛhadāraṇyaka Upaniṣad, may be seen as an exemplification of his programmatic statements on Brahmasūtra I, 1, 2; on the other hand, what he does in such argumentative texts as the second prose chapter of the Upadeśasāhasrī may be seen as his own utilization of those possibilities of reasoning and argumentation that in his view have been authorized by the Veda itself. What the chronological relationship of these "programmatic" statements and actual procedures may be is a question we do not have to discuss in our present context.[134]

10. The Veda not only authorizes a certain limited use of human reasoning, it also employs argumentation and demonstration among its own modes of expression and communication. It uses the language of reason, of "logical" demonstration as a means of explication and persuasion, thus creating the basic patterns of and the openness for legitimate human reasoning. In this manner, reasoning itself is traced back to the Veda, as a dimension of its own impersonal, yet benevolent and skillful manner of speaking to the world.

Śaṅkara says that in all the Upaniṣads ultimate unity is first presented as a thesis and then explicated or illustrated in the sense that the world, "by means of examples and reasons," is explained as a modification or part of the absolute self; finally, unity appears again as a conclusion or summary: *sarvāsu hy upaniṣatsu pūrvam ekatvaṃ pratijñāya dṛṣṭāntair hetubhiś ca paramātmano vikārāṃśāditvaṃ jagataḥ pratipādya punar ekatvam upasaṃharati.*[135] Śaṅkara adds that the cosmological passages dealing with the origination, continuation and dissolution of the world appear generally between "introductions" (*upakrama*) and summarizing "conclusions" (*upasaṃhāra*) concerning the unity of the individual and the absolute self; therefore, he sees it as their purpose to convey and to establish the idea of unity. The terminology which Śaṅkara uses in this context is in part identical with the terminology of the classical theory of inference. But it is also a terminology of persuasion and instruction, and its "logical" connotations cannot be separated from its "pedagogical" implications. That the sacred texts cannot teach their transempirical subject-matter without relying on "worldly words and meanings," or without regard for what is empirically obvious, is emphasized in the preceding passage: *na ca laukikapadapadārthāśrayaṇavyatirekeṇa āgamena śakyam ajñātaṃ vastvantaram avagamayitum.* The use of "examples" is part of a procedure which—whatever its "logical" implications may be—is ultimately didactic or pedagogical: *taddṛṣṭāntopādānena tadavirodhy eva vastvantaraṃ jñāpayituṃ pravṛttaṃ śāstram.*[136] The Veda itself may devise an "inferential procedure" and, "under the guise of a story," teach us in a manner which suits our human understanding: *athavā śrutiḥ svayam eva ākhyāyikāvyājena anumānamārgam upanyasya-asmān bodhayati puruṣamatim anusarantī.*[137]

Śaṅkara's observations on the role of reason *in* revelation are exemplified by his interpretation of specific Upaniṣadic texts, in particular the Bṛhadāraṇyaka Upaniṣad, which he divides into more "śāstric," "proclamative" and more "rational," argumentative sections and which he sees as a sequence of steps corresponding loosely to those in a "syllogism." In his introduction to Bṛhadāraṇyaka Upaniṣad II, 5, which opens the so-called *madhukāṇḍa* (or *madhubrāhmaṇa*), Śaṅkara discusses the function of this section with reference to the threefold procedure of *śravaṇa, manana* and *nididhyāsana* (mentioned before in II, 4, 5 and again in IV, 5, 6). He suggests that its function is to eliminate doubts which arise in connection with the "reasoning," tarka, which is implied by manana, or perhaps to present again as a "conclusion" (*nigamana*) what was first presented as a thesis and then supported by a "reason" (*hetu*): *athavā-ātmā-eva-idaṃ sarvam iti pratijñātasya-ātmotpattisthitilayatvaṃ hetum uktvā punar āgama-pradhānena madhubrāhmaṇena pratijñātasya-arthasya nigamanaṃ kriyate. tathā hi naiyāyikair uktaṃ hetvapadeśāt pratijñāyāḥ punarvacanaṃ nigamanam iti.* He rejects another explanation that his commentator Ānandagiri attributes to Bhartṛprapañca, and he emphasizes again that reasoning has to be in accordance with the sacred texts: *sarvathā-api tu yathā-āgamena-avadhāritaṃ tarkatas tathā-eva mantavyam.* ("Or rather: After presenting the fact that the world has its origin, existence and dissolution in the self as a reason for the thesis that the entire world is nothing but the self, the content of the thesis is restated as a conclusion by the *madhubrāhmaṇa*, which is dominated by authoritative tradition. In this sense, the Naiyāyikas say: The restatement of the thesis, after giving the reason, is the conclusion. . . . But in any case, one has to apply reasoning in accordance with what has been ascertained by the sacred texts.")[138] In the introduction to Bṛhadāraṇyaka Upaniṣad III, 1, in the opening section of the so-called *yājñavalkyakāṇḍa*, Śaṅkara says that this section deals with the same topic as the preceding *madhukāṇḍa*, but that it is not a mere repetition, since it is dominated by reasoning: *upapattipradhānatvād atikrāntena madhukāṇḍena samānārthatve 'pi sati na punaruktatā. madhukāṇḍam hy āgamapradhānam. āgamopapattī hy ātmaikatvaprakāśanāya pravṛtte śaknutaḥ karatalagatabilvam iva darśayitum.*

śrotavyo mantavyaḥ iti hy uktam. tasmād āgamārthasya-eva parīkṣāpūrvakaṃ nirdhāraṇāya yājñavalkīyaṃ kāṇḍam upapattipradhānam ārabhyate. ("Although it deals with the same topic as the preceding *madhukāṇḍa*, there is no repetition, since it relies primarily on argumentation. The *madhukāṇḍa*, on the other hand, relies primarily on authoritative tradition. When both sacred tradition and argumentation are bent upon demonstrating the unity of the self, they are capable of showing it as clearly as a *bilva* fruit on the palm of one's hand; for it has been said that the self should be heard about and reflected upon. Therefore, the *yājñavalkyakāṇḍa*, which relies primarily on argumentation, is introduced in order to determine the meaning of the sacred tradition in accordance with rational reflection.")[139]

In the introduction to IV, 5 (the *maitreyībrāhmaṇa*), the *madhukāṇḍa* is again characterized as being dominated by authoritative tradition (*āgamapradhāna*), the *yājñavalkyakāṇḍa* as being dominated by reasoning (*upapattipradhāna*), and the section on Maitreyī is now presented as a "conclusion" (*nigamana*; with another reference to Nyāyasūtra I, 1, 39): *atha-idānīṃ nigamanasthānīyaṃ maitreyībrāhmaṇam ārabhyate. ayaṃ ca nyāyo vākyakovidaiḥ parigṛhīto, hetvapadeśāt pratijñāyāḥ punarvacanaṃ nigamanam iti.* ("Now the maitreyībrāhmaṇa is introduced, which represents a conclusion. And this is the rule adopted by the experts in dialectics: The restatement of the thesis, after giving the reason, is the conclusion.") In addition, the possibility of a somewhat modified explanation is suggested, and the concordance and cooperation of āgama and upapatti is again emphasized.[140] In his commentary on Bṛhadāraṇyaka Upaniṣad II, 4, 10, which presents the Vedas and their auxiliary texts (sc. *itihāsaḥ purāṇaṃ vidyā upaniṣadaḥ ślokāḥ sūtrāṇy anuvyākhyānāni vyākhyānāni*) as an "exhalation of this great being," that is, brahman (*asya mahato bhūtasya niḥśvasitam*), Śaṅkara explains that this eightfold variety of auxiliary texts is part of the mantras and brāhmaṇas, that it is the Vedic revelation itself which encompasses these ways of discourse and instruction.

Such didactic paths and structures are part of the inner richness and variability of the Veda, which is not just a "source of knowledge" side by side with other such sources, but a comprehensive framework, a universe of discourse adjusted to the requirements of those who rely on it. Repeatedly, Śaṅkara almost personifies the Veda, as if it were a good, skillful teacher, reacting to the needs of students, or a loving, caring mother.[141] But it is, of course, an impersonal structure which fulfills these "personal" aspirations, and which is not only the source of truth, but also the prototype of good teaching. The Veda teaches the ultimate truth by reaching down into the world of appearance and illusion, by relating its statements and its methods of instruction to the way reality appears to those who are still in ignorance.[142] It "translates" its proclamation of ultimate unity into the language of vyavahāra, of worldly practice and orientation. The employment of inferential or quasi-inferential procedures is part of this; anumāna itself has its genuine place in the context of vyavahāra and its practical patterns of analogy and regularity.[143] Only the Veda can legitimize the "transworldly" use of worldly inferential "marks" (liṅga) and can validate worldly "examples" (dṛṣṭānta) as indications or illustrations of the absolute self or brahman.

By pointing out "examples" and "inferential" methods *in* the Veda and by using such devices himself, Śaṅkara appeals to what the world accepts as proof and demonstration; but in terms of his understanding of the Veda, these are only illustrations, basically didactic devices, and there is no claim on his part to add proof and validity to what the Veda teaches.

11. As we have seen, the inferential demonstrations of the self which the Naiyāyikas and Mīmāṃsakas claim as their own achievements are, in Śaṅkara's view, based upon Vedic "marks" or "reasons" (liṅga, hetu). Śaṅkara's two references to Nyāyasūtra I, 1, 39, which figure so prominently in H. Brückner's presentation, have to be understood accordingly.[144] Quoting the Nyāya definition of *nigamana* does certainly not imply a commitment to the Nyāya theory of knowledge and reasoning, or to the metaphysical background of the Nyāya system. This is quite obvious from other passages where Śaṅkara quotes the Nyāyasūtra text, for example, in his commentary on Brahmasūtra I, 1, 4 (quoting Nyāyasūtra I, 1, 2) and II, 2, 37 (quoting Nyāyasūtra I, 1, 18). In both these cases, Śaṅkara uses the Nyāya formulations with approval and as convenient devices for appealing to those whom he wants to instruct and convince. But instead of accepting them as authoritative statements in their own context, he includes them in and adjusts them to his context of Advaita Vedānta. This is quite evident in his reference to

Nyāyasūtra I, 1, 2, where he adds or even substitutes *brahman* in the Nyāya enumeration of decisive soteriological factors.

Moreover, we have to remember that by the time of Śaṅkara *nigamana* had found its way into the exegetic terminology of the Pūrvamīmāṃsā. The following resonance of Nyāyasūtra I, 1, 39, applied to an exegetic context, is found in Śabara's commentary on Mīmāṃsāsūtra VII, 1, 12: *nigamanaṃ ca pratijñāyā hetoś ca punarvacanam.* Nigamana is often used as the counterpart of upakrama, "commencement," "initial statement," usually concerning the relationship between an initially stated general rule and its subsequent specification. The following passage from Śabara's commentary on Mīmāṃsāsūtra I, 4, 24 exemplifies the correlation of upakrama and nigamana in the context of ritual exegesis: *añjanasāmānyena vākyasya-upakramo, ghṛtena viśeṣeṇa nigamanaṃ, yathā-upakramaṃ nigamayitavyam ekasmin vākye.* In such contexts, upakrama may be replaced with *ārambha* and nigamana with *upasaṃhāra*, which, together with upakrama, is also a significant term in Śaṅkara's description of the structure of the Upaniṣads, in particular in his commentary on the Bṛhadāraṇyaka Upaniṣad.

The exegetic role of upakrama and upasaṃhāra, not sufficiently noticed by H. Brückner, is later formalized by their inclusion into the Uttaramīmāṃsā list of the six exegetic "marks" (*liṅga*), which are supposed to establish the purport (*tātparya*) of scriptural, specifically Upaniṣadic, teachings. The following verse is frequently quoted by later Vedāntins of all schools:[145] *upakramopasaṃhārāv abhyāso 'pūrvatā phalam arthavādopapattī ca liṅgam tātparyanirṇaye.*

In his sixteenth-century compendium *Vedāntasāra*, Sadānanda exemplifies the relationship between upakrama and upasaṃhāra by referring to Chāndogya Upaniṣad VI, 2, 1 (*ekam eva-advitīyam*) and VI, 8, 7–16, 3 (*aitadātmyam idaṃ sarvam*). He explains upapatti, the sixth and final "mark," as follows: *prakaraṇapratipādyārthasādhane tatra tatra śrūyamāṇā yuktir upapattiḥ*; and he illustrates this by citing the example of the clay from Chāndogya Upaniṣad VI, 1, 4.[146]

As stated earlier, the Veda, as understood by Śaṅkara, speaks the language of direct enunciation and authoritative testimony as well as of illustration and argumentation. Words like āgama, śruti, śāstra not only refer to the Veda as such and in its totality; they can also refer to one particular type of statement which occurs in the Veda,[147] one of the "languages" which it speaks. It speaks a language that requires simple listening and obedience, and another one which has to be accompanied by reflection, reasoning or meditation. However, Śaṅkara rejects the view, apparently presented by Bhartṛprapañca, that the threefold scheme of *śravaṇa, manana, nididhyāsana* corresponds to clearly separable portions of the Upaniṣads.[148] In his view, the different levels and modes of instruction which are reflected by these three ways or levels of responding to the Vedic revelation cannot be described in terms of such a mechanical separation. In general, the scheme of śravaṇa, manana, and nididhyāsana does not play a very significant part in Śaṅkara's writings.[149]

With reference to Śaṅkara's programmatic statements in his commentary on Brahmasūtra I, 1, 2, we have suggested that his notion of an "alliance" between the Veda and human reason, his understanding of the didactic dimensions of the Veda and his way of finding the basis of legitimate reasoning in revelation itself provide a framework that includes most of his different observations on "reason and revelation." What may be perceived as inconsistency by Śaṅkara's modern readers, need not appear as such in this context. Śaṅkara may use "reason" and "argumentation" to the extent that he presents an entirely "argumentative" section such as the second prose chapter of the *Upadeśasāhasrī*, without abandoning or compromising his underlying conception of the Vedic roots of legitimate reasoning and without contradicting his numerous explicit statements on the ultimate authority of the Veda.[150]

This does, of course, not imply that Śaṅkara could not have held more genuinely different positions in other periods of his life.[151] Even within the context of his fully developed Advaita Vedānta (i.e., excluding his Gauḍapāda commentary), there is room for ambiguity and oscillation, which is inherited and made more obvious and explicit by some later Advaitins. This may be illustrated by the role which *anvayavyatireka*, the method of "positive and negative concomitance" ("continuity-and-discontinuity," "coordinate presence and absence") plays in the thought of Śaṅkara and of his successors.

The Concept of *anvayavyatireka*

12. Since P. Hacker's pioneering monograph on the disciples of Śaṅkara, the meaning and functions of anvayavyatireka in Advaita Vedānta have been discussed by several scholars. Hacker's own statements are brief and somewhat evasive. He characterizes anvayavyatireka as a "logical method" aimed at clarifying the meaning of the "great sayings," such as *tat tvam asi*, and as "reflection on the fact that the contents of the words as well as of the sentence are well-established and that the contrary is logically impossible."[152] Whatever the exact implications of Hacker's statements may be, it seems clear that he sees anvayavyatireka as a method to be applied to the interpretation of the *tat tvam asi*, that is, to the single words of this sentence as well as to their interrelation in the sentence. This is stated more categorically by J. A. B. van Buitenen. He interprets anvayavyatireka as an exegetic device designed to bring about the understanding of *tat tvam asi* as an identity statement, the positive procedure of *anvaya* determining what is identical in the meanings of *tad* and *tvam* and the negative procedure of *vyatireka* excluding from *tad* what is not in *tvam* and vice versa.[153]

S. Mayeda discusses the method of anvayavyatireka in the introduction to his English translation of the *Upadeśasāhasrī*. In accordance with van Buitenen's interpretation, he characterizes the "*anvaya* method" as the "positive formulation" of what is compatible in the meanings of *tad* and *tvam*, and *vyatireka* as "a negative formulation used to exclude all the incompatible meanings."[154] Mayeda, whose presentation is not always very precise, seems to regard anvayavyatireka in its Vedāntic sense as a somewhat peculiar method introduced by Śaṅkara himself and used exclusively in the Upadeśasāhasrī. He describes it as a "meditational method rather than an exegetical method" and associates it with what he calls "*parisaṃkhyāna* meditation";[155] he adds that it is "essentially the same as *jahadajahallakṣaṇā*," but that it was already "neglected" by his own pupils and "dropped by later Advaitins" because of "a defect in logical exactitude."[156] T. Vetter considers various aspects of anvayavyatireka without committing himself to any particular systematic or historical thesis.[157]

The interpretation by S. Mayeda and his predecessors has been carefully reviewed by G. Cardona, to whom we also owe a thorough and comprehensive study of the role of anvayavyatireka in grammatical literature.[158] Against Mayeda, Cardona emphasizes that "reasoning from *anvaya* and *vyatireka*" is not a kind of meditation and that it does not serve "directly to exclude incompatible meanings and to retain compatible ones" in *tat tvam asi* and similar sentences. Moreover, he rejects the contention that anvayavyatireka has a peculiar meaning in Advaita Vedānta or, even more specifically, in Śaṅkara's thought. Instead, he sees it as a much more widely used "mode of reasoning" which "involves the continued presence (*anvaya*) and absence (*vyatireka*)" of related entities and which in Advaita Vedānta "serves to discriminate between what is and is not the self as well as to show what meanings may be attributed to given terms" He characterizes its basic pattern as follows:

"1) a. When X occurs, Y occurs.
b. When X is absent, Y is absent.
2) a. When X occurs, Y is absent.
b. When X is absent, Y occurs."[159]

At this point, there is no need to discuss Cardona's stimulating argumentation. Instead, we may focus on the implications which the "method" of anvayavyatireka has with regard to our theme of "reason and revelation," and we can supplement Cardona's analysis by adding further historical and philosophical observations. This wider context may then lead us to a somewhat modified view of the role of anvayavyatireka in Advaita Vedānta as well as in other areas of Indian thought.

In Śaṅkara's own writings, the references to anvayavyatireka are much less conspicuous than in those of his disciple Sureśvara. The most significant occurrences are found in verse-chapter XVIII of the *Upadeśasāhasrī*, which deals with the interpretation of *tat tvam asi*. After several references to "discrimination" or "distinction" (*viveka*) between self and non-self in the preceding verses, the method of anvayavyatireka is introduced in verse 96 (which is quoted as verse IV, 22 in Sureśvara's *Naiṣkarmyasiddhi*):

anvayavyatirekau hi padārthasya padasya ca
syād etad aham ity atra yuktir eva-avadhāraṇe.

S. Mayeda translates this important verse as follows: "The logical means by which to ascertain [the meanings of] 'this' [and] 'I' should indeed be the method of agreement and difference of the words and of the meanings of the words." T. Vetter translates: "Anvaya-und-Vyatireka von Wortinhalt und Wort, um damit festzustellen, was 'ich' [bzw. 'du'] bedeutet dürfte nämlich in subtiler Überlegung (yukti) bestehen [und nicht jedermann zugänglich sein]."[160] The inaccuracies in these two translations are instructive and symptomatic: Mayeda's "'this' and 'I'," which mixes the *etad* in *syād etad* with the *tad* in *tat tvam asi,* is obviously prompted by his erroneous assumption that anvayavyatireka deals directly with the semantic compatibility of *tad* and *tvam.* Vetter's reversal of the subject (*yukti*) and the predicate nominative (*anvayavyatirekau*)—against the obvious intentions of Śaṅkara and the explicit understanding of Sureśvara—reflects his interpretation of yukti as a peculiar kind of "subtle deliberation," supposedly capable of establishing the existence and nature of the ātman.[161]

What the verse says can be rendered as follows: "(The method of) continuity-and-discontinuity ('coordinate presence and absence') of meanings and words, that should be the method, indeed, (which applies) here in the case of the ascertainment of the meaning of 'I.'" The word "I" with reference to its contexts and predicates as well as the corresponding entity with reference to its properties have to be investigated according to this method. This is then immediately exemplified by the reference to deep sleep (*suṣupta*) in verse 97 (cited in *Naiṣkarmyasiddhi* IV, 23), where the word *aham* is linked to a predicate (*na-adrākṣam*) which excludes all connotations of spatio-temporal particularity and where the continuity of "seeing" (*dṛṣṭi*), that is, of the awareness as such, is coordinated with the discontinuity or absence of all its objective contents (*pratyaya*). The anvaya of one element is juxtaposed with the vyatireka of all others, and its continued presence is seen as indicating its independence from these other factors. Verse 98 adds scriptural legitimacy by quoting from Bṛhadāraṇyaka Upaniṣad IV, 3, where śruti itself demonstrates how to achieve discrimination (*viveka*).

The following verses, although dealing with other questions, remain connected with the theme of viveka, until anvayavyatireka is again explicitly mentioned in verse 176. The subsequent discussion is summarized in verse 193, which emphasizes the necessity of clarifying the meaning of *tvam* before the "great saying" *tat tvam asi* can have its proper epistemic (and soteriological) impact. This refers, of course, to the situation in Chāndogya Upaniṣad VI, where only the meaning of *tad*, i.e. the non-dual absolute "being" (*sat*) has been explained before the *tat tvam asi* is introduced. "If it were not aided by the remembrance of the (proper) meaning of *tvam*, the statement could not produce authoritative knowledge" (*tvamarthasmṛtyasāhāy-yād vākyaṃ na-utpādayet pramām*). In the preceding verses, Śaṅkara has explained that it is for this very purpose of recalling the proper word-meaning that anvayavyatireka has been referred to (*anvaya-vyatirekoktiḥ padārthasmaraṇāya tu*); without a discriminating understanding of the word *tvam* (*tvampadārthāvivekataḥ*), the purport of the sentence, i.e. the eternal freedom of the self, would not become manifest. The reference to anvayavyatireka is for the sake of such discriminative understanding and for no other purpose (*anvayavya-tirekoktis tadvivekāya, na-anyathā*): Śaṅkara emphasizes this again since he is obviously aware that such or similar methods of analysing the phenomena of awareness and of "extracting" the meaning of "I"/ "you" have also been used in the context of extra-Vedic argumentations. For example, we may think of a statement such as *Vaiśeṣi-kasūtra* III, 2, 9, which claims that the ātman can be known without the sacred texts because of the separability of the word "I" from all physical connotations (*aham iti śabdavyatirekān na-āgamikam*). Śaṅkara's own references to the role of anvayavyatireka in Yogācāra etc. will be discussed later.[162]

13. Anvayavyatireka supports the "hearing" (śravaṇa) of the Upaniṣadic "great sayings" insofar as it serves to eliminate confusions and superimpositions from our self-understanding and from our usage of such words as "I" and "you." It does this by juxtaposing the continued presence of the pure subject of awareness with the discontinuity of its objective or objectifiable contents and by exposing the continued applicability of the word "I" in contexts where the connotations of spatio-temporal particularity which are habitually associated with this word have disappeared. It does not anticipate that insight which can only result from the "hearing" of the Upaniṣadic statements; but it is an essential prerequisite insofar as it helps to bring about the receptivity for the meaning and the liberating impact of the "great sayings."

Śaṅkara does not always use the expression anvayavyatireka when he refers to "continuity-and-discontinuity" as a means of achieving viveka, "discrimination." He may also use such terms as *vyabhicāra/avyabhicāra.* This is the case in the second prose-chapter of the Upadeśasāhasrī, which represents a highly concentrated effort to separate the essential nature of the ātman from everything that is "adventitious" or "accidental" (*āgantuka*), that is, from the changing phenomena of the states of waking and dreaming and in general from all objective data. Vyabhicāra/avyabhicāra are the guidelines of this analytic procedure. What is essential never "deviates" or "departs" (*vyabhicar*), while what is "accidental" may always be discontinued and cease to accompany what is essential: *kiṃ ca svapnajāgarite na tava-ātmabhūte, vyabhicāritvād, vastrādivat. na hi yasya yat svarūpaṃ tat tadvyabhicāri dṛṣṭam. svapnajāgarite tu caitanyamātraṃ vyabhicarataḥ.* ("The states of dreaming and waking are not your essence, since they may depart from you, just as your clothes, etc. It never occurs that the essence of something departs from it. But the states of dreaming and waking depart from pure consciousness.")[163]

Śaṅkara goes on to emphasize that this "nondeviating" essence persists in deep sleep, since only the objective contents (*dṛṣṭa*) are denied in this state, but not awareness or "seeing" (*dṛṣṭi*) itself: *paśyaṃs tarhi suṣupte tvaṃ, yasmād dṛṣṭam eva pratiṣedhasi, na dṛṣṭim.*[164] This corresponds to the statement in XVIII, 97 (*na vārayati dṛṣṭiṃ svāṃ, pratyayaṃ tu niṣedhati*), which, as we have seen, is meant to illustrate the "method" of anvayavyatireka introduced in the preceding verse. In this analysis based upon vyabhicāra/avyabhicāra, the grammatical procedure of extracting identical word meanings from different sentence contexts does not play the role which it plays in the presentation of anvayavyatireka in chapter XVIII. But the appeal to the grammatical implications of anvayavyatireka is primarily didactic, and as far as the analysis of phenomena and its goal of viveka are concerned, the two procedures are not essentially different.

The terminology of *vyabhicāra* is already used in Śaṅkara's description of the relationship between "the fourth" (*turīya*) and the three worldly states (*avasthā*) of consciousness. Turīya, identified with the ātman or absolute awareness, never "deviates" from the other three (i.e. never leaves them unaccompanied).[165] In the same sense, the "known" or "knowable" (*jñeya*) may be said to "deviate" from "knowledge" (*jñāna*), while on the other hand *jñāna* never leaves *jñeya* unaccompanied: *na jñānaṃ vyabhicarati kadācid api jñeyam.*[166]

It should be noted that in these passages Śaṅkara does not use *vyabhicāra* in the logical or epistemological perspective, i.e. in the sense of the logical "deviation" of an inferential reason (hetu) being present without its inferendum (sādhya). In Śaṅkara's usage, vyabhicāra and the corresponding verb forms do not indicate an unaccompanied presence, but a failure to be present in a relationship of concomitance, and an ontological defect rather than a logical one.

Another important text dealing with the separation of what is essential from what is nonessential, i.e. with the isolation of pure awareness, is Śaṅkara's commentary on Bṛhadāraṇyaka Upaniṣad IV, 3 (specifically IV, 3, 7). This is the Upaniṣadic section which Śaṅkara invokes after introducing anvayavyatireka in his Upadeśasāhasrī, stating that here the Veda itself teaches the discrimination of awareness and its contents.[167] While neither vyabhicāra/avyabhicāra nor anvayavyatireka are explicitly mentioned in the commentary on this section, the words vyatireka and vyatirikta are frequently used.[168] Moreover, Śaṅkara refers repeatedly to the simile of the extraction of the *muñja* grass from its stalk, which is already found in the Śatapatha Brāhmaṇa and the Kaṭha Upaniṣad and which is subsequently used as one of the most familiar illustrations of the purpose as well as of the procedure of anvayavyatireka.[169]

Upadeśasāhasrī XVIII is not the only text where Śaṅkara uses the term anvayavyatireka; and although the contexts and connotations of these other usages may vary, they illustrate and supplement the statements of the Upadeśasāhasrī. In his commentary on Brahmasūtra II, 1, 5, Śaṅkara relates the story of Prajāpati and the vital organs.[170] In order to determine which among them is superior to the others, Prajāpati asks them to depart successively from the body. It turns out that only "breath" (*prāṇa*) is indispensable, since the body and all the other organs could not subsist without it. Thus, "through this successive departure, the superiority of *prāṇa* is ascertained according to the method of continuity-and-discontinuity" (*ekaikotkramaṇena-anvayavyatirekābhyāṃ prāṇaśraiṣṭhyapratipattiḥ*). This is obviously not a "technical" context. Still, the expression *ekaikotkramaṇa* may be taken as a graphic paraphrase of what Śaṅkara seems to have in mind when he refers to anvayavyatireka as a method of clarifying the meaning of *tvam*: the nonessential elements may leave; what is essential, will stay.

Anvayavyatireka and the "Rule of Co-Apprehension"

14. In his commentary on Gauḍapāda's Kārikā III, 31, Śaṅkara refers to the theory that *manas* is the principle of all plurality, or that all this plurality is nothing but manas, and he says, paraphrasing Gauḍapāda's argumentation: *anvayavyatirekalakṣaṇam anumānam āha . . . sarvaṃ mana iti pratijñā, tadbhāve bhāvāt tadabhāve caabhāvāt.*

The final statement corresponds clearly to Cardona's first proposition:

1) a. When X occurs, Y occurs.
   b. When X is absent, Y is absent.

Although Śaṅkara calls this an anumāna, it is a more stringent relationship than what is ordinarily presupposed for an "inference," that is, "positive and negative concomitance" in the sense of a statement and its contraposition: "When X occurs, Y occurs. When Y is absent, X is absent." In this case, manas is not simply inferred from plurality, but plurality is reduced to manas in a manner which amounts to identification.

It is this kind of reductive, identifying argumentation, applied to the relationship between "body" and "soul" (i.e., life, awareness, etc.), which Śaṅkara attributes to the materialists in his commentary on Brahmasūtra III, 3, 53–54. Just like Śabara before him, Śaṅkara refers to the dead body as a case against the universal and reversible concomitance,—sometimes called "homogeneous concomitance" (*samāvinābhāva*, etc.) and amounting to what is known as "equipollence" in the terminology of traditional Western logic—, between the organic body and the soul-constituents, life, etc.[171] In this case, the positive concomitance *tadbhāve bhāvād* has been proven wrong, since the dead body, while still being an organism, is without the soul-constituents life, etc. Although the compound anvayavyatireka does not occur in this section, the word vyatireka is not only used by Śaṅkara, but also by Śabara and already by Bādarāyaṇa in Sūtra III, 3, 54; as we have seen, it is also a key-word in the Vaiśeṣika argumentation about the existence of the ātman.[172]

Corresponding to what we said about vyabhicāra, vyatireka can indicate an "exception to" or a "deviation from" a relationship of concomitance either in the sense of occurring without its relatum or in the sense of leaving the relatum unaccompanied; in either case, we are dealing with a concomitance of presence and absence, that is, a discontinuity. However, vyatireka, as used in the commentary on Gauḍapāda's Kārikā III, 31, can also indicate a concomitance of absences (in the sense of *tadabhāve ca-abhāvād* or Cardona's "when X is absent, Y is absent"). In accordance with the different meanings of vyatireka, as well as with a more or less stringent usage of anvaya, we have different "modes" of anvayavyatireka, which serve different, although not always clearly distinguished, functions in the history of Indian thought. Anvayavyatireka as a combination of concomitant presences and concomitant absences may be used to support claims of identity and mutual reducibility, if it applies "concomitance" in the strict sense of a fully reversible, "homogeneous" relationship. In a less stringent manner, i.e., in the sense of a statement and its contraposition, it is widely used in inferential reasoning, which does not normally require a reversible or homogenous concomitance between the inferential reason (hetu) and the inferendum (*sādhya*). In an essential, though often problematic and ambiguous sense, anvayavyatireka is related to the empirical ascertainment of causality (*kāryakāraṇabhāva*) or the relationship between means and ends (*sādhyasādhanabhāva*), and in general to the idea of order, regular succession and predictability in the universe.[173] In this sense, Śaṅkara refers to fortunetellers as *anvayavyatirekakuśala*, since they know how certain dream-phenomena are accompanied or followed by actual events.[174] The second "mode" of anvayavyatireka, which uses vyatireka in the sense of "discontinuity" or "concomitance of absence and presence," is primarily a method of differentiation and discrimination, designed to separate one element from its association or identification with others.

Although the word anvayavyatireka has clearly distinguishable connotations in its different contexts, it seems that in Śaṅkara's view these different connotations and usages converge in their basic implications and constitute variations of one basic phenomenon: thinking in terms of continuities and discontinuities.[175] This is not just one specific "mode of reasoning," but the basic structure and orientation of "reasoning" as such, of what Śaṅkara calls yukti, tarka, or anumāna. Anvayavyatireka is certainly not Śaṅkara's "own method." It is something he finds being used in numerous legitimate and illegitimate, i.e. extra-Vedic or anti-Vedic contexts; and he adopts its various "modes" cautiously and only insofar as they contribute to the clarification of the Vedic revelation or to the refutation of opposing views. This can be further illustrated by Śaṅkara's treatment of the teaching of the Buddhist Yogācāra school, which he combines with those of the school of Dignāga.

The Yogācāra-Vijñānavāda "rule of co-apprehension" (*sahopalambhaniyama*) proclaims the universal and reversible concomitance, that is, the utter inseparability of awareness (*vijñāna*) and its contents or objects (*viṣaya*). As understood by Śaṅkara, it is used to support the "consciousness-only" theory, i.e., the reductive identification of extramental entities with elements of awareness. There can be no doubt that this is a much more significant challenge to Śaṅkara's own thought than its radical counterpart, the somewhat archaic materialistic *dehātmavāda* discussed in the commentary on Brahmasūtra III, 3, 53–54. It applies the principle of concomitant presences and concomitant absences in the context of a phenomenology of awareness, thus, an area which is much closer to Śaṅkara's own awareness-oriented thought.

In his commentary on Brahmasūtra II, 2, 28, Śaṅkara characterizes the Yogācāra argumentation as follows: *api ca sahopalambhaniyamād abhedo viṣayavijñānayor āpatati. na hy anayor ekasya-anupalambhe 'nyasya-upalambho 'sti.* In his commentary on Bṛhadāraṇyaka Upaniṣad IV, 3, 7, he says, paraphrasing the "rule of co-apprehension": *yad dhi yadvyatirekeṇa na-upalabhyate, tat tāvanmātraṃ vastu dṛṣṭam.* Already Kumārila, without knowing Dharmakīrti's concept of *sahopalambhaniyama*, has argued against the Yogācāra idea of "co-apprehension" and for the separation (*bhinnatā*) of the "apprehending" (*grāhaka*) and the "apprehended" (*grāhya*) element of awareness (i.e., of vijñāna and viṣaya) by invoking anvayavyatireka. As an instance of an "apprehending" part continuing to be present, while the "apprehended" element is absent, he mentions the case that somebody remembers that he has perceived something, but does not recall the content of his perception:

> *na smarāmi mayā ko 'pi gṛhīto 'rthas tadā-iti hi*
> *smaranti grāhakotpādaṃ grāhyarūpavivarjitam.*
> . . . .
> *tadatyantāvinābhāvān na-ekākāraṃ hi jāyate*
> *anvayavyatirekābhyāṃ siddhā-evaṃ bhinnatā tayoḥ.*

("'I do not remember whether I perceived any kind of object at that time.' In such situations, people remember the occurrence of an act of perception without its content. . . . Thus an identical form cannot be derived from an invariable co-occurrence; rather, their difference is established by positive and negative concomitance.")[176]

Earlier in the same chapter of his *Ślokavārttika*, Kumārila has presented the Yogācārin himself arguing in terms of anvayavyatireka: Contact with external objects cannot be the cause of the definite forms or contents of awareness, since these "forms" (*ākāra*) occur also in memories, dreams, etc., when there is no such contact. On the other hand; they can never, not even in the waking state, occur without consciousness and its dispositions or impressions (*vāsanā*); therefore, they are caused by the impressions:

> *na hi tatra-arthasaṃsargaḥ, kevalā vāsanā-eva tu*
> *hetutvena-upapannā-iti sā-eva jāgraddhiyām api.*
> *anvayavyatirekābhyām evaṃ jñānasya gamyate*
> *ākāraḥ, na hi bāhyasya jñānāpeto nidarśyate.*

("In such cases as dreams etc., there is no contact with external objects; the disposition alone is established as the cause. Therefore, it is also the cause for the cognitions in the waking state. Thus it is ascertained by positive and negative concomitance that the form belongs to the cognition, since no such form can be shown for an external object devoid of cognition.")[177]

There is a noticeable, though somewhat evasive difference between the two usages of anvayavyatireka. As used in the Yogācāra pūrvapakṣa, it serves primarily to establish vāsanā as the cause of ākāra; but it also exposes the contrast between the continued presence of jñāna and the discontinuity of the alleged "contact with external objects." In Kumārila's own argument, anvayavyatireka is not meant to establish or to refute a causal relationship between the "apprehending" and the "apprehended" element, but to demonstrate their separability. In this sense, i.e. as a challenge to the "rule of co-apprehension" (*sahopalambhaniyama*), Kumārila's statements are quoted and refuted in Śāntarakṣita's *Tattvasaṃgraha.*[178]

Unlike Kumārila, Śaṅkara does not explicitly mention anvayavyatireka in his discussion of the "rule of co-apprehension"; but he mentions it repeatedly in his critique of the vāsanā theory. Referring to dreams etc., his Yogācāra pūrvapakṣin argues: *api ca anvayavyatirekābhyāṃ vāsanānimittam eva jñānavaicitryam ity avagamyate.* ("Furthermore, it is ascertained by positive and negative concomitance that the variety of cognitions depends solely on the dispositions.") Against this view, Śaṅkara claims that the perception of external objects is possible without any prior dispositions (*vāsanā*), while a vāsanā, being basically an "impression" (*saṃskāra*) from the outside, is always dependent upon objects: *api ca vinā-api vāsanābhir arthopalabdhyupagamād, vinā tv arthopalabdhyā vāsanotpattyanabhyupagamād arthasadbhāvam eva-anvayavyatirekāv api pratiṣṭhāpayataḥ.* ("Moreover, positive and negative concomitance, too, establish the existence of external objects, since one admits the perception of objects even without dispositions, but no occurrence of dispositions without the perception of objects.")[179] In this section, Śaṅkara argues largely ad hominem and in the context of ordinary worldly assumptions, and he applies anvayavyatireka as a worldly dialectical device that can easily be turned around. Earlier in his refutation of the pūrvapakṣa and in reference to the "rule of co-apprehension" (*sahopalambhaniyama*) as well as to the causal argument for the vāsanā theory, Śaṅkara characterizes his opponent's procedure as "fabrications concerning discontinuities, continuities, etc." (*vyatirekāvyatirekādivikalpa*):[180] This is what reasoning from anvayavyatireka in all its variations amounts to, if it is used without the guidance of the Vedic revelation.

We cannot and need not discuss here the extent to which Śaṅkara's presentation corresponds to the actual argumentation and the intentions of the Yogācārins and, more specifically, of the "Buddhist Logicians" of the Dignāga school who are included in this presentation; nor can we discuss the important and complex role which anvayavyatireka plays in Buddhist philosophical literature in general.[181]

Anvayavyatireka, the Self, and the Indispensability of Revelation

15. Śaṅkara may be aware of the specific technical implications which the various "modes" of anvayavyatireka have in grammar, logic, epistemology, or psychology, and of their specific functions as devices of analysis and discrimination or of coordination and identification. But it is not essential for him to define one such mode and to distinguish it from others. Whatever its specific technical details may be, anvayavyatireka has to do with positive and negative concomitance, deals with constants and variables, with the cooccurrence and noncooccurrence of various types of phenomena: words, meanings, entities or events. As such, it exemplifies the nature of human reasoning (yukti, tarka, upapatti, anumāna), which is groundless in itself and has no legitimate direction, if it is not guided by the Vedic revelation.

Reasoning in terms of anvayavyatireka, of the "mutual deviation" (*itaretaravyabhicāra*) of states of consciousness etc., has to be legitimized by the Veda itself. This is what Śaṅkara emphasizes again in connection with his programmatic statements against "dry," "fruitless" reasoning (śuṣkatarka) in his commentary on Brahmasūtra II, 1, 6: *śrutyanugṛhīta eva hy atra tarko 'nubhavāṅgatvena-āśrīyate. svapnabuddhāntayor ubhayor itaretaravyabhicārād ātmano 'nanvāgatatvam.* ("Only such reasoning which is approved by the Veda is here referred to as being conducive to true experience. Because of their mutual deviation, both dreaming and waking do not belong to the essence of the self.") In his commentary on Bṛhadāraṇyaka Upaniṣad IV, 3, 23, he invokes the "revelation of the continuity of vision" (*dṛṣṭyaviparilopaśruti*), that is, of the continued presence of the witnessing subject in deep sleep, etc., against "worldly" argumentation. In the words of Sureśvara, anvayavyatireka has no "basis" (*āśraya*) apart from the Vedic "words and meanings."[182]

In Sureśvara's writings, specifically in his *Naiṣkarmyasiddhi*, but also in his extensive subcommentaries (vārttika) on Śaṅkara's Bṛhadāraṇyaka and Taittirīya Upaniṣad commentaries, anvayavyatireka plays a much more conspicuous and explicit role than in Śaṅkara's own writings. Sureśvara quotes Śaṅkara's most important statements on anvayavyatireka in the fourth chapter of his Naiṣkarmyasiddhi or elsewhere,[183] and he adds numerous statements of his own. It is obvious that the relationship between anvayavyatireka and the authority of the Veda is a central issue in Sureśvara's thought. While he tries consistently to be faithful to Śaṅkara's intentions, he often goes beyond Śaṅkara's explicit statements, and he supplements and expands his observations in various directions. A brief review of his contributions to this theme seems to be appropriate at this point.

In accordance with Śaṅkara's usage, Sureśvara often refers to the grammatical connotations of anvayavyatireka.[184] But its essential function is to separate the self from anything that is not the self. In this function, it is also introduced in connection with the theory of the "sheaths" (*kośa*) in the *Taittirīyopaniṣadbhāṣyavārttika*, which also combines anvayavyatireka and *vyabhicāra/avyabhicāra* in an important sequence of verses concerning the "states of consciousness."[185] It is a method of analysis and discrimination, which appears in close terminological association with yukti and anumāna (not in the strict sense of "inference"); these terms may even be used as if they were its interchangeable synonyms.[186] The Vedic texts, though "sentences," can produce the knowledge of the ātman, which is not the meaning of any sentence, if their "hearing" is preceded by *anvayavyatireka: anvayavyatirekapurassaraṃ vākyam eva-avākyārtharūpam ātmānaṃ pratipādayati.*[187] But this liberating knowledge can certainly not be brought about by anvayavyatireka alone: *na tv anvayavyatirekamātrasādhyo 'yam arthaḥ.*[188]

He who has practised the method of "continuity-and-discontinuity" with reference to the problem of "self" and "non-self" has met an essential preliminary requirement of liberating knowledge. It is part of his *adhikāra*, his soteriological "qualification" or "competence," and it can be added to other requirements, such as "inner control" (*śama*), "restraint" (*dama*), etc.[189] The discriminative knowledge achieved through the method of "continuity-and-discontinuity" does not anticipate the liberating insight which comes from the Vedic word, nor is there a gradual transition from one to the other. In a sense, reasoning in terms of anvayavyatireka produces only an openness which has to be filled, or perhaps even a confusion which has to be eliminated, by the Vedic revelation. To him who has freed himself from false superimpositions by reasoning in this way, who has discarded the whole sphere of objects, who asks in bewilderment (*vīkṣāpanna*) "Who am I?" (*ko 'smi*), who may even think that he himself has been discarded (*tyakto 'ham*) in this process: to him the Veda speaks in a meaningful and soteriologically effective manner when it says: *tat tvam asi.*[190] The discriminative knowledge which is the result of such reasoning remains in the sphere of difference (*bheda*), of mutual exclusion and nonbeing (*abhāva*), and it cannot realize the absolute nonduality of the "witness" (*sākṣin*) or self.[191]

At this point, Sureśvara seems to be ready to recognize a certain positive potential not only in the differentiating philosophy of the Sāṃkhya school, but even in the more radical way in which the Buddhists have discarded all superimpositions and objectifying identifications of the self, in fact pursuing the unguided, extra-Vedic use of anvayavyatireka to the extreme consequence of their denial of the self (*anātmavāda*). However, this extreme of reasoning is also an extreme of delusion (*moha*); not paying any attention to the Veda and trying to see through "the eye of reason alone" (*anumānaikacakṣus*), the Buddhists remain in darkness.[192] Just as Śaṅkara himself, Sureśvara believes that the Veda not only authorizes legitimate anvayavyatireka, but actually uses it as a means of instruction and illustration; his commentator Ānandagiri refers to the "Vedic method called *anvayavyatireka*" (*anvayavyatirekākyhaśrautayukti*).[193]

The statements in the *Naiṣkarmyasiddhi* are supplemented by numerous references in the *Bṛhadāraṇyakopaniṣadbhāṣyavārttika*, specifically in its massive introductory part, the *Sambandhavārttika*. Here, Sureśvara deals more explicitly with the *prasaṃkhyānavādin*, who teaches that the Veda, instead of directly revealing the truth, enjoins certain meditational and intellectual activities that, if properly performed, will lead to the realization of truth. Again and again, Sureśvara emphasizes that the Veda is self-sufficient, that its power and authority of revelation is neither dependent upon nor paralleled by worldly verification, and that the supreme truth that it teaches and that transcends all result-oriented "works" (*karman*) cannot and need not be mediated by worldly activities. The analytic and discriminative understanding brought about by the "rational" procedure of anvayavyatireka should in no way be confused with the Vedic revelation of the brahman-nature of the self.[194] That the Veda itself speaks "with arguments" (*yuktibhiḥ sārdham*) does not mean that it attempts to justify the soteriological message which it emits "naturally" (*prakṛtyā*), as an outflow of its own essence; it only means that it offers "rational," "intellectual" incentives to accept this message. In this respect, the role of yukti in the *jñānakāṇḍa* is analogous to that of arthavāda in the *karmakāṇḍa*, which, without adding to the authoritativeness of the vidhi, is conducive to its execution.[195] The more systematizing account of anvayavyatireka which Vidyāraṇya gives centuries later in his *Pañcadaśī* is no longer so close to Śaṅkara's own ideas as Sureśvara's statements; around 1600, Madhusūdana Sarasvatī presents a fivefold classification of anvayavyatireka, referring to *dṛgdṛśya, sākṣisākṣya*, etc.[196]

Padmapāda, the other famous disciple of Śaṅkara, pays much less attention to anvayavyatireka than Sureśvara; but he tries to provide a more formal description or even definition of *tarka* than either Śaṅkara or Sureśvara. Reasoning, reflection (tarka) "supports the means of knowledge" (*pramāṇānām anugrāhakas tarka iti*) insofar as it contributes to the subjective certitude concerning the objects of valid knowledge, specifically the nondual ātman/brahman which is the "object" (viṣaya) of the Vedic revelation. Tarka cannot add to or subtract from the validity (*prāmāṇya*) and objective certainty of this revelation. It can only make us ready to accept it without doubt and hesitation by demonstrating its possibility (*sambhava*) and by removing apparent contradictions (*virodha*) from the Upaniṣadic "great sayings."[197] Later on in his *Pañcapādikā*, Padmapāda discusses *manana*, the more directly exegetic "reflection" which traditionally follows the "hearing" (*śravaṇa*) of the Vedic texts (or, according to Padmapāda, of the *śārīraka*, that is, Brahmasūtra text). He defines it as "pondering" (*anusandhāna*) over the "examples" (*dṛṣṭānta*) and "argumentative explications" (*yuktyarthavāda*) found in the Vedic texts, as well as over other "inferences which are not incompatible with the Vedic statements" (*vākyārthāvirodhyanumāna*).[198]

16. Anvayavyatireka as a method of separating the "nonself" from the "self" and of analysing the meaning of *tvam* in *tat tvam asi* illustrates the significance that reasoning has in Śaṅkara's and Sureśvara's exegetical and soteriological thought. But does this mean that yukti alone is capable of uncovering the ultimate, though indirect referent of *tvam*, that is, the nondual self? In his interpretation of Śaṅkara's commentary on Brahmasūtra IV, 1, 2, T. Vetter says: "Śāstra (Schriftzitate und das mit ihnen begründete theologische System) macht das Absolute zugänglich, Yukti (rationale Überlegung) den Kern der Person." He refers to "Śāstra and Yukti" as "theologische und rational-psychologische Untersuchung der Wortinhalte" respectively, and he adds: "Während in diesem Textstück eine klare Verteilung der Aufgaben erreicht ist: Yukti ist für den Inhalt von 'du', Śāstra für den Inhalt von 'jenes', liegt dies im Hinblick auf andere Stellen etwas komplizierter."[199]

In Vetter's view, such "clear division of responsibilities" seems to be the implicit goal of Śaṅkara's thought about the relation between śruti and yukti, something which he approximates more or less successfully in his writings. Interpreted in this sense, the Upaniṣads, which contain the *tat tvam asi* etc., would be authoritative and indispensable only insofar as the meaning of the *tad* is concerned. The *tvam*, however, would be, more or less explicitly, left to "rational," "rational-psychological" investigation, which would lead us to the discovery of what we really are, the "core of the person," and thus enable us to understand the liberating message of identity. It is obvious that there are problems in this approach. If yukti alone can reveal the true meaning of *tvam*, that is, that reality which is also the meaning of *tad*, what then is left as the content of the Vedic message? If, on the other hand, scripture alone can teach us the identity of the meaning of *tvam* and *tad*, that is, the true reality of the *tvam*, would it not be inconsistent to claim another, "rational" way of discovering this reality?

Vetter admits that in his interpretation the role of the Veda is somewhat precarious and redundant: "Man kann nun auch noch fragen, wozu hierbei der Satz 'du bist jenes' nötig ist, wenn er sowieso die eventuell von Śrutisätzen unterstützte rationale Untersuchung (yukti) des Ich, das in diesem Satz angesprochen wird, voraussetzt, und diese Untersuchung schon dessen Natur der Geistigkeit und Leidlosigkeit ans Licht bringt; in USG II wird ja auch der Yukti der gesamte Erlösungsweg anvertraut."[200] But does Śaṅkara ever credit "rational investigation" alone with making accessible the true reality of the *tvam*? And it is really yukti alone which accomplishes liberating knowledge according to the second prose chapter of the Upadeśasāhasrī? This certainly does not follow from the mere absence of scriptural quotes. Our preceding investigations have shown to what extent Śaṅkara sees legitimate reasoning itself within the horizon of revelation, as something not independent in its "rationality," but received and revealed as a pedagogical device and as a means of explication. This may be problematic for us, but it has to be recognized as a constituent factor of Śaṅkara's own orientation, and as something that might help us to understand why he did not see or take seriously as inconsistency or contradiction what we tend to see as such.

In what sense and why does Śaṅkara consider human reason inadequate to reach truth and certainty? What exactly does the priority and superiority of the Veda mean to him? Why is the Veda epistemologically and soteriologically indispensable, and in what sense does human thought depend on it? As we have seen, these questions have many implications and ramifications, and we have to avoid a one-dimensional answer.

First of all, Śaṅkara criticizes the factual and inescapable groundlessness and vacuity of tarka in the sense of hypothetical, speculative reasoning. But he also questions the reliability of anumāna, inference in general, and he emphasizes the incalculable character of the empirical world of appearance, with which it is concerned and on the regularity of which its own validity is based. In fact, Śaṅkara's criticism of reason often blurs the distinction between merely hypothetical reasoning and inference in a more positive sense. Moreover, the goal of Vedāntic thought and teaching, the self or brahman, is such that, even if reason were fully reliable in the worldly sphere, it could certainly not establish knowledge of this transworldly, transempirical reality. Without the aid of revelation, human reason cannot discover reliable worldly signs or analogues of this reality.

In claiming its own methods and criteria, human reason displays an anthropocentric attitude of self-confidence and arrogance that is incompatible with that receptivity and openness which is a condition of liberating knowledge. Relying on his own "worldly potential" (*sāmarthyaṃ laukikam*[201]) of intelligence and reasoning alone, man remains attached to that very world from which he seeks final liberation. No effort of "worldly" reflection by the ego upon itself will yield the liberating insight into the reality of the ātman as the one absolute witness.[202] Confusion and contradiction arise when the thinker thinks of himself in an inference-oriented and self-objectifying manner; and the "tenth man" who is not reminded of his own identity by somebody else will count and re-count the other nine without ever taking notice of himself.[203] Knowledge of the ātman, which coincides with the ātman itself, is not the result of mental activities. Only in listening to the apparently external voice of the Vedic revelation can man transcend the network of result-oriented activities and see himself as what he is and has always been, i.e., as the ātman. Those who believe in the "power of their own thought" (*svacittasāmarthya*) and "rely on their own intellectual skills" (*svabuddhikauśalānusārin*), will never attain the "state beyond nescience" (*avidyāyāḥ pāram*).[204]

Revelation, the Veda, is the indispensable source of liberating knowledge; it is the condition of its possibility. In Śaṅkara's view, this relates to the soteriology of each single individual as well as to the structure of the authoritative tradition; and it has implications of validity and legitimacy as well as of factual genesis and derivation. The Veda alone can lend final validity to statements about the self or the absolute; it is the basis of certainty and clarity in this matter. Moreover, the very legitimacy of "hearing" and studying the Veda is determined by the Veda itself, insofar as it lays down the conditions of qualification, the "mandate" (adhikāra) for liberating knowledge.[205] The Vedic revelation is not a neutral, universal message that could be separated from its original source; the soteriological efficacy of this message depends on its being legitimately received from its original and continuous source. On the other hand, the individual may not always be aware to what extent he is factually indebted to the Veda, that is, to what extent the Veda is the ultimate factual source of certain insights and ways of thinking, even of "reasoning" and inference, which he takes for granted or claims as human accomplishments.[206] Legitimate reasoning itself is rooted in and has to be measured against the Veda.

In Śaṅkara's understanding, the Upaniṣads, the "knowledge portion" of the Veda, respond to human reason, appeal to it, provide it with a context, goal, and basis. They contain so many hints and implicit patterns of reasoning that they seem to anticipate all merely human intellectual efforts. Thus the Upaniṣads are not a set of dogmas against which human reason would have to revolt or assert itself, but rather a source to which it traces itself and its own legitimacy, a universe of meaning in which it can exercise its potential without having to proclaim its autonomy, and to which it can subordinate itself without having to sacrifice itself.[207]

It is obviously impossible for a modern Western reader to follow Śaṅkara into all the details of his Vedic exegesis. But it is equally impossible to understand his thought in its philosophical as well as in its historical dimensions without fully recognizing and respecting its fundamental commitment to the Vedic revelation.[208]

Epilogue

17. In the preceding chapter, we have dealt with the thought of Śaṅkara and some of his successors, in particular Sureśvara. Śaṅkara is a historical person, but also a powerful myth. What we know about the person and his life, and about the number and genesis of his works, is entirely insufficient. We cannot accept the mythified Śaṅkara of the Indian legendary tradition, nor the superhuman saint and national leader proclaimed by the Neo-Vedāntins. Quite obviously, we need more historical and philological work, authenticity studies, search for biographical clues, and so forth. Yet there is little hope that such work will, in the foreseeable future, produce a definitive biography or list of works. Does this mean that we have no basis for a philosophical evaluation of Śaṅkara's thought, its unity and its inner tensions?

No doubt, the philological and historical basis of our investigations is incomplete. We do not have all the certainties our historical and philological orientation seems to require. Yet this does not mean that we have no basis for meaningful philosophical reflections and generalizations. Moreover, the lack of precise historical and biographical contours is in itself an integral part of the phenomenon we are dealing with, and it ought to be respected as such.

We do not have an authoritative corpus of Śaṅkara's works. But we have a textual core area from which we may proceed in various directions. The *Brahmasūtrabhāṣya* defines Śaṅkara's identity. The *Bṛhadāraṇyakopaniṣadbhāṣya*, the most significant of all Upaniṣad commentaries, has the support of Sureśvara's subcommentary; so does the *Taittirīyopaniṣadbhāṣya*. The *Upadeśasāhasrī*, the only noncommentarial work in this group, has been quoted by Sureśvara. In addition to this central group, we have used other works in a more casual and selective manner, and in some cases in a strictly hypothetical sense. Here, different accents would have been possible and legitimate. All this has been supplemented by comments and paraphrases of Sureśvara, Śaṅkara's disciple who tried to coordinate the widely scattered statements of his master, and to make explicit what he found inherent in these statements.

Our perspective has not been a developmental one. We have not tried to find biographical clues or signs of personal and doctrinal change in Śaṅkara's works. Instead, we have tried to understand and explore certain pervasive structures in Śaṅkara's thought and self-understanding, and to see his various statements and procedures concerning reason and revelation within his own context and horizon of thought. In particular, we have tried to understand Śaṅkara's idea of the Veda, that is his idea of an epiphany of transcendent truth which adjusts itself to worldly ways of thought and may use and legitimize argumentation and reasoning to convey its central message of ultimate unity. Śaṅkara's approach has to be seen in the wider historical context which is marked by the rivalry and interaction between Buddhism, Pūrvamīmāṃsā and Nyāya, and by Bhartṛhari's powerful metaphysics of the Vedic word.[209]

In this connection, we have discussed the meaning of *anvayavyatireka.* This concept seems to have only marginal importance in Śaṅkara's works; yet it is of central and symptomatic significance for the entire issue of "reason" and "revelation" as it appears in the classical Indian tradition, and it is the closest approximation to the Indian definition of the nature of rationality and reasoning.

Chapter 5: Notes

1. Cf. *India and Europe*, ch. 12.

2. Cf. *India and Europe*, ch. 21.

3. E.g. T.R.V. Murti, "The Rational Basis of Advaitism." *Philosophical Quarterly* 6 (1930), 57–81.

4. Cf. P. Schreiner, "Some Remarks about the Function of Reason in Modern Advaita Philosophy." *Ānvīkṣikī* 6 (1973), 114–122; ib., 119 (quote from G.R. Malkani).

5. R.S. Naulakha, *Shankara's Brahmavada.* Kanpur, 1964, 36.

6. S.K. Mukherjee, "Śaṅkara on the Relation between the Vedas and Reason." *Indian Historical Quarterly* 6 (1930), 108–113; ib., 113.

7. *An Introduction to Śaṅkara's Theory of Knowledge.* Delhi, 1962, 62; 65; on p. 68, Devaraja suggests that Śaṅkara's insistence on the ultimate authority of the Vedas was due to certain "ultra-orthodox moods."

8. Cf. also M. Hiriyanna, "The Place of Reason in Advaita," in his *Indian Philosophical Studies* I. Mysore, 1957, 45–52.

9. *The System of the Vedānta,* transl. by Ch. Johnston. New, York 1973, 96 (German original: Leipzig, 1883; third ed. 1920).

10. Cf. *India and Europe*, ch. 9.

11. E. Deutsch, *Advaita Vedānta: A Philosophical Reconstruction.* Honolulu, 1969, 5; cf. 6: "We want to find in Advaita Vedānta that which is philosophically meaningful to a Westerner and to articulate this content in universal philosophical terms." According to Deutsch, this amounts to an interpretation of Śaṅkara in terms of levels of "experience."

12. "Conflict between Traditionalism and Rationalism: A Problem with Śaṅkara." *Philosophy East and West* 12 (1962), 153–162; especially 157.

13. *A Thousand Teachings*, 48.

14. Cf. *India and Europe*, ch. 15.

15. Other terms which may be mentioned in this context and which refer either to "reflection" or to "methodical examination" are *manana; vicāra; nyāya; ānvīkṣikī; parīkṣā*; another important term with a wide range of connotations—from "conjectural modification" (in Mīmāṃsā) to "reasoning" in the sense of *yukti—is ūha* (sometimes combined with *apoha*; e.g. Vyāsa and Vācaspati on Yogasūtra II, 18; Medhātithi on Manu II, 6; ed. J.H. Dave. I, 163; already *Avadānaśataka*, ed. J.S. Speyer, I, 209).

16. There is also a broader sense, in which it appears in the title of several Nyāya works, e.g. in Keśavamiśra's *Tarkabhāṣā*.

17. Cf. S. Bagchi, *Inductive Reasoning*. Calcutta, 1953, 4 ff.

18. Nyāyasūtra I, 1, 39, which precedes the definition of *tarka*, is quoted twice in Śaṅkara's commentary on the Bṛhadāraṇyaka Upaniṣad; see below, § 10 f.

19. Cf. *India and Europe*, ch. 15; Maitrī Upaniṣad VII, 8 has the expression *vṛthātarka*.

20. See below, n. 89 f; also Mallavādin, ed. Jambuvijaya, vol. 2. Bhavnagar, 1976, 736 f.

21. This verse from Kumārila's *Bṛhaṭṭīkā* is quoted, e.g., in Śāntarakṣita's *Tattvasaṃgraha* (v. 3242 etc.) and Ratnakīrti's *Sarvajñasiddhi* (cf. G. Bühnemann, *Der allwissende Buddha*. Vienna, 1980, 71; 146). A modified version is found in Yāmuna's *Saṃvitsiddhi* (in: *Siddhitraya*, ed. Rāmamiśra Śāstrin. Benares, 1910, ChSS, 88). - According to TV, 80 (on I, 3, 2), the Mīmāṃsā is an "array of methods" (*yuktikalāpa*).

22. *Lokatattvanīrṇaya* I, 38 (ed. L. Suali, *Giornale della Società Asiatica Italiana* 18, 1905, 278); the verse is quoted by Guṇaratna and Maṇibhadra in their commentaries on Haribhadra's *Ṣaḍdarśanasmuccaya*, v. 44 (by Guṇaratna also in the introduction). Cf. also L. de La Vallée Poussin,

"Une stance jaina et bouddhique." *Journal Asiatique* X/17 (1911), 323–325.

23. Most of the occurrences in this text are in negative formulations, such as *na-upapadyate* or *na yujyate*; cf., e.g., VII, 20 ff.; II, 7; 16 ff.; also XXIV, 14; and Gauḍapāda, Kārikā III, 27.

24. See above, n. 7.

25. Cf. BSBh I, 1, 2 (*Works* III, 8).

26. See below, § 8.

27. Cf. the contributions by G. Oberhammer in: *Offenbarung, geistige Realität des Menschen*, ed. G. Oberhammer. Vienna, 1974. YD, 14 (on Kārikā 2) mentions several definitions of the Veda, one of which includes *tarka*: *aṅgāni vedās tarkā vā, yathā-āha -vedavedāṅgatarkeṣu vedasaṃjñā nirucyate*; a definition which includes *tarka* is also mentioned by Bhartṛhari in his Vṛtti on VP I, 10.

28. See below, § 10.

29. Cf. the contributions on Śaṅkara and Advaita Vedānta in: *Kleine Schriften*, ed. L. Schmithausen. Wiesbaden, 1978.

30. Cf. also my review of Vetter's *Studien* in: *Orientalistische Literaturzeitung* 78 (1983), 493–495.

31. Cf. my review in: *Journal of the American Oriental Society* 100 (1980), 43–45.

32. Cf. *Beweisverfahren*, 51 ff.; 57 ff., also 35: "Vorherrschen der Beweisfunktion"; 41: "Beweisfunktion im Vordergrund", etc. Brückner does not refer to the discussion of "examples" in BSBh III, 2, 20 or to Sureśvara's discussion of the compatibility between "comparison" (*upamāna*) and non-duality in his BUBh-Vārttika II, 4, 459 ff.

33. *Beweisverfahren*, 163: "Sein eigenes Verfahren scheint mir Śaṁkara selbst am besten zu beschreiben, wenn er über das der śruti sagt: . . .

sarvāsu hy upaniṣatsu pūrvam ekatvaṃ pratijñāya dṛṣṭāntair hetubhiś ca paramātmano vikārāṃśāditvaṃ jagataḥ pratipādya punar ekatvam upasaṃharati." For the translation of this passage from BUBh II, 1, 20, cf. 51 f., n. 5.

34. Cf. *Beweisverfahren*, 55; also 58 f.; 68; 74; 181.

35. See below, § 6 f.

36. To reduce Śaṅkara's critique of "inference," "reason" etc. in BUBh to "polemical invectives" ("polemische Ausfälle," *Beweisverfahren*, 128, n. 1) against misuses of argumentation is as misleading as N.K. Devaraja's references to Śaṅkara's "ultra-orthodox moods" (see above, n. 7).

37. *Beweisverfahren*, 56.

38. Cf. BUBh I, 1, introduction.

39. Cf. the reference to the work of P. Hacker and S. Mayeda in Vetter's preface.

40. Cf. "Erfahrung des Unerfahrbaren bei Śaṅkara"; in: *Transzendenzerfahrung, Vollzugshorizont des Heils*, ed. G. Oberhammer. Vienna, 1978, 45–59.

41. On Gauḍapāda, cf. also T. Vetter, "Die Gauḍapādīya-Kārikās: Zur Entstehung und zur Bedeutung von (a)dvaita." *Wiener Zeitschrift für die Kunde Südasiens* 22 (1978), 95–131.

42. It is referred to in several of Vetter's eight interpretive key questions (*Studien*, 17 f.), most explicitly in question E: "Wo kommt der Inhalt des erlösenden . . . Wissens her?"

43. Cf. the presentation and discussion by Vetter, *Studien*, 38 ff.

44. Cf. *Works* I, 196; 208; 227 f.

45. Cf. also *Works* I, 227: *āgamataḥ pratijñātasya-advaitasya* . . .

46. But cf. *Kārikā* II, 3: *niścitaṃ yuktiyuktaṃ ca yat*; Śaṅkara explains *niścitam* as *śrutyā niścitam.*

47. Cf. *Studien*, 34 ff.

48. See below, § 10.

49. *Studien*, 38.

50. *Studien*, 46; on p. 47, Vetter notes that *yukti/tarka* are used more freely than *anumāna* in the formal sense.

51. *Studien*, 71.

52. *Studien*, 89.

53. Cf. *Studien*, 89: "der vielleicht bedeutendste denkerische Versuch."

54. Cf. *Kleine Schriften*, ed. L. Schmithausen. Wiesbaden, 1978, 214.

55. Cf. *Studien*, 107: "Klärung des Inhalts von 'du' bzw. von 'ich' durch Überlegung (*yukti*)"; 114: "Kern des Individuums."

56. *Studien*, 104 ff.

57. *Studien*, 118; on Vetter's interpretation of this and related passages, see below, § 16.

58. In USG I, which according to Vetter would be later than BSBh IV, 1, 2, the relationship is again found to be less clear and definite.

59. *Studien*, 15.

60. Cf. *Studien*, 17.

61. Cf. also *Studien*, 18: "Ausserdem ist festzustellen: je älter ein Text, desto schwieriger ist die Unterscheidung zwischen Theorie und Praxis . . ."

62. Cf. *Studien*, 8; 17; 19, where "theory" is paraphrased accordingly.

63. Cf. *Studien*, 19: "Er verschmäht dann zwar nicht die Vorteile, welche der Advaita-Begriff in Exegese und Polemik bisweilen bietet, es erscheint mir aber als umgekehrte Welt, wenn man diese Episoden seinem sich überall als sehr ernsthaft darbietenden Streben nach dem Heil unterordnen will." The second part of this statement is somewhat surprising, if not incomprehensible, in its context; it seems to involve a typographical error.

64. Cf. "Erfahrung des Unerfahrbaren bei Śaṅkara" (see above, n. 40), 56.

65. Cf. *Studien*, 17.

66. Cf. *India and Europe*, ch. 15, § 12.

67. However, this is a pedagogical orientation without the temporal urge of "saving souls."

68. Cf., e.g., BSBh III, 3, 1; and below, § 9 (specifically n. 128).

69. Vetter himself modifies his earlier assessment of the feasibility of a complete relative chronology of Śaṅkara's writings; cf. *Studien*, 18.

70. There may, indeed, be "(at least) six positions" concerning "being" in Śaṅkara's writings (cf. *Studien*, 13 f.); but this does not mean that there is no basic unity of orientation in this matter.

71. The *Yogasūtrabhāṣyavivaraṇa* may be disregarded in the context of this presentation; but see below, ch. 6.

72. Cf. "Śaṅkara der Yogin und Śaṅkara der Advaitin: Einige Beobachtungen"; in: *Kleine Schriften*, ed. L. Schmithausen, Wiesbaden 1978, 213–242 (originally *Wiener Zeitschrift für die Kunde Süd- und Ostasiens* 12–13, 1968/69).

73. Cf. BUBh II, 1, 20 (*Works* I, 743 ff.); also on Taittirīya Upaniṣad III, 10, 4.

74. Cf., e.g., BSBh II, 1, 11.

75. Cf., e.g., US XII, 18; XVI, 65; XVIII, 43; 88; XIX, 25; USG I, 44; BUBh I, 4, 10 (*Works* I, 676); II, 5, intr. (*Works* I, 770); IV, 5, intr. (*Works* I, 939); on Taittirīya Upaniṣad III, 4, 10; on Kaṭha Upaniṣad I, 2, 20.

76. Cf. USG I, 43; BUBh I, 4, 10 (*Works* I, 676); this is a *pūrvapakṣa; śruti, yukti* etc. are repeatedly combined in *pūrvapakṣa* sections). As a matter of fact, appeals to the concordance or coordination of *śāstra/āgama* and *yukti/tarka* are not at all unusual in the philosophical literature of Śaṅkara's time and of the period prior to it. On the Buddhist side, they appear, e.g., in the works of the Madhyamaka commentators Bhāvaviveka (Bhavya) and Candrakīrti; cf. Sh. Iida, "Āgama (Scripture) and Yukti (Reason) in Bhāvaviveka"; in: *Kanakura kinenronbunshū* (Kanakura Festschrift). Tokyo, 1966, 79–96; also *Reason and Emptiness.* Tokyo, 1980, 105; 226f.; 231; Candrakīrti, *Prasannapadā* on *Madhyamakakārikā* I, 1 (ed. L. de La Vallée Poussin, 42: *yuktyāgamābhyām*); Dharmakīrti, *Pramāṇavārttika* I (Pramāṇasiddhi), 135. See also L. de La Vallée Poussin, "Dogmatique bouddhique. La négation de l'âme et la doctrine de l'acte." *Journal Asiatique* IX/20 (1902), 237–306; especially 253 f. (n. 3). On the Hindu side, see, e.g., Uddyotakara, *Nyāyavārttika* on NS I, 1, 14 (ed. V.P. Dvivedin, Calcutta 1914, 75), where the word *śāstra* (as juxtaposed with *yukti*) refers to the Sūtra text; also Maṇḍana, *Sphoṭasiddhi*, v. 36, where *āgama* refers to the tradition of grammatical philosophy. - Cf. in general *India and Europe*, ch. 15.

77. On Taittirīya Upaniṣad III, 10, 4 (*Works* I, 320): *kāpilakāṇādāditarkaśāstravirodha iti cet, na. teṣāṃ mūlābhāve vedavirodhe ca bhrāntatvopapatteḥ. śrutyupapattibhyāṃ ca siddham ātmano 'saṃsāritvam.*

78. BSBh I, 1, 1 (*Works* III, 6); cf. here also Manu XII, 106 (*vedaśāstrāvirodhinā tarkeṇa*) with commentaries.

79. Cf. US XVI, 65; XVIII, 88. - Cf. also *Vivekacūḍāmaṇi*, v. 474 ff., which is probably not authentic.

80. BSBh II, 2, 1 (*Works* III, 220).

81. See below, § 10.

82. BSBh II, 1, 6 (*Works* III, 188); cf. also *India and Europe*, ch. 15, § 19.

83. Cf. BSBh II, 1, 11: II, 2, 6; on Kaṭha Upaniṣad I, 2, 8 (*kevalena tarkeṇa, kevalābhir yuktibhiḥ*, etc.).

84. On Kaṭha Upaniṣad I, 2, 9 (*na-eṣā tarkeṇa matir āpaneyā*).

85. Cf. BUBh I, 4, 6 (*Works* I, 653): *tārkikais tu parityaktāgamabalair asti na-asti kartā-akartā-ityādi viruddhaṃ tarkayadbhir ākulīkṛtaḥ śāstrārthaḥ*; on the other hand, everything becomes clear to those who follow the sacred texts alone (*kevalaśāstrānusārin*) and who are without conceit (*śāntadarpa*).

86. Cf. on Kaṭha Upaniṣad I, 2, 8: *tarkyamāṇe 'ṇuparimāṇe kenacit sthāpita ātmani tato 'ṇutaram anyo 'bhyūhati, tato 'py 'ṇutaram iti na hi tarkasya niṣṭhā kvacid vidyate*; cf. also the problems and confusions concerning the self described in the commentary on Aitareya Upaniṣad II, 1, intr.

87. BSBh II, 1, 11: cf. also the attack against the "reasoners," BUBh II, 1, 20 (*Works* I, especially 743 ff.).

88. This *pūrvapakṣa* also quotes Manu XII, 105 f. (. . . *vedaśāstrāvirodhinā yas tarkeṇa-anusandhatte* . . .).

89. Cf. VP II, 484 (ed. W. Rau); Vṛtti on I, 30 and on I, 137/129 (I, 153, ed. W. Rau).

90. Cf. Bhāsarvajña, *NBhūṣ*, 393; also the expressions *śuṣkavāda, śuṣkavigraha*: Bhāgavatapurāṇa XI, 12, 20; 18, 30. Maitrī Upaniṣad VII, 8 has *vṛthātarka*; Jayanta, NM 4, uses *kṣudratarka*; NM, 109 also quotes Bhartṛhari, VP I, 34.

91. Cf., e.g., BSBh II, 1, 1 ff.; BUBh IV, 3, 22.

92. Cf. BUBh I, 1, intr. (*Works* I, 608).

93. Cf. BSBh II, 1, 1 ff.; among the philosophical systems, only Sāṃkhya and Yoga are commonly referred to as *smṛti*, but analogous questions are asked with reference to Vaiśeṣika and other systems.

94. Cf. BS I, 4, 1; I, 1, 18; 3, 3; on the other hand, *pradhāna* can also be called *smārta* (BSI, 2, 19). On the special role of the Sāṃkhya tradition, which combines some recognition of the Veda with an extensive use of reasoning, cf. BSBh II, 1, 12.

95. BSBh II, 1, 3 (*Works* III, 184); on the relation of *tarka* and *smṛti*, cf. also BSBh II, 1, 4.

96. Insofar, the coordination of *śruti, smṛti, nyāya* etc. in *dvandva* compounds does certainly not imply that they have the same weight or function at the same level; see above, n. 75 f.

97. Cf. BS I, 3, 28 with BSBh (*Works* III, 123: *pratyakṣaṃ śrutiḥ, prāmāṇyaṃ praty anapekṣatvāt. anumānaṃ smṛtiḥ, prāmāṇyaṃ prati sāpekṣatvāt*); cf. BSBh II, 1, 1, (*Works* III, 182): *vedasya hi nirapekṣaṃ svārthe prāmāṇyaṃ, raver iva rūpaviṣaye.*

98. Cf. BS I, 3, 28; III, 2, 24; IV 4, 20; cf. also the Mīmāṃsā use of *pramāṇa* in the sense of "standard of exegesis" and the list of six such exegetic *pramāṇas* (starting with *pratyakṣa* as direct and explicit scriptural statement).

99. Cf. BUBh I, 1, intr. (*Works* I, 608); II, 1, 20 (*Works* I, 734); II, 5, 15 (*Works* I, 775, where the expression *paṇḍitaṃmanya* refers to the Mīmāṃsakas).

100. BUBh I, 1, intr. (*Works* I, 608); in his commentary on MS I, 1, 5, Śabara uses primarily inference or hypothetical reasoning to establish the existence of the soul, but he refers also to Bṛhadāraṇyaka Upaniṣad IV, 3, 7; Kumārila says with reference to this section: *ity āha nāstikyanirākariṣṇur ātmāstitāṃ bhāṣyakṛd atra yuktyā* (ŚV, 515; the final verse of the *Ātmavāda* chapter). - See also below, n. 204.

101. BSBh III, 3, 53 (*Works* III, 424): *ita eva ca-ākṛṣya-ācāryeṇa śabarasvāminā pramāṇalakṣaṇe varṇitam* (followed by a reference to Upavarṣa). We cannot discuss here the implications which this passage may have concerning the original status and mutual relations of MS and BS; cf. A. Parpola, "On the Formation of the Mīmāṃsā and the Problems concerning Jaimini." *Wiener Zeitschrift für die Kunde Südasiens* 25 (1981), 145–177; specifically 153. Even if Śaṅkara assumed an original continuity of Pūrva- and Uttaramīmāṃsāsūtras, he found this unity and continuity abandoned by the later Pūrvamīmāṃsā commentators.

102. Cf. BUBh II, 1, 20 (*Works* I, 734): *tathā ca nyāyavidaḥ sāṃkhyamīmāṃsakādayo 'saṃsāriṇo 'bhāvaṃ yuktiśataiḥ pratipādayanti.* This statement corresponds to Śaṅkara's own view, although it does not appear in a *siddhānta* section.

103. A satisfactory systematic and historical analysis of this important and problematic concept has not yet been written.

104. Cf. his Vṛtti on VP I, 8, where the expression *arthavādarūpāṇi* is illustrated by a number of Upaniṣad quotes; the authenticity of this Vṛtti has been disputed.

105. Cf. TV, 80 (on I, 3, 2): *lokārthavādopaniṣatprasūta*; 81: *upaniṣadarthavādaprabhavatva* (v. l.: *upaniṣatprabhavatva*). See also TV, 12 (on I, 2, 7): *etena kratvarthakartṛpratipādanadvāreṇa-upaniṣadāṃ nairākaṅkṣyaṃ vyākhyātam*; Someśvara, NSudhā, 24 f., explains: *paralokaphaleṣu karmasu vināśidehādivyatiriktakartṛbhoktṛrūpātmajñānaṃ vinā pravṛttyanupapatteḥ*; Pashupatinath Shastri, *Introduction to the Pūrva Mīmāṃsa.* Varanasi, 1980, 115 ff.

106. Cf. *Vidhiviveka*, ed. M.L. Goswami. Benares, 1978, 199; *Brahmasiddhi*, ed. Kuppuswami Sastri. Madras, 1937, 74. In a corresponding passage of Prabhākara's *Bṛhati* (ed. Chinnaswami Sastri, fasc. 1, Benares 1929, ChSS, 18 f.), the Upaniṣads are not mentioned.

107. Cf., e.g., Maṇḍana, *Vidhiviveka*, 192: *vedānteṣu tāvad ātmatattvapratipattikartavyatā*; Vācaspati paraphrases in his *Nyāyakaṇikā*: *ātmā jñātavya iti hi pratipattir ātmani vidhīyate, tatparatvaṃ ca vedāntānām.* In

his following statements, Vācaspati analyses and critizes this view, first pointing out the threefold implication of *pratipatti* (*tisraḥ khalv imāḥ pratipattayaḥ sambhavanti, śrutamayī, cintāmayī, sākṣātkāravatī ca-iti*) and then the problems of correlating "injunction" and "liberation," which is not something "to be accomplished" (*sādhya*). The followers and commentators of Kumārila, e.g. Pārthasārathi, indicate more or less explicitly that the Upaniṣads should not be seen as amounting to mere arthavādas, but the relationship remains somewhat elusive; cf. *Śāstradīpikā*, ed. Laxman Shastri Dravid, Benares 1916 (ChSS), 372 ff.; also Someśvara, *NSudhā*, 24 f.

108. Cf. *Gītābhāṣya* XVIII, 66 (*Works* II, 295): *yathā-arthavādānāṃ vidhiśeṣāṇām*. . . ; BUBh I, 2, 5 (*Works* I, 697) paraphrases the word *praśaṃsā: na-apūrvārtho 'nyo 'sti*. The most conspicuous passage using the concept of *arthavāda* (or *stuti*) is BUBh IV, 4, 22 (*Works* I, 934 f.). Śaṅkara argues against Pūrvamīmāṃsā attempts to construe Vedic references to renunciation as arthavādas, and he insists that renunciation is enjoined by genuine vidhis, which are accompanied by arthavādas. What is accompanied by an arthavāda in such a manner cannot itself be a mere arthavāda; renunication (*pārivrājya*) is something to be practised, just as the new and full moon ceremony: *yadi pārivrājyam anuṣṭheyam api sad anyastutyartham syāt, darśapūrṇamāsādīnām apy anuṣṭheyānāṃ stutyarthatā syāt*. Śaṅkara's argumentation in this passage is obviously *ad hominem* and does not indicate an abandonment of his basic conviction that the message of the Veda has ultimately to be understood in terms of information, and not of injunction. - Cf. also YD, 16 ff., on vidhi and "renunciation."

109. Cf. BSBh I, 3, 33 (*Works* III, 138): *vidyamānavāda āśrayaṇīyo, na guṇavādaḥ*.

110. Cf. BSBh I, 1, 1–4; II, 1, 6; BUBh 1, 4, 7; US I, 12 ff.; *Gītābhāṣya* XVIII, 66.

111. See also the references to Sureśvara in § 15 (especially n. 195).

112. See below, n. 198.

113. Cf. BUBh IV, 3, 6 (*Works* I, 867); with specific reference to "analogous" (*sāmānyato dṛṣṭam*) inferential reasoning.

114. Cf. BSBh II, 1, 6 (*Works* III, 188): *rūpādyabhāvād dhi na-ayam arthaḥ pratyakṣasya gocaraḥ. liṅgādyabhāvāc na-anumānādinām*; cf. also BSBh I, 1, 2.

115. Cf. BUBh III, 3, intr. (*Works* I, 802): *na ca pramāṇāntaraviruddhārthaviṣaye śruteḥ prāmāṇyaṃ kalpyate yathā* (printed: *tathā*) *śīto 'gniḥ kledayati-iti*; similarly II, 1, 20 (*Works* I, 737): even more strongly *Gītābhāṣya* XVIII, 66 (*Works* II, 294 f.): *na hi śrutiśatam api śīto 'gnir aprakāśo vā-iti bruvat prāmāṇyam upaiti. yadi brūyāc chīto 'gnir aprakāśo vā-iti, tathā-apy arthāntaraṃ śruter vivakṣitaṃ kalpyaṃ, prāmāṇyānyathānupapatteḥ, na tu pramāṇāntaraviruddhaṃ svavacanaviruddhaṃ vā.* Śaṅkara's presentation of this matter may, of course, vary according to the dialectical situation and the opponent whom he addresses. See also Sureśvara, *Naiṣk.* III, 82 ff., for a concise statement on the "division of domains."

116. BSBh II, 1, 13 (*Works* III, 194); this *pūrvapakṣa* adds: *tarko 'pi svaviṣayād anyatra-apratiṣṭhitaḥ syāt.* Ultimately, the Veda is not one among other "means of knowledge," but transcends and supersedes all worldly *pramāṇas*.

117. Cf. Pārthasārathi, *Śāstradīpikā*, ed. Laxman Shastri Dravid. Benares, 1919 (ChSS), 312: *na ca-āgamena pratyakṣabādhaḥ sambhavati, pratyakṣasya śīghrapravṛttatvena sarvebhyo balīyastvāt.* - Cf. also US XVIII, 14 (*pūrvapakṣa*): *śrutānumānajanmānau sāmānyaviṣayau yataḥ / pratyayāv akṣajo 'vaśyaṃ viśeṣārtho nivārayet*; similarly: Vyāsa's Bhāṣya on Yogasūtra I, 49; also on I, 42 (and YSBhV, 103).

118. Cf. Madhusūdana Sarasvatī, *Advaitasiddhi*, ed. Anantakṛṣṇa Śāstrin. Bombay, 1917, 373 f.: *vyāvahārikaprāmāṇyamātram . . . na-advaitāgamena bādhyate,bādhyate tu tāttvikaṃ prāmāṇyam.*

119. Cf., e.g., BUBh I, 1, intr. (*Works* I, 609); BSBh III, 2, 3 (*Works* III, 344 f.; on *deśakālanimitta* and dreaming); also BUBh IV, 4, 22 (*Works* I, 934): *sādhyasādhanādisarvasaṃsāradharmavinirmukta.*

120. See below, ch. 9 (originally in: *Karma and Rebirth in Classical Indian Traditions*, ed. W.D. O'Flaherty. Berkeley, 1980, 268–302; ib., 299 f. with reference to BSBh III, 1, 1).

121. Cf. BUBh II, 1, 20 (*Works* I, 742 f.): *tasmāt puruṣamativaicitryam apekṣya sādhyasādhanasambandhaviśeṣān anekadhā-upadiśati. tatra puruṣāḥ svayam eva yathāruci sādhanaviśeṣeṣu pravartante, śāstraṃ tu savitṛpradīpādivad udāsta eva.* Śaṅkara's ideas are expanded and radicalized in such works as Ānandabodha's *Nyāyamakaranda.*

122. BSBh II, 1, 27 (*Works* III, 213); Śaṅkara adds that in the case of brahman the inadequacy of reason is even more obvious. - Concerning the incalculable variability of this world, see also Bhartṛhari, VP I, 32 f. (*avasthādeśakālānāṃ bhedād*).

123. BSBh II, 1, 15 (arguing against the *asatkāryavāda*); Śaṅkara has no notion of strictly deductive reasoning.

124. Cf. BSBh I, 1, 2 (*Works* III, 8), where Śaṅkara emphasizes that the Sūtra *janmādy asya yataḥ* should not be understood as an attempt to infer the existence of īśvara or brahman.

125. BSBh II, 2, 38 (*Works* III, 257).

126. Cf., e.g., BSBh I, 4, 27; IV, 4, 8.

127. Cf. BSBh II, 1, 13 f. (waves and ocean and other similes); also II, 1, 6, where the reference to "worldly experience" (*Works* III, 187: *dṛśyate hi loke . . .*) and its "examples" serves as a convenient dialectical device.

128. BSBh III, 3, 1 (*Works* III, 375); on the other hand, Śaṅkara emphasizes that the principle of contradiction cannot be used as a basis of questioning the authority of the Veda, and that it should not be applied in a narrow sense; cf. BSBh II, 1, 27.

129. US XVII, 9.

130. Cf. *The Problem of Two Truths in Buddhism and Vedānta*, ed. M. Sprung. Dordrecht, 1973.

131. See above, § 7.

132. BSBh I, 1, 2 (*Works* III, 8).

133. BSBh II, 1, 6 (*Works* III, 188 f.).

134. On the chronological hypotheses of P. Hacker and T. Vetter, see above, § 4 f.

135. BUBh II, 1, 20 (*Works* I, 738).

136. BUBh II, 1, 20 (*Works* I, 737).

137. BUBh IV, 3, 2 (*Works* I, 862); for a discussion of the conspicuous and significant term *ākhyāyikā*, see H. Brückner, "Śaṃkara's Use of the Term *ākhyāyikā* in His *Bṛhadāraṇyakopaniṣadbhāṣya*." *Proceedings of the Fifth World Sanskrit Conference* (Benares, 1981), 100–109.

138. BUBh II, 5 intr. (*Works* I, 770); Śaṅkara quotes NS I, 1, 39.

139. BUBh III, 1, intr. (*Works* I, 782).

140. BUBh IV, 5, intr. (*Works* I, 939). - BUBh IV, 3, intr. (*Works* I, 860 f.) states that in the preceding sections Janaka has first been instructed briefly by scriptural references, that then the four states of consciousness have been referred to, and that now an understanding has to be brought about—in the context of the Upaniṣad itself—by means of reasoning: *evam abhayaṃ pariprāpito janako yājñavalkyena-āgamataḥ saṃkṣepataḥ. atra ca jāgratsvapnasuṣupta-turīyāṇy upanyastāny. . . . idānīṃ jāgratsvapnādidvāreṇa-eva mahatā tarkeṇa vistarato 'dhigamaḥ kartavyaḥ.* IV, 3, 21 (*Works* I, 891) again presents the sacred texts as explicating and reinforcing authoritative statements by argumentation: . . . *ity āgamataḥ. iha tu tarkataḥ prapañcitaṃ darśitāgamārthapratyayadārḍhyāya.* See also *Padabhāṣya* on Kena Upaniṣad, intr. (*Works* I, 15) and II, 1 ff. (*Works* I, 25 f.; on the Upaniṣadic use of the form of the dialogue).

141. Cf. US XVIII, 3: *mātṛvac chrutir ādṛtā*; on Kaṭha Upaniṣad II, 1, 15: *mātṛpitṛsahasrebhyo 'pi hitaiṣiṇā vedena-upadiṣṭam ātmaikatvadarśanam.* Repeatedly, the Veda appears as the subject of "mental acts," i.e. intentions, assumptions, etc.; cf. on Chāndogya Upaniṣad VIII, 1, intr. (*Works* I, 566), which emphasizes the Upaniṣad's consideration for people of slow understanding (*mandabuddhi*) and concludes: *san-*

mārgasthās tāvad bhavantu, tataḥ śanaiḥ paramārthasad api grāhayiṣyāmi-iti manyate śrutiḥ. Various examples of this type are found in BUBh, e.g. I, 5, 17 (*Works* I, 706): *etasya-arthas tirohita iti manuvānā śrutir vyākhyānāya pravartate . . . pitur abhiprāyaṃ manvānā-ācaṣṭe śrutiḥ.* - See, on the other hand, Bhāsarvajña, *NBhūs*, 393: *vedas tv ājñāsiddhatvena-upadiṣṭaḥ pitrādivākyavat. na hy atra yuktyā kaścid arthaḥ pratipāditas . . .* - The doctrine of *apauruṣeyatva* leaves, of course, no room for Vedic "intentions" in a literal sense; cf. Maṇḍana, *Vidhiviveka*, v. 5: *apauruṣeye praiṣādir nṛdharmo na-avakalpate*; Sureśvara, *Sambandhavārttika*, v. 503 f.; 594 f. (on *abhiprāya* and the Veda).

142. Cf. *Gītābhāṣya* XVIII, 66 (*Works* II, 295); BUBh II, 1, 20 (*Works* I, 742 f.) - See also Sureśvara, *Taittirīyopaniṣadbhāṣyavarttika* II, 19 ff., specifically the metaphor of the "mother" in v. 23.

143. Cf. BUBh IV, 3, 6 (*Works* I, 867): inference and the daily activities of eating and drinking.

144. See above, n. 100; H. Brückner, *Beweisverfahren*, 27, calls the Nyāya quotes "schöne Funde."

145. Cf., e.g., Madhva, Bhāṣya on BS I, 1, 4, where the verse appears as a quote from a "Bṛhatsaṃhitā" (not Varāhamihira's work); Vidyāraṇya, *Vivaraṇaprameyasaṃgraha*, ed. Rāmaśāstrī Tailaṅga, Benares 1893, 2; 229 (cf. also the Pūrṇaprajña, i.e. Madhva chapter in Mādhava-Vidyāraṇya's *Sarvadarśanasaṃgraha*); Sadānanda, *Vedāntasāra*, § 184.

146. Cf. *Vedāntasāra*, § 185; 191. - *Upakrama* and *upasaṃhāra* together constitute *one* of the six "marks."

147. Cf. the use of the term *śruti* as one of the six exegetic criteria (*pramāṇa*) in Pūrvamīmāṃsā.

148. BUBh II, 5, intr.; the name of Bhartṛprapañca is mentioned by the commentator Ānandagiri.

149. On Padmapāda's treatment of this scheme, cf. P. Hacker, *Schüler Śaṅkaras*, 152. There is a similar scheme in Yoga (cf. *Yogabhāṣya* on Sūtra I, 48: *āgama, anumāna, dhyānābhyāsa*), which Vācaspati (*Tattvavaiśāradī*

on I, 48) identifies with *śravaṇa, manana, nididhyāsana*; cf. also YSBhV, 114.

150. See above, § 9; Śaṅkara does usually not include scriptural quotes in his argumentation against extra-Vedic groups; cf., e.g., BSBh II, 2, 18–36 (against Buddhists and Jainas); he may, of course, invoke the authority of Vedic revelation in a general sense when he is dealing with the "independent reasoning" of the Buddhists etc.; BSBh II, 2, 24 has one casual reference to the Taittirīya Upaniṣad.

151. See above, § 4 (on Śaṅkara's commentary on the Māṇḍūkya Upaniṣad and on Gauḍapāda's Kārikās).

152. Cf. *Schüler Śaṅkaras*, 74: "Reflexion darüber, daβ der Inhalt der Wörter und des Satzes wohlbegründet und das Gegenteil logisch unmöglich ist"; in another section (93 f.), Hacker emphasizes the affinity between this "logical method" and the distinction (*viveka*) between self and non-self.

153. Cf. *Rāmānuja's Vedārthasaṃgraha*. Poona, 1956, 63.

154. *A Thousand Teachings*, 53.

155. *A Thousand Teachings*, 52; 56; p. 66, n. 23 suggests that this method is only found in US XVIII. - Cf. also K.S. Murty, *Revelation and Reason in Advaita Vedānta*. Delhi, second ed., 1974, 152: "It was Śaṅkara himself who first gave rise to this type of tarka."

156. *A Thousand Teachings*, 57; 55.

157. Cf. *Studien*, 104 ff.

158. "*Anvaya* and *vyatireka* in Indian Grammar." *Adyar Library Bulletin* 31/32 (1967/68), 313–352.

159. "On Reasoning from *anvaya* and *vyatireka* in Early Advaita;" in: *Studies in Indian Philosophy*, Memorial Vol. Sukhlalji Sanghvi, ed. D. Malvania and N.J. Shah. Ahmedabad, 1981, 79–104; specifically 79; 87; 93; 96 f.

160. *Studien*, 104 ff.

161. Cf. Sureśvara's introduction to *Naiṣk.* IV, 22 (US XVIII, 96): *tasya ca yuṣmadasmad-vibhāgavijñānasya kā yuktir upāyabhāvaṃ pratipadyate*; also to IV, 23 (US XVIII, 97); *kathaṃ tau yuktir* . . . .

162. See also VS III, 2, 13: *aham iti pratyagātmani bhāvāt paratra-abhāvād arthāntarapratyakṣaḥ*. In Advaita Vedānta, the individual ego-sense has, of course, to be discarded; cf. Sureśvara, *Naiṣk.* III, 32, denying the *ahaṃdharma* in deep sleep (*suṣupta*).

163. USG II, 89 (ed. S. Mayeda, p. 210); the reading *caitanyamātram* which Mayeda gives in his critical apparatus seems to be preferable to the-*mātratvād* printed in the text. - See also *Gītābhāṣya* II, 16 (*Works* II, 14 f.) and below, ch. 6, n. 65: "being" (*sat*) in correlation with *avyabhicāra* and as irreducible ingredient of all cognition.

164. USG II, 93 (ed. S. Mayeda, p. 211); cf. 209 (p. 215): *advaitabhāvaś ca sarvapratyayabhedeṣv avyabhicārāt. pratyayabhedās tv avagatiṃ vyabhicaranti.* In these words of the "pupil," the usage of this "method" seems to be carried further than in any other text by Śaṅkara.

165. On Māṇḍūkya Upaniṣad VII (*Works* I, 187); apart from his Gauḍapāda commentary, *turīya* plays virtually no role in Śaṅkara's writings (but cf. US X, 4). *Anvayavyatireka* and *vyabhicāra*/*avyabhicāra* are combined in Sureśvara's *Taittirīyopaniṣadbhāṣyavārttika* II, 656.

166. On Praśna Upaniṣad VI, 2 (*Works* I, 133).

167. Cf. US XVIII, 98: *svayam eva-abravīc chāstraṃ pratyayāvagatī pṛthak*; in BUBh IV, 3, 2 (*Works* I, 862), Śaṅkara suggests that, in this section, the Veda itself may have chosen the *anumānamārga* in accordance with our ways of thinking.

168. Cf. BUBh IV, 3, 7 (especially *Works* I, 871 ff.); *vyabhicar* in the sense of "occurring without" is used on p. 872: *vyatiriktacaitanyāvabhāsyatvaṃ na vyabhicarati* (sc. *pradīpaḥ*); cf. IV, 3, 6 (*Works* I, 865): *anumānasya vyabhicāritvād.*

169. Cf. Śaṅkara, loc. cit., 869 f.; Śatapatha Brāhmaṇa V, 1, 2, 18; XII, 9, 2, 7; and more specifically Kaṭha Upaniṣad II, 3, 17: *taṃ* (sc. *puruṣaṃ*) *svāc charīrāt pravṛhen muñjād iva-iṣīkām*; Sureśvara, *Naiṣk.* III, 46; Vidyāraṇya, *Pañcadaśī* I, 42; on the Buddhist side, see Dīghanikāya II (*Sāmaññaphalasutta*), 86; Aśvaghoṣa, *Buddhacarita* XII, 64. The simile of the "bilva-fruit on the hand" (US XVIII, 180) appears also in the introduction to BUBh.

170. Cf. Chāndogya Upaniṣad V, 1, 6 ff.; a parallel version (with Brahmā instead of Prajāpati) is found in BU VI, 1, 7 ff.

171. Cf. Śabara on MS I, 1, 5; also Śaṅkara, BUBh IV, 3, 6.

172. See above, § 12 (references to VS III, 2, 9: *śabdavyatireka*).

173. Cf. Jayanta, NM, 226 ff.; in this section, Jayanta argues against the attempt to establish the authority of the medical tradition (*āyurveda*) in a purely empirical manner, i.e. based upon the "concurrent testimony of sense-perception etc." (*pratyakṣādisaṃvāda*), and to ascertain the causes and cures of diseases by means of "positive and negative concomitance" (*anvayavyatireka*) alone. Cf. also NM, 2 (*śāstra* and *anvayayavyatireka*); 139 ff. (relation between *śabda* and *anumāna*); Bhāsarvajña, *NBhūṣ*, 514 ff.; Vācaspati, *Tattvavaiśāradī* on Yogasūtra I, 24; Medhātithi on Manu II, 6 (ed. J.H. Dave, I. Bombay, 1972, 165); and specifically Abhinavagupta, *Tantrāloka* XXXV, 1 ff. (with commentary by Jayaratha; indebted to Bhartṛhari, VP I, 32; with Vṛtti). See also Muir I, 180 (Kullūka's quote from the Mahābhārata).

174. BSBh II, 1, 14 (*Works* III, 199).

175. Cf. Bhartṛhari, Vṛtti on VP 137/129 (=I, 153, ed. W. Rau): *sādharmyavaidharmya* and "dry reasoning" (*śuṣkatarka*). In Nyāya, *sādharmyavaidharmya* is specifically associated with the dialectical device called *jāti* (used in the sense of "sophistic rejoinder"); cf. NS I, 2, 18 and commentaries.

176. ŚV, 208 f. (v. 83; 85; in v. 83, *grāhakotpādaṃ* has to be substituted for *grāhakotpāda-*). The problematic half-verse 85 a (*-vinābhāvād*?) is missing in Śāntarakṣita's quote of this passage (TS, v. 2070 ff.). In most

cases, Kumārila uses *anvayavyatireka* with linguistic connotations; cf., e.g., ŚV, 357 (v. 25); 628 (v. 157). ŚV, 493 (v. 28 of the *Ātmavāda*) describes the *ātman/puruṣa* as *vyāvṛttyanugamātmaka*, i.e. as"continuing (persistent) in the discontinuities" (of the states of consciousness); this is refuted by Śāntarakṣita, TS, v. 222 ff. Cf. Śālikanātha, *Prakaraṇa-pañcikā*, ed. A. Subramanya Sastri. Benares, 1961, 85; *anvaya-vyatirekābhyāṃ hi vastvantaratvam avasīyate.*

177. ŚV, 202 (v. 52 f.); *tatra* refers to memories, dreams, etc.

178. TS, v. 2070 ff., Kamalaśīla paraphrases: *anvayavyatirekābhyām iti, grāhyagrāhakasmaraṇayor bhāvābhāvābhyām.* Cf. v. 1691 f. (on Caraka's concept of *yukti*).

179. BSBh II, 2, 28 (*Works* III, 248); II, 2, 30 (251).

180. Works III, 249. See also the references to the Buddhist analysis of consciousness, US XVIII, 141 ff.; however, the quote from Dharmakīrti in v. 142 seems to be an interpolation; cf. S. Mayeda, *A Thousand Teachings*, 200, n. 101 (the verse is not questioned by T. Vetter, *Studien*, 100). Yet a knowledge of Dharmakīrti may be assumed for US XVIII and BSBh II, 2, 28 ff. - *Anvayavyatireka* is also mentioned by Jayanta in his presentation and refutation of Vijñānavāda; cf. NM II, 106f.; 109; see also 13 (on materialism).

181. Cf., e.g., Dharmakīrti's *Nyāyabindu* or *Pramāṇavārttika* for numerous occurrences; more specifically, cf. Prajñākaragupta, *Pramāṇavārttikabhāṣya*, ed. R. Sāṅkṛtyāyana, Patna 1953, e.g. III, 428 f. (p. 295); III, 614 ff. (p. 344 ff.); also Y. Kajiyama, "Tripañcakacintā." *Miscellanea Indologica Kiotiensia* 4/5 (1963), 1–15.

182. Cf. *Naiṣk.* II, 8: *anvayavyatirekau ca tāv ṛte stāṃ kimāśrayau.*

183. For a survey of the US quotes in *Naiṣk.*, cf. US, crit. ed. S. Mayeda. Tokyo, 1973, 45 ff. Mayeda does not list the US quotes in Sureśvara's other works. US XVIII, 189 is quoted at least three times: Naiṣk. IV, 32; *Sambandhavārttika*, v. 207; and again *Bṛhadāraṇyakopaniṣadbhāṣya-vārttika* II, 4, 112 (Poona 1892–1894, Ānandāśrama Sanskrit Ser., p. 1051).

184. Cf., e.g., *Naiṣk.* III, 31.

185. Cf. II, 335; 656 f.; Śaṅkara himself does not refer to *anvayavyatireka* in his Bṛhadāraṇyaka and Taittirīya Upaniṣad commentaries. See also Sureśvara's interpretation of the example of the lost hand (US VI, 1) as *anvayavyatirekodāharaṇa* (Naiṣk. IV, 26); on *tārkika* (*kutārkika*) cf. *Taittirīyopaniṣadbhāṣyavārttika* I, 2; *Sambandhavārttika*, v. 2.

186. Cf. Naiṣk. III, 33 ff.

187. Naiṣk. III, 39, intr.

188. III, 33, intr.; cf. II, 8 (necessity of Vedic "support"); against this, see the *pūrvapakṣa* view in *Sambandhavārttika*, v. 441 ff., that *anvayavyatireka* alone is sufficient.

189. Cf. Naiṣk. III, 4.

190. Cf. Naiṣk. III, 5: 53; IV, 9; 18; see also *Taittirīyopaniṣadbhāṣyavārttika* III, 30; II, 656 f.

191. Cf. Naiṣk. III, 6 (with introduction); III, 113 ff.

192. Cf. Naiṣk. III, 34; also III, 6, intr. (on Sāṃkhya).

193. Cf. Naiṣk. III, 40, intr.; Ānandagiri on *Taittirīyopaniṣadbhāṣyavārttika* II, 656 f. (ed. Poona 1889, Ānandāśrama Sanskrit Ser., p. 175).

194. Cf. BUBh-Vārttika II, 4, 114: *anvayavyatirekataḥ niṣkṛṣya; Sambandhavārttika*, v. 810 ff.; 816 f.; and specifically v. 857 (on the essential distinction between "revealed" and "rational" knowledge of the self; cf. the pūrvapakṣa reference to the "states of consciousness," v. 441 f.).

195. Cf. v. 854 ff.; yukti cannot be the "cause of validity" or "validating factor" (*mānakāraṇa*) for the Vedic revelation.

196. Cf. *Pañcadaśī* I, 37 ff.; VII, 210 (anvayavyatireka as a method of understanding the "witness," *sākṣin*); Madhusūdana, *Siddhāntabindu*, ed. and trans. P. G. Divanji. Baroda, 1933, 70.

197. *Pañcapādikā*, ed. Rāmaśāstrī Bhāgavatācārya. Benares, 1891 (Vizianagram Sanskrit Ser.), 39; *yukti* is presented as a synonym (*paryāya*) of *tarka*. Cf. also Rāmānuja on BS II, 1, 4: *sarveṣām pramāṇānāṃ kvacit kvacit tarkānugṛhītānām eva-arthaviniścayahetutvam.*

198. *Pañcapādikā*, 93; cf. P. Hacker, *Schüler Śaṅkaras*, 152 ff.

199. *Studien*, 118; 122; cf. also 103 ff. (on US XVIII, 90–101). Vetter admits that the search for the meaning of *tvam* is already guided by its association with *tad*; cf. *Studien*, 107; 123.

200. *Studien*, 111.

201. Cf. BSBh I, 3, 34 (as cited in n. 205); see also below, ch. 8, § 8.

202. Cf. BSBh I, 1, 4 (*Works* III, 20): *nanv ātmā-ahaṃpratyayaviṣayatvād upaniṣatsv eva vijñāyata ity anupapannam. na, tatsākṣitvena pratyuktatvāt.*

203. Cf. on Aitareya Upaniṣad II, 1, intr.; especially *Works* I, 340: . . . *yena ca mantavya ātmā-ātmanā, yaś ca mantavya ātmā, tau dvau prasajyeyātām.* On the "tenth man," cf. the references given by S. Mayeda, *A Thousand Teachings*, 131, n. 2.

204. Cf. BUBh II, 5, 15 (*Works* I, 776); see also above, ch. 2, n. 60.

205. In this respect, Śaṅkara follows the basic principles of the Pūrvamīmāṃsā theory of *adhikāra*, cf. BSBh I, 3, 34, where the śūdras are excluded from the access to the Veda (especially *Works* III, 236: *sāmarthyam api na laukikaṃ kevalam adhikārakāraṇaṃ bhavati, śāstrīye 'rthe śāstrīyasya sāmarthyasya-apekṣitatvāt*).

206. See above, § 7 (n. 100; on BUBh I, 1, intr.; *Works* I, 608).

207. Śaṅkara does not develop the notion of the Veda as the self-manifestation of the Absolute in the manner of Bhartṛhari and the tradition of *śabdādvaita*; but see his somewhat casual remarks in BSBh I, 1, 3. Occasionally, Śaṅkara associates the idea of "grace" (*prasāda*) with the Veda; see, for instance, BUBh II, 1, 20 (*Works* I, 744), where he calls his opponents, the dialecticians, "devoid of the grace of the sacred texts and a teacher" (*śāstraguruprasādarahita*) and refers to the

idea that the truth is to be attained through choice and grace (*vara-prasādalabhyatva*).

208. Several studies dealing with reason and revelation in Śaṅkara came to my notice after the completion of the original version of this chapter (1982), among them the following ones: J. Taber, "Reason, Revelation and Idealism in Śaṅkara's Vedānta," *Journal of Indian Philosophy* 9 (1981), 283–307; A. Sharma, "Śaṅkara's Attitude to Scriptural Authority as Revealed in His Gloss on Brahmasūtra I, 1, 3," *Journal of Indian Philosophy* 10 (1982), 179–186; H. Brückner, "Revelation and Argumentation. Some References to the Relation of *śruti* and *tarka* in Śaṅkara's Bṛhadāraṇyakopaniṣadbhāṣya," in: *India and the West* (H. Goetz Memorial Vol.), ed. J. Deppert. Delhi, 1983, 209–220; A. Rambachan, "Śaṅkara's Rationale for *śruti* as the Definitive Source of *brahmajñāna*: A Refutation of Some Contemporary Views," *Philosophy East and West* 36 (1986), 25–40. These articles did not produce any results which would require a modification or even re-examination of my interpretation. In particular, A. Sharma's textual basis and philosophical perspective are far too narrow, and his references to the *tatpuruṣa* and *bahuvrīhi* interpretations of the expression *śāstrayoni(tva)* in BS I, 1, 3 are quite insufficient to account for this complex issue. The unpublished dissertation by B. H. Wilson, *Śaṅkara's Use of Scripture in His Philosophy* (University of Iowa, 1982) shows effort and dedication, but misrepresents the role of *anubhava* in Śaṅkara's thought.

209. See above, ch. 2.

CHAPTER 6

Śaṅkara, the Yoga of Patañjali, and the So-Called Yogasūtrabhāṣyavivaraṇa

Historical and Philological Introduction

1. The so-called *Yogasūtrabhāṣyavivaraṇa*, which is more properly called *Pātāñjalayogaśāstravivaraṇa*,[1] was published in 1952 as volume 94 of the Madras Government Oriental Series. Its editors, who worked on the basis of a single manuscript preserved in Madras, did not hesitate to recognize this work as a genuine work of the great Śaṅkara.[2] In a stimulating study, and taking an approach otherwise completely different from that of the editors, P. Hacker also accepted, at least hypothetically, the authenticity of the text, presenting it as an early work by Śaṅkara, who later on would have "converted" from Yoga to Advaita Vedānta.[3] Hacker tried to provide evidence from Śaṅkara's later writings that would indicate a thorough familiarity with, and possibly an early allegiance to, the Yoga tradition of Patañjali. Apart from these general doctrinal observations, his argumentation for the authenticity of the text is primarily based upon the fact that the colophons of the manuscript give Śaṅkarabhagavat (or Śaṅkarabhagavatpāda) as the author; the general significance of the appearance of this name instead of Śaṅkarācārya had been pointed out by Hacker in an earlier article.[4] Hacker did *not*, as T. Leggett claims, examine the authenticity of the text by applying "linguistic and ideological tests devised by himself."[5] By and large, the text of the *Yogasūtrabhāṣyavivaraṇa* and its doctrinal and commentarial peculiarities remain unexplored in Hacker's study.

Several years later, another leading Vedānta expert, H. Nakamura, agreed that the Vivaraṇa might indeed be a work by Śaṅkara himself, but he questioned Hacker's assumption that this would imply a "conversion" from Yoga to Vedānta.[6] S. Mayeda also tends to regard the text as authentic, although there is a certain vacillation in his statements.[7] T. Vetter, who follows Hacker's view, characterizes the Vivaraṇa as a work of little originality in his *Studien zur Lehre und Entwicklung Śaṅkaras.*[8] Other authors who have worked with the text also seem to accept its authenticity.[9]

However, neither the editors of the 1952 edition nor P. Hacker and his successors seem to have paid attention to the fact that a part of the text was already published in 1931 (in volume 6 of the Madras University Sanskrit Series), as an appendix to Maṇḍana's *Sphoṭasiddhi* with the commentary *Gopālikā* by Parameśvara, and that its editor, S. K. Rāmanātha Śāstrī, was not at all inclined to accept the Vivaraṇa as a work by the famous Śaṅkara, author of the *Brahmasūtrabhāṣya.* In his Sanskrit introduction to the edition, Rāmanātha Śāstrī deals not only with Parameśvara, the author of the *Gopālikā*, but also with several other authors by this name, all members of the Payyūr family of Kerala, which flourished in the fourteenth and fifteenth centuries. He refers to the fact that Parameśvara I, author of the commentary *Svaditaṅkaraṇī* on Vācaspati's *Nyāyakaṇikā* (itself a commentary on Maṇḍana's *Vidhiviveka*) and grandfather of the author of the *Gopālikā*, presents himself as a disciple of "Śaṅkarapūjyapāda" (*śaṅkarapūjyapādaśiṣya*[10]). From his consultation of the unpublished *Nītitattvāvirbhāvavyākhyā* by the author of the *Gopālikā* (i.e., Parameśvara II), Rāmanātha Śāstrī concludes that Śaṅkarapūjyapāda—one of several persons in the Payyūr family whose name was Śaṅkara—was not only the *vidyāguru*, but also the paternal uncle (*pitṛvya*) of Parameśvara I.[11] He suggests that this Śaṅkara is the author of the *Yogasūtrabhāṣyavivaraṇa: ayam eva śrīmacchaṅkarapūjyapādaḥ pātañjalayogabhāṣyavivaraṇakartā-iti asmākam abhyūhaḥ.*[12] He adds the *sphoṭa* section of the Vivaraṇa (i.e., pages 167–178 of the 1952 edition) as an appendix to his edition of the *Sphoṭasiddhi.* This section quotes and refutes a sequence of verses from Kumārila's *Ślokavārttika* that is also found in the *Sphoṭasiddhi.* The section of the *Gopālikā* by Parameśvara II that deals with these verses as presented by Maṇḍana may well have been written with a knowledge of the Vivaraṇa's treatment of this topic.[13] On the other hand, Parameśvara I is also credited with a commentary on Vācaspati's *Tattvabindu* that criticizes the *sphoṭa* theory.[14]

Rāmanātha Śāstrī did not notice that Parameśvara I actually

gives a number of quotes from the Vivaraṇa in the introductory portion of his *Svaditaṅkaraṇī*, where he deals with Vācaspati's benedictory verses.[15] No such Vivaraṇa quotes appear in the corresponding passages of the *Juṣadhvaṅkaraṇī*, Parameśvara's own earlier commentary on the *Nyāyakaṇikā*. The quotes in the *Svaditaṅkaraṇī* are highly conspicuous insofar as they constitute the earliest available references to this work, which seems to have been largely unknown outside of Kerala until a transcript was made in 1918/19 and subsequently deposited in the Government Oriental Manuscripts Library of Madras. This was again transcribed for the Adyar Library, from which Rāmanātha Śāstrī published his excerpt.[16] Based upon the information currently accessible to us we may say that there is no conclusive evidence why the quotes in the *Svaditaṅkaraṇī* could not have been taken from a work by that same Śaṅkara whom Parameśvara himself presents as his teacher later in this text. This would imply that the Vivaraṇa is a product of the (possibly earlier) fourteenth century. On the other hand, there is nothing in the form or contents of the Vivaraṇa that would exclude the possibility that it is a work by the author of the *Brahmasūtrabhāṣya*. On the contrary, there are numerous affinities between the Vivaraṇa and Śaṅkara's commentaries on the Brahmasūtras and the Bṛhadāraṇyaka Upaniṣad; these will be illustrated by our following observations. There is, of course, more than one explanation for such affinities; and they do certainly not constitute an adequate basis for Hacker's "conversion" thesis and for his assessment of the commentary on Gauḍapāda's Kārikās as a turning-point in Śaṅkara's development.

2. In general, quotes from or references to the Vivaraṇa are conspicuously absent where one would expect them if this were in fact a work by the great Śaṅkara of the period before or around A.D. 800, or if it had been widely known or recognized as such. It seems that there are no such references in the works of the greatest representative of the Sāṃkhya-Yoga renaissance, Vijñānabhikṣu, or of the great encyclopedic Vedāntins Appayadīkṣita and Madhusūdhana Sarasvatī,[17] who would be likely candidates to utilize a source of this kind in their attempts to establish a concordance or alliance of Vedānta and Sāṃkhya-Yoga. It is at least equally conspicuous that Vācaspatimiśra (ninth or tenth century), a Yoga commentator as well as a commentator on Śaṅkara's *Brahmasūtrabhāṣya* and in general a man of comprehensive learning, gives no indication whatsoever in his commentary *Tattvavaiśāradī* on Vyāsa's *Yogabhāṣya* that he is aware of this supposedly older commentary on the same text. On the other hand, the Vivaraṇa does not show any acquaintance with the Vaiśāradī, which would be surprising if this were in fact, as Rāmanātha Śāstrī suggests, a work written in the fourteenth century by the teacher of Parameśvara I; by this time, Vācaspati's reputation had obviously reached a high level in Kerala. The two commentaries differ considerably in character and orientation; moreover, they are based upon versions of the Yogabhāṣya that are often not identical, a fact which was already noticed by the editors of the Vivaraṇa. In some cases, Vācaspati and the author of the Vivaraṇa have different readings of the Sūtra text; II, 7 and II, 8 read *sukhānujanmā rāgaḥ* and *duḥkhānujanmā dveṣaḥ* in the Vivaraṇa instead of *sukhānuśayī rāgaḥ* and *duḥkhānuśayī dveṣaḥ* respectively in the Vaiśāradī. But unlike Vācaspati, the author of the Vivaraṇa is aware that there are alternative readings in this case, and he mentions them explicitly.[18] It should, however, be noted that Vācaspati's *Yogabhāṣya* text itself, just like that of this *Tattvavaiśāradī*, is not always well established and that it is not necessarily identical with the text, which is commonly and conventionally accepted in the modern printed editions.

The editors of the Vivaraṇa have listed many, but certainly not all significant Yogabhāṣya variants in the footnotes of their edition, and their system of notation is not consistent: In numerous instances, they print the "standard" text of the Yogabhāṣya as supposedly commented upon by Vācaspati and cite (or fail to cite) conspicuous Vivaraṇa variants in the footnotes; even more frequently, this procedure is reversed. The variants seem to be more frequent and significant in such complex and intricate sections as the discussion on *dharma/dharmin* and the "three times" past, present, and future (on III, 13–16). One example is the passage which reads *dharmānabhyadhiko dharmī* according to Vācaspati and the "standard" version, but *dharmābhyadhiko dharmī* according to the Vivaraṇa. In the interpretation of the Vivaraṇa, this is a reference to the view that the substance is something over and above its constituents (*dharmavyatirikta*), while according to Vācaspati it refers to the Buddhists.[19]

Very significant, at times crucial variants are found in the sections dealing with karma and rebirth, specifically on II, 13 and IV, 9. One of these important variants in the Bhāṣya on Sūtra II, 13 has not been cited by the editors, although it is crucial to the interpretation of the term *ekabhavika* and an adequate understanding of the mechanism of rebirth according to the Yogabhāṣya. In this case, the Vivaraṇa is based upon the reading *tatra-adṛṣṭajanmavedanīyasya niyatavipākasya-eva-ayaṃ niyamo*, while Vācaspati, as presented in the modern printed editions of the Yogabhāṣya and the Vaiśāradī, has *tatra dṛṣṭajanmavedanīyasya*; the reading of the Vivaraṇa, which seems to be clearly preferable in the context of the Yogabhāṣya, is again found in the version of the *Yogavārttika* by Vijñānabhikṣu.[20] Other variants in this section have been indicated by the editors, but they need not concern us here.[21] The *karman* sections of the fourth *pāda*, specifically on IV, 9, also contain significant and characteristic variants. According to the Vivaraṇa, the introductory statement has *vṛṣadaṃśavipākādayaḥ svakarmavyañjakāñjanāḥ*, while Vācaspati reads: *vṛṣadaṃśavipākodayaḥ svavyañjakāñjanābhivyaktaḥ*. In the following, the Vivaraṇa has *yathā-anubhavās tathā saṃskārāḥ, te ca vāsanānurūpāḥ*, instead of Vācaspati's *te ca karmavāsanānurūpāḥ*. There can be no doubt that these Vivaraṇa readings, too, deserve careful consideration; they may, in fact, allow for a more coherent interpretation of the karmic mechanism than Vācaspati's text.[22]

However, a further discussion of these and related problems is beyond the scope of this inquiry. Our primary purpose is to draw attention to such sections that are thematically related to other chapters in this volume and that have not yet been explored in the previous studies of the Vivaraṇa. This may also help to illustrate the philosophical rank and character of this work, whoever its author may have been. Specifically, we shall refer to the following problems: the attitude toward Kumārila in the Vivaraṇa; the evaluation of sacrificial *hiṃsā*; the assessment of the role of reason and of sacred, in particular Vedic texts; the argumentation against Buddhism and for the existence of an irreducible "witness" in this text, as compared to that in the Brahmasūtra and Bṛhadāraṇyaka Upaniṣad commentaries.

The Vivaraṇa and the Sacred Texts

3. By and large, the evidence for Śaṅkara's acquaintance with the works of Kumārila is surprisingly scarce; clearly identifiable references, if they exist at all, are very rare, as far as Śaṅkara's generally recognized works are concerned. However, the Yogasūtrabhāṣyavivaraṇa quotes and refutes Kumārila (without mentioning his name) extensively in a remarkable section on the *sphoṭa* theory.[23] First, it presents a sequence of verses from the *sphoṭa* chapter of the *Ślokavārttika*; this same sequence is also quoted and criticized in Maṇḍana's *Sphoṭasiddhi*.[24] Subsequently, it not only defends the *sphoṭa* theory against Kumārila's criticism, but also modifies and rephrases his verses in such a manner that they support the *sphoṭa* theory. The same section mentions the old Mīmāṃsā (and Vedānta) teacher Upavarṣa by name and adds a short quote that is, however, already found in Śabara.[25] It is well known that there is a discussion of the *sphoṭa* theory in Śaṅkara's *Brahmasūtrabhāṣya*, which also contains a quote from and references to Upavarṣa. However, this quote is not identical with Śabara's quote; in general, the treatment of the *sphoṭa* theory in the Brahmasūtrabhāṣya is different from that in the Vivaraṇa.[26] In addition to the *sphoṭavāda* quotes, the Vivaraṇa also contains one shorter quote from the *vākya* chapter of the Ślokavārttika.[27]

Concerning the problem of bloody rituals, i.e., of sacrificial hiṃsā, the author of the Vivaraṇa appears as an advocate of basic tenets of classical Sāṃkhya and Yoga that are explicitly criticized by Kumārila and that are equally incompatible with the views expressed in Śaṅkara's commentaries on the Brahmasūtras and the Chāndogya Upaniṣad.[28] He states that Vedic rituals may indeed have an "ambiguous causality" (*ubhayahetutva*), that is, produce demerit as well as merit, because they imply an element of harming (*pīḍā*). According to the Vivaraṇa, *hīṃsā* will produce bad *karman* even if it takes place "for the sake of sacrifice" (*kratvartha*): *kratvarthā-api satī hiṃsā-aniṣṭabhūtā-eva tadarthatāṃ pratipadyate*.[29] The correlation of helping with dharma and of hurting with adharma applies in all cases: *punaś ca tataḥ parānugrahaparapīḍanābhyāṃ dharmādharmau*.[30]

While in this respect the Vivaraṇa follows the basic attitude of the classical Sāṃkhya and Yoga texts, it is generally much more scripture-oriented than the *Yogabhāṣya* or even Vācaspati's *Tattvavaiśāradī*. Compared to these texts, it exhibits a conspicuous tendency to invoke the Upaniṣads, specifically the Bṛhadāraṇyaka and the Chāndogya Upaniṣad, as well as the Bhagavadgītā. The distribution of Vedic quotes is somewhat uneven. While there are long portions without Vedic quotes or references, they appear in unusual concentration in such sections as the lengthy discussion on the existence of the "Lord" (*īśvara*; on Sūtra I, 25 ff.).

Although Vyāsa's Yogabhāṣya does contain several references to Upaniṣadic statements,[31] it never invokes the Upaniṣads explicitly as sources of authority or validation. It does not dwell upon the problem of the authority of the Veda, nor does it seem concerned about avoiding conflicts with the Vedic revelation. Vācaspati invokes the Upaniṣads occasionally, specifically the Śvetāśvatara Upaniṣad, which is traditionally associated with Sāṃkhya and Yoga.[32] He does not show the Vivaraṇa's predilection for the Bṛhadāraṇyaka and the Chāndogya Upaniṣad, which are, of course, Śaṅkara's favorite Upaniṣads. In general, scriptural references are much less conspicuous and significant in the *Tattvavaiśāradī* than in the *Yogasūtrabhāṣyavivaraṇa*.[33]

In addition to its Upaniṣadic references, the Vivaraṇa also presents some theoretical considerations concerning the authority and the metaphysical status of the sacred texts, or more specifically its dependence on and inherence in the omniscience and pure "goodness" (*sattva*) of the "Lord." Although this proceeds from commentarial observations, it goes far beyond the explicit statements of Vyāsa's Bhāṣya.[34] In general, the Vivaraṇa seems to associate the terms *śāstra* and *āgama* more closely with the Veda, specifically the Upaniṣads, than the Bhāṣya does; it paraphrases, e.g., Vyāsa's expression *mokṣaśāstrādhyayana* as *upaniṣadādyadhyayana*.[35]—The discussion of karma and rebirth is much more scripture-oriented in the Vivaraṇa than in the Bhāṣya; there is a conspicuous concern that there should be no conflict with śruti and smṛti, and that these matters should be explicated in such a manner that there is no "infuriation of all sacred texts" (*sarvaśāstraviprakopa*) and, moreover, no "uselessness of the texts on ritual works" (*karmaśāstrānarthakya*).[36] In general, the Vivaraṇa is less susceptible than the Bhāṣya to the kind of criticism Śaṅkara raises against Sāṃkhya and Yoga in his commentary on Brahmasūtra II, 1, 1 ff. On the other hand, there is no such attempt to distinguish the absolute, self-sufficient authority of the Veda from the conditional, limited authority of the *smṛti* texts as we find it in the *Brahmasūtrabhāṣya*;[37] and the authoritative Yoga texts, etc., are listed side by side with the Veda itself.[38]

The Vivaraṇa also argues in terms of a concordance of reasoning or inference (*anumāna*) and authoritative texts (*āgama*).[39] Concerning the exegesis of the sacred texts, it employs the Mīmāṃsā concepts of *vidhi, pratiṣedha, stuti/arthavāda*, etc., but it rejects, in a manner clearly reminiscent of what we find in various passages in Śaṅkara's "classical" works,[40] the Mīmāṃsā attempt to reduce scriptural statements concerning the existence of the "Lord" to merely auxiliary statements, "praises" (*stuti*), supplements to instructions on ritual performances or to "meditational injunctions" (*upāsanāvidhi*).[41] Still in the context of Sāṃkhya and Yoga, and without identifying meditational activities as "works" (*karman*), the Vivaraṇa advocates "knowledge" (*jñāna*), which it identifies with "detachment" (*vairāgya*) and which it contrasts with "works"; it associates final liberation with knowledge alone.[42]

The Vivaraṇa and Buddhism

4. Among the most remarkable features of the Vivaraṇa is its vigorous and elaborate criticism of Buddhism, specifically of Vijñānavāda. While the Yogabhāṣya contains some critical references to the Buddhist theories of "consciousness only," momentariness, etc., it does not present any broad and comprehensive criticism of Buddhist thought. In general, it remains open and indebted to Buddhist influences.[43] Here again, the so-called Yogasūtrabhāṣyavivaraṇa shows an obvious affinity with what we know from Śaṅkara's commentaries on the Brahmasūtras and the Bṛhadāraṇyaka Upaniṣad.

The status of the Buddha as a teacher and the problems resulting from the plurality of Buddhas are discussed in the context of the long chapter on the "Lord" (*īśvara*), which is one of the most conspicuous sections of the whole work.[44] Buddhist concepts and doctrines—the identification of the mind with its ideas, the denial of a subject or witness of experience, the theory of momentariness, the Vijñānavāda denial of material things, problems concerning the relationship between ideas and objects—are then discussed in the commentary on Sūtra I, 32 and in several subsequent sections, specifically in the fourth pāda.[45]

The section on I, 32 focuses on the necessity of an identical, unifying subject of awareness, in order to account for the possibility of mental discipline and concentration as well as for the facts of daily life and experience. The subject cannot simply coincide with a "stream" of momentary data of awareness, with mere consciousness understood as a continuous flux.[46]

As stated earlier, the author of the Vivaraṇa argues specifically against the Yogācāra-Vijñānavāda school of Buddhism. On Sūtra IV, 14, the Vijñānavāda arguments for the nonexistence of the material world and the exclusive existence of consciousness are presented, including the dream argument and the "rule of co-apprehension" (*sahopalambhaniyama*). However, the term *sahopalambhaniyama*, which Śaṅkara uses in the *Brahmasūtrabhāṣya*, apparently after becoming aware of Dharmakīrti's *Pramāṇaviniścaya*, does not occur in this passage.[47]

Explicating Vyāsa's formulation *na-asty artho vijñānavisahacaraḥ* the Vivaraṇa states the Vijñānavāda position as follows: *tasmād artho vijñānavyatirekeṇa na-asti-iti pratijānīmahe, pramāṇam apy atra bhavati, vijñānavyatirekeṇa na-asti grāhyaṃ vastu, vijñānavyatirekeṇa-anupalabhyamānatvāt, vijñānasvarūpavat.*[48] Against this, the Vivaraṇa first presents a soteriological *prasaṅga*: If being an object of awareness (*upalabhyamānatva*) coincides with mere appearance (i.e., with illusory existence), then awareness itself, as it is also an object of apprehension, would be unreal, and there would be no subject of awareness. Whose would be liberation? How could there be separation from anything? How would bondage and liberation be possible?[49] Various other arguments follow that seem to be worth mentioning: The thesis that there is no object apart from consciousness is simply contradicted by perception. Consciousness is perceiving, that is, illuminating (*avabhāsaka*); the object has to be illuminated (*avabhāsanīya*). These are essentially different attributes that cannot belong to one and the same substratum. Object and cognition are being "grasped" (i.e., understood) as essentially different, and there can be no suspicion of inseparability; the reason claimed by the Vijñānavādin is invalid.[50]

The Vijñānavādin refutes himself when he argues against others: How can he deny the existence of him against whom he tries to establish his position? If, however, the opponent exists as distinct from the Vijñānavādin's consciousness, then the existence of pots, etc. is also established.[51] Moreover, followers of this doctrine could not legitimately converse with one another, by instructing disciples, etc.;[52] in general, the whole realm of daily activities (*vyavahāra*) could not be accounted for by this and similar views; a "breakdown of *vyavahāra*" (*vyavahāravilopa*) would result.[53]

Even in dreams, consciousness is not really without extramental support, since it relates to objects that *have been* perceived: *svapnajñānam api upalabdhārthaviṣayatvāt na nirālambanam.*[54] This is a point already emphasized in the *Nirālambanavāda* section of Kumārila's *Ślokavārttika.*[55] In general, the anti-Buddhist argumentation in the Vivaraṇa is obviously indebted to Kumārila; yet it can by no means be reduced to what is already found in the Ślokavārttika, and it remains characteristically different in style and substance.

The author of the Vivaraṇa supplements his arguments against Vijñānavāda with others, which apply also to similar and affiliated standpoints, specifically the theory that, although objects may have an existence apart from consciousness, they arise and disappear simultaneously with acts of awareness, since whatever exists must have a relation to experience: *evaṃ ghaṭādir artho 'pi vijñānasamānasamayajanmavināśa eva, bhogyatvāt iti.*[56] Here, no less than in the case of strict Vijñānavāda, the author of the Vivaraṇa sees a denial of the "commonness" (*sādhāraṇatva*) of objects, that is, their accessibility to different subjects, and, moreover, the loss of their identity and continuity in the temporality of one's own consciousness. In general, we find here a sharp critical sense of problems concerning the temporal constitution of acts and contents of awareness. In the context of past, present, and future, where past phenomena may be objects of present acts of awareness, etc., the object cannot just coincide, or be strictly synchronous, with the apprehending or intending act: *tasmāt idānīntano 'rtho na-idānīntanajñānasahabhūr eva-iti, grāhyatvāt, atītārthavat, atīto vā na-atītajñānasahanāśajanmā, grāhyatvāt, idānīntanārthavat. bhūtabhavisyajjñānagrāhyā arthā adhunā-api santi, grāhyatvāt, adhunātanapratyayagrāhyavat, idānīntanam api vastu purvottarakṣaṇeṣu tathā-eva.*[57]

5. Enlarging upon a remark made in the Yogabhāṣya, the Vivaraṇa presents the Vijñānavādins as deserving compassion, as their minds are subject to a basic karmic defect. The materialists and Śūnyavādins, on the other hand, do not deserve such compassion, as they are only bent upon deceiving people: *kevalajagadvañcanārtha-*

pravṛttatvāt tu na-eteṣv anukampā kartavyā.[58] According to the Vivaraṇa, the Vaiśeṣikas and others are also subject to a fundamental confusion, insofar as they see consciousness (*caitanya*) as a mere attribute of the self, to be eliminated in the state of release. But unlike the Buddhist "destructionists," they accept at least a stable, identical subject or substratum: *vaināśikebhyas tv ayaṃ viśeṣaḥ-sthiram ekaṃ dharmiṇam icchanti-iti.*[59]

Whatever the specific target of argumentation or criticism may be, the Vivaraṇa tries to establish the identity and distinctness of the conscious, "witnessing" self (*puruṣa, ātman*) against everything that is merely "visible" (*dṛśya*), and occurs as objective content (*pratyaya*) of awareness; the illuminator (*prakāśaka*) has to be distinguished from what is to be illuminated (*prakāśya*), the perceiver (*grāhaka*) from the perceived or perceivable (*grāhya*). This is obviously in accordance with the Sāṃkhya-Yoga dualism of *puruṣa* and *pradhāna*,[60] where the objective "nature" (*pradhāna* or *prakṛti*) includes the objectifiable processes of the mental sphere (*citta*). But the Vivaraṇa goes beyond what one would expect in a Yoga text, and the style of argumentation is again reminiscent of what we find in Śaṅkara's "classical" works, such as the anti-Buddhist passages in the commentaries on the Brahmasūtras and the Bṛhadāraṇyaka Upaniṣad. On the other hand, dualistic implications are not always avoided in these "classical" texts, where the distinctness and internal unity of the *ātman* often seems to be a more serious and direct concern than the ultimate nonduality of all reality.

Among the relevant peculiarities of the Vivaraṇa argumentation, we may mention, for example, its references to the metaphor of the lamp (*pradīpa*) and its constant and conspicuous usage of the terms *vyatireka* and *vyatirikta*, as occurring in such compounds as *vijñānavyatireka, cittavyatirikta, vyatiriktagrāhyatva, viṣayavyatirikta, vyatiriktapuruṣa, vyatiriktadṛśyatva.*[61] Some of this refers to the separability of external objects from actual empirical awareness; but in most cases, it is the distinctness and absoluteness of the witnessing self that is at stake. There is no exception to the rule that whatever is "given" or perceived, must be given to, perceived by a distinct, nonobjectifiable subject or witness: *na tu vyatiriktagrāhyatvaṃ vyabhicarati.*[62] While physical objects may exist without "empirical" acts or states of consciousness, i.e., without the *vijñāna* of Vijñānavāda or the *citta* of Yoga, neither physical objects nor acts of consciousness, mental states, or "perceptions" (*pratyaya*)[63] can be "graspable" or "visible" (*grāhya, dṛśya*) without a separate witnessing subject.

Already in the second pāda, we find a remarkable attempt to infer the existence of an irreducible "seer" or "witness" from the "visibility" (*dṛśyatva*) of whatever can be "seen"; it is based upon the premise that whatever appears as an objectifiable datum can do so only by reflecting a "light" that is not its own. The relationship between objects and sources of manifestation is pursued through different stages up to the ultimate source of light and awareness, the puruṣa or ātman. Visible external objects, such as pots, etc., as well as the "lights" (*āloka*) which illumine these objects, and the "perceptions" (*pratyaya*) which in turn illumine (i.e., let appear in cognition) these lights and all other objects: all this requires, in order to be "visible," visibility for and manifestation by an essentially different principle: *etat tu tadastitvānumānam. katham? ghaṭādīnāṃ dṛśyānāṃ svarūpavyatiriktena-anyena dṛśyatvadarśanāt, tatprakāśakānāṃ ca-ālokānāṃ vyatiriktadṛśyatvāt, sarvārthāvabhāsakānām api pratyayānāṃ svarūpavyatiriktadṛśyatvam avagamyate, ghaṭāditadālokādivad iti.*[64] The basic conditions of "visibility" or objectivity are the same in the case of external objects like pots and "inner" data, that is, perceptions; external objects are valid inferential "examples" for the latter.

The "proof" for the existence of a witnessing subject is certainly not meant to disprove or question the existence of the objects. What is denied to the objects is not their independent existence, but their independent manifestness. However, this hierarchy of objects and factors of manifestation also has ontological connotations. The objects of manifestation may change; the "lower" levels of manifestation may turn out to be dependent on higher manifestors: What is indispensable, irreducible and constantly present in this structure of appearance is the witness. The witness or spirit (*puruṣa*) is unchanging (*apariṇāmin*) and does not "deviate" from any given content of awareness. The contents may change; the puruṣa does not, and this establishes his separate existence: *tadavyabhicāreṇa-eva puruṣasya vyatiriktatvasiddhiḥ.*[65]

There is an obvious connection with the *anvayavyatireka* "method" introduced in the *Upadeśasāhasrī*, although the term itself is not used in this context.[66] Even more significant is the affinity with Śaṅkara's interpretation of Bṛhadāraṇyaka Upaniṣad IV, 3, 1 ff., which describes the successive elimination of "lights" up to the ultimate source of light and witnesshood, the pure ātman.[67] And it is in Śaṅkara's commentary on this passage (specifically on IV, 3, 7) that we find some of the most striking correspondences to the argumentation of the Vivaraṇa. We referred earlier to the following statement in the Vivaraṇa: *na tu vyatiriktagrāhyatvaṃ vyabhicarati, pradīpayor dṛśyatvād ghaṭādivat. etena vyatiriktagrāhyatvaṃ jñānasya dṛśyatvāt pradīpādivat siddhaṃ bhavati.*[68] On Bṛhadāraṇyaka Upaniṣad IV, 3, 7, Śaṅkara says: *yady api pradīpo 'nyasya-avabhāsakaḥ svayamavabhāsātmakatvāt tathā-api vyatiriktacaitanyāvabhāsyatvaṃ na vyabhicarati, ghaṭādivad eva. yadā ca-evaṃ, tadā vyatiriktāvabhāsyatvaṃ tāvad avaśyambhāvi.*[69]

There are remarkable analogies also in the manner in which common sense and daily life (*vyavahāra*) are invoked against Vijñānavāda, which is depicted as entailing a "breakdown of *vyavahāra*." The Vivaraṇa uses the expression *vyavahāravilopa*, the commentary on the Bṛhadāraṇyaka Upaniṣad *sarvasaṃvyavahāralopa*; both refer specifically to the impossibility of accounting for the activities of debate, etc., in terms of the "consciousness-only" theory.[70] The readiness to rely on common sense and vyavahāra is, of course, also a striking feature of Śaṅkara's argumentation against Vijñānavāda in his Brahmasūtra commentary (II, 2, 28ff.).

Implications for the Conversion Theory

6. All this is conspicuously different from the treatment of Vijñānavāda and Buddhism in general in the commentary on Gauḍapāda's Kārikās (specifically IV, 24ff.). It throws suspicion on Hacker's assessment of this work as a transitional work between the *Yogasūtrabhāṣyavivaraṇa* and Śaṅkara's "mature" works, such as his commentaries on the Brahmasūtras and the Bṛhadāraṇyaka Upaniṣad. In several significant respects, the Vivaraṇa is closer to these works than the commentary on Gauḍapāda but, as noted before, such affinities are open to different interpretations.

Both P. Hacker and T. Vetter suggest that in the course of his development Śaṅkara turned away from an early indebtedness to Buddhist ideas. Vetter states that Śaṅkara's anti-Buddhist polemics in his Brahmasūtra commentary might be an attempt to disassociate himself from something he himself wrote earlier, in his commentary on Gauḍapāda.[71] Hacker maintains that, in his commentary on the Bṛhadāraṇyaka Upaniṣad, Śaṅkara turned against a "Buddhist" theory he had previously accepted: the theory of the apparent disintegration of pure consciousness into subject and object.[72] But the argumentation is just as vigorous in the Vivaraṇa as it is in the Bṛhadāraṇyaka Upaniṣad commentary. In a recent article, F. Whaling claims that "Hacker has shown by literary analysis" that in his early days Śaṅkara was "much closer to Buddhism than he was later when he wrote the commentary on the Vedānta Sūtras."[73] Trying to elaborate Hacker's thesis further, Whaling speculates on an "early Vijñānavāda phase" in Śaṅkara's thought, and he finds a "Buddhist Gauḍapāda phase" in his "commentaries on the Māṇḍukya Upaniṣad and Kārikās, his commentary on the Taittirīya Upaniṣad, and parts of the Upadeśasāhasrī, and also possibly in his commentary on Vyāsa's commentary on the Yoga Sūtras."[74] Whaling has obviously not paid any attention to the anti-Buddhist passages of the Vivaraṇa, and his statements are definitely less cautious than those of Hacker and Vetter.

There is nothing in the Vivaraṇa passages under discussion that would exclude Śaṅkara's authorship. As we have seen, they correspond to and supplement what we find also in his "mature," "classical" works. Of course, there are also statements in the Vivaraṇa that would not be acceptable in the context of these works. Basic teachings of Sāṃkhya and Yoga, which are expressly rejected in Śaṅkara's Advaita Vedānta works, are simply taken for granted in the Vivaraṇa, for example, the existence of "primal matter" (*pradhāna*) and the plurality of "selves" or "spirits" (*puruṣa*). However, the Vivaraṇa does not give any prominence to Sāṃkhya and Yoga teachings incompatible with Advaita Vedānta. Apart from strictly commentarial statements,[75] "primal matter" and the plurality of selves do not play a significant role.

Other themes lead the author of the Vivaraṇa to long digressions and far beyond the text on which he comments: for instance, problems of awareness; the search for the pure, irreducible subject or witness; the critique of Buddhist teachings; the existence of a supreme, omniscient "Lord" (īśvara). Moreover, the tendency to rely on the Upaniṣads and a conspicuous allegiance to the Vedic tradition are peculiar and untypical features of this "Yoga" text.

Whether it is by Śaṅkara or not, there is lively, intellectually stimulating argumentation in the Vivaraṇa, and its author demonstrates a remarkable level of philosophical reflection and considerable dialectical skills.[76] In particular, there is nothing stereotypical or scholastic in the argumentation against Buddhism, although there is, of course, some misunderstanding or misrepresentation of specific Buddhist teachings. Buddhism is taken as a fresh, living challenge to be dealt with in direct and problem-oriented argumentation. The Vivaraṇa does not attempt an explicit coordination or reconciliation of "reason" and "revelation"; nor does it try to find "reason" in "revelation." But rational argumentation and reliance on authoritative, specifically Vedic, instruction often appear side by side and in factual coordination or combination.[77]

All this would indicate a remarkable degree of "originality" if it were certain that the Vivaraṇa is by the young and developing Śaṅkara himself and not by a much later author who would be indebted to and borrowing from the works of the "mature" Śaṅkara.

The Vivaraṇa, Vācaspati, and the Traditions of Kerala

7. It has not been the purpose of this chapter to solve the problem of the authorship of the so-called Yogasūtrabhāṣyavivaraṇa or to refute Hacker's hypothetical reconstruction of Śaṅkara's development. However, a few final considerations concerning this matter seem appropriate. As noted earlier, Hacker's authenticity thesis is, apart from more general and obviously inconclusive observations concerning Śaṅkara's familiarity with Yoga teachings, primarily based upon the fact that the colophons present Śaṅkarabhagavat and not Śaṅkarācārya as the author of the Vivaraṇa. Hacker himself recognizes that this alone is not a sufficient criterion of authenticity.[78] It is furthermore evident that his stimulating investigations have to be supplemented by a broader sampling of texts and manuscripts, which may be based upon numerous new manuscript catalogues not available to him. Among the cases not considered by Hacker is the commentary *Jayamaṅgalā* on Īśvarakṛṣṇa's *Sāṃkhyakārikā*. According to the colophons, this is also by Śaṅkarabhagavat, and just as the Vivaraṇa, it was preserved, and probably composed, in Kerala.[79]

Readers of this work will hardly feel tempted to attribute it to the author of the *Brahmasūtrabhāṣya*, or, on the other hand, to the author of the *Yogasūtrabhāṣyavivaraṇa*.[80] In Kerala, the name Śaṅkara has apparently been more common than elsewhere.[81] One might suspect that, if there was a confusion of authors, it was not so much a matter of confusing the author of the Brahmasūtrabhāṣya with the institutionalized Śaṅkarācāryas, but rather with other authors whose name was Śaṅkara. Several "Yoga" works, e.g. the *Yogatārāvalī*,[82] are, of course, traditionally ascribed to "Śaṅkarācārya."

It seems obvious that the Vivaraṇa had a special and possibly unique relationship with Kerala; it is here where the text was preserved and, at least to a certain extent, studied. Even if the Vivaraṇa should be by the author of the Brahmasūtrabhāṣya, it would still be true that it did not have any significant impact outside Kerala. This would obviously constitute a conspicuous and probably exceptional case among the writings of the great Śaṅkara. May we accept the Indian tradition that Śaṅkara came from Kerala, and may we speculate that the Vivaraṇa, a youthful work of his,[83] found a certain recognition only in his homeland, while the fame of his other works spread all over India?

A merely regional impact would, however, be more normal for a work produced by a member or affiliate of the Payyūr family, such as Śaṅkara, the teacher and possibly uncle of Parameśvara I. In this case, it would also be unnecessary to dismiss the final verse of the text, which pays respect to the "venerable original Śaṅkara," as an addition made by a scribe or eager disciple.[84] If the author of the Vivaraṇa was not identical with the author of the Brahmasūtra and Bṛhadāraṇyaka Upaniṣad commentaries, he was certainly familiar with these works and indebted to their author. In general, medieval Kerala was rich in local and somewhat parochial traditions of learning, which remained virtually unknown in the rest of India. The extraordinary contributions to mathematics and astronomy in medieval Kerala, which had no impact upon the development of these sciences in other parts of India, illustrate this insularity.[85] In Mīmāṃsā and other branches of traditional learning and literature, the members and affiliates of the Payyūr family made significant contributions that remained unknown outside of Kerala.[86]

Yet the assignment of the Vivaraṇa to such a late date as the fourteenth century is far from satisfactory. The style of the argumentation against Buddhism, the fact that Kumārila is the latest author explicitly referred to, and, more specifically, the absence of any identifiable reference to Vācaspatimiśra could easily be invoked as arguments for an earlier date.[87] How much earlier? Are there criteria that would allow us to come to a definitive chronological conclusion, even if we cannot resolve the authorship problem?

8. In a recent study of the Vivaraṇa, which contains numerous significant philological observations and which has already been referred to, A. Wezler agrees that the question of the authorship of the Vivaraṇa or, more specifically, the question whether its author is identical with the author of the *Brahmasūtrabhāṣya*, has to remain unanswered for the time being.[88] Nevertheless, so he argues, it can be determined that the Vivaraṇa must be considerably older than Vācaspati's *Tattvavaiśāradī*. He asserts that "the text of the Bhāṣya as known to Vācaspatimiśra shows clear vestiges of an influence exercised on it by the Vivaraṇa."[89] In support of his thesis, he cites several variant readings in the Yogabhāṣya texts on Sūtra I, 5 and II, 32. According to Wezler, the statement *kliṣṭapravāhapatitā apy akliṣṭāḥ* in the section on I, 5 was added to the Yogabhāṣya text under the influence of the Vivaraṇa's explication of the section. In his view, it is not only the fact that the Vivaraṇa does not cite this statement, but also the context of the Yogabhāṣya itself which suggests its spuriousness. He finds its contents "but repeated by the following phrase, viz. *kliṣṭacchidreṣv apy akliṣṭā bhavanti*," and he sees a "striking discrepancy as regards the image, i.e. *pravāha* (*patita*) on the one hand and *chidra* on the other, that can hardly be accounted for convincingly."[90] But the idea and imagery of a "gap in a series" or "succession" of (temporal) phenomena, or of an interruption in the "flow" of mental modes, is certainly not unnatural in the context of classical Yoga thought. The conjunction of *chidra* and *pravāha* appears again in the Bhāṣya on Sūtra IV, 27, which introduces the word *chidra*.[91] The issue of redundancy is more serious. But the statement starting with *kliṣṭacchidreṣu* is certainly not merely repetitious; it explains and justifies what has been said before in a more general sense. It would, however, not be repetitious at all if, in accordance with a possibility considered by Wezler himself, the preceding sentence could be read as implying a question or objection. If the author of the Vivaraṇa, unlike Vācaspati and other commentators, should have taken it in this sense, his following *tasmād āha* would be less problematic insofar as it could be understood as introducing Vyāsa's response to this question or objection, which the Vivaraṇa has paraphrased in detail although without quoting the exact wording in which it was presented in the Bhāṣya.[92] In general, it is evidently impossible to reconstruct a complete text of the Yogabhāṣya from the Vivaraṇa, which does not always quote the text on which it comments in its entirely.

It may certainly be granted that the phrase *kliṣṭapravāhapatitā* . . . , together with the Vivaraṇa's failure to cite it, raises legitimate questions; and the idea of a later interpolation may indeed "suggest itself."[93] Yet, this alone is not enough for a strong and compelling argument; further evidence, at least of a cumulative type, is called for. Is such evidence provided by the variants in Yogabhāṣya II, 32?

Concerning this section, Wezler argues that Vācaspati's reading *mṛjjalādijanitam* instead of the Vivaraṇa's *mṛdādijanitam* originated under the influence of the explanation of the *ādi* given by the Vivaraṇa, i.e. the phrase *ādiśabdād udakaṃ ca,* and that "similarly" the "irritating plural" *abhyavaharaṇāni* was "eliminated, i.e. replaced by" *abhyavaharaṇādi* in Vācaspati's version. But without further evidence, can we really say more than that *abhyavaharaṇāni* is the *lectio difficilior* that may or may not be the correct one? Finally, the combined reference to "earth" and "water" is very common, if not stereotypical in texts dealing with purity;[94] and water is the most familiar of all purifying substances. There is obviously no compelling reason why the *mṛjjala* in Vācaspati's version should reflect any specific influence of the Vivaraṇa. Vācaspati himself uses the compound *mṛjjalādikṣālana* in his commentary on Yogabhāṣya II, 5. In general, enumerative compounds with *ādi* are, of course, very susceptible to variants, which may result from omissions as well as from additions.[95]

As we have stated earlier, there are a large number of significant cases where Vācaspati's reading and interpretation of the Yogabhāṣya are clearly incompatible with that of the Vivaraṇa. How do the instances of an alleged influence relate to the numerous incompatibilities? Why did Vācaspati, if he had a Bhāṣya text influenced by the Vivaraṇa, follow this text in some cases, but disregard it in numerous other and apparently more significant cases? What exactly did he have? A Yogabhāṣya text which showed only occasional traces of the Vivaraṇa's interpretation, or one consistently shaped by it? Or did he have the Yogabhāṣya together with and embedded in the Vivaraṇa?[96] Whatever the answer to these hypothetical questions may be, it remains undeniable that there is no coherent pattern in the Yogabhāṣya variants that would support the thesis of a general influence of the Vivaraṇa upon Vācaspati's or the "standard" version of the Yogabhāṣya. Much further study of the textual tradition or traditions, of possible regional varieties, of versions other than the Vaiśāradī version is needed before definite conclusions concerning the relative chronology of the Vivaraṇa and the Vaiśāradī and the role of the Vivaraṇa in the textual tradition of the Yogabhāṣya can be drawn. Borrowing a phrase from Wezler's assessment of Hacker's authorship thesis, we may assert that so far the available evidence is not sufficient to turn "possibility into certainty."[97]

Nevertheless, we may readily agree with Wezler's observation that the Yogabhāṣya text as found in the Vivaraṇa is in many instances better than Vācaspati's version; it may indeed have preserved a significant number of older readings. In general, it is undeniable that Wezler's philological investigations have opened promising prospects for future research, that would not only affect our understanding of the Vivaraṇa, but also of the Yogabhāṣya itself.

For the time being, the so-called *Yogasūtrabhāṣyavivaraṇa* remains a puzzle. Basic questions concerning its philological status, its historical role, and its philosophical position are still open. Hacker's challenging and intriguing hypothesis that Śaṅkara, the author of the *Brahmasūtrabhāṣya*, wrote this text as a Yogin and before "converting" to Advaita Vedānta is, indeed, nothing but a hypothesis, one appealing, yet somewhat unlikely possibility among others.[98] In order to arrive at a definitive solution of the authorship problem, we may have to wait for a fortunate textual discovery. In the absence of this, the only way to approach the problem seems to be the continuation of that type of patient and thorough philological work for which the recent studies by A. Wezler provide a model.[99] Even if such investigations may not reveal the identity of the author of the Vivaraṇa, they will certainly contribute to a better understanding of its place in the history of Indian thought.

Śaṅkara and Classical Yoga

9. As a postscript to the preceding observations, we may now briefly comment on the question how the Yoga system is treated in those writings which are generally accepted as Śaṅkara's genuine works, above all in the *Brahmasūtrabhāṣya*. Regardless of the authorship of the so-called *Yogasūtrabhāṣyavivaraṇa*, we may still ask what kind of transition (or, according to Hacker, "conversion") would have been involved if the author of the Brahmasūtrabhāṣya had, indeed, first produced a commentary on the Yogaśāstra. In doing so, we may also consider H. Nakamura's suggestion that even if these works had one and the same author, he could have combined and reconciled them without undergoing any "conversion" or change of allegiance.[100]

In approaching our topic, we have to distinguish between Śaṅkara's evaluation and critique of the theoretical, metaphysical teachings of Patañjali's Yoga, on the one hand, and his attitude towards Yoga practices (as well as other meditational techniques), on the other hand. As far as its metaphysical basis is concerned, classical Yoga is inseparable from the Sāṃkhya system. Accordingly, and following the lead of Brahmasūtra II, 1, 3,[101] Śaṅkara presents his critique of Yoga metaphysics as an extension of his critique of Sāṃkhya, or as being implied in it. How does he deal with Sāṃkhya?

Our most important source for Śaṅkara's understanding and critique of Sāṃkhya is his Brahmasūtrabhāṣya, specifically the following sections: I, 1, 5–11 (and 18); I, 4, 1–28; II, 1, 1–11; II, 2, 1–10. These sections may be supplemented by more casual statements in other parts of the Brahmasūtrabhāṣya, as well as in other works, such as the *Bṛhadāraṇyakopaniṣadbhāṣya*, the *Upadeśasāhasrī*, and the *Gītābhāṣya*.

In the first *adhyāya* of this *Brahmasūtrabhāṣya*, Śaṅkara tries to establish that brahman is the one ultimate subject of all Vedic texts, and that this brahman is the omniscient, omnipresent, and omnipotent cause of a world with no true reality of its own. In contrast with this view, the Sāṃkhya school asserts that a nonmanifest and unconscious "nature" or "matter" (*pradhāna, prakṛti*) is the ultimate cause of the manifest universe, and that this concept of pradhāna has the support of the Veda. Śaṅkara argues in detail against this claim, and against the concomitant theory that there are many "spirits" (*puruṣa*); he tries to demonstrate that it is entirely incompatible with the Upaniṣads, and that the true meaning of those Vedic passages which have been invoked by the Sāṃkhya teachers is *brahman*, not *pradhāna*.[102]

Furthermore, Sāṃkhya claims that its views have the additional independent and extra-Vedic support of reasoning (*tarka*) and tradition (*smṛti*). Against this, Śaṅkara argues that wherever there is conflict between śruti and smṛti, "revelation" takes precedence over "tradition," and that no human reasoning and experience has any independent metaphysical or soteriological validity apart from the authority of the Veda.[103] Sāṃkhya and Yoga themselves are nothing but "traditions" (smṛti); their teachings have to be measured against the standard of śruti, and if necessary, they have to be corrected or discarded.[104] But even without considering their compatibility or incompatibility with the Veda, the Sāṃkhya (and Yoga) theories can, according to Śaṅkara, be shown to be inconsistent within themselves; accordingly, he concludes his argumentation with an "autonomous" (*svatantra*) "rational refutation" (*yuktipratiṣedha*) of these theories.[105]

All this does not mean that Sāṃkhya and Yoga have to be discarded in their entirety: "We willingly allow room for those portions of the two systems which do not contradict the Veda."[106] But no compromise is possible when it comes to the Sāṃkhya theory of pradhāna, the "plurality of spirits" (*puruṣabahutva*), or the derivation of "cognition" (*buddhi*) etc. from the unconscious pradhāna. Such ideas are incompatible with the Advaitic message of the Veda; they postulate, moreover, an authority and sovereignty of human knowledge that Śaṅkara finds entirely unacceptable. The followers of Sāṃkhya and Yoga, who advocate these ideas, remain committed to the illusion of plurality; they fail to recognize the unity of the self: *dvaitino hi te sāṃkhyā yogāś ca na-ātmaikatvadarśinaḥ*.[107]

10. Śaṅkara's treatment of Yogic practice, and of meditational techniques in general, is more ambiguous than his assessment of

Sāṃkhya-Yoga metaphysics. To be sure, there is no independent "Yogic path" towards final liberation; only pure knowledge, as revealed by the Veda, can bring about liberation. "Works" (*karman*) and techniques, even Yogic or similar "mental acts" (*mānāsī kriyā*), cannot lead to this goal. Yet they can pave the way for the occurrence of liberating knowledge. They have an important preparatory and provisional function within the context of the "two truths." Their significance for the elusive ascent from the "lower," empirical realm towards the ultimate, absolute truth of nondualism is undeniable and legitimate.[108]

In a broad sense, Yogic practice is simply part of Śaṅkara's world. He accepts the "greatness of Yoga" (*yogamāhātmya*)[109] insofar as its potential for extraordinary, even superhuman powers and accomplishments is concerned. He believes that the Veda itself authorizes and encourages acts of inner discipline, the focusing of the mind (*upāsana*), etc.[110] Most specifically, he advocates the meditative concentration on the sacred syllable *om* as a Vedic method of preparing oneself for liberating knowledge. Such meditation is most sigificant and beneficial for persons of slower understanding.[111] The "method of meditation" (*dhyānayoga*) is inherently conducive to perfect, liberating insight (*samyagdarśanasya-antaraṅgam*).[112] It has great therapeutic significance for those who try to overcome their "afflictions" (*kleśa*), such as passion and hate (*rāga, dveṣa*), as well as other obstacles on the way to liberating knowledge. Śaṅkara obviously shares a deep therapeutic concern with the Yoga. However, P. Hacker has drawn unwarranted conclusions from this common therapeutic dimension in his argumentation concerning the authorship of the so-called *Yogasūtrabhāṣyavivaraṇa.*[113]

Even with regard to Yoga practice as such, Śaṅkara is ultimately obliged to disassociate himself from it. Regardless of its doctrinal ties with the dualistic Sāṃkhya system, Yoga practice itself, in its methodic performance of "mental acts," its application of certain techniques of self-control in order to reach the soteriological goal, involves an inherent dualism, that is, the dualism of means and ends, of the goal and the seeker, and of actions and results.

Śaṅkara's treatment of Yoga practice is not so much an extension of his critique of Sāṃkhya, but an expression and application of his general attitude toward "works" (*karman*), and more specifically, of his rejection of the "work orientation" of the Pūrvamīmāṃsā. The "mental acts" (*mānasī kriyā*) that constitute Yogic meditation are not physical activities motivated by personal desires, and they are not rituals in a literal sense. They are nevertheless "works," and they are oriented towards results. They are part of that network of means and ends which keeps us in saṃsāra. Bondage itself is of the nature of means and ends: *sādhyasādhanalakṣaṇo bandhaḥ.*[114] Final liberation, which coincides with the pure identity of the self (*svātmasvarūpatva*), is nothing to be attained (*āpya*) or produced (*utpādya*); it cannot be contingent upon mental (*mānasa*), vocal (*vācika*) or physical (*kāyika*) acts and duties.[115]

In performing acts of meditation and concentration (*upāsana*), one does not transcend that status of being an agent (*kartṛtva*) which is an ingredient of saṃsāra itself. The teaching that the absolute brahman is the ātman presupposes such transcendence (*kartṛtvādisarvasaṃsāradharmanirākaraṇe hi brahmaṇa ātmatvopadeśaḥ*), while directives to perform meditative acts apply only as long as transcendence has *not* taken place (*tadanirākaraṇena ca-upāsanavidhānam*).[116] Yogic meditation as such is incapable of transcending or superseding its own underlying premises. Śaṅkara states explicitly that the "calming of the fluctuations of the mind" (*cittavṛttinirodha*) which *Yogasūtra* I, 2 presents as the very essence of Yoga cannot be considered as a means (*sādhana*) to achieve final liberation (*mokṣa*).[117] He refers specifically to a mental and intellectual exercise known as *prasaṃkhyāna* which according to classical Yoga attenuates and removes the "afflictions" (*kleśa*) and finally brings about "metaphysical discrimination" (*vivekakhyāti*).[118] It appears that this method was adopted and perhaps reinterpreted by certain Vedāntins who employed it as a technique to realize the meaning of the Upaniṣadic "great sayings" (*mahāvākya*).[119] Śaṅkara's critique of *prasaṃkhyāna* focuses on its implication of methodic repetition and accumulation (*abhyāsa*) and mental effort and performance (*ceṣṭita*).[120] According to his faithful disciple Sureśvara, no such mental exercise and repetition (*āmreḍana*, etc.) can lead to that "knowledge" which is the pure presence of reality itself.[121]

In spite of their great and indispensable role at the earlier stages of development, Yoga practices and techniques may even turn into obstacles if the seeker becomes attached to their pursuit and believes that such "result-oriented," inherently dualistic and saṃsāric activities can bring about final liberation. Śaṅkara shows little appreciation of the fact that Yoga itself is keenly aware of the need to overcome its own initial "result-orientation" and acquisitiveness. The Yoga teachers themselves emphasize that the identity of the self (*puruṣa*) is not something to be acquired (*upādeya*).[122] He for whom the awareness of the metaphysical distinction between *puruṣa* and *prakṛti* (*vivekakhyāti*) and the sheer presence (*kaivalya*) of the spirit is supposed to arise cannot in any way be "acquisitive" (*kusīda*).[123] Such statements or concessions cannot change Śaṅkara's basic position: neither Sāṃkhya theory nor Yoga practice can lead us to the ever-present goal of final liberation without the guidance of the Veda (*na sāṃkhyajñānena vedanirapekṣeṇa yogamārgena vā niḥśreyasam adhigamyata iti*).[124]

What is the relationship between such statements and the presentation and interpretation of Patañjali's and Vyāsa's Yoga in the *Vivaraṇa*? Assuming that the author was identical, what kind of reorientation, reevaluation, or change of position would have been required? Could he have reconciled (as H. Nakamura seems to suggest) the presentation of Yoga we find in the *Vivaraṇa* with his advocacy of Advaita Vedānta? It seems hardly conceivable that Śaṅkara the Advaitin could have retained or repeated all the statements made in the *Vivaraṇa* or that he could have explicated Yoga and Sāṃkhya thought without referring to what he saw as its basic defects. The author of the *Brahmasūtrabhāṣya* and the *Bṛhadāraṇyakopaniṣadbhāṣya* was in no way inclined towards compromise and syncretism. Even the didactic dimension of his thought would not have given him such flexibility. Śaṅkara the Advaitin was committed to the one ultimate truth of nondualism, and he saw the Veda as its unique and indispensable source.[125]

Yet it is hardly appropriate to characterize the reorientation and change of allegiance we would have to assume if Hacker's hypothesis were true as a "conversion." In accordance with Śaṅkara's Advaitic self-understanding, it would rather have been an act of progression and transcendence, that is, of relegating Yoga practice and Sāṃkhya theory to a lower, preliminary level of insight and orientation.[126]

Chapter 6: Notes

1. Cf. A. Wezler, "Philological Observations on the So-Called Pātañjalayogasūtrabhāṣyavivaraṇa." *Indo-Iranian Journal* 25 (1983), 17–40. The shorter title *Yogasūtrabhāṣyavivaraṇa*, which is already found in the preface by the editors and, even earlier, as the title of the excerpt published by Rāmanātha Śāstrī in 1931 (see n. 10), has been used by P. Hacker and subsequently adopted by other authors, e.g. T. Vetter and S. Mayeda; it has become the most familiar name of this work.

2. Cf. YSBhV, XIII ff.

3. "Śaṅkara der Yogin und Śaṅkara der Advaitin, einige Beobachtungen." *Wiener Zeitschrift für die Kunde Süd-und Ostasiens* 12/13 (1968; Festschrift E. Frauwallner), 119–148; also in: *Kleine Schriften*, ed. L. Schmithausen. Wiesbaden, 1978, 213–242.

4. "Śaṅkarācārya and Śaṅkarabhagavatpāda. Preliminary Remarks concerning the Authorship Problem." *New Indian Antiquary* 9 (1947), 175–186; revised version: *Kleine Schriften*, 41–58.

5. *The Chapter of the Self*. London, 1978, 174.

6. Cf. T. Leggett, ibid.—In two recent articles in Japanese, H. Nakamura has investigated various textual and doctrinal issues in the Vivaraṇa, but without systematically reviewing the authenticity problem; cf. *Indogaku Bukkyōgaku kenkyū (Journal of Indian and Buddhist Studies*, Tokyo) 25/1 (1976), 70–77; 26/1 (1977), 119–126. For information concerning these two articles, which do not have an immediate bearing upon the issues discussed in this chapter, I am indebted to my colleague W. Tyler. In a further contribution in English, Nakamura discusses what he calls "noteworthy ideas" in the Vivaraṇa; cf. "Śaṅkara's Vivaraṇa on the Yogasūtra-Bhāṣya." *Adyar Library Bulletin* 44/45 (1980/81), 475–485. Nakamura has also begun, but subsequently discontinued, a Japanese translation of the Vivaraṇa in the Buddhist journal *Āgama*. After the completion of the first version of this chapter, T. Leggett has published an English translation of the first two Pādas of the Vivaraṇa: *Śaṅkara on the Yoga-sūtra-s* (vol. 1: Samādhi; vol. 2: Means). London, 1981–1983. As far as the more intricate and technical portions of the

text are concerned, this translation is often quite unsatisfactory; cf., e.g., vol. 1, 107 f., where crucial Mīmāṃsā implications and obvious inaccuracies in the printed text have been overlooked. Moreover, several scriptural references in this passage are incorrect, although they had been correctly identified by the editors (cf. YSBhV, 68). A. Wezler has continued his valuable philological studies of the text in several articles; see "On the 'varṇa' System as Conceived of by the Author of the Pātañjala-yogaśāstravivaraṇa." *Dr. B. N. Sharma Felicitation Volume.* Tirupati, 1986, 172–188; and in particular: "On the Quadruple Division of the Yogaśāstra, the Caturvyūhatva of the Cikitsāśāstra and the 'Four Noble Truths' of the Buddha." *Indologica Taurinensia* 12 (1984), 289–337; on this, see below, ch. 7.

7. Cf. *A Thousand Teachings.* Tokyo, 1979, 4: "It is likely that he was familiar with Yoga, since he is the author of the *Yogasūtrabhāṣya-vivaraṇa . . .";* but 65, n. 63: "The authenticity of this text has not yet been established, but as far as I can see now, there is no conclusively negative evidence."

8. Cf. *Studien,* 2 1: "das mit Ausnahme der Gotteslehre wenig originelle YViv."

9. Cf. G. Oberhammer, *Strukturen yogischer Meditation.* Vienna, 1977; but see the cautionary remark on p. 135: "Śaṅkaras Subkommentar. . . . von dem P. Hacker glaubt, dass er dem bekannten Advaitin dieses Namen zuzuschreiben und daher in die erste Hälfte des 8. Jahrhunderts n. Chr. zu datieren ist."

10. Cf. *The Sphoṭasiddhi of Ācārya Maṇḍanamiśra with the Gopālikā of Ṛṣiputra Parameśvara,* ed. S.K. Rāmanātha Śāstrī. Madras, 1931, XIII.

11. Ibid., XIV.

12. Ibid., XV.

13. Cf. *Gopālikā,* 193 ff.

14. Cf. *Tattvabindu by Vācaspatimiśra with Tattvavibhāvanā by Ṛṣiputra Parameśvara,* ed. V.A. Ramaswami Sastri. Annamalainagar, 1936; for a discussion of the "three Parameśvaras of Kerala," see the editor's intro-

duction, 87 ff. The work of the Payyūr family is also discussed by K. Kunjunni Raja, *The Contribution of Kerala to Sanskrit Literature.* Madras, 1958, 90 ff.; Kunjunni Raja criticizes the view accepted by Ramaswami Sastri that the Śaṅkara referred to in the Svaditaṅkaraṇī was not only the teacher, but also an uncle of Parameśvara I, and he refers to C. Kunhan Raja's suggestion "that Śaṅkara may be the author of the Niruktavārttika from which Parameśvara quotes" (93).

15. E. Stern (Philadelphia) has prepared an annotated edition of this unpublished text and the *Juṣadhvaṅkaraṇī* by the same author (together with the *pūrvapakṣa* of the *Vidhiviveka* and the *Nyāyakaṇikā*). Mr. Stern deserves much credit for having identified not only these Vivaraṇa quotations, but also numerous other significant references in the texts he has edited for his doctoral dissertation (University of Pennsylvania, 1988). Maṇḍana's own refutation of the Yogic proof for the existence of God (*Vidhiviveka*, ed. M.L. Goswami. Benares, 1978, 146 ff.) may seem to go beyond the argument in YBh I, 25; but there is certainly no need to assume that he knew the extensive YSBhV on I, 25.

16. Cf. YSBhV, VII (general editor's introduction): also *Descriptive Catalogue of Sanskrit Manuscripts, Adyar Library and Research Centre*, vol. 8 (1972; compiled by K. Parameswara Aithal), 8 f. (nos. 25–26). -For one passage of the text, a manuscript "available with the Oriental Manuscripts Library, Trivandrum," was also consulted (YSBhV, VIII). This seems to be identical with the "Trivandrum manuscript" of which A. Wezler made a much more systematic use; see below, n. 88.

17. In the case of Madhusūdana, his commentary on the Bhagavadgītā, which follows Śaṅkara but also gives much room to Patañjali's Yoga, may be mentioned specifically as a work in which one might expect, but does not actually find references to the Vivaraṇa.

18. Cf. YSBhV, 139 (on II, 7): *sukhānuśayī tathā duḥkhānuśayī-iti anyeṣam pāthaḥ.* In this same section, the Vivaraṇa states: *tathā ca vakṣyati dharmāt sukhaṃ sukhād rāgaḥ iti.* This seems to refer to YBh IV,11 where, however, the Vivaraṇa (p. 331) reads *dharmāt sukham. sukānuśayī rāgaḥ*, while Vācaspati's version has, indeed, *dharmāt sukham . . . sukhād rāgo. . . .* In Vācaspati's version, YBh I, 11 has *sukhānuśayī rāgaḥ duḥkhānuśayī dveṣaḥ*; this is, however, not found in the Vivaraṇa.

19. YSBhV, 246 (on III, 13); cf. also the different versions of YBh II, 18 and III, 6. An important variant not pointed out by the editors occurs in YBh I, 36, where the Vivaraṇa reads *vaiṣamya* instead of *vaiśāradya*. In several cases, the Yogabhāṣya variants of the Vivaraṇa are supported by other manuscripts. On II, 13 (YSBhV, 151), the Vivaraṇa has a phrase *trivipākārambhī vā janmāyurbhogahetutvāt* which is missing (perhaps due to a scribal error caused by the repetition of *hetutvāt*) in Vācaspati's version and in most of the printed editions, but which occurs in some of the manuscripts and one printed text consulted by R. S. Bodas (see below, n. 20).

20. Cf. YSBhV, 155, line 1; on p. 157, a further YBh variant concerning *(a)dṛṣṭajanmavedanīya* has been noted by the editors, while other variants on the same page remain unmentioned.-It should not be taken for granted that Vācaspati himself read *tatra dṛṣṭajanmavedanīyasya niyatavipākasya* instead of . . . *adṛṣṭajanmavedanīyasya* etc. According to the edition by R.S. Bodas, so far the only edition of the Bhāṣya and Vaiśāradī which attempts to be "critical," the reading *dṛṣṭa*-does not seem to have any clear manuscript support. Cf. *The Yogasūtras of Patañjali with the scholium of Vyāsa and the comm. of Vācaspatimiśra*, ed, by R.S. Bodas. Revised and enlarged by the addition of the comm. of Nāgojī Bhaṭṭa by V.S. Abhyankar. Bombay, 1917 (Bombay Sanskrit and Prakrit Series), 71, notes on lines 7 and 21. It seems that in preferring the reading *dṛṣṭa*-, Bodas has followed the lead of earlier printed editions (and perhaps an attempted emendation); cf. his survey of published and unpublished sources, *Prastāvanā*, X f. Nāgojībhaṭṭa obviously presupposes the reading *adṛṣṭa*- (Bodas, 275, lines 22 ff.).—Cf. also Y.K. Wadhwani, "Ekabhavika karmāśaya in: in: Yogabhāṣya 2.13." *Proceedings of the All-India Oriental Conference* 28 (1976), 473–480; the authoress compares Vācaspati's and Vijñānabhikṣu's readings and interpretations, but she has not consulted the Vivaraṇa, and she seems to be unaware of the existence of the variant readings in the Vācaspati manuscripts. This is also the case with P. K. Guptā, *Pātañjala Yogasūtra: eka samālocanātmaka adhyayana, Tattvavaiśāradī evaṃ Yogavārttika ke paripreksya meṃ*. Delhi, 1979, 252 ff. Both Vācaspati and Vijñānabhikṣu give occasional references to Yogabhāṣya variants. On II, 13, Vācaspati mentions an alternative to *ekabhavika; kvacit pāṭha aikabhavika iti*; in the Vivarana, this occurs once instead of *ekabhavika* (cf. YSBhV, 151). However, on III, 22, the Bhāṣya itself as well as Vācaspati (with one variant *ekabhavika* being listed by R.S. Bodas) have *aikabhavika*.

Vijñānabhikṣu notes a variant reading *kaivalinaḥ* (instead of *kevalinaḥ*) in his commentary on I, 24 (*Pātañjalayogadarśana*, ed. Nārāyaṇa Miśra. Benares, 1971, 71), as well as *aikabhavika* on II, 13 (p. 169).

21. Cf., e.g., the different versions of the final statement of YBh II, 13. That the author of the Vivaraṇa considers his own reading problematic in this case, is indicated by the fact that he offers alternative explanations; but Vācaspati's "standard" version is by no means easier or more satisfactory.

22. I hope to discuss these matters in detail in a monograph on the history of the philosophical karma theories in Hinduism which is now under preparation. On karma and rebirth, see also below, ch. 9.

23. YSBhV, 268 ff. (on III, 17); Kumārila's verses are found ŚV, 383 f. (v. 131 ff.).

24. Cf. *Sphoṭasiddhi* on v. 27; ed. and trans. K. A. Subramania Iyer. Poona, 1966, 69; ed. S.K. Rāmanātha Śāstrī (see above, n. 10), 193 f.

25. YSBhV, 264 (on III, 17); this quote (*gakāraukāravisarjanīyāḥ*) is also given by Śabara on MS I, 1, 5; cf. E. Frauwallner, *Materialien zur ältesten Erkenntnislehre der Karmamīmāṃsā*, Vienna, 1968, 38. In YBh III, 17 the phrase occurs without reference to Upavarṣa.

26. Cf. BSBh I, 3, 28 (*Works* III, 125), where the Upavarṣa quote is: *varṇā eva tu, na śabdaḥ*; YSBhV, 267: *na varṇāḥ padam* is perhaps a (critical) reference to this teaching which is reviewed more positively in BSBh.

27. YSBhV, 275 (on III, 17).

28. See above, ch. 4, § 3 ff.; 8.

29. YSBhV, 323 (on IV, 7).

30. YSBhV, 331 (on IV, 11).

31. Cf. YBh III, 35: *vijñātāram are kena vijānīyāt* (i.e. BU II, 4, 14 and IV, 5, 15); see the commentary on this, YSBhV, 291 f.; in YBh II, 23, the phrase *iti śruteḥ* refers to a "scriptural" claim made by others.

32. Cf. *Tattvavaiśāradī* on YS/YBh II, 22 (reference to Śvetāśvatara Upaniṣad IV, 5).

33. Cf., e.g., YSBhV, 183 (on II, 19): *āgamavirodha* (with reference to Taittirīya Upaniṣad II, 1) and *smṛtivirodha*; 184: *śrutiprasiddhatva* (with reference to BU, II, 4, 11).

34. Cf. YSBhV, 55 f. (on I, 24).

35. YSBhV, 216 (on II, 32); and similarly; 123 (on II, 1): *mokṣaśāstrāṇāṃ ca-upaniṣatprabhṛtīnām*; see also 78 (on I, 27), where the word *āgamin* is paraphrased as *vedavādin*. On p. 250 (on III, 13), the Gītā is referred to as *āgama*. In this connection, we may also mention the phrase *avadyotakatvād āgamasya* (75; on I, 26), which is reminiscent of Śaṅkara's references to the Veda as a source of light; see above, ch. 5, n. 97 (BSBh II, 1, 1); n. 121 (BUBh II, 1, 20).

36. Cf. YSBhV, 148 ff (on II, 13); specifically 153: *sarvaśāstraviprakopaś ca syāt . . . karmaśāstrānarthakye ca mokṣaśāstre 'py anāśvāsaprasaṅgaḥ*; also 151: *sarvaśrutismṛtiviprakopa*.—Cf. the discussion of *karman*, BSBh III, 1, 1 ff.

37. See above, ch. 5, § 6; 9.

38. Cf. YSBhV, 73 (on I, 25): *vedetihāsapurāṇayogadharmaśāstrādyāgamataḥ*.

39. Cf. YSBhV, 67 (on I, 25): *anumānāgamaprasiddheśvara; anumānāgamavirodha*. See also 114 (on I, 48).

40. See above, ch. 5, n. 108.

41. Cf. YSBhV, 68 (on I, 25); the printed text requires several emendations; most conspicuously, l. 7 should read: *śrutīnāṃ vidhipratiṣedhārthatvād īśvarāpratyāyakatvam*, instead of: . . . . *vipratiṣedhārthatvād*. . . .

42. Cf. YSBhV, 46 (on I, 16): *vairāgyasya jñānaprasādamātratve jñānavairāgyayor ananyatvāt tadviparītayoś ca rāgājñānayor anarthāntaratvam eva siddham*; but also 334 (on IV, 22): *yāgena svargo bhaviṣyati, samādhyādinā mokṣo bhaviṣyati*.

43. Cf., e.g., L. de La Vallée Poussin, "Le Bouddhisme et le Yoga de Patañjali." *Mélanges chinois et bouddhiques* 5 (1936/37), 223–242.

44. Cf. YSBhV, on I, 25 (specifically 71 f.).

45. Cf. YSBhV, on IV, 14 f.; 19; 21–24.

46. YSBhV, 83 ff.

47. BSBh II, 2, 28; Vācaspati uses the term *sahopalambhaniyama* in his *Tattvavaiśāradī* on YS IV, 14.

48. YSBhV, 340 (on IV, 14).

49. Ibid.

50. Cf. YSBhV, 341 (on IV, 14): *svalakṣaṇabhedena-arthajñānayor upalabhyamānatvān na-avyatirekagandho'pi. tataś ca vyatirekeṇa-anupalabhyamānatvād ity asiddho hetus tava.*

51. Ibid.: *na ca-asau na-asti-iti śakyaṃ pratijñātuṃ, yaṃ prati sisādhayiṣasi. sa cet tadvijñānavyatiriktaḥ, tathā ghaṭādir api sidhyati.*

52. Cf. YSBhV, 345 (on IV, 16).

53. YSBhV, 351 (on IV, 19); cf. 343 (on IV 15): *sādhyasādhanādivyavahāravilopa.*

54. YSBhV, 341 (on IV, 14).

55. Cf. ŚV, 173 f. (v. 107 ff.).

56. YSBhV, 343 (on IV, 15); that there has to be relation to experience, follows from a radical application of the karma theory, which turns the whole world into a vehicle of reward and punishment.

57. YSBhV, 344 (on IV, 15).

58. YSBhV, 356 (on IV, 23).

59. Ibid.

60. Cf. also YSBh V, 358 ff. (on IV, 24), where the argument from "visibility" (*dṛśyatva*) is supplemented by the "teleological" Sāṃkhya-Yoga argument that all "aggregates" must be "for the sake of *puruṣa*" (*puruṣārtha*); on the use of this argument, cf. also USG II, 56; 70.

61. Cf. YSBhV, 340 ff. (on IV, 14 f.); 349 f. (on IV, 19); 358 ff. (on IV, 24).

62. YSBhV, 350 (on IV, 19).

63. The word *pratyaya* appears in YS II, 20: *draṣṭā dṛśimātraḥ śuddho 'pi pratyayānupaśyaḥ*; cf. also YS III, 35, and YSBhV, 291: *pratyaya* as reflecting the light of the *puruṣa* (*puruṣābhāsa*).—On *pratyaya* see also US XII, 6 ff.; XVIII, 97 f.; 109 ff.

64. YSBhV, 189 (on II, 20).

65. YSBhV, 190 (on II, 20); cf. 192: *buddhipratyayasākṣitvasya siddhatvāt.*—On the use of *vyabhicāra, vyabhicar-*, cf. also *Gītābhāṣya* II, 16 (*Works* II, 14 f.), where "being" is presented as the pure irreducible objective factor in cognition; cognition "deviates" and fluctuates with reference to particular and changing, i.e. unreal, contents, but not with reference to "being" as such: *yadviṣayā buddhir na vyabhicarati, tat sat.* This is not, as P. Hacker (see article mentioned in n. 3, p. 131, n. 29) seems to think, a "spiritualistic" reduction of being to awareness.

66. In its "logical" connotation, the term is used YSBhV, 26; 29 (on I, 7).

67. Cf. BUBh IV, 3, 7; (*Works* I, 871), where the "light of the *ātman*" is described as *buddhivijñānāvabhāsaka* and *vyatirikta*.

68. YSBhV, 350 (on IV, 19); see above, n. 62.

69. *Works* I, 872; see above, ch. 5, n. 168. Cf. also BSBh II, 2, 28 (*Works* III, 250): *ataḥ pradīpavad vijñānasya-api vyatiriktāvagamyatvam asmābhiḥ prasādhitam.*

70. Cf. YSBhV, on IV, 15 (specifically 341; 343); on the other hand, BUBh IV, 3, 7; (*Works* I, 873 f.); see also above, n. 53.

71. "Zur Bedeutung des Illusionismus bei Śaṅkara." *Wiener Zeitschrift für die Kunde Süd- und Ostasiens* 12/13 (1968; Festschrift E. Frauwallner), 407–423; ib., 409.

72. "Śaṅkara der Yogin und Śaṅkara der Avaitin, einige Beobachtungen" (see above, n. 3), 133.

73. "Śaṅkara and Buddhism." *Journal of Indian Philosophy* 7 (1979), 1–42; especially 25.

74. Ibid., 25 f.; 28.

75. Cf., e.g., YSBhV, 194 (on II, 22).

76. Insofar, T. Vetter's characterization of the Vivaraṇa as "wenig originell" (see above, n. 8) is somewhat surprising if measured against his assessment of USG II (which the Vivaraṇa would anticipate to a certain extent if it were an early work by Śaṅkara) as "der vielleicht bedeutendste denkerische Versuch" of Śaṅkara (see above, ch. 5, n. 53).

77. See also above, n. 39 (*anumānāgamaprasiddha*, etc.); there is, however, an occasional tendency in the Vivaraṇa to use reason and inference independently, very often by presenting formal schemes of inference (*anumāna*).

78. Cf. "Śaṅkara der Yogin und Śaṅkara der Advaitin, einige Beobachtungen" (see above, n. 3), 124.

79. Cf. *Jayamaṅgalā*, ed. H. Śarmā. Calcutta, 1926, Preface.

80. However, the identity of the authors of the Vivaraṇa and the *Jayamaṅgalā* seems to be assumed by Rāmanātha Śāstrī (see above, n. 10), XI: *ayam eva śaṅkaro vā syāt yogabhāṣyavivaraṇasāṃkhyajayamaṅgalādīnāṃ kartā.*

81. In the Payyūr family alone, this name occurs repeatedly; it is also common among the representatives of the Kerala tradition of mathematics and astronomy.

82. The *Yogatārāvalī* has been published in: *Minor Works of Śrī Śaṅkarāchārya*, ed. H. R. Bhagavat. Poona, second ed., 1952.

83. In this case, we would have the problem that there is already a good deal of "mature," fully developed argumentation in this work, as illustrated by our preceding observations.

84. This is done by the editors of the text; cf. YSBhV, 370, n. 1; the statement *praṇamāmy. . . . bhagavatpādam apūrvaśaṅkaram* can, of course, not be attributed to the "original Śaṅkara" himself.

85. Cf. D. Pingree, *Jyotiḥśāstra. Astral and Mathematical Literature* (A History of Indian Literature, VI/4), Wiesbaden, 1981, 47ff.

86. Cf. K. Kunjunni Raja, *The Contribution of Kerala to Sanskrit Literature.* Madras, 1958; specifically XV; XIX; 90 ff. (on the Parameśvaras).

87. But cf. the lively and extensive argumentation against the Buddhists in Cidānanda, *Nītitattvāvirbhāva*, ed. P. K. Narayana Pillai. Trivandrum, 1953, 116–124; 201–211; on this work, which may have been composed around 1300, Parameśvara II wrote his unpublished *Vyākhyā*.—The assumption that the Vivaraṇa is deliberately "archaic," avoiding references to more recent authors, would appear artificial.

88. "Philological Observations on the So-Called Pātañjalayogasūtrabhāṣyavivaraṇa" (see above, n. 1). In a number of significant cases, Wezler has compared the printed text with the manuscript transcript on which it is based, as well as with the "Trivandrum manuscript," the existence of which was already known to the editors, but which was only consulted in one instance; see above, n. 16. In his article, Wezler also refers to a YSBhV manuscript kept in the Woolner collection, Lahore; according to his kind information, this is a palm-leaf manuscript in Malayalam script, thus also from Kerala.

89. Wezler, 34; cf. Ibid.: "to prove that the Vivaraṇa is in fact the oldest extant YS commentary it is not at all necessary to assume that its author was the famous Advaitin Śaṅkara."

90. Wezler, 33.

91. There are again characteristic variants in the Vivaraṇa and the Vaiśāradī versions of this section; on *pravāha*, cf. also II, 32 (Buddhist usage); III, 2; 52.

92. Cf. YSBhV, 18; cf. also the usages of *iti* in the YBh section, 17 f.

93. A. Wezler (see above, n. 1; 88), 34; cf. 32, on *mṛjjalādijanitam.*

94. Cf., e.g., Manu V, 105 ff.

95. Cf., e.g., S. Mayeda's critical apparatus on US II (USG), 1 (p. 261 ff., n. 3; 180; 206; etc.).

96. Could Vācaspati have chosen not to acknowledge his acquaintance with the Vivaraṇa? But why should he have disregarded many of its more helpful readings? Wezler presents the reading *akāṣṭhamauna* instead of *ākāramauna* in YBh II, 32 as an illustration of the superiority of the Vivaraṇa version. But in this case, possession of the Vivaraṇa, which clearly repeats the word *akāṣṭhamauna*, should have prevented the acceptance of *ākāramauna*—a word which according to Wezler owes its very existence to a scribal error.

97. Wezler, 36.

98. For some useful, though incomplete and inconclusive, information and discussion on citations in the Vivaraṇa, cf. T. Leggett's introductions to his English translation of Pādas 1 and 2 of the text (see above, n. 6).

99. See above, n. 1; 6.

100. See above, n. 3; 6.

101. BS II, 1, 3: *etena yogaḥ pratyuktaḥ.*

102. Cf. BSBh I, 1, 5–11; 18; I, 4, 1–28. See also G. J. Larson, *Classical Sāṃkhya*, second ed. Santa Barbara, 1979, 212 ff.; on texts apparently claimed or utilized by Sāṃkhya teachers: 218.

103. Cf. BSBh II, 1, 1–11.

104. Cf. BSBh IV, 2, 21 (*yoginaḥ prati ca smaryate*).

105. Cf. BSBh II, 2, 1 (*Works* III, 220): *iha tu vākyanirapekṣaḥ svatantras tad yuktipratiṣedhaḥ kriyata iti eṣa viśeṣaḥ.*

106. BSBh II, 1, 3 (trans. G. Thibaut).

107. BSBh II, 1, 3 (*Works* III, 183); cf. II, 1, 1 (*Works* III, 181): *kapilo hi na sarvātmatvadarśanam anumanyate, ātmabhedābhyupagamāt.*

108. Such "gradual" ascent relates ultimately to the *saguṇa brahman* only; cf. BSBh IV, 3, 14 f.

109. Cf. BSBh I, 3, 33 (*Works* III, 135).

110. Cf. the definitions of *upāsana*, BUBh I, 3, 9; GBh XII, 3.

111. Cf. BSBh I, 3, 13 (on *om* and the "lower" and "higher" *brahman*); IV, 1, 2 (especially *Works* III, 463: *yas tu svayam eva mandamatir. . . .*).

112. GBh V, 26.

113. See the convincing critique of Hacker's arguments by A. Wezler, "Quadruple Division" (see above n. 6), 290–294; see also below, ch. 7.

114. BUBh III, 2, introduction (*Works* I, 792).

115. Cf. BSBh I, 1, 4 (*Works* III, 16 f.): *yasya tu-utpādyo mokṣas, tasya mānasaṃ, vācikaṃ kāyikaṃ vā kāryam apekṣata iti yuktam. . . . na ca-āpyatvena-api karmāpekṣaḥ, svātmasvarūpatve saty anāpyatvāt.*-On "mental acts"

(*mānasī kriyā*), see BSBh I, 1, 4 (*Works* III, 18); also Padmapāda, *Pañcapādikā*, ed. Rāmaśāstrī Bhāgavatācārya. Benares, 1891, 11: *mānasī kriyā-eṣā, na jñānam.*

116. BSBh IV, 1 4 (*Works* III, 466); cf. BUBh IV, 4, 22 (*Works* I, 934): *na ca-asya-ātmanaḥ sādhyasādhanādisarvasaṃsāradharmavinirmuktasya sādhanaṃ kiṃcid eṣitavyam.* See also the definitions of *upāsana*, BUBh I, 3, 9; GBh XII, 3.

117. Cf. BUBh I, 4, 7 (*Works* I, 663): *mokṣasādhanatvena-anavagamāt.*

118. Cf. YS IV, 29; YBh I, 2; 15; II, 2; 11; IV, 29. The term is also found in other systems, such as the Nyāya, as well as in the *Mahābhārata.* The Vivaraṇa on YBh I, 15 paraphrases *prasaṃkhyāna* as *darśanābhyāsa.*

119. Cf. Sureśvara, Naiṣk. III, 89 f. See also Maṇḍana, *Brahmasiddhi*, ed. S. Kuppuswami Sastri. Madras, 1937, 30; 33 ff.; 134; referring to the passage on p. 30, the commentators paraphrase *prasaṃkhyāna* as *viveka* or *vivekajñāna.*

120. Cf. US I, 18, 9; 12; 17; for the term *ceṣṭita* (US I, 18, 12), see also YBh I, 50: *khyātiparyavasānaṃ hi cittaceṣṭitam.* However, BSBh IV, 1, 1 f. recognizes the relative value of "repetition" (*āvṛtti*) for those of "slower understanding" (*mandamati*).

121. Naiṣk. III, 89 f.; see also BUBhV I, 818–848; III, 796–961; and T.M.P. Mahadevan, *Saṃbandha-Vārtika of Sureśvarācārya.* Madras, 1958, XXIII ff.

122. Cf. YBh II, 15; and below, ch. 7. Sāṃkhya itself postulates complete freedom from *kartṛtva* as well as *bhoktṛtva* for the state of *kaivalya.*

123. Cf. YS IV, 33: *prasaṃkhyāne 'py akusīdasya sarvathā vivekakhyāter dharmameghaḥ samādhiḥ*; Vyāsa paraphrases: *tato 'pi na kiṃcit prārthayate. . . .*

124. BSBh II, 1, 3 (*Works* III, 183). However, GBh III, introduction (*Works* II, 42) lists the Yogaśāstra among those sources that teach the "renunciation of all actions" (*sarvakarmasaṃnyāsa*).

125. See above, ch. 3. Śaṅkara is not in the category of the more flexible "pandit commentators," for whom Vācaspatimiśra seems to provide the prototype; yet, even Vācaspati does not merely juxtapose different commentarial presentations, but seems to aim at their convergence towards, or inclusion in, Advaita Vedānta.

126. Cf. Madhusūdana Sarasvatī, *Vedāntakalpalatikā* I, 4; and *India and Europe*, 358.

CHAPTER 7

The Therapeutic Paradigm and the Search for Identity in Indian Philosophy

Introduction: Philosophy, Soteriology, Therapy

1. Until several decades ago, general histories of philosophy used to assure their readers that philosophy originated in Greece, that it was a genuinely and uniquely European phenomenon, and that there was no philosophy in the true and full sense in India and other "Oriental" cultures. The "Orientals," according to this view, did not pursue "pure theory"; they did not seek knowledge for the sake of knowledge, regardless of its practical or soteriological implications.[1] Many centuries earlier, the Greeks themselves had claimed that they possessed a capacity for *theoria* that distinguished them from other cultures, a unique freedom to ask questions about themselves and the world that were motivated by wonder and curiosity alone.[2]

In their own way, modern Indian writers have accepted and echoed this assessment. However, from their angle, the pursuit of knowledge for its own sake appears as idle curiosity, and as a useless academic enterprise. Meaningful knowledge has to serve a purpose; it has to be a means (*sādhana*) towards an end. Accordingly, the fact that Indian philosophy does not advocate knowledge for the sake of knowledge, but instead proclaims its commitment to a spiritual and soteriological purpose, appears as a fundamental strength.[3] Indeed, the classical and traditional texts themselves often refer to their soteriological and religious commitment and to their nontheoretical goals and purposes (*prayojana*), and they emphasize that merely factual knowledge as such is not a desirable human goal (*puruṣārtha*). The ultimate destination of philosophical inquiry should be final liberation (*mokṣa*) from suffering, rebirth, and the other imperfections of worldly existence (*saṃsāra*).[4]

Numerous metaphors and similes in Indian religious and philosophical literature illustrate the instrumental, practical, and pedagogical function of doctrines and theories. According to a familiar Buddhist metaphor, a good doctrine is like a raft or a boat that can be used to cross a river. The good teacher is like a boatman who steers his disciples to the other shore.[5] The same illustration is also found in the Mahābhārata and in Vedānta literature.[6] Most conspicuous and significant, specifically in Buddhism, are those metaphors and comparisons that associate philosophy with therapy and medicine, the good teacher with the good doctor, the metaphysician with the physician. The most relevant Buddhist materials have been collected, and are easily accessible in, P. Demiéville's classical article "byō" in the encyclopedia *Hōbōgirin*; this article is now also available in English translation.[7] We may therefore limit ourselves to some brief and general reminders.

The Buddhist teaching is a strong, efficient therapy and medicine against the *kleśas*, that is, the afflictions of greed, hatred and delusion (*lobha, dveṣa, moha*). The Bodhisattvas are great medical experts (*bhaiṣajyaguru*); they know how to remove the "poisoned arrows," the afflictions and defilements that have struck the suffering human being; they know how to procure peace and well-being.[8] The Buddha Siddhārtha Gautama himself is the "king of physicians" (*vaidyarāja*). Good teaching is healing; the disciples are like patients. Merely theoretical instruction and speculation would be a waste of time. As the simile of the wounded man in the ancient canonical dialogue between the Buddha and Māluṅkyāputta demonstrates, it would not only be irrelevant, but soteriologically harmful.[9]

Medical metaphors are significant not only in Buddhism. The Vedānta, too, presents its teachings and methods as an efficient treatment of the "fever of desires." Its "medicine of knowledge and detachment" (*jñānavirāgabheṣaja*) is supposed to cure the ailment of desires and illusions, above all that fundamental "eye-disease" (*timira*) which is our false way of seeing and understanding the world and ourselves and which is known as *avidyā*.[10]

The most intriguing illustration of the relationship between therapy and theory, medicine and philosophy is provided by the fundamental Buddhist teaching of the "four noble truths": (1) that worldly existence coincides with *duḥkha,* i.e. pain and frustration; (2) that this condition has an origin (*samudaya*); (3) that it has also an end or cessation (*nirodha*); and (4) that there is a way leading to this goal, the "noble eightfold path."[11] The oldest extant sources present this as the message of the Buddha's first sermon, the *Dhammacakkappavattanasutta* which he delivered in the Deer-Park near Sārnāth. It has remained the basic framework of Buddhist thought and teaching ever since, in Mahāyāna as well as in Hīnayāna.

Since H. Kern's *Geschiedenis van het Buddhisme in Indië* (1882), numerous scholars, including H. Zimmer, E. Frauwallner, and A. Bareau, have argued or tacitly assumed that the scheme of "four noble truths" was "borrowed from the medical method," and that the Buddha followed "the procedure for the physician of his day."[12] Without arguing for an actual historical borrowing, other scholars have emphasized the therapeutic paradigm underlying the four truths, for instance E. Conze: "The holy doctrine is primarily a medicine. The Buddha is like a physician. Just as a doctor must know the diagnosis of the different kinds of illnesses, must know their causes, the antidotes and remedies, and must be able to apply them, so also the Buddha has taught the *Four Holy Truths,* which indicate the range of suffering, its origin, its cessation, and the way which leads to its cessation."[13]

The Fourfold Division of Medicine and Philosophy

2. In a thorough and comprehensive analysis of this issue, A. Wezler has shown that there is no evidence for an actual "borrowing" of the "four noble truths" from any corresponding fourfold scheme of medical teaching. As a matter of fact, there is no evidence whatsoever that such a scheme did exist prior to the time of the Buddha.[14] To Wezler's convincing arguments, we may add the following general consideration: If the "four noble truths" had, indeed, been borrowed from an earlier medical scheme, the intense sense of discovery, of a new and overwhelming insight, which the early Buddhists and apparently the Buddha himself attached to the "four truths," would be hard to understand. We have no reason to question the genuineness of this sense of discovery, which was accompanied by an unprecedented awareness of causality, a new understanding of the interrelatedness of events and phenomena in this world - and which in turn could have had an impact upon the self-understanding of medicine.[15]

Nevertheless, the "four truths" provide us with an inherently therapeutic paradigm; and the comparisons of the Buddha with a good doctor are certainly ancient and genuine. As P. Demiéville notes, the medical principles of diagnosis, etiology, recovery and therapeutics can be easily associated with, or even substituted for, the "four truths."[16] The Buddhist tradition itself has elaborated the analogy very explicitly and tried to establish a precise correspondence. Buddhaghosa's *Visuddhimagga* paraphrases the "four truths" in a medical fashion as *roga, roganidāna, rogavūpasama*, and *bhesajja.*[17] In Aśvaghoṣa's *Saundarananda* we read: "Therefore, in the first truth think of suffering as disease, in the second of the faults (i.e., *kleśas*), in the third of the cessation of suffering as good health, and in the fourth of the path as the medicine."[18]

Other old and important texts that make explicit reference to the medical paradigm include the *Ratnagotravibhāga* and the *Yogācārabhūmi.*[19] Furthermore, Yaśomitra's *Abhidharmakośavyākhyā* cites an old canonical *Vyādhisūtra* that seems to correspond to a section in the Chinese *Saṃyuktāgama.*[20] The commitment to healing in a metaphysical sense (i.e., to dealing with the entire worldly mode of existence as with a disease) is, indeed, central for the self-understanding of Buddhism and, as far as we can see, without precedent in pre-Buddhistic Indian literature.[21] Yet, in spite of the systematic elaboration of the therapeutic and medical paradigm in Buddhism, "the Buddha is *merely compared* to a physician or the doctrine to a medicine, etc.; nowhere can be found any traces of an awareness that the Buddha in conceiving the Four Noble Truths could have drawn on a similar systematic division of the Cikitsāśāstra!"[22]

With certain variations and modifications, the fourfold scheme of "noble truths" was also adopted by, or at least echoed in, several schools of Hindu philosophy. The relevant materials have been surveyed and explored by A. Wezler.[23] Once again, we may limit ourselves to some brief reminders and observations.

Vātsyāyana Pakṣilasvāmin, the author of the *Nyāyabhāṣya* (ca. A.D. 400), supplements his discussion of the sixteen "categories" or "fundamental topics" (*padārtha*) of the Nyāya system by referring to another set of important topics or significant terms which he calls *arthapada.* These are "what ought to be abandoned" (*heya*, corresponding to *duḥkha*); "that which produces" or causes the undesirable condition of the *heya* (*tasya nirvartakam*, corresponding to *samudaya*); its "final abandonment" (*hānam ātyantikam*, i.e., *nirodha*); and the "means" to bring about such abandonment (*tasya-upāyaḥ*, i.e., *mārga*, the "path").[24] Later Nyāya commentators, in particular Udayana,[25] discuss the implications of Vātsyāyana's presentation in greater detail.

Bhāsarvajña, whose interpretation of the Nyāya stands apart from the tradition of Vātsyāyana, Uddyotakara, and Udayana, confirms in his *Nyāyabhūṣaṇa* that this scheme corresponds to the Buddhist "knowledge relating to the four noble truths" (*cāturāryasatyaṃ jñānam*).[26] He also refers to two sections in Patañjali's *Yogasūtra*, that is, II, 16–17, and II, 24–26, which speak about *heya, heyahetu, hāna* and *hānopāya*, that is, the suffering (*duḥkha*) which ought to be discarded, the misconception and confusion which is its cause, its abandonment, and the method to bring about such stoppage or abandonment. Introducing these sections, Patañjali's commentator Vyāsa makes the following programmatic statement:

> As medical science (*cikitsāśāstra*) has four divisions: illness, cause of illness, recovery, and therapeutics - so this teaching (i.e., Yoga) has four parts (*caturvyūha*), i.e., cycle of births (saṃsāra), its cause (*hetu*), liberation (*mokṣa*), and the means of liberation. Of these the cycle of births, *saṃsāra*, is *heya*, to be discarded, the association of *puruṣa* and *pradhāna/prakṛti* is *heyahetu*, or the cause of what is to be discarded; perpetual stoppage of this association is *hāna* or liberation; and right knowledge is the means of liberation (*hānopāya*).[27]

This fourfold scheme plays an even more prominent role in the *Yogaśāstravivaraṇa* (also known as *Yogasūtrabhāṣyavivaraṇa*) attributed to Śaṅkara. Here it appears at the very beginning of the text and is used to explain the purpose (*prayojana*) of the Yoga system.[28] The unwarranted conclusions P. Hacker has drawn from this passage in his argumentation concerning the authenticity of the *Vivaraṇa* have been exposed by A. Wezler.[29] Among later philosophical texts, Madhusūdana Sarasvatī's famous *Prasthānabheda* refers to the fourfold medical scheme.[30]

While there is no identifiable medical model for the original "four noble truths" of the Buddha (and, in fact, little likelihood that there was such a model in pre-Buddhist medicine), the case seems to be different as far as the medical references in the Yoga texts are concerned. As noted by A. Wezler, "it is hardly conceivable that the *caturvyūhatva* of the Cikitsāśāstra as expounded in the Yogabhāṣya and the Vivaraṇa is simply a fabrication made for the sole purpose of establishing a parallel to the fourfold division of the Yogaśāstra as implied already by the Sūtra itself." Wezler adds that the medical model was apparently not simply cited as an illustration. Although it does exemplify the similarity between Yoga and medicine, it also implies a claim of superiority, that is, the idea that Yoga provides health in a superior sense which transcends all merely physical healing. This would certainly agree with the introductory statements of Īśvarakṛṣṇa's *Sāṃkhyakārikā*.[31]

There are, indeed, several references to a fourfold division of medicine, or a fourfold medical knowledge, in older medical literature itself. The most significant one is found in the *Carakasaṃhitā:*

> *hetau liṅge praśamane*
> *rogāṇām apunarbhave*
> *jñānaṃ caturvidhaṃ yasya*
> *sa rājārho bhiṣaktamaḥ*[32]

Although the terminology as well as the order of enumeration are different, the basic correspondence seems undeniable; *rogāṇām apunarbhavaḥ*, the nonrecurrence of diseases, is the goal; *praśamana*, tranquilizing, curing indicates the means; *liṅga* means the symptom and the disease itself; *hetu* is its cause and refers to etiology.[33] Yet this statement appears isolated and casual in its context. Its implications remain unexplained; it had evidently no significant impact upon the contents of medical teaching or upon medical practice itself. Whatever the role of such fourfold divisions in medicine may have been, it was certainly in no way comparable to that of the "four noble truths" in Buddhism, or even of the "fourfold division" (*caturvyūhatva*) in Yoga.

If Yoga adopted the fourfold scheme from medicine, it certainly gave it a new meaning and emphasis; in doing so, it must have been aware of the role of the "four noble truths" in Buddhist soteriology. The same can be said about the fourfold scheme in Nyāya; here, Bhāsarvajña explicitly recognizes the correspondence with the "four truths" of the Buddhists.[34] Neither in Yoga nor in Nyāya was the "fourfold scheme" simply "borrowed" from the medical tradition; here as elsewhere, the historical relations between philosophers and doctors, physicians and metaphysicians are more complex and ambiguous.[35]

Health and Identity

3. Regardless of the historical connections, we have now to address and clarify the conceptual and structural relationship between philosophical and medical "therapy," and specifically between the medical and philosophical applications of the "fourfold scheme." How far does the analogy go? How deep and significant is it? These questions suggest themselves, first of all, with reference to the goal of medical and philosophical "therapy," that is, to the desired state of health, or freedom from affliction and disease. What is the nature of the "health" and "well-being" which the doctors are seeking? What does it mean to the philosophers and soteriologists who invoke the therapeutic, medical paradigm? How does it correspond to the goal to which they are committed?

Here, it is conspicuous that Caraka's verse on the fourfold medical knowledge (*jñānaṃ caturvidham; Sūtrasthāna* IX, 19) does not mention "health" as such; instead, it refers to the "nonrecurrence of diseases" (*rogāṇām apunarbhavaḥ*). While this is a negative manner of expression and presentation, it also contains a remarkable absolutist claim. It is obviously reminiscent of the claims and ideas of the philosophers, who try to achieve final liberation from all cyclical recurrences, from rebirth and repeated existence (*punarjanma, punarbhava*), from *saṃsāra* in general. Does this appeal to the "nonrecurrence of diseases" represent a "borrowing" on the part of the medical tradition?

The philosophers themselves, when referring to the medical goal of health, often use another term: *ārogya*.[36] While this term, too, implies an "absence of disease," it does so in a different manner. As A. Wezler notes, it "literally means the state of 'being *again* free of disease'; a previous state of health is presupposed." Wezler adds that this is "palpably different" from the understanding of existence in Buddhism as well as Yoga, which both try to terminate a state of suffering and confusion without presupposing a "previous" state of wholeness and health. Accordingly, he sees here a certain incongruity of the analogy.[37]

Yet it is precisely at this point that we may also find some of the deeper implications of the medical metaphor, and perhaps the most significant common denominator between the medical concept of health and the goal of philosophical soteriology. While the "philosophers" may not presuppose a "previous" state of health and perfection (i.e., a past state in a temporal sense), they nevertheless appeal to the idea of a "return" in a nontemporal sense, a rediscovery and retrieval of an identity and inherent, underlying perfection that has always been there, and that has to be freed from obscuration, confusion, and disturbance. Medical ideas of healing as a reemergence of freedom from disease, as a regaining of a "natural," "inherent" state of health, balance, and harmony, would certainly be compatible with this understanding. We may, indeed, assume that it was such a conception of health that offered itself as a bridge between the therapeutic paradigm and the other two important paradigms that dominate the self-understanding of Buddhism, Yoga and other schools of classical Indian thought: the ideas of "awakening" and final "liberation."

4. Among the Sanskrit words for health, the terms *svāsthya* and *svasthatā*[38] provide an even stronger connotation of a natural, original state and condition than *ārogya*. *Svāsthya* is "coinciding with oneself," being in one's own true, natural state, free from obstruction; it is a state of health and balance as well as of identity and true self-understanding, "being oneself" in a physical as well as cognitive sense. It is significant that both Śaṅkara and his disciple Sureśvara have used *svāsthya/svasthatā* to refer to their soteriological goal, the unobstructed presence and identity of the ātman. At the same time, they have used these terms to argue for their soteriological reliance on *jñāna*, "knowledge," and for their theory that liberation coincides with cognitive realization, that is, with the reemergence of the ever-present ātman. However, with their radicalization of this view, they ultimately transcend the therapeutic paradigm altogether. Instead of being a therapeutic goal, their goal of liberation turns out to be an awakening from those very conditions under which therapy would have been meaningful.

One of the most characteristic passages concerning *svāsthya* is found in Sureśvara's *Sambandhavārttika*, i.e., the introduction to his commentary on Śaṅkara's *Bṛhadāraṇyakopaniṣadbhāṣya*. Arguing against the ritualistic and "work-oriented" Pūrvamīmāṃsā school, and rejecting the thesis that final liberation (*mukti*) is as much subject to ritualistic injunctions (*vidhi*) as mere "prosperity" (*abhyudaya*), Sureśvara says: "No; prosperity and release, which are (respectively) what is to be accomplished and what is not (subject to) being accomplished, what is impermanent and what is permanent, are opposed to each other. Therefore, (this thesis) that they have the same means is not correct."[39]

In support of his view, Sureśvara quotes the sharp distinction between what is "more pleasant" (*preyas*) and truly "better" or good (*śreyas*) from the *Kaṭha Upaniṣad*,[40] as well as the *Muṇḍaka Upaniṣad* on the contrast between that which is "brought about" (*kṛta*) and that which is not brought about or produced (*akṛta*).[41] These distinctions epitomize the claim of the Upaniṣads to supersede the ritualism of the Brāhmaṇas, and to substitute the higher value of true, permanent identity for the temporary results of ritual acts. "Final release" (*mukti*) or "isolation" (*kaivalya*) of the self (i.e., the manifestation of its true identity), is not to be produced or accomplished (*sādhya*) in a literal sense, but only in a figurative sense (*upacārāt*), just as the regaining of the natural state of health (*svāsthya*) through medical therapy is not the accomplishment or acquisition of something new, but only a return to a "previous" state, a removal of disturbances and obstacles: "From medical treatment, the natural state (*svāsthya*) results for one who is afflicted by disease; likewise, isolation (*kaivalya*; i.e. final liberation) results once the misconception of the self has been destroyed through knowledge".[42]

The "natural state of the self" (*ātmanaḥ svāsthyam*), which may also be called "resting of the self in its own true nature" (*svarūpe 'vasthitir . . . ātmanaḥ*, i.e. establishment of the self in its identity), is the state of final release (*mukti*), and it is what the *Kaṭha Upaniṣad* had characterized as the truly good (*śreyas*).[43] It is a state not subject to processes of production, and inaccessible to means, instruments and causes: "Was the self not established in its identity before, so that, in order to be established in it, it would depend on a means through effort? But then this would not be its (true) identity."[44] True identity is not of such a kind that it could ever be absent; nor can it be changed or newly acquired: *na hi svabhāvo bhāvānāṃ vyāvartyeta.*[45]

Śaṅkara himself, Sureśvara's teacher and master, mentions the "natural state" (*svasthatā*) as the goal of both medical and nondualistic "philosophical" soteriology in the introduction to his *Māṇḍūkyabhāṣya: rogārtasya-iva roganivṛttau svasthatā, tathā duḥkhātmakasya-ātmano dvaitaprapañcopaśame svasthatā.*[46]

The Limits of the Therapeutic Paradigm

5. The "natural state" that Sureśvara and Śaṅkara proclaim as their soteriological goal is, indeed, not a "previous state" in a literal, that is, chronological sense; but it is an underlying condition or substratum with a continuous, though obscured and forgotten presence.[47] It is something to be restored and rediscovered from a state of forgetfulness and superimposition, from that fundamental "disease" with which the philosophers are dealing, the cognitive disease or affliction *avidyā*, "nescience," "misconception." This *avidyā* is deep-rooted metaphysical confusion, a radical misunderstanding of the world and one's own true nature. It is essentially self-deception, self-alienation, apparent loss of one's own identity.[48] But such true identity and and selfhood (*ātman, svabhāva, kaivalya*), such fundamental "resting" and "existing in oneself" (*svarūpe 'vasthānam, svāsthya, svasthatā*) cannot be really lost, forgotten or newly acquired. In a strict sense, it cannot and need not even be reacquired or reattained. Ultimately, it transcends the categories of acquisition and avoidance (*upādāna* and *hāna*), and of means and ends (*sādhana* and *sādhya*) altogether.

One of the most radical articulations of this orientation towards inalienable identity, this view that true identity can never be lost, and that nothing can or needs to be acquired or accomplished in the self-effacing "process" of liberating knowledge, is found in the work of Śaṅkara's predecessor Gauḍapāda: That "nature" (*prakṛti*), which is truly "natural" and "original" (*sahaja, akṛta*, etc.), that is, the ātman itself, is such that it never abandons its identity (*svabhāvaṃ na jahāti yā*).[49] Trying to obtain it as a "fruit" or result (*phala*), striving towards it in terms of "means and ends," is in itself a part and symptom of saṃsāra, of that ignorance and affliction from which liberation is sought. The realm of saṃsāra itself is coextensive with the domain of involvement in causes and effects, means and results: *yāvad dhetuphalāveśaḥ, saṃsāras tāvad āyataḥ*.[50]

It is well known that Gauḍapāda is greatly indebted to Nāgārjuna's Madhyamaka Buddhism. And paradoxically, this most radical presentation of the Buddhist denial of selfhood and identity (ātman, svabhāva) expresses at the same time, though in a negative and elusive manner, an intense search for, and uncompromising commitment to, identity, through such terms as *dharmatā* and *tathatā*, but above all in its concept of *śūnyatā*, "voidness." It commits itself to an identity (*svabhāva*) that is not an "identity of entities" (*bhāvānaṃ svabhāvaḥ*), that cannot be found in particular things or specific phenomena, and that cannot be reached as the result of causal methods or techniques.[51] It is a goal that seems to be incompatible with the very idea of "being reached," and which transcends the most basic presuppositions of the therapeutic paradigm.

In a less radical and paradoxical sense, a "trans-causal" and "supra-therapeutic" commitment to identity is also found in other systems, specifically in Sāṃkhya and Yoga. Having presented the "fourfold division" of Yoga and medicine, in which *hāna*, "discarding," and, implicitly, *upādāna*, "obtaining," function as the central categories, Vyāsa himself adds the following clarification: "Here, the identity of the knower (i.e., *puruṣa*) cannot be something to be obtained or discarded" (*tatra jñātuḥ svarūpam upādeyaṃ heyaṃ vā na bhavitum arhati*.[52]

With this, the medical paradigm has reached the limits of its applicability. The denial of *hāna* and *upādāna* with regard to the ultimate goal of Yoga is a denial of fundamental premises of the medical, therapeutic orientation; in a sense, it revokes the "fourfold scheme" and the therapeutic paradigm itself. Indeed, it is not only through the adoption of this paradigm, but also through its transcendence, that Yoga and other schools of Indian thought articulate their self-understanding. Their goal is not well-being as such, nor is it the avoidance of suffering per se. It is, rather, the freedom from attachment, that is, the positive attachment to pleasure and the negative attachment to pain. *Icchā* and *dveṣa*, desire and aversion themselves are "afflictions" (*kleśa*), and it is from these that philosophical soteriology seeks liberation.[53] Such liberation is supposed to transcend the motivation by pleasure and pain, well-being and suffering, and to replace it with a genuinely different, purely cognitive, and, in a sense, "theoretical" orientation towards reality and identity (i.e., primarily the identity of the knowing subject itself). As the introductory verses of the *Sāṃkhyakārikā* state, this "cognitive" approach is superior to, and essentially different from, medicine, Vedic rituals, etc.[54] Medicine itself, as seen from this perspective, is an integral part of the fundamental "disease" of avidyā and saṃsāra.

But how can we be interested in a kind of knowledge that transcends pleasure and pain, attachment and aversion? What is the kind of motivation that commits us to the search for identity? It cannot be desire of the ordinary type. It cannot be the anticipation of a pleasant result. "Identity" (*svabhāva, svarūpa*) is not a "result" nor is it a "rewarding experience." It is an ontological category, not a mental, subjective state of enjoyment. How can we be interested in it? Can there by any interest, any motivation at all, that will not keep us entangled in the network of *saṃsāra*? How can there be striving for liberation from *saṃsāra*, and for the goal of absolute freedom and identity? Is this absolute goal "attractive"? How do the *preyas* and the *śreyas, abhyudaya* and *niḥśreyasa* really differ?[55]

These questions indicate one of the great and persistent, though often implicit, themes of Indian soteriological and psychological thought. A few brief observations, primarily on Advaita Vedānta, may suffice.

Desire and the Search for Identity

6. Maṇḍanamiśra discusses this matter at the beginning of his *Brahmasiddhi* with special reference to *ānanda*, "bliss," which is one of the familiar epithets of brahman. Isn't the desire to know brahman, if it is oriented towards "bliss," itself attachment and passion (*rāga*), and thus incompatible with the idea of liberation? Maṇḍana says that not all wishing (*icchā*) is passion and attachment. The clarity and readiness of the mind (*cetasaḥ prasādaḥ*), a cognitive wishing and inclination (*abhiruci*) towards ultimate truth, that is, the reality and identity of brahman, does not constitute attachment.[56]

The greatest and strictest Advaita Vedāntin, Śaṅkara, is even less inclined to admit any kind of "wishing" (*icchā*) in approaching the ultimate identity of brahman. Accordingly, he is very reserved with regard to the bliss aspect of brahman; as far as possible, he tends to avoid it.[57]

Śaṅkara's statements on *ānanda* are generally very brief; he hardly ever mentions it if not required to do so by specific Upaniṣadic passages on which he comments. He seems reluctant to recognize "bliss" as an essential property of brahman, which would be of the same rank as existence (*sat*) and consciousness (*cit*). He never uses the famous formula *saccidānanda*. Even if there is ānanda in brahman, it certainly cannot be enjoyed or experienced in any way similar to the experience of worldly pleasure. Deep sleep (*suṣupta, suṣupti*) is the closest analogue or approximation to "bliss" according to Śaṅkara's Advaita Vedānta. What they have in common is that both of them are effortless, "natural" ways of "resting in oneself," of coinciding with one's identity. They are entirely free from desire, attachment, aversion and fear.

The most explicit discussion of ānanda in its relation to brahman/ātman is found in Śaṅkara's explication of the doctrine of the five "sheaths" (*kośa*) in the *Taittirīya Upaniṣad*. According to Śaṅkara, ānanda as a mode of brahman's existence, and thus of our own ultimate identity, is not just different in degree from worldly forms of pleasure, but different in essence. It is accessible only to pure knowledge, i.e. self-knowledge, and not to any kind of enjoyment or practical acquisition.[58] In his commentary on the *Brahmasūtra*, Śaṅkara indicates furthermore that the "self" (ātman) which is, in the terminology of the *Taittirīya Upaniṣad*, "consisting of bliss" (*ānandamaya*), is not the highest brahman.[59] The highest, absolute brahman is the ground of all modifications, including the *ānandamaya* modification or "sheath." It is without duality and does not leave room for any enjoyment of or interest in pleasure and "bliss." It is the "work portion" (*karmakāṇḍa*) of the Veda that addresses desires. The *jñānakāṇḍa*, the Upaniṣadic "knowledge portion," teaches the utter transcendence of desires, of all *upādāna* and *hāna*. It deals with identity instead of well-being.[60]

Of course, Śaṅkara's position is by no means representative of

Indian thought in general, not even of its nondualistic traditions. As we have seen, Maṇḍana's position is less radical. In Tantric nondualism, there is even less caution and reluctance to view the identity of the absolute as something to be desired and acquired. *Icchā* itself is a "potentiality" (*śakti*) of the absolute; "desire" and "acquisition" are not incompatible with its identity. In a characteristic and programmatic statement, Abhinavagupta declares that true—and that means necessarily nondual—identity (*svabhāva*), which he identifies as the one self-illuminating presence of consciousness (*prakāśa*), is the highest goal "to be acquired" (*upādeya*): *tatra-iha svabhāva eva paramopādeyaḥ, sa ca sarvabhāvānāṃ prakāśarūpa eva, aprakāśasya svabhāvatānupapatteḥ, sa ca na-anekaḥ prakāśasya taditarasvabhāvānupraveśāyoge svabhāvabhedābhāvāt.*[61]

Here as elsewhere, the general tendency of the Hindu tradition is towards inclusion, balance and compromise. It attempts to combine and reconcile *abhyudaya* and *niḥśreyasa*, the pursuit of well-being and the search for ultimate identity, within the one comprehensive structure of dharma.[62] Yet, in the view of the philosophers, medicine is to be superseded by metaphysics, just as dharma itself is to be transcended by mokṣa. Health in the ultimate sense is the manifestation of identity, just as the deepest meaning of *duḥkha* is "alienation."

7. In conclusion and retrospect, we may say that the therapeutic paradigm, the association of "philosophy" and "medicine," is, indeed, highly significant in Indian philosophical thought and self-understanding, not only in Buddhism, but also in the major schools of Hinduism. The references to a "fourfold division" of medical therapy in Yoga, Nyāya, and Buddhism are most conspicuous and significant. Yet the use of this analogy and of the therapeutic paradigm in general has its limits. As we said earlier, "it is not only through the adoption of this paradigm, but also through its transcendence, that Yoga and other schools of Indian thought articulate their self-understanding."[63]

Philosophical soteriology deals with the cognitive affliction of *avidyā*, self-deceit, mistaken identity. It attempts to rediscover and restore the true identity. This seems to be in fundamental accordance with the view that medical therapy is ultimately nothing but the restoration of an original "natural state" (*svāsthya*), and not the accomplishment of something new. However, the most radical philosophical soteriologies, such as Śaṅkara's Advaita Vedānta, ultimately transcend any kind of therapeutic, medical orientation, with its inherent causal methods and techniques. The therapeutic paradigm as such, together with the entire saṃsāric network of "means and ends" (*sādhana, sādhya*), "causes and results" (*hetu, phala*), "acquisition and avoidance" (*upādāna, hāna*), has to be discarded by a purely "cognitive," radically "theoretical" commitment to the identity of the self (ātman).

It remains true that India has not proclaimed "pure theory," knowledge for the sake of knowledge in the manner in which this was done in Europe, and it has not produced the same dichotomy of "theory" and "practice." Yet this does not mean that it did not pursue other directions of "theoretical" orientation. In its search for identity, and in its explication of the relationship between therapeutic practice and liberating knowledge, the Indian tradition has developed its own distinctive perspectives on the relationship between "theory" and "practice."[64]

Chapter 7: Notes

1. Cf. *India and Europe*, ch. 9.

2. Cf. *India and Europe*, ch. 1.

3. See, for instance, Bankim Chandra Chatterji (Caṭṭopādhyāya), *Racanāvalī* II, 217ff.; H.P. Sinha, *Bhāratīya darśana kī rūparekhā*. Calcutta, 1963, 4 ff.

4. The introductory sections of the *Sāṃkhyakārikā* and the *Nyāyasūtra* and numerous other documents of classical Indian philosophy illustrate this point.

5. Cf. W. Rahula, *What the Buddha Taught*. New York, second ed. 1974, 11 ff.

6. Cf. Śaṅkara, USG 1,3: *ācāryaḥ plāvayitā, tasya jñānaṃ plava iha-ucyate*; and *Mahābhārata* XII, 313, 23.

7. *Buddhism and Healing*. Demiéville's Article "Byō" from *Hōbōgirin*, trans. M. Tatz. Lanham, 1985.

8. This may imply the postulate that the Bodhisattva should first cure the bodily diseases, as a prerequisite for the cultivation of awakening; cf. *Buddhism and Healing*, 45 (from the *Gaṇḍavyūhasūtra*).

9. See *Majjhimanikāya*, 63.

10. Cf. US XIX, 1: *tṛṣṇājvaranāśakāraṇaṃ cikitsitaṃ jñānavirāgabheṣajam*: USG 1, 40: *avidyādṛṣṭer anekavad avabhāsate, timiradṛṣṭyā-anekacandravat*; and Sureśvara, *Taittirīyopaniṣadbhāṣyavārttika* II, 105; 149 ff.

11. Cf. *Mahāvagga* 1, 6, 10ff.; for a recent study on the different versions, with special reference to questions of syntax, see K. R. Norman. "The Four Noble Truths: A Problem of Pāli Syntax." *Indology and Buddhist Studies* (Festschrift J.W. de Jong). Canberra, 1982, 377–391.

12. Cf. A. Wezler in the article quoted below, n. 14, 312 f.

13. E. Conze, *Buddhism. Its Essence and Development.* Oxford, 1951, 17.

14. See A. Wezler, "On the Quadruple Division of the Yogaśāstra, the Caturvyūhatva of the Cikitsāśāstra and the 'Four Noble Truths' of the Buddha." *Indologica Taurinensia* 12 (1984), 289–337.

15. That there is a significant affinity between the pursuit of medicine and the awareness of causal relations (both in terms of etiology and therapy) can hardly be questioned; cf. Dasgupta II, 396: "It was in this connection that the principle of causality was first from a practical necessity applied in Āyurveda."

16. Cf. *Buddhism and Healing* (see above, n. 7), 1.

17. Cf. *Visuddhimagga* XVI, 87 (ed. C.A.F. Rhys Davids, PTS, 512; as quoted by Wezler, "Quadruple Division," 317); see also R. Birnbaum, *The Healing Buddha.* Boulder, 1979, 22.

18. *Saundarananda* XVI, 41.

19. Cf. A. Wezler, "Quadruple Division," 311; quoted from the Patna manuscript of the *Yogācārabhūmi* (*Śrāvakabhūmi* section). See also the extensive use of the medical paradigm in the *Bodhisattvabhūmi*, ed. N. Dutt. Patna, 1966, 182; also 100; 121.

20. Cf. Yaśomitra, *Sphuṭārthā Abidharmakośavyākhyā*, ed. U. Wogihara. Tokyo, 1971, 514 f. On the problems concerning the correspondence between this text and the *Saṃyuktāgama* section, see A. Wezler, "Quadruple Division," 319 f.

21. The closest approximation to the Buddhist awareness of *duḥka* which we find in the older Upaniṣads is the notion of the "six waves" (i.e. hunger, thirst, sorrow, delusion, old age, death); cf. BU III, 5, 1: *ātmā . . . yo 'śanāyāpipāse śokam mohaṃ jarāṃ mṛtyum atyeti*). Śaṅkara often refers or alludes to the "six waves"; cf. US XIV, 12; XVIII, 103; 203; XIX, 4. But in general a striving for "fullness" is more characteristic of the Upaniṣads; cf., e.g., Chāndogya Upaniṣad VII, 23 ff. (*bhūman*); also G. Gispert-Sauch, *Bliss in the Upaniṣads.* Delhi, 1977, specifically 194 f.; 204.

22. A Wezler, "Quadruple Division," 321.

23. As the title of his article indicates, Wezler focuses on the role of the therapeutic paradigm in the Yoga system. On the "therapeutic" ideas of the *saṃsāramocaka* (referred to by Wezler, 316, n. 74; 317, n. 81), see above, ch. 4.

24. Cf. NBh on NS I, 1, 1; IV, 2, 1; according to Uddyotakara's *Vārttika* on I, 1, 1, the four "fundamental topics" are discussed by all authoritative teachers in all soteriological traditions of learning: *etāni catvāry arthapadāni sarvāsv adhyātmavidyāsu sarvācāryair varṇyanta iti* (ND, ed A. Thakur, 14). See also *India and Europe*, ch. 15.

25. Cf. Udayana, *Pariśuddhi* on NS I, 1, 1 (ND, ed. A. Thakur, 103 f.).

26. Cf. Bhāsarvajña, NBhūṣ, 442.

27. See YBh II, 15: *yathā cikitsāśāstraṃ caturvyūham, rogo rogahetur ārogyam bhaiṣajyam ity; evam api śāstraṃ caturvyūham eva.*

28. Cf. YSBhV, 2; on the Vivaraṇa, see above, ch. 6.

29. See A. Wezler, "Quadruple Division," 290 ff.

30. Cf. *Prasthānabheda*, ed. Gurucandra Tarkadarśanatīrtha. Calcutta, 1939, 13: *cikitsāśāstrasya rogatatsādhanaroganivṛttitatsādhanajñānaṃ prayojanam*; the same section refers to the soteriological implications of *kāmaśāstra*. Madhusūdana's presentation emphasizes the dichotomy of etiological and therapeutic causality, which corresponds to the *anuloma* and *pratiloma* presentations of the *pratītyasamutpāda* formula.

31. Cf. A. Wezler, "Quadruple Division," 307.

32. *Carakasaṃhitā, Sūtrasthāna* IX, 19.

33. Cf. A. Wezler, "Quadruple Division," 309.

34. See above, n. 26.

35. As another aspect of this relationship, we may mention the claims of the medical tradition to contribute to the soteriological goals of the philosophers, i.e. ultimately *mokṣa*; see, for instance, *Carakasaṃhitā, Śārīrasthāna V*, 10; *Sūtrasthāna* I, 15 f.

36. See, for instance, YBh II, 15 (as quoted above, n. 27), together with its commentaries. Cf. also Vasubandhu, *Abhidharmakośabhāṣya* IV, 8 (ed. P. Pradhan, second ed., Patna 1975, 202): *nirvāṇam . . . paramārthena kuśalam ārogyavat.*

37. Cf. A. Wezler, "Quadruple Division," 304 f.

38. For the adjective *svastha*, "self-abiding," see, for instance, Śaṅkara, US XIV, 23; XVII, 74.

39. Cf. *Sambandhavārttika*, v. 23 (ed. and trans. T.M.P. Mahadevan. Madras, 1958, 14):

na, abhyudayasya mukteś ca sādhyāsādhye dhruvādhruve
vailakṣaṇyān na yuktā-iyaṃ tulyasādhanatā tayoh.

40. *Kaṭha Upaniṣad* II, 1 (quoted in v. 24). But see also the use of *priya*, BU II, 4; IV, 5.

41. *Muṇḍaka Upaniṣad* I, 2, 12 (quoted in v. 25).

42. V, 28 (Mahadevan, 17 f):

cikitsayā-iva saṃprāpya svāsthyaṃ rogārditasya tu
ātmāvidyāhater bodhāt tat kaivalyamavāpyate.

43. Cf. v. 32; 47 (Mahadevan, 20; 30).

44. V, 48 (Mahadevan, 30):

tatra-ātmā kiṃ svarūpe prāṇ na sthito yena tatsthitau
hetuṃ vyapekṣate yatnāt, svarūpaṃ hi na tad bhavet.

45. V. 56; (Mahadevan, 34); cf. Gauḍapāda, *Kārikā* IV, 29: *prakṛter anyathābhāvo na kathaṃcid bhaviṣyati.*

46. Cf. A. Wezler, "Quadruple Division," 301. See also US XIX, 1: *tṛṣṇā-jvaranāśakāraṇaṃ cikitsitam.*

47. In this context, we may refer to the concept of *turīya*, as found in the work of Gauḍapāda.

48. Cf. the familiar Vedāntic parables of the "prince in the jungle," the "tenth man," etc. For references, see S. Mayeda, *A Thousand Teachings*, 131, n. 2; J. A. B. van Buitenen, *Rāmānuja's Vedārthasaṃgraha*. Poona, 1956, 308 ff.

49. Cf. *Kārikā* IV, 9.

50. Cf. *Kārikā* IV, 56; cf. Śaṅkara, BUBh III, 2, introduction (*Works* I, 792): *sarvo 'yaṃ sādhyasādhanalakṣaṇo bandhaḥ.*

51. See, for instance, chapters 15 (*svabhāva*) and 25 (*nirvāṇa*) in Nāgārjuna's *Madhyamakakārikā*, together with Candrakīrti's *Prasannapadā*.

52. Cf. YBh II, 15 (see above, n. 27).

53. Cf. the "wheel of *saṃsāra*" (*saṃsāracakra*), YBh IV, 11.

54. Cf. SK, v. 1 f.; according to the commentators, a reference to medicine is implied in the word *dṛṣṭa*.

55. Cf., e.g., Manu XII, 88 (*pravṛtta* and *nivṛtta dharma*); VS I, 1, 2 (*abhyudaya* and *niḥśreyasa*); see also W. Slaje, "*Niḥśreyasam* im alten Nyāya." *Wiener Zeitschrift für die Kunde Südasiens* 30 (1986), 163–177 (on *niḥśreyasa* and *apavarga* in Nyāya); and Udayana, *Pariśuddhi* I, 1, 1 (ed. A. Thakur, 86ff.; 103f.).

56. Cf. *Brahmasiddhi*, ed. S. Kuppuswami Sastri. Madras, 1937, 1ff.; see also A. Thrasher in *Encyclopedia of Indian Philosophies*, ed. K.H. Potter, vol. 3 (Advaita Vedānta). Princeton, 1981, 348 ff., especially 350; P. Hacker, *Kl. Schr.*, 284 f.

57. Cf. P. Hacker, *Kl. Schr.*, 284: "Der sehr nüchterne Śaṇkara schätzte diese Lehre nicht . . ."; see also A. Fort, "Beyond Pleasure: Śaṅkara on

Bliss". *Journal of Indian Philosophy* 16 (1988), 177–189. Śaṅkara states repeatedly that there can be no desire with regard to the knowledge of *brahman*, since it is the unity and identity of everything; cf. BUBh I, 5, 2 (*Works* I, 693): *brahmavidyāviṣaye ca sarvaikatvāt kāmānupapatteḥ.*

58. See Śaṅkara's commentary on *Taittirīya Upaniṣad* II, 5 ff.; especially II, 8.

59. Cf. BSBh I, 1, 19.

60. See, for instance, BUBh, introduction. *Mokṣa*, absolute freedom as absolute identity, is nothing to be obtained or brought about; cf. BSBh I, 1, 4 (*Works* III, 17): *na ca-āpyatvena-api kāryāpekṣā, svātmasvarūpatve saty anāpyatvāt.*

61. Cf. Abhinavagupta, *Tantrasāra*, ed. Mukunda Ram Sastri. Srinagar, 1918(reprint Delhi, 1982), 5 f. (Upodghāta). But see, on the other hand, Uddyotakara, NV, introduction (ed. A. Thakur, 11): *na saṃvidd heyā, asukhaduḥkhatvāt, ataddhetutvāc ca. na-apy arthyate, aphalatvāt.*

62. Cf. the characteristic reconciliation of medicine and philosophical soteriology (personified as Vijñānaśarman and Jñānaśarman) in Ānandarāya Makhin's allegorical drama *Jīvānandana* (written around 1700 at the court of Tanjore).

63. See above, § 5.

64. Cf. *India and Europe*, ch. 15. See also above, ch. 2, § 3, on Udayana's statement that there would be no "human goal" (*puruṣārtha*) and no meaningful soteriological striving without examination and reflection (*Pariśuddhi* I, 1, 1; ed. A. Thakur, 146).

CHAPTER 8

Man and Self in Traditional Indian Thought

Introduction

1. What is the role of man in Indian and European thought? Are there any fundamental and historically decisive differences? Are there differences that might help us to understand, correlate and contrast the Indian and the Western traditions in general?

At the beginning of the nineteenth century, and in the early days of modern Indological research, one of the most influential and most controversial of all Western thinkers, Georg Wilhelm Friedrich Hegel, claimed that "man . . . has not been posited"[1] in India and that Indian thought sees the concrete human individual only as a "transitory manifestation of the One," of an abstract Absolute, and as being without any "value in itself."[2] Hegel was not an Indologist, nor did he try to understand non-Western traditions in a neutral, impartial manner. He was one of the most effective philosophical spokesmen of history, progress and European supremacy. Are his statements about the role of man in Indian thought just a symptom of his general Eurocentric bias?

More than a hundred years later, Betty Heimann, a Western Indologist who tried to do exactly what Hegel had failed or avoided to do, namely, do justice to the peculiarities and own internal standards of Indian thought, emphasized in her own way the Indian indifference towards man as man, the lack of interest in singling him out among other living beings. While the West has proclaimed man's uniqueness as a thinking and planning creature, propagating and promoting his domination over the natural world and his unique capacity for cultural development and historical progress, Indians, according to Betty Heimann, have never tried to separate him from the natural world and the unity of life: "No human *hybris*, self-elevation and self-deceit, can here develop where man is but another expression of Nature's all-embracing forces."[3]

Is Hegel right? Is Betty Heimann right? Is what they are saying the same basic truth, only seen from two different angles? Indeed, among those central themes of Western thought, which seem to be conspicuously absent in Indian, specifically Hindu thought, man appears as one of the most conspicuous ones. There is no tradition of explicit and thematic thought about man as man in India, no tradition of trying to define his essence and to distinguish it from other forms of life. There is nothing comparable to the Western fascination with man as "rational animal" ("animal rationale," "homo sapiens"); there is no emphasis on the unity of the human species, no notion of a uniquely human dignity, no proclamation of human rights or of human sovereignty over nature. There is, in general, nothing comparable to that tradition in the West which has its roots in ancient Greek as well as Biblical sources and leads through the Renaissance and Enlightenment periods to the growing anthropocentrism of modern Western thought. There is no suggestion in any of the religious traditions of India that *only* man is endowed with an immortal soul or an irreducible personal and spiritual identity.

In the context of *saṃsāra*, i.e. transmigratory existence through innumerable births and deaths, there is no basic difference between men and other living beings: The transition from human to animal existence is as much a possibility as that from animal to human or superhuman existence. Of course, there has been some disagreement on the exact extent of saṃsāra or the realm of transmigration, karma, and rebirth in which a "soul" may exist in innumerable embodiments. The inclusion of plants in this realm of karmic embodiments has not always been taken for granted.[4] But the standard description of saṃsāra in later "orthodox" Hinduism is *brahmādistambaparyanta*, "extending from (the highest individual God) Brahma to the tufts of grass." On the other hand, the Indian tradition has not produced anything comparable to the modern secular anthropocentrism of the West, which leaves man to himself alone, depriving him of a metaphysically, theologically, or cosmologically privileged position and proclaiming him instead as the goal and center of his own temporal, cultural, and technological world, as the maker of history and progress. In general, the ideas of historical progress, of cultural and technological development, of man's growing mastery of nature, of a man-made dignity of man seem to be conspicuously absent from traditional Indian thought.

Traditional Indian thought seems to be preoccupied with the *ātman*, that "self" and immortal principle *in* man which it also finds in animals and other forms of life; *manuṣya*, man as a particular species of living beings, man as homo sapiens, seems to be insignificant compared to this self *in* man and other beings.

Man in Vedic Thought

2. So we have to ask again: Is Hegel right? Has man "not been posited" in India? The question has far-reaching implications and ramifications; and Hegel's and Heimann's observations are certainly not without basis: The role of man *is* different in India and the West. However, much further clarification and differentiation is required before we can draw general conclusions. The anthropological content of the rich and complex Indian philosophical tradition has to be reexamined; and before we can compare and contrast the Indian and Western ideas, we have to determine more precisely: What is the role of man in Indian thought? To what extent has it changed and developed in different directions? Indian thought is not monolithic; and its historical developments and transformations, while less spectacular than those of Western thought, are by no means negligible.

What *has* actually been said about man, the human species in the different schools and periods of Indian philosophical thought? This topic has not yet met with the scholarly interest which it deserves. Obviously, a full and comprehensive treatment cannot be attempted within the narrow limits of this presentation. Instead, we will give some exemplary textual references and suggest some basic historical and philosophical perspectives. We will be selective; by and large, Buddhist and Jaina thought will not be included in this presentation.[5]

The peculiar and intriguing differences between the Vedic texts and the documents of later and classical Hinduism are generally recognized, though interpreted in different ways. It has often been noticed that there is a more worldly, earthly, temporal atmosphere in the older Vedic texts than in later Indian thought; this has obvious implications for the understanding of man. As a matter of fact, man as an earthly, temporal being plays a more significant role in these texts; and words like *ātman* or *puruṣa,* which in later thought are commonly associated with the absolute self, are in their Vedic usage often closer to the embodied person, to man in his concrete individuality. Moreover, there are various explicit attempts to define man as man and to draw that borderline between man and animal that seems to be so much less important in later philosophical literature.[6]

In accordance with the general character of the Vedic and older Upaniṣadic texts, we cannot expect philosophically coherent discussions on the nature of man. The descriptions, definitions, classifications, and genealogical explanations of man we find in these texts are embedded in and inseparable from their mythical and ritualistic contexts. In a basic and general sense, the Vedic texts, in particular the Brāhmaṇas, classify man (*manuṣya, puruṣa*) as a *paśu,* a domesticated animal; he appears frequently in a fivefold group together with cows, horses, goats, and sheep.[7] Other species, such as camels and dogs, also mules and asses, are sometimes added to this group.[8] However, in subsuming manuṣya under paśu and in including man in the category of domestic animals, the Brāhmaṇas do not present him as a mere animal among other animals: On the contrary, he appears as a very special and distinguished animal. The *Śatapatha Brāhmaṇa,* one of those texts which classify man as a paśu, has, on the other hand, numerous statements on his special role and preeminence among the animals. The animals "come after" man;[9] man is the first one among the animals (*prathamaḥ paśūnām*).[10] He is the "two-footed animal," animal bipes (*paśur dvipād*),[11] and his vertical, upright posture and orientation is contrasted with that of the "horizontal," four-footed creatures.[12] In short, man is like a ruler, an Indra among the animals;[13] and all animals somehow belong to him.[14] More specifically, man is distinguished and preeminent because he is the only one among the animals that performs rituals or sacrifices.[15]

Man is called *sukṛta,* "well-made,"[16] and presented as the most appropriate abode for the cosmogonic powers; he is closer to the origin of the world than the other creatures.[17] In a genetic sense, too, he is first and foremost among the animals; occasionally, the four-footed animals are even presented as fallen men, fallen brothers of man, creatures that were originally two-footed and had an upright posture.[18] Man has a special relationship with those cosmic and divine forces invoked in the rituals; he is "nearest" (*nediṣṭha*) to the "Lord of Creatures" (*prajāpati*).[19] Several hymns of the *Atharvaveda*, in particular X, 2, celebrate man's special ritual powers, his unique access to the sacred texts, his ability to influence the universe; and they trace his preeminence in the world, which corresponds to his special ritual mandate, to his peculiar association with brahman, the supreme cosmic principle.[20]

Vedic Ideas and the Soteriological Privilege of Man

3. The most explicit, coherent and emphatic Vedic statements on the uniqueness of man are found in the *Aitareya Āraṇyaka* (11, 3, 2): In man (*puruṣa*), we are told, the self (*ātman*) exists in a more manifest manner (*āvistarām*) than elsewhere. He is almost endowed with intelligence (*prajñā*); he alone understands, discerns (*vijānāti*) what he sees; and he knows how to express what he understands. The intelligence, the cognitive power (*abhivijñāna*) of the other animals is bound by or coincides with their hunger and thirst (*aśanāpipāse*); they are unable to plan for the future. Man, on the other hand, knows the tomorrow (*veda śvastanam*), the "world and the nonworld" (*lokālokau*, i.e., this world as well as what is beyond this world); and "by the mortal he desires the immortal" (*martyena-amṛtam īpsati*). A. B. Keith translates this whole passage as follows:

> The self is more and more clear in man. For he is most endowed with intelligence, he says what he has known, he sees what he has known, he knows to-morrow, he knows the world and what is not the world. By the mortal he desires the immortal, being thus endowed. As for the others, animals, hunger and thirst comprise their power of knowledge. They say not what they have known, they see not what they have known. They know not to-morrow, they know not the world and what is not the world. They go so far, for their experiences are according to the measure of their intelligence.[21]

In this passage, the term *ātman* refers to the absolute self, while *puruṣa* stands for man as homo sapiens, that earthly, temporal creature in which, as we are told, the absolute self, the center and ground of the universe, finds its supreme manifestation and embodiment. In this sense, these two words which are often used interchangeably in later philosophical texts (e.g., in Nyāya-Vaiśeṣika or Sāṃkhya), are clearly distinguished in the *Aitareya Āraṇyaka*.

Man is more intelligent than the other creatures. He is less subject to his immediate desires. He can think about tomorrow and plan for the future. In a number of places, this idea is connected with an etymological explanation of the most specific word for "man": *manuṣya*. It is derived from the verbal root *man*, "think," "consider,"[22] and associated with *manas*, a word that refers to the mind as the cognitive organ and the seat of intelligent planning;[23] man's humanity (*manuṣyatva*) is said to be rooted in the thought or reflection (*man-*) of the "Lord of Creatures" (*prajāpati*).[24] Of course, all this refers primarily to the *ārya*, the member of the ethnic and ritual community of the Veda, the descendent of its mythical ancestor *manu*. The word *manu* itself, which can also mean "intelligent," functions occasionally as a virtual synonym of *ārya* and stands in the same contrast to *dāsa* or *dasyu*, two familiar Vedic terms for those aborigines of the Indian subcontinent whom the "Āryan" invaders considered as enemies and impure barbarians.[25] However, it would be quite wrong to conclude from this that the cognate word *manuṣya* is always a basically ethnic or ethnocentric term.

It seems that the passage from the *Aitareya Āraṇyaka* (probably before 600 B.C.) does not yet presuppose a fully and clearly developed theory of karma and rebirth; it does not have the notion of saṃsāra, the cycle of death and birth as it is generally taken for granted in later Indian thought. Once this theory has become a basic premise, it provides a new background and context for, and gives a potentially new meaning to, the idea of man's openness for the "tomorrow" and the more distant future. This openness, this potential freedom from immediate desires can now be interpreted as a special qualification and mandate for final liberation from the cycle of death and rebirth and worldly existence in general: a unique freedom to strive for the distant goal of *mokṣa*, of liberating the self from its embodiments, a goal that transcends all worldly desires and any temporal horizon of expectations. The idea that being human implies a unique capability for final liberation, a rare or even exclusive soteriological privilege, is indeed quite familiar in such texts as the *Mahābhārata* and the Purāṇas. According to a familiar and somewhat stereotyped phrase, it is difficult or extremely difficult to achieve human existence (*mānuṣyaṃ durlabham*, or *atidurlabham*), and even the gods may envy the humans and desire their state of being. In a soteriological perspective, there is nothing higher than man, nothing better than being human (*na mānuṣāc chreṣṭhataraṃ hi kiṃcit*).[26] And the *Viṣṇu Purāṇa* and other Purāṇas tell us how rare and precious this opportunity is, occurring only once in "a thousand times thousand births."[27] Human existence may be full of misery; yet it is the only gateway to liberation, the only opportunity to choose one's future instead of simply living in accordance with the karma accumulated in the past. It is a rare privilege, even if it means existence as a *caṇḍāla*, an outcaste.[28] The *Bhāgavata Purāṇa* states that those who exist as humans can see the Lord Viṣṇu more clearly, more manifestly (*āvistarām*) than other creatures.[29] This appears almost as an adaptation of the glorification of man in the *Aitareya Āraṇyaka* to the theistic thought of Vaiṣṇavism.

4. In addition to its repeated statements on the special religious and soteriological significance of being human, the *Mahābhārata* also refers to man's earthly, secular capabilities and to his dominating role among the creatures of this world. In a story told by Bhīṣma in the *Śāntiparvan* (XII, 173), the god Indra appears in the shape of a jackal and speaks to Kāśyapa who is in a suicidal mood. He tries to convince him that being human is a very favorable earthly situation and that, compared to the animals such as the jackals, man enjoys very special privileges and advantages. In particular, he can use his hands as instruments, which enable him to protect himself from insects, to extract thorns, etc., to find shelter from cold, rain and heat, to provide for himself clothing, food and housing. Human beings enjoy their lives as masters of the earth, letting other creatures work for them; using various means, they win power over them (v. 15: *adhiṣṭhāya ca gāṃ loke bhuñjate vāhayanti ca / upāyair bahubhiś ca-eva vaśyān ātmani kurvate*). However, this same chapter of the Mahābhārata continues by suggesting that it might be better not to use such special abilities and powers and not to get involved in worldly affairs at all (v. 31: *aprāśanam asaṃsparśam asaṃdarśanam eva ca / puruṣasya-eṣa niyamo manye śreyo na saṃśayaḥ*). The jackal concludes by saying that, should he once more have the opportunity of being human, he would use it for sacrifices, giving and austerities (v. 49: *yajña, dāna, tapas*), instead of exercising worldly skills and powers.[30]

Man's potential for intelligent planning, for applying tools and techniques, for subduing other creatures and for dominating the earth, that is, his potential as rational animal ("animal rationale"), appears as a temptation to be resisted. Exploiting this potential would be a misuse of a unique soteriological opportunity. The true privilege of man is not to be the master of his world, but to be liberated from it; his mandate is not to employ other creatures as instruments for his own needs and desires, but to use himself, his own human existence, as a vehicle of self-transcendence.

This presentation deals with the development of Hindu thought about man; it would not be feasible to include Buddhism in all its richness and variety. However, at this point I cannot resist referring to the story of the rabbit in the *Avadānaśataka*, a collection of legends probably compiled around A.D. 100: The animal declares that it is, indeed, *ūhāpohavirahita*, deprived of the ability of abstract reasoning, of inference and calculation. It is inferior to man; yet it insists that inferiority in this area does not constitute an essential difference and should not give a sense of special dignity or uniqueness to man.[31]

Whatever may have been said about man's special or even exclusive soteriological qualification, we should not forget that the idea that man alone has the spiritual capacity for final liberation is by no means a universally recognized premise or principle in Indian thought and literature. It is not difficult to find texts in all three major religious traditions of India—Hinduism, Buddhism and Jainism—that credit nonhuman beings, too, with the attainment of final liberation. Numerous stories in the Purāṇa and Māhātmya literature, or in the Buddhist Jātakas (cf. the *Sasajātaka* in Pāli or the *Hastijātaka* in the Sanskrit *Jātakamālā*) deal with ethical and soteriological achievements of animals, even if they are not just ordinary animals. While the idea of man's special soteriological qualification or mandate may be widely accepted, there is an equally obvious reluctance to credit him with exclusive access and to simply deny such access to all other creatures. After all, the same type of life and self is present in all creatures; any strict demarcation would appear artificial. In the Indian context, the tendency to keep the borderline between men and animals permeable at least to some extent is not surprising. No rigorous anthropocentrism or human self-elevation, even of a soteriological type, can develop in a tradition of thought that takes the idea of *saṃsāra* and the unity of life for granted.

On the other hand, increasingly rigid internal differentiations of mankind, i.e., demarcations and classifications of different types of human beings, interfere with and overshadow the notion of a fundamental unity of mankind that seems to be implied in the proclamation of man's special or unique capability for liberation. Traditional Hinduism develops a whole complex system of formalistic and legalistic restrictions, of rules of ritualistic qualification (*adhikāra*), which divide mankind into fundamentally different groups and also determine their access to sacred knowledge and final liberation. Being human may be an important prerequisite; but it is not enough according to orthodox Hinduism. It is not man as man who is eligible for liberation. Numerous qualifications and restrictions limit the soteriological privilege not to man in general, but to specific classes of human beings. It is often taken for granted that only Bhārata, India, is a *karmabhūmi*, a region in which liberation from the cycle of death and birth is possible. And the *Viṣṇu Purāṇa* which, as we have seen earlier, glorifies human birth as a rare privilege qualifies this by referring to Bhārata as the only "land of responsible action" (*karmabhū*) and characterizing other regions as mere "areas of enjoyment," i.e. of paying off old karma (*bhogabhūmi*).[32] It is thus clear that human existence is a true soteriological privilege only if it takes place in India. It should also be remembered that the Vedic usage of the terms *manu, manuṣya,* etc., does not necessarily refer to "mankind" in its totality, but primarily to the Vedic *ārya,* who is contrasted with the barbarian *dāsa* or *dasyu.*[33] Other restrictions and specifications relate to caste membership, sex, etc.[34] Natural and empirical criteria, such as intelligence, discipline, restraint, are not considered sufficient to determine somebody's religious and soteriological qualification; as Śaṅkara says, adhikāra is not based upon worldly competence alone.[35]

Man in Pūrvamīmāṃsā

5. The orthodox *smārta* tradition of Hinduism interprets the four varṇas,—brahmins, kṣatriyas, vaiśyas and śūdras—as quasi-biological species, postulating that the differences between these groups, although less conspicuous, are as significant as those between cows and elephants. These divisions within the human species tend to overshadow the demarcation of the human species as such. It may appear ironic that occasionally this fact that mankind is divided into castes is itself presented as a characteristic of the human species, something that distinguishes men from other living creatures, such as cows.[36] Furthermore, it cannot always be taken for granted that the foreigners, non-Indian barbarians (mleccha) to whom the varṇa structure does not apply, should really be regarded as human beings.[37]

Even without considering such fragmentation of the idea of mankind, and regardless of the restrictive and limiting impact which considerations of adhikāra have upon man's access to final liberation, we may say that preoccupation with soteriology, with liberation from worldly, temporal existence, can hardly be expected to be conducive to anthropology in the Western sense, that is, to interest in man as an earthly, temporal, historical creature. The openness for mokṣa, final liberation, which seems to lend a new dimension of meaning to the old Vedic notion of man as a planning, future-oriented being, also leads to an evaporation of the anthropological motivation. Man may be privileged in terms of his capacity for liberation, but his soteriological aptitude is comparable to a ladder that ought to be thrown away after being used. Man is soteriologically privileged insofar as he is a vehicle of self-transcendence and self-negation. The openness for the future in the *Aitareya Āraṇyaka* is openness for the future in a temporal sense; mokṣa, absolute liberation, on the other hand is supposed to be freedom from, transcendence of, temporality, worldliness and worldly, temporal planning as such.

Even if being human constitutes a unique opportunity, it remains at the same time a transitory role and disguise. Being human is, according to a familiar Indian metaphor, just one among many roles which the self (or *jīva*, etc.), regarded as a dramatic actor, can play. Other familiar similes present the body as a temporary vehicle of the self, as some kind of machine operated by it, as its changeable and disposable garment, or as a nest which it will leave sooner or later. The human condition is only one, though special, garment or vehicle of the self; it is just one among many possible accessories. Although it may indeed constitute a special soteriological opportunity, it is also a special case of bondage. It is not man as man, as animal rationale, who ought to be liberated, but the self *in* man; and liberation of the self is liberation from being human as well as from any other limiting worldly condition. Accordingly, we can hardly expect genuine anthropological interest in those classical systems of Indian thought which are increasingly preoccupied with final liberation.

There is, however, one Hindu system that takes up the old notion of man as a thinking and planning creature and applies it explicitly to describe man as manuṣya, and to single him out among other living beings. This system is the Pūrvamīmāṃsā, a school of ritual thought and Vedic exegesis less concerned with final liberation (mokṣa) than the other so-called orthodox systems of Hindu philosophy. The Mīmāṃsā deals primarily with dharma, with ritual duty and sacrificial performances, which are supposed to produce religious merit and appropriate reward for the sacrificer either in his current existence or after death. It specializes, so to speak, in ritualistic and religious planning, both for this life and the hereafter; its aims are not beyond time and space. Accordingly, it provides a much more congenial atmosphere for dealing with man as manuṣya and as a temporal, worldly creature.

6. The Mīmāṃsā school is, of course, not interested in anthropology per se, as a branch of theoretical learning. What it presents is a kind of ad hoc anthropology, a by-product of its theory and methodology of ritual, sacrificial action. Why is it that, as stated in the *Śatapatha Brāhmaṇa*, man alone performs sacrifices? Why is it that he has a special aptitude and responsibility for dharma, ritual duty and propriety? Is it really true that only man has the adhikāra, the qualification and mandate to perform sacrificial acts?

These and similar questions form the background of an interesting section in Śabara's commentary on the *Mīmāṃsāsūtras*.[38] The focal point in Śabara's discussion (approximately A.D. 500) is again man's openness for the future, the open temporal horizon that allows him to go beyond the fulfillment of immediate needs and desires and to make plans not only for this life, but also for future lives. It may be true that also animals, just like human beings, desire happiness and try to attain it. However, as Śabara tells us, animals are not able to nurture hopes and expectations and plan for results that are to occur in a different or remote period of time (*kālāntaraphala*); they desire only what is immediately at hand (*āsanna*). Śabara mentions and dismisses apparent exceptions to this rule: What folk tradition and popular belief tend to interpret as fasting or other religious observances on the part of certain animals (such as dogs and kites) is in reality nothing but an avoidance of food due to illness, and it is in all cases to be explained as an immediate bodily reaction. Man's knowledge of dharma, of ritual duty and of the methods of accumulating religious merit, is based upon the Veda. But the animals do not and cannot study the Veda, nor do they have access to any other relevant textual sources. Therefore, they have no idea of what dharma is. And without any knowledge of dharma, how could they legitimately and competently perform ritual acts? How could they attempt to accumulate merit and to make plans for the more distant future and the hereafter? They are simply not open for the future in this sense; they are not free to pursue distant goals in the wide temporal horizon of dharma. Unlike man, they are caught in the network of their immediate biological needs and urges.

Śabara's word for "man" in this section on the difference between men and animals is usually puruṣa. In philosophical terminology, puruṣa is a familiar synonym of ātman, and as such, it refers not so much to men as distinct from animals, but to that eternal spiritual principle which is found in men as well as animals. As a matter of fact, Śabara uses the word puruṣa not only with reference to man in his earthly, bodily existence, but also with reference to that self or soul that is supposed to survive after death and to reap the heavenly results of the accumulated sacrificial merit. However, even after death, and supposedly disembodied, Śabara's puruṣa remains a quasi-worldly actor and enjoyer, and a much more concrete and temporal being than the self or ātman in other philosophical systems. It remains, as Madeleine Biardeau states, "the subject of empirical life" ("le sujet de la vie empirique"), enjoying the sacrificial rewards in heaven very much in the manner in which there is enjoyment for man while alive on earth: "Même si, alors, il est dépouillé de son corps, il garde au moins la possibilité de jouir du ciel d'une manière tout à fait analogue à celle du vivant."[39]

Śabara's great commentators add very little to his exposition. Kumārila's *Ṭupṭīkā*, the appendix to his *Tantravārttika*, skips it altogether. Prabhākara's *Bṛhatī* is, as usual, very brief; the subcommentary of Śālikanātha Miśra observes that the animals, since they are unable to comprehend the meaning of words and incapable of verbal communication, cannot be the addressees of, and cannot respond to, those Vedic injunctions which are the one and only source of dharma.[40]

There are several reasons why questions concerning the definition of man and his distinction from the animals are not further elaborated upon in later Mīmāṃsā. The most important and obvious one among these has been referred to earlier: the division of mankind into hereditary groups, quasi-biological species such as the four main castes, and the exclusion of such groups as the śūdras from the Vedic rituals. From the angle of brahminical orthodoxy, which the Mīmāṃsā advocates, certain distinctions within mankind appear far more significant than the definition and demarcation of mankind as such. This can hardly be conducive to searching for common features of all human beings. On the contrary, any emphasis on the unity of the human species as contrasted with the animals could compromise the argumentation against the admission of the śūdras to the rituals, and thus weaken or undermine the position of the Mīmāṃsakas.[41]

7. Kumārila, the greatest and most influential Mīmāṃsā commentator, is a leading representative of the view that the four main castes (varṇa) are genuinely different species; and he tries to support this view by postulating real universals "brahmin-ness" (*brāhmaṇatva*), "kṣatriya-ness" (*kṣatriyatva*), etc., which distinguish these groups from one another.[42] The school of Kumārila's rival Prabhākara does not accept this theory of "caste-universals"; it sees "humanness," *puruṣatva*, as a basic universal that constitutes a final, indivisible species.[43] But while the followers of Prabhākara do not try to provide a metaphysical and biological basis for the exclusion of the śūdras, they nevertheless accept it as valid; they do not further pursue the implications of their suggestion that "humanness" or "humanity" is a universal and distinguishing feature shared by all human beings. Generally, we may say that even those systems of traditional Hindu thought that represent a less restrictive, more universalistic orientation than the Pūrvamīmāṃsā of Kumārila do not attempt to question or abolish the varṇa structure and other fundamental divisions of mankind as such. In Buddhism, the situation is, of course, somewhat different; but this would be a different topic and out of place in a presentation which focuses on traditional Hindu philosophy.

In general, the understanding of man is inseparable from the notion of dharma and its different interpretations. But this relationship is also very ambiguous and evasive. That the mandate for dharma distinguishes men from animals is often taken for granted: Only man is open for the "ought"; regardless of what he has in common with the animals, he finds himself faced with norms and duties, i.e. with dharma. He has to live up to these norms and duties to be truly and fully human. In this sense, the concept of man becomes a normative concept: without living up to dharma, men would just be like beasts: *dharmeṇa hīnāḥ paśubhiḥ samānāḥ*.[44] But again, we have to emphasize that the concept of *varṇāśramadharma*, the "dharma for the principal castes and stages of life," which dominates traditional Hindu thought *not* only in Pūrvamīmāṃsā, leaves little room for universal or "egalitarian" applications of the idea of human self-perfection or self-fulfillment through dharma. The mandate for dharma is specified in accordance with hereditary group membership; and large segments of the biological species "man" are factually excluded from any access to dharma (i.e., to ritual and ethical norms and duties), and that means, from the very possibility of self-perfection as humans.[45]

Śabara's statements on the nature of man and the difference between men and animals find a remarkable echo in the thought of Śaṅkara, the great representative of Advaita Vedānta. In general, Advaita Vedānta or Uttaramīmāṃsā is the metaphysical, knowledge-oriented counterpart of the ritualistic Pūrvamīmāṃsā; it advocates an absolutism and nondualism ultimately incompatible with ritual works. However, in worldly and social matters, though in a somewhat provisional sense, Advaita Vedānta usually follows the lead of the Pūrvamīmāṃsā; and it also claims strict allegiance to the teachings of the Veda. Śaṅkara accepts the division of society into the four basic varṇas, and he agrees that there are irreducible differences of adhikāra, religious qualification or mandate. Just as Śabara and other Mīmāṃsakas argue for the exclusion of the śudras from the Vedic rituals, Śaṅkara argues for their exclusion from the liberating soteriological revelation of the Upaniṣads.[46] However, as we have seen earlier, Śabara nevertheless has a very explicit notion of man as man, as planning, future-oriented creature, in a sense that obviously includes the śūdras while excluding the animals and demarcating men as one special group of creatures. Śaṅkara's response to this notion illustrates his peculiar attitude towards "anthropology" and the idea of man as "rational animal."

Śaṅkara and the Transcendence of the Animal Rationale

8. In the introduction to his *Brahmasūtrabhāṣya,* Śaṅkara tells us that there is no basic difference between the practical worldly behavior of humans and animals. Men as well as animals try to obtain what is pleasant and avoid what is unpleasant; fear and desire govern their actions. And just as Vātsyāyana Pakṣilasvāmin in his *Nyāyabhāṣya,* Śaṅkara notes that the animals, too, make use of the "means of knowledge" (*pramāṇa*).

> Animals, when sounds or other sensible qualities affect their sense of hearing or other senses, recede or advance according as the idea derived from the sensation is a comforting or disquieting one. A cow, for instance, when she sees a man approaching with a raised stick in his hand, thinks that he wants to beat her, and therefore moves away; while she walks up to a man who advances with some fresh grass in his hand. Thus men also—who possess a higher intelligence—run away when they see strong fierce-looking fellows drawing near with shouts and brandishing swords; while they confidently approach persons of contrary appearance and behavior. We thus see that men and animals follow the same course of procedure with reference to the means and objects of knowledge (*pramāṇaprameyavyavahāra*). Now it is well known that the procedure of animals bases on the non-distinction (of Self and Non-Self); we therefore conclude that, as they present the same appearances, men also—although distinguished by superior intelligence—proceed with regard to perception and so on (*pratyakṣādivyavahāra*), in the same way as animals do.[47]

In his following remarks, Śaṅkara refers to ritual activities and indicates that such actions, though based upon the study of Vedic texts and meant to ensure a pleasant hereafter, are not fundamentally different from other human activities. In his view, *dharma* itself is an ingredient of the world of *māyā*. In its egocentric structure, it is not genuinely different from *artha* and *kāma*, the "human orientations" toward success and sensuous pleasure. Only *mokṣa* represents an essentially different *puruṣārtha* ("goal of man," "orientation of the self").[48]

According to Śaṅkara's commentators, the purpose of this passage is to illustrate the all-pervasive presence of *avidyā*, "ignorance," "misconception," in this world of practical, empirical life, its presence and influence in humans no less than in animals. This may be true; but there are also other implications in this passage that have not been made explicit by the commentators such as Padmapāda, Vācaspati Miśra, and their successors. It is Śabara's distinction between men and animals in terms of intelligence and long-term planning, that is being rejected here, as amounting to nothing more than a difference in degree. The basic egocentric mechanism of worldly life and action is the same, regardless of the degree of intelligence and foresight, and whether or not Vedic rituals and methods aiming at the hereafter are involved or not. Man remains an animal—even if he is a rational animal. His rationality may make him more successful than the other creatures; but it does not constitute an essential difference. It is not sufficient to account for his access to mokṣa, final liberation, which lies beyond all horizons of worldly intelligence, of temporal planning, of means and ends. Of course, Śaṅkara recognizes the natural, empirically obvious intellectual deficiencies of the animals, their inability to learn and study and comprehend the sacred texts. Living beings differ vastly from one another insofar as the "manifestness of knowledge, sovereignty, and so forth" (*jñānaiśvaryādyabhivyakti*)[49] is concerned; the animals *are* inferior in this hierarchy. Śaṅkara is also fully aware of the glorification of man in the *Aitareya Āraṇyaka*, which we quoted earlier. In his commentary on the *Taittirīya Upaniṣad*[50] he presents it as an illustration of man's natural preeminence and superiority (*prādhānya*).

Yet, in order to be open for mokṣa, man has to abolish any attempt to establish himself as a superior earthly creature, as rational animal. Planning itself, thinking in terms of means and ends, the ability to dominate the earth and the other creatures which we found described in the *Mahābhārata*: all this has to be discarded. It amounts to a merely instrumental, deceptive superiority.[51] Man cannot ascertain his soteriological privilege by claiming and exercising his natural capabilities, his superior intelligence, and so forth. Śaṅkara is quite explicit on this point: Whatever we may discover as man's "worldly competence" (*sāmarthyaṃ laukikam*) is not sufficient to explain his adhikāra, his qualification for liberating knowledge.[52] To attain liberating knowledge means to discover one's own true identity. But man's true identity is not his role as reasoning, reckoning, planning animal rationale, nor is it anything specifically or uniquely human. His identity is that of the self (ātman), which he shares with all creatures and which is neither the subject nor the object of planning and reasoning. In trying to discover this self, man has to abandon his humanity; he has to discard himself as rational animal.

Animal rationale, "rational animal," is the leading definition of man in the Western tradition of thought. According to Martin Heidegger, it is conditioned by, reflects and expresses the fundamental nature of European metaphysics which it accompanies from its Greek beginnings to its culmination in modern science and technology.[53]

One does not have to be a Heideggerian to see the central and symptomatic role of this definition in Western thought: Anthropocentrism in this sense, the emphasis on man as thinking, planning, organizing creature, as potential "master and owner of nature" ("maître et possesseur de la nature"),[54] is a conspicuous and deeply significant phenomenon of the European tradition.

The notions of history, progress, technological mastery, as well as of secularism, nihilism, and relativism, are closely associated with this understanding of man. What counts is what man has made of himself in history and culture, and the possibilities he sees for further efforts of organizing his world and himself. In this perspective, the absolute timeless self (ātman) we find at the center of the soteriological thought of traditional Hinduism, must appear as a mere abstraction; as we have seen in our introductory remarks, it has been dismissed as such by Hegel.

Hegel claims that "man . . . has not been posited"[55] in India. Indeed, there is nothing like the European anthropocentrism in India; there is no comparable fascination with man as planning, thinking, temporal creature, as rational animal. Yet, our preceding survey has shown that it would be a simplification and inappropriate generalization to state that man as man has never been "posited" or proclaimed in India, or that the notion of man as animal rationale has never been considered in traditional Indian thought. The idea of man as planning, intelligent, future-oriented creature has, indeed, been articulated and considered, beginning in such early texts as the *Aitareya Āraṇyaka*. But the interest in this idea has remained ephemeral.[56] It was dismissed by Śaṅkara and his followers, and disregarded by the majority of philosophical schools. In a sense, it simply evaporated in the climate of Indian ritual and soteriological thought.

Chapter 8: Notes

1. *Vorlesungen über die Philosophie der Weltgeschichte* II (*Die orientalische Welt*), ed. G. Lasson. Hamburg, third ed., 1968, 399.

2. Ibid.; and *Vorlesungen über die Geschichte der Philosophie I* (*Einleitung*), ed. J. Hoffmeister. Leipzig, 1944, 267 (not included in the new edition by F. Nicolin, Hamburg 1959).

3. *Facets of Indian Thought*. London, 1964, 116.

4. See below, ch. 9.

5. The following presentation will focus on explicit thematizations of man, and not deal with what might be called "implicit anthropology," i.e., general anthropological implications of metaphysical or cosmological theories or religious world-views. Much of what has been written on "man" in Indian thought deals primarily with such "implicit anthropology," or with certain non-conceptualized "images" of man. This may be said about the majority of the contributions in the special issue of *Studia Missionalia* (19, 1970) which was published under the title "Man, Culture, and Religion." Some basic observations on the relationship between man and animal in India are found in J. Gonda, "Mensch und Tier im alten Indien." *Studium Generale* 20 (1967), 105–116. Very little precise information is contained in: *The Concept of Man, A Study in Comparative Philosophy*, ed. by S. Radhakrishnan and P.T. Raju. London, 1960; various other "comparative" studies are equally vague and generalizing. The following presentation borrows freely from my earlier study: "Anthropological Problems in Classical Indian Philosophy." *Beiträge zur Indienforschung, Ernst Waldschmidt zum 80. Geburtstag gewidmet*. Berlin, 1977, 225–236. For additional perspectives, see P. Hacker, *Kl. Schr.*

6. On "anthropological" ideas in the Veda, see also: C.A. Scharbau, *Die Idee der Schöpfung in der vedischen Literatur*. Stuttgart, 1932, 145 ff; R. N. Dandekar, *Der vedische Mensch*. Heidelberg, 1938; L. Monteiro, *L'homme d'après la Ṛgveda Saṃhitā*. Goa, 1980 (Diss. Fribourg-Suisse, 1973). On the older usage of the words *ātman, puruṣa* etc., see P. Deussen, *Allgemeine Geschichte der Philosophie* I/1, Leipzig 1894, 282–336. For useful quotes and references, see also Muir I.

7. For instance, *Śatapatha Brāhmaṇa* VI, 2, 1, 2; VII, 5, 2, 6; X, 2, 1, 1.

8. See the Sanskrit dictionaries of Boehtlingk/Roth ("Petersburger Wörterbuch") and Monier-Williams, s.v. *paśu*.

9. *Śatapatha Brāhmaṇa* II, 3, 1, 20.

10. *Śatapatha Brāhmaṇa* VI, 2, 1, 18; VII, 5, 2, 6. See also W. Rau, *Staat und Gesellschaft im alten Indien*. Wiesbaden, 1957, 46 f.; Rau's suggestion that the classification of man as a *paśu* implies a reference to slavery is not convincing.

11. *Śatapatha Brāhmaṇa* VII, 5, 2, 32; see also II, 5, 1, 1.

12. *Śatapatha Brāhmaṇa* IV, 5, 2, 5.

13. *Śatapatha Brāhmaṇa* IV, 5, 5, 7.

14. *Śatapatha Brāhmaṇa* VII, 5, 2, 6.

15. *Śatapatha Brāhmaṇa* VII, 5, 2, 23.

16. *Aitareya Upaniṣad* I, 2, 3.

17. See *Bṛhadāraṇyaka Upaniṣad* I, 4, 3 f.; a descending genealogical order from humans, *manuṣya*, to ants, *pipīlika*.

18. See, for instance, *Śatapatha Brāhmaṇa* III, 7, 3, 1.

19. *Śatapatha Brāhmaṇa* II, 5, 1, 1.

20. See specifically *Atharvaveda* X, 2, 18 ff.; also XI, 8 and P. Deussen, *Allgemeine Geschichte der Philosophie* 1/1. Leipzig, 1894, 265 ff.; L. Renou, *Études védiques et pāṇinéennes* 2. Paris, 1956, 69–79.

21. *The Aitareya Āraṇyaka*, ed. (with introduction, translation, etc.) by A. B. Keith. Oxford, 1909 (repr. 1969), 216 f.

22. See Yāska, *Nirukta* III, 7 (on *manuṣya*): *matvā karmāṇi sīvyanti*.

23. See *Śatapatha Brāhmaṇa* VII, 5, 2, 1 ff.; specifically 6: Prajāpati producing man out of *manas*, thus giving him special strength.

24. *Maitrāyaṇī Saṃhitā* IV, 2, 1. See also *Kulārṇava Tantra* I, 69: *jñānavān mānavaḥ*.

25. See, for instance, *Ṛgveda* VII, 21, 11; VIII, 87, 5; VI, 21, 11.

26. *Mahābhārata* (crit. ed.) XII, 288, 20; see also VI, 116, 32; XIV, 43, 20; XIV, App. 1/4, 70. In his article "A Note on the Hindu Concept of Man" (*Journal Fac. of Letters, Univ. of Tokyo, Aesthetics* II, 1988, 45–60), M. Hara has collected numerous references to *mānuṣyaṃ durlabham* and the theme of the rarity and difficulty of human birth, not only from the Hindu texts, but also from Buddhist and Jaina literature (including the *Subhāṣitaratnakaraṇḍakakathā* attributed to Āryaśūra, which contains a whole chapter entitled *durlabhamānuṣyakathā*). The desire of the gods to be born as humans is expressed, for instance, in *Mārkaṇḍeya Purāṇa* 55, 6: *devānām api bho viprāḥ sadā-eva-eṣa manorathaḥ/ api mānuṣyam āpsyāmo devatvāt pracyutāḥ kṣitau*. Humans are frequently reminded not to waste or misuse their unique privilege, for instance in the *Pretakalpa* of the *Garuḍa Purāṇa* or in the following verse of the *Mahābhārata* (XII, 286, 34): *yo durlabhataraṃ prāpya mānuṣyam iha vai naraḥ/ dharmāvamantā kāmātmā bhavet sa khalu vañcyate*.

27. *atra janmasahasrāṇāṃ sahasrair api, sattama,*
kadācil labhate jantur mānuṣyaṃ puṇyasaṃcayam.

This verse which is found in the *Viṣṇu Purāṇa* (II, 3, 13/23) and other texts (cf. *Kulārṇava Tantra* I, 69) occurs with several variant readings; see W. Kirfel, *Das Purāṇa vom Weltgebäude*. Bonn, 1954, 19. The most significant variant is *puṇyasaṃcayāt* instead of *puṇyasaṃcayam*. The ablative would imply that human birth itself is the result of merit accumulated in the non-human existences by which it is preceded. This, however, would seem to be in conflict with the premise that human existence, with its unique mandate for *dharma*, is the condition for accumulating merit or "good karma"; for a clear statement of this idea see, for instance, *Mahābhārata* XII, 283, 28:

mānuṣeṣu mahārāja dharmādharmau pravartataḥ,
na tathā-anyeṣu bhūteṣu manuṣyarahiteṣv iha.

It seems that in the later Purāṇic tradition there is less emphasis on man's unique dharmic freedom; at any rate, the question how this old premise would have to be reconciled with the idea that human birth is a reward for accumulating merit (also repeatedly referred to in the *Pretakalpa* of the *Garuḍa Purāṇa*) is not explicitly addressed. Elsewhere, and in a theoretically more consistent manner, human birth is not said to result from an accumulation of "good karma," but merely to occur after a long period of time and the gradual cancellation of previous karma through a succession of non-human existences; see, for example, the Jaina *Uttarādhyayana Sūtra* III, 1, 7. Other descriptions and similes (for example, that of the "blind tortoise" rising from the ocean once every hundred years and accidentally pushing its neck through the hole of a yoke drifting at the surface) imply an irreducible element of blind chance. The attempt to "explain" human birth as the result of an accumulation of merit seems to be a later popularizing "rationalization." But see YSBhV on *Yogasūtra* II, 12 (karma of animals).

28. See *Mahābhārata* XII, 286, 31 f.:

    caṇḍālatve 'pi mānuṣyam sarvathā tāta durlabham.
    iyaṃ hi yoniḥ prathamā yāṃ prāpya jagatīpate /
    ātmā vai śakyate trātuṃ karmabhiḥ śubhalakṣaṇaiḥ.

29. *Bhāgavata Purāṇa* XI, 7, 19 ff.; specifically 21: *puruṣatve ca mām . . . āvistarām prapaśyanti.*

30. *Mahābhārata* XII, 173; specifically 15; 31; 49.

31. *Avadānaśataka*, ed. J. S. Speyer. Petersburg, 1902–1909, 209. According to the *Milindapañha*, ed. V. Trenckner (PTS), 32, animals are capable of "thought" (*manasikāra*), but not of "insight" (*paññā*).

32. *Viṣṇu Purāṇa* II, 3, 11 (22) ff.; see also W. Kirfel, *Bhāratavarṣa*. Stuttgart, 1931, 49; 63.

33. *Ṛgveda* VI, 21, 11; VIII, 87, 5.

34. See below, ch. 10 (originally in: Nachrichten Ak. Wiss. Göttingen, Phil.-hist. Klasse, Jahrg. 1975, Nr. 9). The dharmic significance of the

sexes and the position of women in Indian ritual and soteriological thought would be a topic of its own, deserving a separate detailed discussion.

35. See BSBh I, 3, 34: *sāmarthyam api laukikaṃ kevalaṃ na-adhikārakāraṇaṃ bhavati.*

36. See Bhāruci (ed. J. D. M. Derrett) on Manu X, 42: *eṣa varṇavibhāga utkarṣāpakarṣasambandho manuṣyaviṣaya eva draṣṭavyaḥ, na gavādiṣu.*

37. See *India and Europe*, ch. 11.

38. Śabara on MS VI, 1, 5 ff.

39. "L'ātman dans le commentaire de Śabarasvāmin;" in: *Mélanges d'Indianisme: A la mémoire de L. Renou.* Paris, 1968, 117.

40. *Ṛjuvimalā* on *Bṛhatī* VI, 1, 4; ed. S. Subrahmanya Sastri, vol. 5. Madras, 1967, 55 f.

41. See MS VI, 1, 1 ff. and commentaries; already *Taittirīya Saṃhitā VII*, 1, 1, 6 states: *śūdro yajñe 'navakḷptaḥ.*

42. See below, ch. 10.

43. See Śālikanātha Miśra, *Prakaraṇapañcikā*, ed. A. Subrahmanya Sastri. Benares, 1967 100 f.: *na hi nānāstrīpuruṣavyaktiṣu puruṣatvād arthāntarabhūtam ekam ākāram ātmasākṣātkurvantī matir āvirbhavati.* The two usages of *puruṣa* in this passage have different connotations: "male" and "human"; as indicated, *puruṣa* can also mean the immortal principle in man as well as in other living beings. The fact that the term *puruṣa* has these different connotations has very significant implications for what we have called "implicit anthropology" in the Indian tradition. However, we cannot discuss these implications in the current context.

44. The whole verse reads:

āhāranidrābhayamaithunaṃ ca sāmānyam
etat paśubhir narāṇām /

dharmo hi teṣām adhiko viśeṣo, dharmeṇa
hīnāḥ paśubhiḥ samānāḥ.

This verse is often ascribed to the *Hitopadeśa*, but it is found only in some editions (e.g., Vāsudevācārya Aināpure. Bombay, 1928, p. 3), and it seems to be an interpolation. In a similar fashion, some Tantric texts associate man with *jñāna*, "knowledge"; cf. *Kulārṇava Tantra* I, 69: *nidrādimaithunāhārāḥ sarveṣāṃ prāṇināṃ samāḥ / jñānavān mānavaḥ prokto, jñānahīnaḥ paśuḥ, priye.* Analogous statements presenting various other capabilities or reponsibilities as distinguishing marks of man are found in some versions of the *Śatakatraya* traditionally attributed to Bhartṛhari; cf. *The Nīti and Vairāgya Śatakas of Bhartṛhari*, ed. and transl. by M.R. Kale. Bombay, 1910, p. 5, v. 13, where a man who is not acquainted with poetry, music and the arts is called a "beast without horns and tail" (*sāhityasaṃgītakalāvihīnaḥ sākṣāt paśuḥ pucchaviṣāṇahīnaḥ*); also verse 14, where "learning, austerities, giving" (*vidyā, tapas, dāna*) are identified as normative characteristics of man. These verses are not found in D. D. Kosambi's critical edition of the *Śatakatraya*, which is the basis of B. S. Miller's edition and translation (New York, 1967). But see v. 70 in this edition (i.e., v. 20, ed. Kale): *vidyā nāma narasya rūpam adhikam . . . vidyāvihīnaḥ paśuḥ*; in Miller's translation: "knowledge is man's crowning mark . . . when he lacks it, a man is a brute." On "reasoning" (*vicāra, vicāritā*) as a specific mandate of man, see *Yogavāsiṣṭha, Mumukṣuprakaraṇa* XIV, 46 (ed. L. S. Paṇśīkar. Bombay, 1937, I, 109).

45. This, of course, is far less relevant if seen in the context of karma and rebirth. See also *India and Europe*, ch. 16 (on the concept of dharma in general).

46. Cf. BSBh I, 3, 30 ff.

47. *The Vedānta Sūtras of Bādarāyaṇa with the commentary by Śaṅkara*, translated by G. Thibaut, vol. I. Oxford, 1890 (reprint New York, 1962), 7 f. For the Sanskrit text, see Śaṅkara, *Works* III, 3; the theme of "ne-science" (*avidyā*) and "superimposition" (*adhyāsa*) as comprising "worldly" (*laukika*) as well as "Vedic" (*vaidika, śāstrīya*) transactions has been introduced in the preceding section. Cf. NBh I, 1, 7: *evam ebhiḥ pramāṇair devamanuṣyatiraścāṃ vyavahārāḥ prakalpante.*

48. For various interpretations of the puruṣārthas, see A. Sharma, *The Puruṣārthas: A Study in Hindu Axiology*. East Lansing, Mich., 1982.

49. Cf. BSBh I, 3, 30.

50. Śaṅkara on *Taittirīya Upaniṣad* II, 1, 1.

51. Cf. Sureśvara, *Sambandhavārttika*, v. 1016 f.: The desires of men and animals are similar; but unlike men, the animals "do not know the means" (*na tu jānanti sādhanam*).

52. Cf. BSBh I, 3, 34.

53. See specifically M. Heidegger, *Brief über den "Humanismus" (an Jean Beaufret)*; in: *Platons Lehre von der Wahrheit*. Bern, 1947.

54. Cf. R. Descartes, *Discours de la méthode* ("Discourse on Method"), ch. 6.

55. See above, n. 1.

56. The role of man is, of course, conspicuously different in modern Indian thought as it developed in response to the Western challenge. It may suffice here to refer to the Bengali thinker and writer Bankim Chandra Chatterji (Bankimcandra Caṭṭopādhyāya, 1838–1894), whose "anthropological" thought reflects A. Comte's positivistic "religion of man," trying to apply it to the reinterpretation of the traditional Hindu concepts of *dharma* and *svadharma*. "The Religion of Man" is the title of Rabindranath Tagore's Hibbert Lectures (1930; London, fifth ed., 1958). Even in otherwise rather traditionalistic recent Pandit literature, modified ways of dealing with man may be found; see Maheśacandra Nyāyaratna, *Brief Notes on the Modern Nyāya System* (in Sanskrit). Calcutta, s.d., 8 (on *manuṣyatva*); Vidyāśaṅkara Bhāratī, *Dhārmikavimarśasamuccaya*. Poona, 1944, 142; 206 (man as goal-oriented, responsible actor in the world). See also N. K. Reddy, *The Concept of Man in R. Tagore and S. Radhakrishnan*. Bangalore, 1973. H. J. Klimkeit, "Bipin Chandra Pal- Der Künder eines indischen Humanismus." *Zeitschrift für Religions- und Geistesgeschichte* 32 (1980), 241–254.

CHAPTER 9

Competing Causalities: Karma, Vedic Rituals, and the Natural World

Introduction

1. It is one of the familiar paradoxes of the Indian religious and philosophical tradition that the theory and mythology of transmigration and karma, obviously one of the most basic and most commonly accepted premises of this tradition, is not found in its most ancient and venerable documents. "There is no trace of transmigration in the hymns of the Vedas; only in the Brāhmaṇas are there to be found a few traces of the lines of thought from which the doctrine arose."[1] We cannot and need not discuss here in detail the complex and controversial question of its origins and early developments; a few reminders may be sufficient.[2]

The available sources seem to indicate that the doctrine of rebirth, karma, and *saṃsāra* was preceded by the idea of *punarmṛtyu*, "redeath," "dying again." Provided there is a continuation of our existence after this earthly death—does it come to an end, too? What is the nature of this end? Is it unavoidable? The notion of *punarmṛtyu* leads to that of *punarāvṛtti*, "return" into an earthly existence; the idea of cycles of death and birth, of transmigrations through many lives, of the lasting and retributive efficacy of our deeds becomes more and more prevalent in the Upaniṣads, and it wins almost universal acceptance in subsequent literature. However, its formulations in the older Upaniṣads are still tentative and partial; it is still open to basic questions and doubts, not organized and universalized into one complete and comprehensive world-view. There is an element of controversy, novelty, secrecy, illustrated by a famous passage of the *Bṛhadāraṇyaka Upaniṣad* that tells us how Ārtabhāga received this teaching from Yājñavalkya.[3] Not only here, but to a certain degree even in such texts as the *Mahābhārata*, it appears still in competition with other theories and concepts, for example, those of *kāla* and *niyati*.[4]

There are many different versions, adaptations and approximations of the karma theory. It is neither necessary nor appropriate to search for one true and ultimate version. However, the Indian tradition itself has developed distinctive criteria that reflect a certain level of centralization and theoretical consolidation, and that may be used to distinguish the systematized and "axiomatic" versions of the karma theory from more casual and tentative conceptions of retributive causality. Among these, the allied notions of *akṛtābhyāgama* and *kṛtavipraṇāśa*, i.e., the occurrence of what is not due to karma and the disappearance of karmic results, are most significant. Both of these terms denote *prasaṅgas*, undesirable consequences to be uncovered in the argumentation of an opponent. They presuppose two interrelated premises: there should be no undeserved experience of suffering or well-being; and no effect of a past deed should be lost. This dual criterion of strict karma appears in Hindu, Buddhist, and Jaina sources. It is invoked by Nāgārjuna and Siddhasena Divākara as well as the great teachers of "orthodox" Nyāya, Mīmāṃsā, and Advaita Vedānta; it is also recorded in the Mahābhārata.[5] It would be easy to add numerous references from later texts. They are generally brief and casual and show that this was a recognized premise and basic rule that, though susceptible to exceptions, modifications and reinterpretations, could not simply be disregarded with impunity.

We are not in a position to locate with precision the origin of a strict, systematically committed, "axiomatic" notion of karma. It is, however, safe to assume that the contribution of the Buddha to the consolidation and systematization of the karma theory, that is above all, to its formulation in terms of strict and pervasive causality, was considerable. This is something that seems to be associated with the very idea of his enlightenment. The Buddha, or the early Buddhists, also clarified and redefined the concept of action as ethically relevant conduct in the spheres of the mind, speech, and body; they gave a new emphasis to the role of intention and awareness in the karmic process.[6]

In contrast with its absence in the Vedic hymns and with its still controversial and somewhat tentative status in the most ancient Upaniṣads, the doctrine of karma and *saṃsāra* seems to be fully established and almost universally accepted as a comprehensive world-view in classical and later Indian thought. Only the Cārvākas and other "materialists" appear as rigorous critics of its basic premises[7]—the belief in a continued existence beyond death, in cycles of death and birth, in the retributive, ethically committed causality of our actions. For the materialists, as far as they are known to us from the reports and references of their opponents,[8] death, that is, the dissolution of our physical body, is the end. There is no inherent power of retribution attached to our deeds. There is no goal or value beyond earthly pleasure. "The elements are earth, water, fire, and air. Wealth and pleasure are the sole aims of man. The elements move through original impulse. There is no other world. Emancipation is death."[9] "Dharma and adharma don't exist; there is no result of good and bad actions."[10] "As long as we live, let's have a pleasant life."[11] The awareness of this basically different approach, this materialistic and hedonistic denial of the foundations of the karma theory, is to a certain extent kept alive by the traditions of the Hindus as well as of the Jainas and Buddhists, in particular in doxographic literature. Haribhadra's *Ṣaḍdarśanasamuccaya*, Mādhava's *Sarvadarśanasaṃgraha*, the *Sarvasiddhāntasaṃgraha* falsely attributed to Śaṅkara, and various other works of this type all present the Cārvāka view as one of the traditional world-views and as a fully established *darśana*; other texts deplore the growing influence of materialistic and hedonistic ways of thinking.[12]

However, the doxographic presentation of the Cārvākas is usually highly stereotyped. Their position is far from being a living philosophical challenge to the authors of later times; it appears rather fossilized in its contents and argumentation. There is no "dialogue" between the materialists and their opponents. Their criticism of the ideas of immortality and retribution, which are basic premises of the theory of karma, is preserved by the tradition; but it is not much more than a relic from the distant past. This is true in spite of the fact that materialistic thought in India underwent certain distinctive developments, and that the old ideas attributed to Bṛhaspati and Purandara were adjusted, modified, and refined in response to the arguments presented by the Hindu and Buddhist opponents.[13] As a matter of fact, what the doxographic accounts present as the explicit target of this criticism is in most instances not the theory of karma and *saṃsāra* as such, but rather the belief in immortality and retribution in general or in its older forms. Vedic sacrifices, which relate to the "other world" (*paraloka*), to a continued existence of our ancestors, and so forth, are ridiculed, particularly the *śrāddha* ceremony: There is no "other world," nobody in it for whom our sacrificial activities might be useful.[14] It is this criticism of doctrines and practices of the Vedas and Brāhmaṇas that is carried through the centuries by the doxographic tradition; "materialistic" arguments that relate, in a specific sense, to later developments of the doctrine of karma and saṃsāra are very rare.[15] It should, however, be noted that the Tibetan Buddhist tradition paid more specific attention to the documentation as well as refutation of materialistic arguments against this doctrine.[16]

2. Apart from the Cārvākas and certain other "materialists" and "fatalists,"[17] virtually nobody in the classical and later traditions of Indian religion and philosophy has questioned the basic principles of the theory of karma. There seems to be no explicit awareness and hardly any reflection of the initial absence of the theory in the oldest period of thought, although the texts which document this absence are carefully preserved. The doctrine of karma and saṃsāra is projected into the most ancient texts, including the Vedic hymns;[18] it is always taken as their indispensable background and presupposition. Concepts and theories that were initially used independently of and without reference to the karma theory, and that, in its earlier phases, appear side by side with it and as its possible rivals, are reinterpreted in the light of the karma theory, are accommodated to or even identified with it. Various forms of adjustment combine the Sāṃkhya theory of *prakṛti* and the three guṇas, *sattva, rajas* and *tamas*, with the karma theory. *Daiva, niyati*, and so forth, no longer represent an impersonal cosmic "fate," but are constituted by one's own past actions; *kāla*, "time," is no longer seen as an independent ordaining principle, but becomes a function of karma.[19] Karma explains the causes of our present fate[20] by means of what has been regarded as "one underlying fundamental intuition."[21] But although it may be argued that karma is directed toward a single all-comprehensive world-view,[22] we cannot disregard the concrete historical varieties and deep-rooted tensions and ambiguities which remain with the theory even in its fully developed "classical" versions.[23]

There are symptomatic border problems, "grey zones," questions and ambiguities concerning the scope and limits of karmic causality. It is by no means simply taken for granted that the whole world is just a stage for ethically committed or soteriologically meaningful events, or that natural processes are necessarily governed by or subordinate to retributive causality. The realm of cosmology and even that of biology is not *eo ipso* coextensive with the realm of saṃsāra, that is, of retribution and of possible soteriological progression. There are various ways of specifying and delimiting karma and saṃsāra and of relating karmic causality to other contexts of causality.

The theory of karma and saṃsāra is not, and certainly has not always been, *the* Indian way of thinking. It does not represent one basically unquestioned pattern and premise of thought, and it would be quite inadequate to try to find one master key, one single hermeneutic device that would allow us to understand it all at once and once and for all. As a matter of fact, the understanding of the karma theory has often been hampered by an exclusive and thus misleading search for *one* basic principle or pattern of thought, *one* essential meaning, *one* "underlying intuition," by an exclusive interest in its core and its essence, disregarding its perimeter and its limits, its conflicts and its tensions.[24]

In its concrete totality, the doctrine of karma and saṃsāra is a very complex phenomenon, both historically and systematically. It functions at various levels of understanding and interpretation, as an unquestioned presupposition as well as an explicit theory, in popular mythology as well as in philosophical thought. In its various contexts and applications, it has at least three basically different functions and dimensions: karma is (1) a principle of causal explanation (of factual occurrences); (2) a guideline of ethical orientation; (3) the counterpart and stepping-stone of final liberation. These three functions are balanced, reconciled, and integrated in various manners; they do not form a simple and unquestioned unity.

An analysis of these three functions and their complex relationships is far beyond the scope of this presentation. We will only consider a few central conceptual issues, as we find them reflected in traditional Hindu and Buddhist thought.

Concerning the first function, we may recall here Kant's definition of explanation ("Erklären") as "derivation from a principle which one must be able to comprehend and state clearly";[25] at this point, we do not have to discuss the nature of such a "principle," that is, whether it is a true law, or just a familiar rule or regularity. We may also recall the correspondence of explanation and prediction. Being able to "explain" events or phenomena according to the "principle" of karma and rebirth, just as explanation in general, can relate to the past as well as the present; and extending the process of explanation into the future means extrapolation into prediction. In our present context, this leads us from the first to the second function of the idea of karma. The prediction and expectation of desirable and undesirable karmic results can be transformed into codes of behavior; on the other hand, social and ethical codes or value systems can easily be translated into the language of karmic reward and punishment.

As is well known, the ultimate goal of Indian philosophy is not the conceptual mastery of the realm of karma, but its transcendence. Karma, together with *avidyā*, "nescience," "misconception," is a fundamental condition of our being-in-the-world, i.e., of *saṃsāra* and *duḥkha*. It is a condition that has to be overcome. It is—and this is the third function of karma in Indian thought—the counterpart of the idea of final liberation (*nirvāṇa, mokṣa*, etc.).

In certain Indian texts, most conspicuously in the Dharmaśāstra literature and in some Purāṇas, we find elaborate lists of actions and their appropriate karmic results, specifically forms of karmic punishment for prohibited acts, that is, undesirable modes of existence in this world or in the underworld. As examples, we may mention the twelfth chapter of the *Manusmṛti* and the *Pretakalpa* of the *Garuḍa Purāṇa*. No such lists appear normally in philosophical literature. Instead, the philosophers are more interested in the fundamental condition of our current existence and the general dynamism of motivations, acts and resulting experiences which keep the process of life, death and rebirth going. The Yoga and other systems refer to the "wheel of saṃsāra" (*saṃsāracakra*), which is upheld by the "spokes" (*ara*) of merit and demerit (*dharma, adharma*), pleasure and pain (*sukha, duḥkha*), attachment and aversion (*rāga, dveṣa*).[26] We have, of course, also to mention the Buddhist formula of "dependent origination" (*pratītyasamutpāda*) and its adaptations in various Hindu systems, such as the Nyāya.[27]

In this connection, it is also important to remember that, in spite of their close alliance, the ideas of karma and of rebirth are not identical. The explanatory role of rebirth, i.e., of the alleged fact of previous existences, has to be distinguished from that of karma. The experience gained in previous lives is supposed to account for certain innate abilities and instinctual forms of behavior, such as the newborn baby's ability to breathe and to suck mother's milk, and (specifically in Yoga) the fear of death and clinging to life itself (*abhiniveśa, ātmāśis*).[28] Such argumentation does not necessarily imply any reference to karmic retribution; it can, in a sense, be ethically neutral. On the other hand, the theory postulates that without karma there would be no rebirth.

3. Although the philosophers do not normally put forth specific schemes of karmic retribution, they seem nevertheless convinced of the validity of such schemes. They accept them as warranted by the sacred tradition, or by certain superhuman forms of insight (*yogipratyakṣa*). The explanatory role of karma in which they are interested is, above all, associated with the internal variety (*vaicitrya*) and apparent unevenness and injustice (*vaiṣamya*) in the realm of life. Why is it that living beings, in particular humans, are not alike? Why are some long-lived and some short-lived, some healthy, some sickly, some handsome, and some ugly? The answer is, of course, karma.[29]

Explanation of this kind is obviously not explanation in the modern scientific sense, but something much closer to theodicy. As a matter of fact, the reference to karma in such cases is in some significant instances combined with an explicit vindication and exculpation of the "Lord" (*īśvara*). The commentaries on Brahmasūtra II, 1, 34, in particular that by Śaṅkara, provide an impressive example. Following the clues given by the Sūtra, Śaṅkara states that the Lord, in his role as creator or organizer of an uneven world, takes into consideration the good and bad karma of the creatures, and that therefore there is no unfairness or cruelty (*vaiṣamya, nairghṛṇya*) on his part: "The creation is uneven in accordance with the merit and demerit of the creatures; for this, the Lord cannot be blamed" (*ataḥ sṛjyamānaprāṇidharmādharmāpekṣā viṣamā sṛṣṭir iti naayam īśvarasya-aparādhaḥ*).[30] The association of karma and theodicy is also obvious, though perhaps less conspicuous, in Nyāya and Vaiśeṣika.[31] Of course, the Lord is not bound by the power of karma; he may choose to transcend or supersede it by virtue of his divine grace. This idea is of great significance in the theology of the theistic sects and *bhakti* movements.

To be sure, in old Buddhism (and Jainism), there is no room for an explicit theodicy of this kind. Instead, we may say that the theory of karma and rebirth functions in lieu of a theodicy. One of the earliest examples of this is, in the canon of the Theravāda Buddhists, the *Cūḷakammavibhaṅgasutta* of the *Majjhimanikāya*. Here, a young brahmin wants to know why people are handsome or ugly, rich or poor, short-lived or long-lived, stupid or intelligent. The Buddha instructs him that this is due to the fact that they are owners as well as products of their karma.[32] Many centuries later, a Sinhalese Buddhist tract against Christianity cites the variety of modes of existence not only as evidence for karma, but also against the idea of a divine creator: If the world were the creation of God, "all children born would be of one color, of one disposition, of one nature, the same in wisdom, equal in happiness, and of the same race."[33]

What is karma? What is an "act," and what is the nature of its "unseen" (*adṛṣṭa*) retributive potential? Are all activities, all transactions "acts" or "deeds" in a karmically relevant sense? The ways in which these questions have been answered or addressed vary widely. They range from the Buddhist conception of *karman/kamma* as ethically relevant conduct in thought, speech and physical action to the orthodox brahminical notion of ritual "works." The most restrictive position, extreme even within the Pūrvamīmāṃsā, is that of Bhartṛmitra who is credited with the view that only specifically enjoined and goal-oriented Vedic performances (i.e., *kāmyakarman*), not regular rituals (*nityakarman*) or prohibited acts, produce the invisible potential of *apūrva*.[34] While the other Mīmāṃsakas, including Kumārila, reject this claim, they, too, correlate *apūrva* with Vedic injunctions and prohibitions. To what extent do they recognize general karma, i.e., the retributive potential of ethically relevant deeds, apart from the Vedic *apūrva*? Whatever the specific answers may be, the Mīmāṃsakas, as guardians of Vedic "orthodoxy," tend to subordinate the "general karma" to the special causal power of the rituals. Other philosophers, specifically in the various schools of Vedānta, have tried to find different forms of balance and interaction between the domains of Vedic rituals and ethical conduct (*ācāra*, *caraṇa*). This debate can be traced back to the predecessors of Bādarāyaṇa, such as Kārṣṇājini, and pursued to the later Vaiṣṇava commentators of Bādarāyaṇa's *Brahmasūtra*, for instance Rāmānuja.[35]

What is the scope and nature of karmic causality? Which are the effects karma produces in the world? Where and how can they be located?[36] As a rule, the realm of karmic causality is the realm of life; its effects should be felt by living beings. The experiences (*bhoga*) of pleasure and pain are the primary results of karma. However, these are inseparable from external conditions and do not simply occur (if we disregard certain idealistic, subjectivistic doctrines) in the private mental lives of the subjects of experience. As a matter of fact, *duḥkha* and *sukha* themselves have objective as well as subjective implications. According to Śaṅkara and others, the hierarchy of pain and pleasure, or suffering and well-being, coincides with the objective hierarchy of creatures from the plants and low animals to human and finally divine beings.[37] According to classical Yoga, the results of karma are birth into a particular species (*jāti*), length of life (*āyus*), and experience (*bhoga*).[38]

Karma is supposed to be personal, i.e., attached to one individual being or life-process. But how can this be isolated from the shared and public world in which living beings coexist? How do one's own experiences, together with their external conditions, interfere with the *bhoga* of others? Does one's own personal and private karma contribute to the formation of a public and common reality, so that an appropriate share of pleasure or pain may be derived from it? How literally can the rule that nothing undeserved, that is, not resulting from or corresponding to karma, ought to be experienced (*akṛtābhyāgama*), be taken in a shared natural and social world? To what extent is this entire world itself, this stage for karmic performances and their results, a product of karma? Is the world essentially a karmic show, a projection of retributional causality? What is the reality of objects apart from their capability to provide karmically relevant experiences, i.e., their *bhogyatva*?[39]

Again, we find a variety of answers or implicit assumptions relating to these questions. *Karman/kamma* has clearly cosmogonic implications in some Buddhist schools; at least, the possibility receives serious attention.[40] Śaṅkara, among others, suggests that acts, primarily those affiliated with the Veda, produce and uphold the reality and structure of the empirical world.[41] On the other hand, most systems credit the world with an independent reality and certain regularities of its own. Among these, the Vaiśeṣika provides the example of a system which is committed to the description and explanation of the world, including natural, "physical" phenomena and processes, and to a comprehensive classification of its basic components. What is the place of karma in such a system? How does karmic causality function in this context? How does it relate to, and interact with, what is going on in the "natural world"?

In different ways, the Vaiśeṣika and the Mīmāṃsā illustrate the theme of "competing causalities," that is, competing, overlapping domains of explanation and expectation. In the following, we will try to identify and analyze some of the problems that arise from the encounter and juxtaposition of karma and other contexts of causation. The perspective will be historical. The presentation will focus on cases that reflect historical changes, that illustrate the differences and tensions between older and later levels of thought, and that exemplify the adjustment of pre-karmic and extra-karmic ways of thinking to the theory of karma and *saṃsāra*. We will first discuss the Mīmāṃsā concept of *apūrva*, specifically its interpretation by Kumārila. Then we will deal with some basic problems concerning the Vaiśeṣika concept of *adṛṣṭa*. A short "epilogue" will refer to the "way of the fathers" in the Upaniṣads and to Śaṅkara's consummation and transcendence of the theory of karma and rebirth.

Karma and the Mīmāṃsā Concept of *Apūrva*

4. The Mīmāṃsā, more properly Pūrvamīmāṃsā or Karmamīmāṃsā, presents itself as the advocate of the Vedic foundations against criticisms, changes, and reinterpretations. Divided into various schools, it carries the exegesis and defense of the Vedic sacrificial dharma into the period of the classical philosophical systems, into their framework of methods and presuppositions. It carries with it a set of pre-Upaniṣadic notions and ways of thinking which may appear obsolete in the new atmosphere. On the other hand, it disregards or rejects ideas or doctrines that have become basic premises for the other systems. Final liberation (mokṣa), commonly accepted as a leading theme or even as the basic concern of philosophical thought, does not play any role in the older literature of the system; Mīmāṃsā deals with dharma, not with mokṣa.[42] Familiar ideas like the cyclical destruction of the world (*mahāpralaya*), "yogic perception" (*yogipratyakṣa*), the "Lord" (īśvara), and so forth, remain excluded even in its later literature.[43] For our present discussion, the following is of peculiar significance: the Mīmāṃsā carries the heritage of the "prekarmic" past of the Indian tradition into an epoch for which karma and saṃsāra have become basic premises. As well as their counterpart, mokṣa, the concepts of karma and saṃsāra do not play any role in the *Mīmāṃsāsūtra* and remain negligible in its oldest extant commentary, Śabara's *Bhāṣya*. These texts do not deal with "works" or "deeds" in general, and they do not refer to or presuppose any general theory of an ethically committed, retributive causality inherent in such deeds. They deal only with the specific efficacy of the Vedic sacrificial works.

However, with the transformation of Mīmāṃsā into a comprehensive, fully developed philosophical system, karma and saṃsāra, as well as mokṣa, become more significant and manifest in its thought and argumentation, not so much as explicit themes, but as tacitly accepted presuppositions or as points of reference and orientation.[44] This is exemplified in a very peculiar and complex manner by the writings of Kumārila, the most successful systematizer of the Mīmāṃsā tradition. Kumārila's basic concern in this connection is to explicate and to justify the specific Mīmāṃsā ideas about the efficacy of the Vedic rituals, which are considered to be the core of dharma. He has to do this in the context and atmosphere of ways of thinking for which karma and saṃsāra have not only become basic premises but which have also developed sophisticated theoretical models and a keen sense of problems in this area and with reference to causality in general. Kumārila's procedure presents a remarkable example of a highly specialized and idiosyncratic line of thinking that nevertheless illustrates some of the most basic problems of the functioning of karma and of causality in general. The efficiency of the Vedic rituals entails its own special and "transkarmic" (or rather, "protokarmic") causality; the encounter of this type of causality with the wider causal context of karma and saṃsāra leads to symptomatic questions of correspondence and mutual adjustment. The discussion of these problems centers around the concept of *apūrva*, for Kumārila that particular "potency" that gathers and stores the efficacy of the Vedic rituals and makes it possible for transitory sacrificial performances to have lasting effects in the distant future.

Although the term *apūrva* occurs in both Jaimini's *Mīmāṃsāsūtra* and Bādarāyaṇa's *Vedāntasūtra*,[45] Śabara is the earliest source directly relevant for our discussion. However, before we turn to his *Mīmāṃsābhāṣya* and its commentaries and subcommentaries, it seems appropriate to recall the background and prehistory of the classical Mīmāṃsā usage of apūrva, and a different line of development in the history of the concept. First of all, we have to refer to its usage in grammatical literature where it pertains to "prescriptive rules" (*vidhi*) that teach something new, not said before. More significantly, numerous sources mention an old Mīmāṃsā theory of apūrva which is conspicuously different from its explication in Kumārila's Bhāṭṭa school, and which is in general not well documented in the extant Mīmāṃsā literature. Among these sources, the following ones deserve special attention: Bhartṛhari's *Vākyapadīya* and its commentary by Helārāja; Bhavya's *Madhyamakahṛdayakārikā* and its commentary, or autocommentary, the *Tarkajvālā*; Uddyotakara's *Nyāyavārttika*; Vyomaśiva's *Vyomavatī*; and finally Jayanta's *Nyāyamañjarī*.[46]

According to the theory indicated by these sources, *apūrva* is a synonym of *dharma* itself, and it is an impersonal and substrateless (*anāśrita*) potentiality, a kind of cosmic principle or power to be manifested or actualized by the ritual acts (*kriyāvyaṅgya; yāgādikarmanirvartya*). According to Bhartṛhari's testimony, the action (*kriyā*) itself would have a state of substrateless potentiality. We may assume that it is this theory of apūrva which is alluded to and rejected by Kumārila in his *Ślokavārttika*; Kumārila's commentator Pārthasārathi ascribes it to a faction within the Mīmāṃsā (*ekadeśinaḥ*).[47]

5. The way in which the topic of *apūrva* is introduced and discussed by Śabara and his commentators leaves no doubt that, even within Mīmāṃsā, it is a very controversial concept. It is presented in basically different interpretations and at various levels of thematization and reification. Śabara's brief remarks are commented upon in two widely divergent sections in Prabhākara's *Bṛhatī* and in Kumārila's *Tantravārttika*.[48] Prabhākara's comments are even shorter than Śabara's own remarks; in their brevity, they remain cryptic and deliberately elusive as far as the ontological status of apūrva is concerned; for more explicit statements we have to refer to the writings of Prabhākara's follower and commentator Śālikanāthamiśra.[49] Kumārila's commentary, on the other hand, is very elaborate, and it goes far beyond Śabara's own statements; the *Apūrvādhikaraṇa* of the *Tantravārttika* is the most important and most comprehensive discussion of the topic in classical Mīmāṃsā.

At the beginning of this section, a lengthy *pūrvapakṣa* is presented, according to which the assumption of apūrva is quite unnecessary and unfounded. Kumārila's refutation is a special application of the epistemological device of *arthāpatti*, "circumstantial inference" or "negative implication": Vedic injunctions would be meaningless or misleading if the connection between the sacrificial acts and their future results were not established; apūrva is this indispensable connecting link. Apūrva is a potency produced by the sacrifice that makes it possible that its fruits be reaped at a later time; it is a bridge between the actions and their promised results. In this context, apūrva appears as a specific device to account for a specific exegetic problem. Yet Kumārila himself leaves no doubt that it has wider and more general implications and ramifications: basically, the same problem for which the concept of apūrva is supposed to provide a solution exists also in the case of ordinary, "secular" activities such as farming, eating, studying:[50] the results cannot be expected right after the completion of the acts, but only some time in the future. A certain storable "power" (*śakti*), which may also be interpreted as a potential state of the expected result, is necessary as a connecting and mediating principle between act and result. This is a rule that applies to all cases of instrumentality and to the causal efficiency of actions in general.[51] The actions as such are sequences of vanishing moments. They can gain totality, coherence, and future efficacy only if, in spite of their temporal disparity and constant disintegration, their causal power is accumulated and integrated and remains present up to the completion of the appropriate results. This is even more obvious in the case of complex activities that combine various actual performances at various times and occasions; a favorite example in the sacrificial field is the new and full moon sacrifice, *darśapūrṇamāsa*.[52]

We cannot and need not enlarge here on the technical details and scholastic developments of the theory of apūrva. One of the main issues is how subdivisions in the realm of apūrva are supposed to correspond to the complexities of the rituals and the Vedic pronouncements by which they are enjoined, how certain subordinate, auxiliary actions have or produce their own specific units of apūrva, and how these contribute to the final and comprehensive apūrva of the complete sacrifice, which in turn corresponds to the unity and totality of the result, for example, heaven, *svarga*.[53] Basically, apūrva comes in "units" of higher and lower order; incomplete acts do not produce any apūrva at all; and the subordinate apūrvas of the auxiliary parts of the sacrifice do not accomplish anything independently, if the whole sacrifice is not completed.[54] On the other hand, the distinguishability of the various apūrvas or "units" of apūrva accounts for the multiplicity and variety of the results.[55]

6. In trying to locate apūrva, to account for its lasting presence after the disappearance of the sacrificial act as a physical act, Kumārila ultimately resorts to the soul of the sacrificer—although apūrva remains for him a potency (*yogyatā*) generated by, and in a sense belonging to, not the sacrificing person, but the principal sacrifice (*pradhānakarman*) itself. The causal potencies created and left behind by the sacrificial acts remain present as traces or dispositions (*saṃskāra*) in the person who has performed them; according to Kumārila, there is no other possible substratum in which they could inhere.[56]

Throughout his discussion, Kumārila takes it for granted that in its basic dimensions his discussion of apūrva responds to problems that concern acting in general, in particular the relationship of acts to such results that occur only in the distant future. In a sense, it appears as a case study on the causal efficiency of acts in general. Yet the dividing line which separates apūrva from other types of causal potency remains clear and irreducible. Apūrva is unique insofar as it results exclusively from the execution of Vedic injunctions; and its separation from the juxtaposition with other, "secular" types of acting and of causal potency leads to peculiar though mostly implicit problems of coordination and of possible interference.

There seems to be a basic assumption that if Vedic rites, including all subsidiary acts, are performed in strict accordance with the Vedic rules, they will not fail to produce their proper results. Sacrificial, "apūrvic" causality seems to operate within a finite and well-defined set of conditions, a kind of closed system, in which it seems to be secure from outside interference: in bringing about its assigned result, the power of the sacrifice, that is, apūrva, will prevail over other possible influences, including those which might arise from the general karmic status of the sacrificer.[57]

The standard example of sacrificial result in Kumārila's discussion is the attainment of heaven (*svarga*); in this case it is obviously impossible to challenge empirically the efficacy of the sacrifice, that is, its power to produce the result. However, there are other cases where the actual occurrence of the result is not relegated to a future life or a transempirical state of being. The most notable among these is the *citrā* ceremony,[58] which is supposed to lead to the attainment of cattle (*paśu*) and thus presents itself as an easy target of criticism and ridicule, already referred to and discussed in Śabara's *Bhāṣya*.[59] Kumārila devotes one chapter of his *Ślokavārttika* to presenting the arguments against the *citrā* ceremony (*Citrākṣepa*) and another one to refuting these arguments (*Citrākṣepaparihāra*). In his refutation, he does not resort to any extra-apūrvic factors, such as the bad karma of the sacrificer, to account for the obvious irregularities in the appearance of the assigned result. It is simply the nature of the citrā sacrifice that there is no specified and exactly predictable temporal sequence between its performance and the occurrence of the result. The desired result, the attainment of cattle, may very well occur not in this but in a future life; on the other hand, cases of the acquisition of cattle that are not preceded by empirically ascertainable citrā performances should be seen as results and indicators of performances of this ritual in a previous existence, and the invisible causal agency of apūrva should be taken as directing the visible sequence of events.[60]

In the case of the "rain-producing" *kārīrī* sacrifice, however, relegation of the result to an indefinite future seems to be much less acceptable, since what is at stake here is the production of rain in the immediate future. In this case, Kumārila cannot avoid referring to adverse apūrvic influences, to the counterproductive efficacy of other Vedic actions, which, at least temporarily, prevent the result of the kārīrī ceremony (rain) from appearing. Kumārila's commentator Pārthasārathi adds that we are dealing here with acts prohibited by the Veda, the result of which stands in opposition to the production of rain; at any rate, the obstructive influence should itself be rooted in specific acts enjoined or prohibited by the Veda, not in any general karmic circumstances.[61]

Kumārila's discussion of apūrva remains for the most part restricted to "optional rites" (*kāmyakarman*) and rites for specific occasions, which are aimed at the fulfillment of specific desires and needs and presented in terms of positive injunctions (vidhi). The question whether there is an *apūrva* corresponding to the violation of prohibitions (*pratiṣedha*), that is, resulting from such actions that according to the Veda will lead to punishments or undesirable consequences, is only briefly referred to by Kumārila.[62] Basically, he is ready to accept such a negative counterpart of the positive potential resulting from proper sacrificial enactments: there is an apūrva resulting from violating the prohibition to kill a brahmin, and it will accomplish the punishment of the violator in hell (*naraka*). Yet it is not surprising that Kumārila does not further enlarge on this point. He has obviously reached a rather delicate border area of his theory of apūrva that would make it difficult for him to avoid various conceptual entanglements and to keep his discussion within the limits of a specifically Vedic context of causality and from lapsing into the general field of "karmic," that is, retributive causality: What, for example, is the mechanism governing a violator of a Vedic prohibition who is not entitled to the study of the Veda and thus cannot derive any apūrva from it? What happens to a śūdra killing a brahmin?

Another point not really clarified is the apūrvic status of the "permanent rites" (*nityakarman*), regular performances which are not designed for the attainment of specific results. In the *Ślokavārttika*,[63] Kumārila mentions them casually in connection with the theme of final liberation, which is not really his own concern; their value consists in their contribution to eliminating past demerit and to keeping off such demerit which would result if they were not performed. The systematic implications of these suggestions are not pursued.

Apūrva is a conceptual device designed to keep off or circumvent empirically oriented criticism of the efficacy of sacrifices, to establish a causal nexus not subject to the criterion of direct, observable sequence. Yet, in trying to safeguard metaphysically the apūrvic sanctuary of sacrificial causality, Kumārila repeatedly emphasizes that its basic problems are parallel to those of "ordinary," "secular" causality and action: the "empiricists" are not safe on their own ground; even there they cannot get along without some durable and coordinating "potency" (śakti), which must be analogous to that of apūrva.[64]

Kumārila commits himself much more deeply to developing a comprehensive metaphysical theory of apūrva than his rival Prabhākara, and he goes much more clearly and resolutely beyond Śabara's statements. In presenting the ātman as the "substratum" (*āśraya*) of apūrva, which inheres in it as a saṃskāra, he opens himself to the influence of models of thought developed in Nyāya and Vaiśeṣika and presented in Vātsyāyana's *Nyāyabhāṣya* and elsewhere. Prabhākara not only avoids locating apūrva as a saṃskāra in the sacrificer; he also avoids any comparable theoretical commitment. For him, the basic question raised by the concept of apūrva is not that of a causal mechanism functioning toward the accomplishment of a desired result (*phala*), but that of the unconditional authority and imperative power of the Veda: what is "to be done" (*kārya*) according to the Vedic injunctions has not merely and not even primarily an instrumental value, and it need not be explained or justified in terms of a coherent theory of its causal efficacy; nor does the Veda have to derive any additional motivating power from such a theory.[65] As Rāmānujācārya's *Tantrarahasya* explains in an eloquent summary of the Prābhākara views on this matter, "duty" (*kāryatā*) and "instrumentality" (*sādhanatā*) are essentially different, and the fulfillment of the Vedic injunctions (vidhi) is a purpose in itself.[66] Here, the "optional rites" are themselves interpreted in the light of the "permanent rites," which are not motivated by the expectation of a desired result.

Interaction between Mīmāṃsā and Nyāya-Vaiśeṣika

7. As we noted earlier, Kumārila, though emphasizing the parallels between apūrva and other "stored effects" of actions, does not integrate his notion of apūrva into the general context of the theory of karma, nor does he discuss problems of interaction, overlapping, or conflict between these two types and contexts of causality. There can be no doubt that Kumārila is fully aware of the karma theory and, moreover, that he recognizes it as a generally accepted and basically acceptable presupposition of philosophical thought.[67] Yet his way of dealing with it remains, in spite of a few explicit statements, casual and elusive.

While Kumārila is far from questioning the basic validity of the theory in general, he does reject certain symptomatic applications, specifically in the field of cosmology, and he points out some fundamental difficulties that arise in this context. In accordance with the Mīmāṃsā refusal to accept the doctrine of periodic world destructions and subsequent regenerations, he rejects the attempt of the Vaiśeṣika school to explain these cosmic processes by presenting the retributive power of past deeds, together with the controlling agency of the "Lord," as their efficient cause:[68] karma cannot be the moving force behind the whole world process in the theistic Vaiśeṣika or in the "atheistic" Sāṃkhya context.

On the other hand, it is obvious that the way of thinking which is exemplified by the Vaiśeṣika concept of adṛṣṭa—the retributive potency of past deeds stored as a quality of the soul (ātman)—has served as a model for the explication of apūrva by Kumārila and by subsequent authors. Apūrva and adṛṣṭa are often found in close relationship. They may be used almost interchangeably, or adṛṣṭa may function in specifically sacrificial contexts as a concept which includes apūrva.[69] We may also refer here to Śaṅkara who uses apūrva in such a way that it relates to karma, that is, what is called adṛṣṭa in Vaiśeṣika, in general.[70] However, in this context Kumārila himself uses not the term adṛṣṭa but saṃskāra, which in Vaiśeṣika is restricted to other functions. A possible source for the use of saṃskāra in Kumārila's discussion of apūrva would be the "examination of the fruit" (*phalaparīkṣā*) in the *Nyāyabhāṣya*.[71] This section responds directly to the basic concern of the apūrva discussion: How can actions, specifically sacrificial performances but also actions in a general sense, produce results which occur a long time after the completion and disappearance of the actions? The *Nyāyabhāṣya* answers that the actions leave certain dispositions (saṃskāra), namely, dharma and adharma, in the soul and that these make it possible that the fruit, such as heaven (svarga), is reaped at a much later time. Even in the choice of its examples, the *Nyāyabhāṣya* sometimes comes close to Kumārila's presentation. It is noteworthy that the interpretation of apūrva as a saṃskāra is introduced only in the *Tantravārttika*; it is not found in Kumārila's *Ślokavārttika*, which precedes the *Tantravārttika* and deals with apūrva in a more casual manner.

While Kumārila cautiously adopts for his own context what he finds useful in the Nyāya or Vaiśeṣika discussions, representatives of these systems in turn try to cope with the Mīmāṃsā theory of sacrificial causality or specifically with Kumārila's explication of apūrva. Examples may be found in Śrīdhara's *Nyāyakandalī* and in Jayanta's *Nyāyamañjarī*; a pre-Kumārila version of the theory of apūrva, basically amounting to the idea of a substrateless and impersonal power which is invoked and manifested by the sacrificial performance, was already discussed and refuted by Uddyotakara in his *Nyāyavārttika* on Sūtra I, 1, 7. A major difficulty Śrīdhara sees in Kumārila's apūrva is the way in which it is still supposed to belong to the sacrifice itself and not just to the sacrificer. For him, no real quality or potency can inhere in or belong to an action.[72] A shorter, less specific discussion is found in Vyomaśiva's Vaiśeṣika commentary,[73] in which he still refers primarily to the older view that there is a "dharma without substratum" (*anāśrito dharmaḥ*). In accordance with the main direction of the karma theory, adṛṣṭa as understood in Vaiśeṣika is not only stored in, but also belongs to and is caused by, the acting person (*puruṣa*): we are the responsible causes of our actions, of which we have to bear the consequences as traces in our own soul. In Mīmāṃsā, only the *utsarga*, the official act of initiating the sacrifice, has to be done by the sacrificer; the actual performances themselves may be left to "paid agents." Although Kumārila maintains that the soul (ātman) of the sacrificer is the subject or the "doer" of the sacrificial action, the question of personal authorship and responsibility is less important here: what produces apūrva is rather the impersonal power of the sacrifice itself, which is only unleashed, activated during the actual performance of the sacrifice. Apūrva may be stored and coordinated in the soul; yet it is not merely and not even primarily a quality or subordinate ingredient of the soul; it is and remains the effect and the stored power of the sacrifice.[74] Although Kumārila has made various adjustments to the way of thinking exemplified by the Vaiśeṣika doctrine of categories and to the theories of saṃskāra and adṛṣṭa, the magico-ritualistic world-view of the Brāhmaṇa texts, which presupposes an impersonal mechanism of forces to be invoked by the rituals, remains present as an underlying factor in his discussion of *apūrva*.

In his *Nyāyamañjarī*, Jayanta discusses the problems of sacrificial causality in accordance with the Nyāya tradition of Vedic apologetics. He is far from questioning the specific role and efficacy of Vedic rituals; in a rare case of concrete biographical information in Indian philosophical literature, he mentions an immediately successful *sāṃgrahaṇī* ceremony performed by his own grandfather; yet he does not accept the Mīmāṃsā strategy of defense.[75] Jayanta quotes repeatedly from the sacrificial discussions in Kumārila's *Ślokavārttika*; however, he gives hardly any indication that he is aware of the *Apūrvādhikaraṇa* of the *Tantravārttika*. In his criticism of the Mīmāṃsā theory of sacrificial causality, he constantly refers to a view which, unlike the theory of the *Tantravārttika*, does not recognize the storage of sacrificial effects, of apūrva, as a saṃskāra of the soul. The "saṃskāric" view (*saṃskriyāpakṣa*) is presented as a specialty of the Nyāya school.[76]

Jayanta places the theory of sacrificial efficacy more resolutely in the general framework of the theory of karma and saṃsāra. He does not accept the Mīmāṃsā restriction to specific and exclusively sacrificial contexts of causality, but sees a much more open field of possible interaction and interference with other karmic influences. The possibility of karmic and other personal deficiencies on the part of the sacrificial agent (*kartṛvaiguṇya*) is seen as much more relevant and as a potential cause of delay for the reaping of the sacrificial results. The idea of *kartṛvaiguṇya*, which appears in the *Nyāyasūtra* in the compound *karmakartṛsādhanavaiguṇya* ("deficiency of the act, the agent and/or the means"), is a cornerstone of Nyāya apologetics.[77] Since the varying degrees of immediacy and regularity in the appearance of sacrificial results can be explained by referring to various factors of merit and demerit, it becomes unnecessary for Jayanta to assume, as Kumārila does, any basic distinction in the nature of the sacrifices themselves.[78] Thus, without renouncing the special role of sacrificial causality, Jayanta tries to integrate it into the general framework of karma and saṃsāra.

Finally, we may mention here a section in Vācaspati's *Tattvavaiśāradī* on *Yogasūtra* II, 13, where the relationship between the dominant apūrva of the *jyotiṣṭoma* (the means of attaining heaven) to the negative potential of the act of killing that is subordinate to this sacrifice is discussed in a way characteristically different from Kumārila's way of dealing with this question[79]—that is, integrated into a general theory of merit, demerit, and retributive causality.

The Vaiśeṣika Concept of *Adṛṣṭa*

8. In the development of the Mīmāṃsā concept of *apūrva*, in particular in Kumārila's presentation, we found the encounter of Vedic exegesis and of the theory of the sacrifice with the general theory of karma, the attempt to defend and to explicate the uniqueness of sacrificial causality and at the same time to cope with more general and basic problems of causality and action. The Vaiśeṣika concept of *adṛṣṭa* ("unseen," "invisible"), on the other hand, exemplifies the encounter of a system of cosmology, philosophy of nature, and categorial analysis with soteriological ideas and the attempt to explicate and to justify within its own conceptual framework the theory of karma and saṃsāra.

In classical Vaiśeṣika, as represented by Praśastapāda, *adṛṣṭa* is a comprehensive term for *dharma* and *adharma*, "merit" and "demerit," two of the twenty-four qualities (*guṇa*) enumerated in the list of "categories" (*padārtha*) of the system. However, the basic text of the school, the *Vaiśeṣikasūtra* attributed to Kaṇāda, has only a list of seventeen guṇas that does not include dharma and adharma; and there is no reason to accept the later claim that they were implicitly considered as guṇas, that is, as qualities of the soul.[80] The integration of dharma and adharma into the list of guṇas is a symptomatic step in the process of the final systematization of Vaiśeṣika and of its attempted merger of soteriology and "physics."

Although the *Vaiśeṣikasūtra* does not list adṛṣṭa among the "qualities," the term and concept is nevertheless quite familiar in this text. Most of the occurrences of adṛṣṭa are found in a section[81] that deals with various causes of mostly physical movements (*karman* in the technical meaning of Vaiśeṣika, i.e., the third "category," *padārtha*): adṛṣṭa moves objects in ordeals and magnetic processes; it causes extraordinary movements of earth and water, the circulation of water in trees, the upward flaming of fire, the horizontal blowing of wind or air, the initial movements of atoms and "minds" (*manas*, in the process of forming new organisms). Another section[82] uses adṛṣṭa and dharma/adharma in a more religious and ethical perspective, referring to the "invisible" results and purposes of ritual and ethical activities, to their "merit" and "demerit." Dharma is further mentioned as a causal factor in dreams, in the extraordinary type of cognition known as *ārṣa*, and so forth.[83] It is obvious that adṛṣṭa covers at least two different sets of problems and implications, and it may be questioned whether or to what extent there is an original conceptual unity in these two usages. As far as the physical and cosmological usage of adṛṣṭa is concerned, its primary function seems to be to account for strange and extraordinary phenomena in nature which would not be explicable otherwise (magnetism, upward movement of fire, etc.), as well as for phenomena that seem to be signs or to contain an element of reward and punishment; according to Candrānanda's *Vṛtti*, the oldest extant commentary on the *Vaiśeṣikasūtra*, such events as earthquakes are indicators of good and evil (*śubhāśubhasūcana*) for the inhabitants of the earth.[84] Although there is an obvious ethical implication in the second group of cases, the *Sūtra* text does not indicate in any way that the adṛṣṭa, which is supposed to cause these events, is to be understood as inhering in souls (ātman). This assumption would seem to be even more remote in cases like the upward flaming of fire, for which no ethical, retributive, or psychological implications are suggested.[85] In cases like this, adṛṣṭa appears simply side by side with other causes of physical motions like "gravity" (*gurutva*) or "liquidity" (*dravatva*), which inhere in those material substances which they affect; like adṛṣṭa. "gravity" and "liquidity" are explicitly classified as "qualities" only in the later list of twenty-four guṇas. The most momentous function of adṛṣṭa seems to be referred to in the statement that it causes the initial movements of atoms and "minds"—the function of a "prime mover" when after a period of *mahāpralaya*, during which the whole world process has come to a complete rest, the regeneration of our universe starts again. On the other side and in an obviously different perspective, adṛṣṭa or dharma/adharma is introduced to ensure the retributive efficacy of actions which have a ritual or moral significance. In this sense, it shows a close analogy with apūrva; Śaṅkaramiśra, the author of the *Upaskāra* on the *Vaiśeṣikasūtra*, repeatedly uses the word apūrva in this context.[86]

The *Vaiśeṣikasūtra* does not state that the unseen physical power behind such phenomena as the upward flaming of fire and the retributive power of past deeds stored in the soul are identical, nor does it state that they are different. We do not know when the identity, which is taken for granted by Praśastapāda and later Vaiśeṣika, was first established in an explicit and definite manner. Already the *Nyāyabhāṣya* of Vātsyāyana has a more unified concept of dharma/adharma as being inherent in the soul; and the connection between the retributive efficacy of deeds, stored as "dispositions" (saṃskāra) of the soul, and certain physical processes has been made more explicit.[87] However, it does not consider the specific kinetic functions of adṛṣṭa mentioned in the *Vaiśeṣikasūtra*; and it does not use the term adṛṣṭa as a synonym of dharma/adharma. Instead the term is used with reference to a theory that is rejected by the *Nyāyabhāṣya* and that maintains that there is an "invisible force" (adṛṣṭa) in the material atoms (*aṇu*), also in the "mind" (*manas*), that gives them the kinetic impulse needed for the formation of bodies, and so forth; in this view, adṛṣṭa seems to function primarily as a principle of physicalistic, naturalistic explanation, and its ethical and soteriological implications remain at least very obscure.[88] The theory that adṛṣṭa resides in the atoms and not in the ātman is also referred to and rejected by Praśastapāda's commentator Vyomaśiva.[89]

9. In the tradition of the Vaiśeṣika school, its final systematizer, Praśastapāda, leaves no doubt concerning the unity of adṛṣṭa in its various physical, ethical, and religious functions. He universalizes its application as an indispensable factor functioning in the processes of life and consciousness: dharma and adharma are supporting causes and conditions of life in general (*jīvanasahakārin*), of its basic condition of breathing as well as of mental processes like desire and cognition.[90] In particular, Praśastapāda emphasizes the role of adṛṣṭa in the cosmic processes of the periodic destruction and regeneration of the whole universe.[91] There is no doubt that adṛṣṭa (dharma/adharma) has now become all-pervasive and that it functions as the key factor in reinterpreting the "natural" world as saṃsāra, that is, as a mechanism of reward and punishment, or karmic retribution. Yet, even the great systematizer Praśastapāda has not been able to harmonize completely or cover the ambiguities and dichotomies inherited from the *Vaiśeṣikasūtra*. There remains a tendency to separate the contexts of physical or cosmological explanation and of ethics, soteriology, and Vedic apologetics. The physical functions of adṛṣṭa, in particular the specific examples given by the *Sūtra*, are left out of consideration in the section on dharma and adharma within the systematic survey of the qualities; this section focuses, quite in accordance with the more popular connotations of dharma, on socioreligious duties and their karmic implications. Instead, it is a section in the chapter on "motion" (i.e., *karman* in its technical Vaiśeṣika meaning) which presents adṛṣṭa in its more specifically physical and biological role and which refers to the peculiar kinetic functions attributed to it in the Sūtra. Praśastapāda's commentator Śrīdhara also mentions the upward flaming of fire, the horizontal movement of wind, etc., in the section on the selves (ātman); he argues that these phenomena prove not only the existence of adṛṣṭa, but also the omnipresence of its substratum, the ātman. However, he does not assign any specific retributive function to these movements.[92]

Praśastapāda says that, apart from its other functions, adṛṣṭa has to account for such phenomena in the merely material, physical realm of the elements (*mahābhūta*) which do not have an otherwise ascertainable cause (*anupalabhyamānakāraṇa*) and which can be beneficial or harmful (*upakārāpakārasamartha*) to us.[93] This twofold condition illustrates a basic ambiguity in the meaning of adṛṣṭa: on the one hand, it serves as a kind of gap-filler in the realm of physical causality, providing a principle of explanation where other, "visible" and therefore preferable causes fail. On the other hand, it serves as a device to interpret the world process as saṃsāra, in terms of reward and punishment, of what is beneficial and harmful to us, thus not simply supplementing, but potentially replacing the whole context of "natural" physical causality. As we have seen, Praśastapāda tends to universalize the presence and influence of dharmic, retributive causality, while also trying to accommodate the "Lord," Īśvara.

E. Frauwallner, to whom we owe the most penetrating and reliable analysis of the Vaiśeṣika system, has suggested that in its origins the Vaiśeṣika was a "pure" philosophy of nature, theoretical in its orientation, interested in the explanation of natural phenomena, not in soteriological schemes and methods of liberation from saṃsāra.[94] Whatever the original status of the Vaiśeṣika may have been—whether we accept Frauwallner's stimulating, yet inevitably speculative thesis or not—it remains undeniable that the soteriological orientation is not genuinely at home in Vaiśeṣika. This was clearly felt even within the Indian tradition; the dharmic commitment and the soteriological relevance of the Vaiśeṣika doctrine of categories were repeatedly questioned. Praśastapāda's procedure, as well as that of the final redactors of the *Vaiśeṣikasūtra*, may in part be understood as a response to such charges, found in the *Nyāyabhāṣya* and other texts.[95] Adṛṣṭa, which may primarily have been a gap-filler in the causal explication of the universe, subsequently offered itself as a channel for a much more decidedly dharmic and soteriological reinterpretation of the Vaiśeṣika theory of the universe. At the same time, this theory of the universe and of the categories of reality was presented as a framework and basis for explicating in a theoretically coherent manner the status and functions of retributive causality, to account for karma in terms of a comprehensive metaphysics and categoriology. Insofar as adṛṣṭa is presented as a potentially all-pervasive factor in the universe, in particular as the moving force of its periodic regenerations, a karmic framework has been provided for the functioning of "natural" causality; on the other hand, dharma/adharma, or what is called karma in most of the other systems, has found its theoretical accommodation in a context that remains primarily that of a philosophy of nature and a doctrine of categories. This is a balance that is at the same time a compromise, and it has obviously contributed to the scholastic petrification of the Vaiśeṣika. As we have noticed earlier, this use of karma/adṛṣṭa as a principle of cosmological explanation was rejected by the Mīmāṃsā; it found, however, a more positive response in a school which has a much more genuinely soteriological orientation than the Vaiśeṣika: the Sāṃkhya.[96]

We need not discuss here in detail the more technical problems of how adṛṣṭa is supposed to function in the contexts of physical and mental causation. Our main concern is its status in the general field of causality, the question of how it relates to or interacts with other causal factors. The most common suggestion in Praśastapāda's work is that of a causal aggregate in which adṛṣṭa functions as one among other causes (*kāraṇa*): its absence or presence, just like the absence or presence of other factors, may decide whether an effect, be it an act of perception or a physiological process, takes place or not; or it may add to or subtract from what other causes may bring about.[97] However, sometimes it seems to represent not so much one causal factor among others, but rather another level of causality, or something like a medium and condition of causal efficacy, which may unleash, neutralize, or counteract causal influences in the mental as well as in the physical sphere. In this sense, its function would come closer to that of the "category" of "potency," *śakti*, which is included in the categorial systems of the Prābhākara school and of Candramati's *Daśapadārthī*, but is rejected in classical Vaiśeṣika.[98]

Karma, Adṛṣṭa, and "Natural" Causality

10. An important condition of the understanding of adṛṣṭa is that its substrata, the souls, are supposed to be omnipresent (*vibhu*). Its efficacy is thus not at all restricted to that particular body which is attached to its underlying ātman as an instrument of saṃsāric experience. Since any ātman is omnipresent, its adṛṣṭa can function anywhere and affect all those entities which may become relevant for it in terms of karmic reward and punishment. An illustration of this is given in Uddyotakara's *Nyāyavārttika*: if somebody waters a tree, the success of his action, that is, the process of fertilization and growth, may be influenced by the karma of the person who at a later time will eat the fruits of the tree; it becomes the function of the tree, directed by the karmic potential of a soul that may or may not be that of the person who watered the tree, to provide an opportunity of retributive experience, of enjoyment.[99]

Although any soul's adṛṣṭa may potentially function anywhere, it has, of course, a specific jurisdiction over the particular body which serves as a vehicle of retribution for that soul which is the adṛṣṭa's "own" underlying substratum. The body, together with the sense-organs and the "mind" (manas), provides the ātman with its karmic rewards and punishments, and the adṛṣṭa regulates their appropriate distribution.

The necessity of merit and demerit for the explanation of organic processes and structures is already a theme in the *Nyāyasūtra*, and the *Nyāyabhāṣya* and its subcommentaries give us elaborate and formalized "proofs" for this necessity: there have to be vehicles, instruments of retributive experience; the complex instrumental character of organic bodies (*śarīra*) would remain unexplained if they were not seen as fulfilling this very function and as being shaped by the retributive causality of dharma and adharma.[100] Karmic causality may affect material, physical processes in general; in the realm of life, however, it appears as the most basic and decisive factor, as that which distinguishes living organisms from lifeless matter. The implication seems to be that there is no life without karma, that life and saṃsāra, the realms of biology and of soteriology, are exactly coextensive.

A diametrically opposed view is presented and rejected in the *Nyāyabhāṣya*—the theory that there is no basic distinction between mere matter and living organisms, that all forms of life are just spontaneous configurations of matter, that there is no need to postulate karma as the formative principle of organisms.[101] This radical materialistic denial of karmic causality remains, as we have noted earlier, far from being a living challenge to the general acceptance of the karma theory in classical Indian thought, and its rejection is common to the Hindu, Buddhist, and Jaina schools. Yet there are certain questions and ambiguities concerning the demarcation line between the realms of life and lifeless matter; and it is not always simply taken for granted that life and saṃsāra are exactly coextensive. The special case of Jainism, which includes even minerals in its horizon of living, saṃsāric existence, need not concern us here. Even within Hinduism, there has been some room for questions and disagreements and for historical changes in this matter.

The standard idea of saṃsāra, of transmigratory existence and of retributive causality, is that it comprises the whole sphere "from Brahmā to the tufts of grass" (*brahmādistambaparyanta*). Yet, the inclusion of the plants or vegetables has not always been accepted in all the philosophical schools of Hinduism. In Praśastapāda's systematization of Vaiśeṣika, vegetables are not classified as living organisms (*śarīra*), that is, as receptacles of experience, but as mere "objects" (*viṣaya*); just like stones, they are nothing but special configurations of the element earth.[102] The *Vaiśeṣikasūtra* itself remains ambiguous and poses, moreover, peculiar philological problems in this connection.[103] In later Vaiśeṣika texts, the whole issue is tacitly dropped or its treatment is adjusted to the more comprehensive view of saṃsāra, which includes the vegetables. An explicit discussion of the problem is found in Udayana's *Kiraṇāvalī*: although trees are seats of experience, although they have all the basic attributes of living, experiencing beings, Praśastapāda chose not to include them in the class of śarīra, because their internal awareness is extremely faint (*atimandāntaḥsaṃjñatā*) and because they are mostly mere subsidiaries to other living beings.[104] Udayana still argues for what his successors usually take for granted. Certain borderline problems are also found in the case of the lowest animals, such as worms and insects, creatures which are called *kṣudrajantu, svedaja*, and so forth in the Indian tradition. The most familiar type of biological or zoological classification in India follows the criterion of the origin, the kind of "birth" of the various creatures. In two different versions, this scheme is already found in two of the oldest Upaniṣads, the *Chāndogya* and the *Aitareya*. According to the *Chāndogya Upaniṣad*,[105] all living beings are either "born of an egg" (*aṇḍaja*), "born alive" (*jīvaja*), or "sprout-born" (*udbhijja*, born from something that bursts, splits). Instead of this threefold scheme, the *Aitareya Upaniṣad*[106] has a fourfold one: "egg-born," "sprout-born" (*udbhinnaja*), "born with an embryonic skin" (*jāruja*, later usually *jarāyuja* and corresponding to *jīvaja*), and finally "sweat-born" (*svedaja*, in a more general sense: born from warmth and moisture). The two Upaniṣads neither explain nor exemplify exactly what they mean by these classifications. However, we find these schemes, predominantly the fourfold one, with certain variations in many later texts of different branches of Indian learning, in philosophy, in medicine, in dharma literature.[107] We need not discuss here the implications of the aṇḍaja (birds, fish, etc.) and jīvaja groups (viviparous, mostly mammals), nor even of the more problematic group of the udbhijja creatures (which are not always simply understood as plants or vegetables, but occasionally also as animals coming from a larva, etc.). The group which is of primary interest in the present context is that of the "sweat-born" creatures.

11. The class of "sweat-born" or "heat-born" creatures often coincides more or less with what in other contexts is called *kṣudrajantu*, "little, insignificant creatures." The expression *kṣudrāṇi bhūtāni* is already found in the *Chāndogya Upaniṣad*,[108] where we are told that these creatures live according to the rule "be born and die" and do not enter the "way of the fathers," which is a cycle leading back to an earthly existence, nor the "way of the gods," which is without return to earth. It has been suggested that this means that their existence is a merely ephemeral one and that they do not take any part in the processes of transmigration and retribution.[109] Such an interpretation would go beyond the ambiguous statement of the Upaniṣad, and it would not have the support of the parallel version of this text in the *Bṛhadāraṇyaka Upaniṣad*.[110] It seems that we are dealing here not with completely extra-transmigrational forms of life, but rather with a form of soteriological failure that would relegate these creatures to an endless repetition of their state of being, not giving them any opportunity for soteriological ascent.

At any rate, the biological and soteriological status of the creatures known as *kṣudrajantu* and *svedaja* seems to be rather precarious in several texts, and more than once the possibility of a spontaneous, nonkarmic origin of these forms of life suggests itself. Worms, maggots, lice, and similar creatures are supposed to originate in various disintegrating materials, in rotting food, in corpses, in pus, in excrement, and from other kinds of organic warmth and moisture;[111] we even have the curious case of the small worms (*kṛmi*), which according to some writers on the science of erotics (*kāmaśāstra*) are produced from blood (*raktaja, rudhirodbhava*) in the female sex organs and cause there the "itching" (*kaṇḍūti*) of sexual passion.[112] None of these texts gives us a theory of the spontaneous, nonkarmic origination of certain forms of life; on the other hand, there is no indication of an agency of "souls" and their karma in these processes.

It is not surprising that the appearance of maggots in rotting materials was used by the Cārvākas and other materialists in their argumentation for a nonkarmic, spontaneous origination of life from mere matter. In the canonical writings of the Buddhists as well as of the Jainas, we hear about a materialistic king by the name of Pāyāsi (Prakrit form: Paesi), who conducts various "experiments" to demonstrate the nonexistence of the soul and the soulless origination of living creatures.[113] For example, he has a person executed whose corpse is put in an iron pot which is then sealed up. When the pot is opened again some time later, the corpse is full of maggots. For Pāyāsi/Paesi, this means: no souls could get into the pot, since it had been sealed; so there must have been soulless, spontaneous origination of life. And if this is possible in the case of worms, why not also in the case of humans?

The materialistic reference to the allegedly spontaneous origination of life in rotting materials is still mentioned in the pūrvapakṣa sections of various later texts such as Jayanta's *Nyāyamañjarī*; in Jayanta's own view, there can be no doubt that it is the presence of souls (ātman) and the efficacy of their karma which transforms parts of rotting substances, such as rotting sour milk, into the bodies of worms, thus creating peculiar vehicles of karmic retribution.[114] The Jaina commentator Guṇaratna even turns the appearance of worms in corpses into a direct argument *against* materialism.[115] In such classical and later sources, there is, in fact, an increasingly systematic and rigid superimposition of religious and soteriological schemes and perspectives upon biological, zoological, cosmological observations, and a gradual evaporation of the spirit of observation, of the empirical openness for natural phenomena. The old schemes of biological and zoological classification are not further developed or empirically supplemented.[116] The interest in such classifications is more and more overshadowed by the interest in the ways and levels of saṃsāra; the old schemes of classification are reduced to, or replaced by, soteriological hierarchies.

12. We have discussed earlier how karmic causality, specifically in Vaiśeṣika, interacts with other causes, how it influences or controls physical and other natural processes, how its sovereignty is extended and stabilized in the development of Vaiśeṣika thought. To conclude this discussion, it may be an appropriate experiment to reverse our perspective and to ask whether or to what degree the efficacy of physical and other "natural," nonkarmic causes may extend into what should be the domain of karmic retribution. Since retribution takes place in the realm of awareness, of the experience (*bhoga*) of pleasure or pain, we may formulate this question as follows: is there anything in the realm of experience, of pleasant and unpleasant states of awareness, which is controlled not by karma but by the intrusion of nonkarmic factors? Is there, for example, the possibility of "undeserved" suffering caused by "merely" natural causes? In his presentation of "pleasure" (sukha) and "pain" (duḥkha) as two "qualities" (guṇa) of the soul, Praśastapāda states that they arise "in relation to dharma" (*dharmādyapekṣa*);[117] apart from this, not much explicit attention is paid to the problem in Vaiśeṣika literature.

Some relevant discussions are found in Nyāya literature. Uddyotakara addresses the question why there are delays in the ripening of karma, and he gives a number of reasons. First of all, the obstacle may be past karma which is still ripening (*vipacyamāna*) and whose results have not yet been experienced (*anupabhuktaphala*). Second, it may be the karmic residues of other living beings who may be destined to have similar or shared experiences (*samānopabhoga*) and whose karmic needs may thus interfere with any particular processes of ripening. Third, it may be the activities of "sharers of karma" (*karmabhāgin*, i.e., members of a family or ritual unit who could affect each other's karmic situation). Fourth, the necessary auxiliary causes (*sahakārin*), primarily dharma and adharma themselves, which are required to complete the causal aggregate, may be absent or not function properly. Uddyotakara concludes this section by stating that "the course of karma is difficult to understand" (*durvijñeyā ca karmagatiḥ*).[118] This remark is reminiscent of the statement *karmagatir vicitrā durvijñānā ca* which we find in Vyāsa's *Yogabhāṣya* at the end of another discussion of the question why karma does not always ripen on schedule.[119] Unlike Vyāsa, Uddyotakara considers the mutual interference of the karmic situations of different agents. With his reference to the auxiliary causes, he even seems to leave room for nonkarmic interferences. But even in this case, he emphasizes the role of dharma and adharma and tries to confine the issue basically to the karmic sphere. Ultimately, and in spite of all interferences, karma will bear fruit; appropriate results will appear sooner or later.[120] According to Uddyotakara, there will be no disappearance of karma (*kṛtavipraṇāśa*); nor should we expect the occurrence of unearned, undeserved suffering or well-being (*akṛtābhyāgama*).

The problems arising from the juxtaposition of karmic and nonkarmic causality, and the potential limitations on the principles of *kṛtavipraṇāśa* and *akṛtābhyāgama*, are addressed much more clearly and explicitly in Buddhist thought, specifically in the Theravāda tradition.

In the *Saṃyuttanikāya*, Moliyasīvaka asks whether it is true that all pleasant, painful and neutral feelings (*vedanā*) are caused by deeds committed in the past (*pubbekatahetu*). The Buddha responds by enumerating eight different causes of diseases; the "ripening of karma" (*kammavipāka*) is only one of them.[121] The conclusion is that the view referred to by Moliyasīvaka is not tenable. The *Milindapañha* quotes this passage from the *Saṃyuttanikāya* (which has further parallels in the *Aṅguttaranikāya*[122]) and relates it to the question whether there can still be painful experiences for the Tathāgata whose stock of karma has been eliminated.[123] Similarly, karma is by no means the sole cause of death.[124] Remarkable debates on the scope and limits of karmic causality are also found in the *Kathāvatthu*; they illustrate the controversial status of this theme as well as the basic contrast that was seen between the "private" and experiential processes of the "ripening of karma" and their external and "public" conditions, including such cosmic processes as the formation of the earth.[125] The Andhakas appear as the advocates of a widely extended scope of karmic causality. The Theravādins take a more moderate approach. For them, karma is primarily the cause of experience, not necessarily of its external correlates.[126] As we have seen, not even all "feelings" or "sensations" are necessarily results of karma. Nevertheless, the Theravāda tradition has been reluctant to renounce the relevance of *akṛtābhyāgama* altogether. There have been repeated attempts to preserve it at least as far as feelings of physical pleasure and pain are concerned. In this sense, orthodox Theravādins have dissociated themselves, or tried to reinterpret, the view expressed in the *Milindapañha*.[127] This would, however, not necessarily apply to cognitive or meditational experiences, nor would it cover such phenomena as self-inflicted pain.[128] The case is altogether different when we move from feelings to mental tendencies, intentions and decisions. Here, too, karma is supposed to play a significant role; but Theravādins as well as other advocates of the karma theory have consistently, though more or less explicitly, rejected the view that this involves any strict determination.[129]

The view expressed in the *Milindapañha* may, in fact, show a certain lack of universality and rigidity in the application of the karma principle. Yet in the way in which it exposes even the Buddha to "ordinary," "natural," "neutral" causality, it opens a remarkable dimension of freedom from, and indifference towards, karma and its peculiarly "selfish" and "private" causality. What is more, it shows that the Buddhists, who may have been the first to articulate the idea of karma in terms of strict retributive causality, may also have had the clearest understanding of its limitations and ambiguities.

Epilogue: The "Way of the Fathers" and the Theory of Karma in Śaṅkara's Advaita Vedānta

13. Both the *Chāndogya Upaniṣad* and the *Bṛhadāraṇyaka Upaniṣad* contain, with certain variations, a chapter that P. Deussen has called "the most important and most explicit text on the theory of transmigration which we have from the Vedic period."[130] The text first presents the "five-fire doctrine" (*pañcāgnividyā*), which is supposed to answer, among other questions, the question why the "other world," in spite of so many creatures dying and passing into it, does not become full, that is, how and why there is return from that world into this earthly sphere. In the sacrificial language of the Brāhmaṇas, we learn that man, in his return, has to pass through five stages or transformations which are all considered to be sacrificial fires, or as taking place within the context of sacrificial fires: man (i.e., deceased man) is "sacrificed" by the gods in "that world" as *śraddhā*, "faith"; then he becomes *soma*, rain, food, semen, from which he will again arise as a human being. Subsequently this doctrine is combined with the distinction between the "way of the fathers" (*pitṛyāna*) and the "way of the gods" (*devayāna*). The "way of the gods" is the way of those who, through their knowledge and faith, reach the "world of brahman," beyond the sun, and liberation from earthly existence. The "way of the fathers," on the other hand, is the way of those who have done pious and sacrificial works and have enjoyed the reward resulting from these deeds in heaven, but have ultimately been unable to avoid the return into an earthly existence. A "third abode" (*tṛtīyaṃ sthānam*) is also referred to; it means existence as low animals and is for those who do not reach the "way of the gods" or the "way of the fathers." According to the *Kauṣītaki Upaniṣad*, all those who die proceed at least to the moon from where they may be turned back. The doctrines of the "five fires" and of the "two paths" obviously do not form an original unity; in fact, the "two paths" appear outside this combination, for example, in the *Kauṣītaki Upaniṣad*, and, side by side with the combined version, in the *Jaiminīya Brāhmaṇa*.[131] We cannot and need not enlarge here on the specific problems and highly controversial issues connected with the interpretation of these doctrines.[132] Our primary concern is the character of the sequence of events which constitutes the "way of the fathers," its type and pattern of regularity, and the way in which man is seen as participating in it.

The downward part of the "way of the fathers" coincides basically with the sequence of the "five fires." However, it is more naturalistic in its presentation, describing the sequence of events as a series of natural transformations rather than a sacrificial series: there is transformation into ether, wind, rain, and food—that is, nourishing vegetables; these, being eaten and transformed into semen, may lead the one who has gone through these stages back into human or possibly animal existence.[133] Natural cycles, recurrent, seasonal phenomena are used as vehicles of the migrations or transformations of the human being between its earthly existences. Death and birth, ascent and return: the phases and phenomena of man's existence relate to or even coincide with natural, cosmic, meteorological events, such as the ascent of smoke to the sky, the phases of the moon, the seasons, the seasonal rains. The goal is to get beyond these cyclical, seasonal processes, to a permanent heaven or to the world of brahman. In several ancient texts, the moon is the lord of the seasons, those regularities which imply the recurrence of life and death, which determine the scope and the limits of the "way of the fathers." He is the guardian of heaven. In the *Kauṣītaki Upaniṣad*, he examines the knowledge of those who ascend to him after their death, and he decides whether they may proceed to those spheres where they are free from the seasonal cycles and the repetition of their earthly existence. In the versions of the *Chāndogya* and *Bṛhadāraṇyaka Upaniṣads*, no such function is assigned to the moon; the division of the "two ways" takes place already here on earth. In the *Jaiminīya Brāhmaṇa*, the seasons themselves appear as guardians and conduct the decisive examination.[134]

There are only a few stations in the succession of events where knowledge and merit become relevant. They decide whether one remains confined to the "way of the fathers" or reaches the "way of the gods"; within the "way of the fathers," the merit of past deeds, primarily sacrificial acts, decides how long one is allowed to stay in the realm of the moon. Apart from this, entering upon the "way of the fathers" means to be subject to a succession of events and transformations that follows its own "natural" order and is not directed or kept in motion by the retributive causality of our deeds. To be sent into a plant, a vegetable, is not in itself a form of retribution and punishment; it is just the ordinary, "natural" way of returning to the earth. The texts under discussion are still far from a clear and thorough conception of karmic, retributive causality; other passages in the *Bṛhadāraṇyaka Upaniṣad* may indeed come much closer to such a conception.[135] Problems of the continuity and coherence of act and retribution or of the durability and identity of the subject in the various processes of transformation do not become explicit; the question "who or what transmigrates?" is not really asked.

A transition which seems particularly delicate and problematic, most notably in the version of the *Chāndogya Upaniṣad*, is the transfer from the vegetable being into the organism and to the level of being of its eater, its consumption and appropriation by a human being or by an animal. While natural processes take care of the transportation up to the vegetable existence, the next step is obviously of a different order. The *Chāndogya Upaniṣad* emphasizes that it is a very difficult transition.[136] As a matter of fact, it seems to be left to mere chance which kind of living being will consume a particular vegetable, extract its essence, transform it into the semen of a new creature, its own offspring, and thus raise it to its own level of being. The most exemplary account of the formation of the semen, a "second ātman" in the body of the father, and of the processes of conception and birth, is found in the *Aitareya Upaniṣad*,[137] and it has been taken for granted by the traditional commentators that this has to be understood in the context of the "way of the fathers."

Only the version of the *Chāndogya Upaniṣad* tries to establish a relationship between one's type of birth and the preceding good or bad conduct (*caraṇa*), in a passage that appears somewhat abruptly and seems to be a later addition.[138] Later systematizers, in particular Śaṅkara, refer specifically to this problematic transition, trying to harmonize and to reconcile, but at the same time making explicit the differences and tensions between this scheme of thought and the later, fully developed theory of karma.

14. The most explicit and most coherent discussion of karma and transmigration which we find in Śaṅkara's writings, *Brahmasū-*

trabhāṣya III, 1, 1–27, deals primarily with the exegesis of the "two ways" and the "five fires," specifically the "way of the fathers." Śaṅkara emphasizes that only śruti is a really authoritative source for our knowledge and understanding of the processes of karma and transmigration: attempts to explain this matter in terms of assumptions produced by human thought alone (*puruṣamatiprabhavāḥ kalpanāḥ*) are inevitably futile; the various theories and conceptualizations presented by the Sāṃkhya or the Vaiśeṣika, by the Buddhists or the Jainas, are contradicted by one other as well as by śruti.[139] Nevertheless, Śaṅkara develops a rather elaborate scheme of reasoning designed to harmonize and systematize the teachings of śruti, to reconcile the pattern of the "way of the fathers" with the understanding of transmigration expressed in the metaphor of the caterpillar,[140] an understanding that seems to imply a much more direct transition from one body into the next one, without such a long and complicated interlude as the pitṛyāna. In his explanation and apologetics, Śaṅkara also uses a peculiar interpretation of the theory of apūrva; it states that subtle ingredients or transformations of the sacrificial oblations, specifically of the sacrificial water, constitute the apūrva, which "envelops" the soul of the sacrificer, accompanies it to the heavenly spheres, and keeps it there as long as the sacrificial merit lasts.[141] Following an interpretation which had already been suggested by Bādarāyaṇa's predecessor Kārṣṇājini, Śaṅkara states that once a transmigrating soul (*jīva*) has been led back to earth by the "way of the fathers," into the condition of a vegetable, its karmic residue (*anuśaya*) will determine its further development. The assumption of such a residue that remains after the processes of enjoyment and cancellation of karma in the heavenly spheres is explained and justified in an elaborate discussion. In this way, Śaṅkara tries to bridge what might appear as a gap in the causal sequence, to establish that the transition from the vegetable to its "eater" is not left to mere chance.[142]

It is a familiar phenomenon and need no further concern us here that Śaṅkara in his interpretation and apologetics presupposes and employs doctrines and conceptual devices developed at a much later time than the texts he is dealing with. For our present discussion, it is more significant that his exegesis of the "five fires" and the "way of the fathers" ultimately and explicitly demonstrates the unreconciled disparity of these old Upaniṣadic models and the later systematic understanding of karma and transmigration. Following the lead of Bādarāyaṇa, he arrives at a curious juxtaposition of two different transmigrating entities (*jīva*) in one and the same organism.

The rain which falls to earth nourishes the plants, but it does not give them their life-principle. A jīva that is sent down to earth by, or in the form of, rain is thus attached to an organism which is already occupied and operated by a jīva of its own. It cannot really be embodied in such an organism; it is only located in it as a kind of "guest jīva." Śaṅkara is very explicit on this distinction of different jīvas in one vegetable organism: for the jīva that has been "born into" and is embodied in a vegetable, this means a form of karmic retribution, the allocation of a particular vehicle of retributive experience. For the "guest jīva," on the other hand, no karmic retribution is involved at this particular stage. The descent according to the "way of the fathers" has its own order and regularity, with which karmic processes do not interfere; as far as this part of the journey is concerned, a jīva does not accumulate any new karma, nor does it experience the results of previous karma.[143] The juxtaposition and contrast of the two jīvas illustrate the interference of two different models of thought and, moreover, of different historical layers of the Indian tradition: a scheme that is, apart from certain crucial junctures, primarily left to "natural," seasonal, cosmic regularities interferes with the more comprehensive context of the universalized theory of karma and saṃsāra. Śaṅkara tries faithfully to preserve the peculiar teachings on the "five fires" and the "two ways." Yet, these ancient Upaniṣadic schemes appear as curious epiphenomena or as fossilized relics in a universe now thoroughly governed by karmic causality.

In the wider framework of Śaṅkara's thought, the explication of the peculiarities of karma and the exegesis of the sacred texts on this matter remain confined to the "lower level" of truth, to the realm of *vyavahāra*. Ultimately, the notions of karma and saṃsāra have only one meaning and function: to provide a counterpart and stepping-stone of liberating knowledge, to show us what ultimate reality is *not*, to expose the spatio-temporal universe in its ontological deficiency.

The whole world is only a stage for karmic processes,[144] or rather: it is itself nothing but a karmic play. It owes its very existence to karmic attachment and superimposition, to that ignorance (*avidyā*) which is the root cause of our karmic involvement and in fact coextensive with it. To be in the world, to accept its reality as well as one's own worldly reality, means to *act* in the world, to accept it as a network of causal relations, of desires and results, as a context of practical, pragmatic truth and confirmation.[145] Causality is in its very essence karmic causality; it constitutes the "reality" of the world, a reality that can be defined only in terms of means and ends, of practical consequences, of "reward" and "punishment," and that becomes transparent as soon as the practical involvement in the network of means and ends is terminated. To be in saṃsāra is not just the function of a particular demerit; it is the function of and coincides with the "involvement in causes and results" (*hetuphalāveśa*) as such.[146] The domains of karma and of cosmic ignorance and illusion (avidyā, māyā) are identical. Karma is thoroughly universalized and implemented in Śaṅkara's philosophy. Yet, this radical and uncompromising consummation of the principle of karma is at the same time a radical devaluation.[147] In a sense, the Lord (*īśvara*) is the only subject of transmigration (*saṃsārin*), according to Śaṅkara;[148] in an even more radical sense, there is no saṃsārin at all.

Chapter 9: Notes

1. J. N. Farquhar, *An Outline of the Religious Literature of India.* London, 1920 (reprint Delhi, 1967), 33.

2. On the prehistory and earliest developments of the doctrine of karma and *saṃsāra,* see A.M. Boyer, "Étude sur l'origine de la doctrine du saṃsāra." *Journal Asiatique* 9: 18 (1901, vol. 2), 451–499; T. Segerstedt, "Själavandringslärans ursprung." *Le Monde Oriental* (Uppsala) 4 (1910), 43–87; 111–181; H.G. Narahari, "On the Origin of the Doctrine of Saṃsāra." *Poona Orientalist* 4 (1939/1940), 159–165; P. Horsch, "Vorstufen der indischen Seelenwanderungslehre." *Asiatische Studien/Études Asiatiques* 25 (1971), 99–157.

3. *Bṛhadāraṇyaka Upaniṣad* III, 2, 13.

4. Cf., J. Scheftelowitz, *Die Zeit als Schicksalsgottheit in der indischen und iranischen Religion.* Stuttgart, 1929; H.G. Narahari, "Karma and Reincarnation in the Mahābhārata." *Annals of the Bhandarkar Oriental Research Institute* 27 (1946), 102–113.

5. See Nāgārjuna, MK XVII, 23 (*akṛtābhyāgamabhaya*). Bhāvaviveka, *Madhyamakahṛdayakārikā* IX (Mīmāṃsā), 103 (*kṛtanāśākṛtāgamau*); NS/NBh III, 2, 72 (*na, akṛtābhyāgamaprasaṅgāt*); III, 1, 4 (*kṛtahāna*); Kumārila, ŚV, 490 (v. 12): *kṛtanāśākṛtāgamau;* Śaṅkara, BSBh III, 2, 9 (*akṛtābhyāgamakṛtavipraṇāśau ca durnivārāv anyotthānapakṣe syātām*); Mahābhārata V, 27, 10; XIII, 7, 5; XIII, 6, 10 (*na-akṛtaṃ bhujyate kvacit*). The significance of this principle has not been sufficiently recognized by modern scholars; but see L. de La Vallée Poussin, *Le Muséon* III/1 (1902), 49, n. 187 f. (Siddhasena and the Buddhists according to the *Sarvadarśanasaṃgraha*).

6. The discovery of strict causality itself, specifically in the realm of human existence, and the insight into the causal nature of good and bad existence (*sugati, duggati*) of living beings, figures prominently in the accounts of the Buddha's enlightenment (*bodhi*). In various important texts on karma/kamma, for instance the *Sāleyyakasutta* and the *Cūḷakammavibhaṅgasutta* of the *Majjhimanikāya,* the Buddha instructs brahmins

for whom the karma doctrine is a basically new and unfamiliar teaching.

7. "Cārvāka" is used with more or less specific reference to a particular school, often interchangeably with the more general terms "Lokāyata" and "Lokāyatika." The basic teachings usually attributed to the Cārvākas are also mentioned in the Buddhist canon, where they are associated with the heretic teacher Ajita Kesakambalī; cf., e.g., *Dīghanikāya* II, 22 ff. (*Sāmaññaphalasutta*).

8. Cf. G. Tucci, "Linee di una storia del materialismo Indiano." *Opera Minora*, vol. 1. Rome, 1971, 49–156 (originally published 1923–1929); E. Frauwallner, *Geschichte der indischen Philosophie*, vol. 2. Salzburg, 1956, 295–309 (*History of Indian Philosophy*, vol. 2, trans. V.M. Bedekar. Delhi, 1973, 215–226); S.N. Dasgupta, *A History of Indian Philosophy*, vol. 3. Cambridge, 1940 (reprint 1961), 512–550.

9. Cf. Kṛṇṣnamiśra, *Prabodhacandrodaya*, ed. and trans, S.K. Nambiar. Delhi, 1971, 40 f. (act 2).

10. Haribhadra, *Ṣaḍdarśanasamuccaya*, v. 80.

11. Mādhava, *Sarvadarśanasaṃgra*. Poona, 1906 (Ānandāśrama Sanskrit Series), 5: *yāvaj jīvet sukhaṃ jīvet*. This is also quoted in various other texts.

12. See, for instance, Kṛṣṇamiśra's *Prabodhacandrodaya*, a Vaiṣṇava philosophical drama written in the late eleventh century.

13. On these developments, see E. Steinkellner, *Dharmottaras Paralokasiddhi, Nachweis der Wiedergeburt*. Vienna, 1986, 9ff.; Steinkellner refers to a posthumous and unfinished study of Lokāyata thought by E. Frauwallner which documents a variety of attempts to explain awareness as a product or epiphenomenon of the body. Relevant materials have also been collected by M. Namai in two articles in Japanese on the philosophy of the materialists (i.e., Bārhaspatya) and its critique by the later Buddhists; cf. *Indological Review* 2 (1976), 33–74; 3(1981), 59–78.

14. Cf. *Sarvadarśanasaṃgraha* (see above, n. 11), 2, 5; *Prabodhacandrodaya* (see n. 12), 40 f. (v. 21). According to the Cārvākas, sacrificial performances are nothing but a means of livelihood for the performing priests.

15. For a specific criticism of the transfer of a *jīva* from one body into a new one, see Śāntarakṣita, TS (with Kamalaśīla's *Pañjikā*), v. 1860 ff. (the Lokāyata chapter).

16. Cf. E. Steinkellner, *Nachweis der Wiedergeburt, Prajnāsenas 'Jig rten pha rol sgrub pa*. Vienna, 1988, part 2, 10; Steinkellner emphasizes the special interest of the Tibetans in explicit discussions concerning karma and rebirth, since this was a less familiar topic for them than for the Indians.

17. The most notorious fatalists in the Indian tradition are the Ājīvikas, headed by Makkhali Gosāla; cf. A.L. Basham, *History and Doctrines of the Ājīvikas*. London, 1951.

18. Cf. Ṛgveda IV, 27 (Vāmadeva in the womb).

19. Cf. J. Scheftelowitz (see above, n. 4), 21 ff.

20. See H. von Glasenapp, *The Doctrine of Karman in Jaina Philosophy*, trans. G. B. Gifford. Bombay, 1942, 30 (German original: Leipzig, 1915; Diss. Bonn). See also Aurobindo Ghose, *The Problem of Rebirth*. Pondicherry, 1969, 14. In a negative perspective, Christian and other critics have often emphasized the all-inclusive character of karmic causality; cf., e.g., T.E. Slater, *Transmigration and Karma*. London/Madras, 1898, 36: "Thus Karma or Adrishta becomes the one and only law of the universe."

21. R. Panikkar, "The Law of Karman and the Historical Dimension of Man." *Philosophy East and West* 22 (1972), 26.

22. See above, the references to *akṛtābhyāgama* and *kṛtavipraṇāśa* (cf. n. 5).

23. For a somewhat impressionistic survey of these varieties, see *Karma and Rebirth in Classical Indian Traditions*, ed. W.D. O'Flaherty. Berkeley,

1980. This volume is supplemented by: *Karma. An Anthropological Inquiry*, ed. C.F. Keyes and E.V. Daniel. Berkeley, 1983, as well as *Karma and Rebirth: Post Classical Developments*, ed. R.W. Neufeldt. Albany, 1986.

24. The distinction between "the karma theory" and its different "interpretations" which has been used by K. Potter (*Karma and Rebirth in Classical Indian Traditions*, 241 ff.) may be a helpful and legitimate heuristic device but should be applied with caution and hermeneutic reflection.

25. Cf. *Kritik der Urteilskraft* (*Critique of Judgement*), § 78: "Denn erklären heisst von einem Prinzip ableiten, welches man also deutlich muss erkennen und angeben können." If Kant had been aware of the karma concept, he might have characterized it as a "regulative idea" or "regulative principle," i.e. as something that provides unity and centrality to one's understanding of the world, but is (unlike the "categories") not constitutive of the very structure of reality, nor susceptible of empirical verification.

26. Cf. YBh IV, 11; see also the reference to the "interlinked sequence of existence" (*śliṣṭaparvā bhavasaṃkramaḥ*), YBh I, 16.

27. Cf. NS/NBh I, 1, 2.

28. Cf. YBh II, 9; see also NBh and NV III, 2, 60 ff.

29. Cf. *Milindapañha*, ed. V. Trenckner. London, 1880 (reprint 1962; PTS), 65: *kena kāraṇena manussā na sabbe samakā?*

30. Cf. also Rāmānuja on BS II, 1, 34.

31. See NBh and NV III, 2, 67 (*janmavyāvṛtti*; cf. the entire section III, 2, 60–68); see also NV I, 1, 1 (ed. A. Thakur, 18: *kathaṃ punaḥ karmanimittatā janmanaḥ? bhedavattvāt. kaḥ punar bhedaḥ? sugatir durgatiś ca-iti*); NM, 42 ff. (*jagadvaicitrya*); and Praśastapāda's discussion of the cosmic role of *adṛṣṭa*, PB, 48 ff.

32. *Majjhimanikāya*, No. 135; see also 41 (*Sāleyyaka*) and 136 (*Mahākammavibhaṅga*); in general, however, these and similar texts show more interest in future karmic results.

33. Cf. R.F. Young, "An Early Sinhalese Buddhist Tract against the Christian Doctrine of Creation." *Zeitschrift für Missionswissenschaft und Religionswissenschaft* 69 (1985), 44–53; ibid., 48. The idea of God is a common target of Buddhist critique.

34. Cf. ŚV, 5 (Pārthasārathi on v. 10: *nityaniṣiddhayor iṣṭāniṣṭaphalaṃ na-asti. . . .*).

35. Cf. Rāmānuja on BS III, 1, 8 ff.; see also P. Deussen, *The System of the Vedānta*, trans. Ch. Johnston. Chicago, 1912 (reprint New York, 1973; first German ed.: Leipzig, 1883), 390 ff. ("Ritual and Moral Work").

36. P. V. Kane, *History of Dharmaśāstra*, vol. V/2. Poona, 1962, 1561: "In the physical world, there is the universal law of causation. The doctrine of Karma extends this inexorable law of causality to the mental and moral sphere." Similar statements are familiar in the literature on karma, but they obviously beg the question and avoid all difficulties; and moreover, nothing like this has ever been said in traditional Indian literature.

37. Cf. BSBh I, 1, 4 (*Works* III, 13 f.: *sukhatāratamya, duḥkhatāratamya*; see also, e.g., Udayana, *Kiraṇāvalī*, ed. J.S. Jetly. Baroda, 1971 (GOS), 38 ff.

38. Cf. YS and YBh II, 13; *āyus* and *jāti* may be seen as vehicles of *bhoga*; cf. Udayana, *Kiraṇāvalī* (see n. 37), 38: *tasmāt sarveṣāṃ svakarmanibandhano bhogaḥ, tac ca tannāntarīyakatayā* (instead of—*īkatayā*) *janmāyuṣī ākṣipati.*

39. Cf. YBh IV, 15: *kecid āhuḥ, jñānasahabhūr eva-artho bhogyatvāt sukhādivad iti*; the YSBhV, 343, explains this as the view of certain Buddhists who admit the existence of external objects, but not beyond their role as providers of experience.

40. Cf. *Kathāvatthu* VII, 7–10 (especially VII, 7, on the question whether the earth itself is a result of karma); see also Yaśomitra on Vasubandhu's *Abhidharmakośa* and *Bhāṣya*, ed. Dwarikadas Sastri. Benares, 1981, 567 (Mount Meru, the "continents,'" etc., as karmic products); this passage has been discussed by P. Griffiths, "Karma and Personal Identity: A Response to Professor White." *Religious Studies* 20 (1984), 481–485.

41. Cf. BSBh II, 2, 1 (*Works* III, 221): just like houses, palaces, beds, and other artefacts, the entire world, including the earth, is "suitable for the enjoyment of the results of various works" (*nānākarmaphalopabhoga-yogya*); see also BUBh II, 2, 1 (*Works* I, 790): "villages, cattle, heaven, etc." are "specific instances of the variety of results of works" (*karma-phalavaicitryaviśeṣa*).

42. The Mīmāṃsā neglect of the idea of final, irreversible liberation is still reflected in the teachings of Dayānanda Sarasvatī, the founder of the Ārya Samāj; he recognizes only temporary "paradises," or states of bliss.

43. We do not consider here later, syncretistic tendencies.

44. Cf. Kumārila, ŚV, 475 ff. (*Sambandhākṣepaparihāra*, v. 108 ff.); "previous births" (*janmāntara*) are generally accepted and sometimes casually referred to by the Mīmāṃsā teachers; see, for instance, Śabara on MS I, 3, 2 (non-remembrance of what has been experienced in a previous life).

45. Cf. MS I, 2, 19; III, 4, 12, f.; BS III, 3, 18.

46. Cf. Bhartṛhari, VP III/7 (*Sādhanasamuddeśa*) 34: *apūrvaṃ kālaśaktiṃ vā kriyāṃ vā kālam eva vā*; also VP III/8 (*Kriyāsamuddeśa*), 37, with Helārāja (ed. A. K. Subramania Iyer, 27); Bhavya in: S. Kawasaki, "The Mīmāṃsā Chapter of Bhavya's Madhyamaka-hṛdaya-kārikā, 1: Pūrvapakṣa." *Institute of Philosophy. The University of Tsukuba, Studies 1976*, 1–16 (especially 10, v. 10); Uddyotakara, NV I, 1, 7; Vyomaśiva, *Vyomavatī* (ChSS), 639 ff.; Jayanta, NM, 255. This view should not be identified with the Prābhākara conception of *apūrva* as unconditional *kārya* or *niyoga*; cf. Rāmānujācārya, *Tantrarahasya*. Baroda, 1956, 42: *apūrvarūpaṃ kāryam liṅādipratyayavācyam*); however, there may be connections.

47. See ŚV, 78 (v. 195); see also TV, 241 f.

48. The decisive section is on MS II, 1, 5. It relates to an objection already discussed by Śabara on MS I, 1, 5—that as long as the sacrifice takes place, it does not produce its fruit, and when the fruit occurs, the sacrifice is no longer there. Another relevant section is found in the

Vyākaraṇādhikaraṇa of the *Tantravārttika*; cf. TV on MS I, 3, 24–29. On the use of *apūrva* in grammar, cf. Patañjali, *Mahābhāṣya* on Pāṇini I 4, 3; for further usages of the word, see Bhartṛhari, VP II, 119 (quoted by Kumārila, TV, 241 ff.); III/1, 69; III/7, 34. Three studies in Japanese concerning *apūrva* were published by K. Harikai; see especially *Nihon Bukkyō Gakkai Nenpō* 42 (1977), 1–15; also *Indogaku Bukkyōgaku Kenkyū (Journal of Indian and Buddhist Studies)* 26/1 (1977), 420–426; 28/1 (1979), 459–463.

49. Cf. his commentary *Ṛjuvimalā* on Prabhākara's *Bṛhatī*, part 3, ed. S. Subramanya Sastri. Madras, 1962; also his systematic monograph *Prakaraṇapañcikā*. In Prabhākara's interpretation, Jaimini's word *ārambha* has special significance. As identified with *niyoga*, "obligation," *apūrva* is something that could not be known "prior to" (*pūrva*), or apart from, the Vedic injunctions. Kumārila, TV, 242, explains *apūrva* etymologically as not existing prior to the performance of the sacrifice (*yāgānuṣṭhānāt pūrvam abhūtam*). On the different interpretations, cf. G. Jha, *Pūrva-Mīmāṃsā in Its Sources*. Benares, second ed., 1964, 226 ff.

50. TV, 365.

51. TV, 366: *sarvasādhanānām iṣṭaphalapravṛttāv āntarālikavyāpārāvaśyabhāvitvāt*; cf. 365: *sūkṣmaśaktyātmakaṃ vā tat phalam eva-upajāyate.*

52. TV, 364 f.

53. Cf. G. Jha (see above, n. 49), 240 ff. The most familiar later handbook is Āpadeva, *Mīmāṃsānyāyaprakāśa (Āpadevī)*, ed. and trans. F. Edgerton. New Haven, 1929.

54. On the structural analogy between *apūrva* and the concept of *sphoṭa* as used in speculative grammar, cf. Maṇḍana, *Sphoṭasiddhi*, ed. N.R. Bhatt, trans. M. Biardeau. Pondicherry, 1958, 29; 83 (v. 10).

55. TV, 367: *yasya tv apūrvāṇi kriyante, tasya pratikarma pratiyogaṃ ca tadbhedād upapanne phalanānātvavaicitrye*; on "partial" *apūrvas*, see also TV on MS III, 1, 8 ff.

56. TV, 369: *yadi svasamavetā-eva śaktir iṣyeta karmaṇāṃ, tadvināśe tato na syāt, kartṛsthā tu na naśyati.*

57. On the other hand, it is held that if a particular result is assigned to a particular sacrifice by the Veda, only this, and no other results, will be accomplished; cf. ŚV, 485 f. (*Citrākṣepaparihāra,* v. 16).

58. The defense of the *citrā* sacrifice is one of the most symptomatic cases of Mīmāṃsā apologetics, and it became one of the starting points of Mīmāṃsā epistemology.

59. On MS I, 1, 5.

60. Cf. ŚV, 484 f. (*Citrākṣepaparihāra,* v. 11 f.).

61. Cf. ŚV, 487 f. (v. 26).

62. TV, 368 f.; cf. also Someśvara, N Sudhā, 604.

63. ŚV, 476 f. (*Sambandhākṣepaparihāra,* v, 110 ff.); see also M. Hiriyanna, *Outlines of Indian Philosophy.* London, sixth ed., 1967, 330.

64. See above, n. 50 f.

65. Cf. *Bṛhatī* (see above, n. 49), 319 ff.; M. Hiriyanna (n. 63), 328 ff.

66. *Tantrarahasya,* ed. R. Shama Shastry, second ed. K.S. Ramaswami Sastri. Baroda, 1956 (GOS), 57; 59.

67. Cf. ŚV, 472 f. (*Sambandhākṣepaparihāra,* v. 94 ff.).

68. ŚV, 466 f. (v. 70 ff.), Cf. Pārthasārathi, *Śāstradīpikā,* ed. L.S. Dravid. Benares, 1916 (ChSS), 320 ff.; 327 ff.; although the Sāṃkhya is more in the focus of this argumentation, it seems that the idea which is rejected here was not indigenous to the Sāṃkhya.

69. Cf. Maṇḍana, *Sphoṭasiddhi* (see n. 54), 84 (v. 11); Pārthasārathi, *Śāstradīpikā,* 14; see also the "Glossarial Index" in F. Edgerton's *Āpadevī* (see above, n. 53).

70. Cf. BSBh III, 1, 6; 2, 28 ff.

71. Cf. NS and NBh IV, 1, 44 ff.; see also YS and YBh III, 9 ff.; IV, 8 ff. (on *saṃskāra* and *vāsanā*). Kumārila may have had predecessors also in Mīmāṃsā; it seems that the so-called Vṛttikāra, a pre-Śabara commentator of the Mīmāṃsāsūtras, interpreted merit and demerit as attributes (*saṃskāra, guṇa*) of the soul; cf. E. Frauwallner, *Materialien zur ältesten Erkenntnislehre der Karmamīmāṃsā.* Vienna, 1968, 95.

72. Cf. NK in: *The Bhāshya of Praśastapāda*, together with the *Nyāyakandalī*, ed. V. P. Dvivedin. Benares, 1895 (Vizianagram. Sanskrit Series), 273 ff.; Śrīdhara quotes from the *Apūrvādhikaraṇa* of TV; he also refers to Maṇḍana's *Vidhiviveka.* On Uddyotakara and the old theory of *apūrva*, see above, n. 46.

73. Cf. Vyomaśiva, *Vyomavatī* (ChSS), 639 ff.; this passage does not indicate any acquaintance with TV.

74. TV, 366 ff.: the *puruṣa* is not the efficient or instrumental cause (*sādhana*); the soul is indispensable as an *āśraya*, but remains comparable to a mere carrier (cf. 370, the simile of the camel). A curious discussion of the question of personal authorship in rituals is found in Śaṅkaramiśra's *Upaskāra* on VS VI, 1, 5 (first published Calcutta, 1861; trans. N. Sinha, Allahabad, 1911). Śaṅkaramiśra obviously misunderstands the *pūrvapakṣa* in MS III, 7, 18 (rejected MS III, 7, 19 ff., Śabara) as Jaimini's own view.

75. Cf. NM, 248 ff.; the *sāṃgrahaṇī* ceremony, which was followed by the acquisition of the village Gauramūlaka, is mentioned on p. 250.

76. Cf. NM, 255: ŚV, *Citrākṣepaparihāra*, v. 26, is quoted twice.

77. Cf. NS and NBh II, 1, 56 ff.; see also the explanation of the failure of ordeals, Bhāruci and Medhātithi on Manu VIII, 115. Kumārila does not accept this theory as a satisfactory explanation; cf. TV, 368.

78. The threefold division of sacrifices into those which bear fruit after death (e.g., *jyotiṣṭoma*), those which bear fruit irregularly (e.g., *citrā*), and those which bear fruit in this life (e.g., *kārīrī*) is Jayanta's direct target of criticism (NM, 252 ff.; see specifically 253, for the term *sāmānyādṛṣṭa*, "common *adṛṣṭa*").

79. Cf. ŚV, 87 ff.; and above, ch. 4.

80. The Jaina author Jinabhadra (probably sixth century and apparently not familiar with Praśastapāda's work) states explicitly that the number of qualities in Vaiśeṣika is seventeen; cf. *Viśeṣāvāśyakabhāṣya*, ed. D. Malvania. Ahmedabad, 1966–1968, v. 2972 ff. with commentary.

81. VS V, 1, 15; V, 2, 4; 8; 14; 19. Cf. also IV, 2, 5: *dharma* causing the movement of atoms toward the formation of bodies.

82. VS VI, 2, 1 ff.; VI, 2, 1 is repeated as X, 20 (X, 2, 8 of the *Upaskāra* version).

83. VS IX, 24; 28 (IX, 2, 9; 13 in the *Upaskāra*).

84. Candrānanda on VS V, 2, 2; if this were to be expressed in terms of the karma theory, it would obviously imply some kind of "group karma."

85. Candrānanda's and Śaṅkaramiśra's attempts in this direction are not very convincing; Śaṅkaramiśra on VS V, 2, 13 (14 according to Candrānanda) suggests that only first movements of flaming, etc., at the beginning of a new world period are meant.

86. Cf. also his comments on VS VI, 1, 5, with lengthy remarks on the Mīmāṃsā.

87. NBh on NS III, 2, 63 ff.; cf. also IV, 1, 44 ff.

88. NBh III, 2, 73; the word *adṛṣṭa* is introduced in the commentary on the preceding Sūtra. This may have been a view which, at a certain time, had its proponents in Nyāya or Vaiśeṣika itself, and was not, as suggested by Vācaspati's *Nyāyavārttikatātparyaṭīkā*, a Jaina view. The causality of atomic motion is ambiguous in Jaina thought. Although *dharma* and *adharma* function as media of motion and rest and may even be called their causes (cf. Kundakunda, *Pañcāstikāyasāra*, v. 102: *gamaṇaṭṭhidikāraṇāni*), they are not supposed to be efficient (ibid., v. 95), but only conditional and auxiliary causes (*upagraha*; cf. Umāsvāti,

Tattvārthasūtra V, 17). A certain spontaneous causality is left to the movable things themselves (cf. Kundakunda, v. 96).

89. Cf. *Vyomavatī* (ChSS), 638 ff.; cf. Śaṅkara, BSBh II, 2, 12 (*Works* III, 232): *adṛṣṭam ......ātmasamavāyi vā syād aṇusamavāyi vā.* Once *adṛṣṭa* had been located in the *ātman*, the notion of the "omnipresence" (*vibhutva*) of the souls became inevitable. Jayanta, NM II, 43, refers to a definition of *adṛṣṭa* as an "attribute of the elements" (*bhūtadharma*).

90. Cf. Praśastapāda (PB; see above, n. 72), 308 ff. On the role of *adṛṣṭa/dharma* in the process of sense perception, cf. 186; in dreams: 184; *adharma* as a factor in the occurrence of doubt: 175. In general, *adṛṣṭa* appears in the explanation of phenomena like desire, aversion, pleasure, etc. VS IV 1, 9, which deals with the conditions of perception and corresponds to PB, 186, does not mention *dharma.*

91. Cf. PB, 48 ff. We cannot discuss here the role of the "Great Lord" (*maheśvara*) in this process.

92. Cf. Praśastapāda, PB, 308 ff.; Śrīdhara, NK, 88 f. My interpretation of the role of *adṛṣṭa* in Vaiśeṣika, as presented in the original version of this chapter (see above, Preface) finds support in an article by A. Wezler, "A Note on the Concept *adṛṣṭa* as used in the *Vaiśeṣikasūtra.*" *Aruṇa-Bhāratī, Prof. A.N. Jani Felicitation Volume.* Baroda, 1983, 35–58.

93. PB, 308 ff. There is a rule in Vaiśeṣika that "invisible" causes should not be invoked as long as "visible" causes are available; see e.g., NK, 145 f.

94. Cf. E. Frauwallner (see above, n. 8), 90 (trans. V. M. Bedekar, 60); cf. my critical review of Frauwallner's thesis, *Journal of the American Oriental Society* 106 (1986), 857 f. See also Bhartṛhari, VP III/3, 18 (on *adṛṣṭa* and the omnipresent souls).

95. NBh I, 1, 9 contrasts the Vaiśeṣika categories, as mere neutral objects of knowledge, with the soteriologically relevant Nyāya category of *prameya.*

96. Cf. E. Frauwallner, vol. 1. Salzburg, 1953, 404 ff. (trans. V. M. Bedekar, 318 ff.).

97. See above, n. 90; the usual term for the causal aggregate is *kāraṇasāmagrī*.

98. Cf. E. Frauwallner (see above, n. 8), 154 (trans. V. M. Bedekar, 109). *Śakti* is rejected by Vyomaśiva, *Vyomavatī* (ChSS), 194, and Śrīdhara, NK (see above, n. 72), 144 ff. Bhartṛhari, VP III/7 (*Sādhanasamuddeśa*), 9 ff. (with Helārāja's commentary) may be taken as an indication that *śakti* once played a more prominent role in Vaiśeṣika.

99. Cf. NV IV, 1, 47 (Bibliotheca Indica): *mūlasekādikṛtam bhoktuḥ karmāpekṣaṃ pṛthivyādidhātum anugṛhṇāti.* NV III, 2, 67 calls the functions of karma with reference to the body "restrictive" (*niyāmaka*). According to PB, 107 (and NK, 108; see above, n. 72), the *adṛṣṭa* of persons who are destined to derive certain experiences from artefacts such as jars is also operative in their production.

100. Cf. NBh III, 2, 63 ff. The definition of *śarīra* is already given in I, 1, 11.

101. Ibid. This *pūrvapakṣa* is already referred to in NS III, 2, 63: *bhūtebhyo mūrtyupādāvat tadupādānam.*

102. Cf. PB (see above, n. 72), 27.

103. The Sūtra which divides the products of earth into organisms, sense organs, and objects is found only in the *Upaskāra* version (IV, 2, 1).

104. *Praśastapādabhāṣyam* with the comm. *Kiraṇāvalī* of Udayanācārya, ed. J. N. Jetly. Baroda, 1971 (GOS), 39. Cf. 39 f.: *vṛkṣādayaḥ pratiniyatabhoktrādhiṣṭhitāḥ, jīvanamaraṇasvapnaprajāgaraṇarogabheṣajaprayogabījasajātīyānubandhānukūlopagamapratikūlāpagamādibhyaḥ prasiddhaśarīravat*: trees, etc., are inhabited by particular experiencers since they show all the characteristics such as living, dying, sleep, waking, disease, curability, seeds, attachment to their own species, seeking what is favorable, avoiding what is unfavorable, which we find also in the case of

what is generally accepted as *śarīra*. In a different context, the question is referred to by Vyomaśiva, *Vyomavatī* (ChSS), 404; cf. also Śaṅkaramiśra, *Upaskāra* on VS IV, 2, 5. Śrīdhara, NK (see above, n. 72), 83, denies the existence of souls in trees, etc. See also A. Wezler, "On the Term *antaḥsaṃjña-*." *Annals of the Bhandarkar Oriental Research Institute* 68 (1987), 111–131; and below, n. 148.

105. *Chāndogya Upaniṣad* VI, 3, 1.

106. *Aitareya Upaniṣad* III, 3.

107. Cf. Manu I, 43 ff. A classification of four types of birth (*yoni*) is also found in Buddhism: *aṇḍaja, jalābuja, saṃsedaja, opapātika*; see *Majjhimanikāya* 12; ed. V. Trenckner, vol. 1. London, 1888, 73. *Opapatika* refers to the "sudden" origination of superhuman beings. On Jaina classifications, see E. Frauwallner (see above, n. 8), 266 ff. (trans. V.M. Bedekar, 193 ff.); and P.S. Jaini in *Karma and Rebirth in Classical Indian Traditions* (see above, n. 23), 222 ff. On plant life, see G.P. Majumdar, *Vanaspati.* Calcutta, 1927; R.P. Das, *Das Wissen von der Lebensspanne der Bäume: Surapālas Vṛkṣāyurveda.* Stuttgart, 1988; A. Wezler, "Bemerkungen zu einigen von Naturbeobachtung zeugenden Textstellen und den Problemen ihrer Interpretation." *Studien zur Indologie und Iranistik* 13/14 (1987), 321–345.

108. *Chāndogya Upaniṣad* V, 10, 8. Cf. Pāṇini II, 4, 8: *kṣudrajantavaḥ*; Patañjali has various suggestions as to the exact meaning of the term; see also *Vyomavatī* (ChSS), 229: *kṣudrajantavo yūkādayaḥ*; Udayana, *Kiraṇāvalī* (GOS), 39: *kṣudrajantūnāṃ maśakādīnāṃ yātanāśarīrāṇi.*

109. Cf. H. von Glasenapp, *Indische Geisteswelt*, vol. 2. Baden-Baden, no date, 209.

110. *Bṛhadāraṇyaka Upaniṣad* VI, 2, 1–16 (especially VI, 2, 16).

111. Cf. Patañjali, *Mahābhāṣya* on Pāṇini I, 4, 30: a casual reference to the origination of scorpions (*vṛścika*; dung beetles?) from cow-dung; on the same "phenomenon," cf. Śaṅkara (also Bhāskara and Rāmānuja) on BS II, 1, 6; and G.A. Jacob, *A Second Handful of Popular Maxims.* Bombay, second ed., 1909, § 81.

112. Cf. R. Schmidt, *Beiträge zur indischen Erotik*. Berlin, second ed., 1911, 257 (quoting from the *Ratirahasya* and the *Anaṅgaraṅga*). For the role and origination of "worms" (*kṛmi*) in the medical tradition, see the detailed classification in G.J. Meulenbeld, *The Mādhavanidāna and Its Chief Commentary*. Leiden, 1974, 285–295.

113. Cf. E. Frauwallner (see above, n. 8), 297 ff. (trans. V.M. Bedekar, 216 ff.).

114. Cf. NM II, 13: *śukraśoṇitādivad dadhyavayavān vikṛtān upādāsyate*; when Udayana, *Kiraṇāvalī* (GOS), 38, calls worms etc. "heat-born" (*uṣmaja*), he does not deny the involvement of a *jīva*.

115. *Tarkarahasyadīpikā* on Haribhadra's *Ṣaḍdarśanasamuccaya*, v. 49; ed. M.K. Jain. Calcutta, 1969 (Jñānapīṭha Mūrtidevī Jaina Granthamālā), 224 ff.; cf. also *Ācārāṅgasūtra* I, 1, 6.

116. This does, of course, not exclude the accumulation of empirical observations in certain specific areas. However, in various important disciplines, including medicine (*āyurveda*), the expansion of the karmic and soteriological schemes has interfered with, or even superseded, the empirical orientation.

117. Cf. PB (see above, n. 72), 259 f. In the case of *duḥkha*, reference is made to *adharma*.

118. Cf. NV III, 2, 61; ed. V. P. Dvivedin. Calcutta, 1914 (Bibliotheca Indica), 442.

119. Cf. YBh II, 13; karma whose ripening is undetermined (*aniyatavipāka*) may take three different courses: it may be destroyed without ripening (sc. through practices of atonement); it may merge with a dominant karma; it may be suppressed by a dominant karma whose ripening is determined, and remain dormant for a long time (*kṛtasya-avipakvasya nāśaḥ, pradhānakarmaṇy āvāpagamanaṃ vā, niyatavipākapradhānakarmaṇā-abhibhūtasya vā ciram avasthānam*). The karma which Vyāsa calls *niyatavipāka* is supposed to produce its results either in the present or in the immediately subsequent existence.

120. This is analogous to the orthodox view that in spite of all obstacles and delays a correctly executed ritual will ultimately not perish without having produced a result (*adattaphala*); cf. Jayanta, NM, 254.

121. *Saṃyuttanikāya* 26, 21; ed. L. Feer, vol. 4. London, 1894 (PTS), 230 ff.

122. Cf. *Aṅguttaranikāya*, ed. R. Morris and E. Hardy. London, 1885–1900 (PTS), vol. 2, 87 f.; 3, 131 (*yāni kho pana tāni vedayitāni pittasamuṭṭhānāni*); 5, 110 (diseases, *ābādha*, produced by the same series of causes).

123. *Milindapañha* (see above, n. 29), 134 ff.

124. Cf. Buddhaghosa, *Visuddhimagga* VIII, 1 ff.

125. *Kathāvatthu* VII, 7–10; specifically VII, 7: *paṭhavī kammavipāko ti*? VII, 10 establishes a sharp distinction between *kamma* and *kammavipāka*.

126. Cf. J.P. McDermott, "The *Kathāvatthu* Kamma Debates." *Journal of the American Oriental Society* 95 (1975), 424–433.

127. Cf. the statements of leading Sinhalese authorities referred to by Nyānatiloka, *Die Fragen des Milinda*, vol. 1. Leipzig, 1919, 216 f. (n. 121).

128. That one cannot mechanically pay off bad karma by means of systematic self-torture seems to be taken for granted by the Theravāda Buddhists as well as most representatives of "orthodox" Hindu thought. In accordance with this premise, Śaṅkara emphasizes that the pain or discomfort of performing "permanent rites" (*nityakarman*) is not a fruit (*phala*) of past karma and therefore cannot accomplish its cancellation; cf. GBh XVIII, 66 (*Works* II, 290).

129. The issue of karma and "freedom" has been avoided in this chapter and would be a topic for a different paper. However, its significance has sometimes been exaggerated in the secondary literature.

130. *Sechzig Upanishads des Veda*. Leipzig, third ed., 1921 (reprint Wiesbaden, 1963), 137. The two sections are found in *Chāndogya Upaniṣad*

V, 3–10 and *Bṛhadāraṇyaka Upaniṣad* VI, 2 (*Śatapatha Brāhmaṇa* XIV, 9, 1). There have been numerous adaptations of this mythology in later or extra-brahminical literature, for instance in the *Mahābhārata* I, 85, 10–20; on this section, see J. A. B. van Buitenen, "Some Notes on the Uttara-yāyāta." *Adyar Library Bulletin* 31/32 (1967–1968; V. Raghavan Felicitation Vol.), 617–635 (reprint in: *Studies in Indian Literature and Philosophy*, ed. L. Rocher. Delhi, 1988, 281–292).

131. *Kauṣītaki Upaniṣad* I, 1 ff.; *Jaiminīya Brahmaṇa* I, 18; for the "combined" version, see I, 45 ff. The Jaiminīya versions differ in various ways from the other versions. On the transformation into water, food, seed, cf. *Śatapatha Brahmaṇa* III, 7, 4, 4.

132. For a good survey, cf. H. W. Bodewitz, *Jaiminīya Brāhmaṇa* I, 1–65. Translation and Commentary. Leiden, 1973, 243 ff.

133. The version of the *Chāndogya Upaniṣad* is more detailed, introducing several additional stages of transformation.

134. *Kauṣītaki Upaniṣad* I, 1; *Jaiminīya Brāhmaṇa* I, 18, 146; with the notes by H. W. Bodewitz, 55 ff.; 117 ff. on the connection between life and death and day and night, the phases of the moon, and so forth, cf. BU III, 1, 3 ff.

135. Cf. BU III, 2, 13; IV, 4, 3, ff.

136. *Chāndogya Upaniṣad* V, 10, 6.

137. *Aitareya Upaniṣad* II, 1 ff. (= *Aitareya Āraṇyaka* II, 5, 1 ff.).

138. *Chāndogya Upaniṣad* V, 10, 7.

139. Cf. BSBh III, 1, 1.

140. As used in BU IV, 4, 3.

141. BSBh III, 1, 6. This or a similar theory is already referred to and rejected by Prabhākara, *Bṛhatī* (see above, n. 49), 323. Śaṅkara criticizes the Mīmāṃsā concept of *apūrva* in BSBh III, 2, 38 ff.

142. Cf. BSBh III, 1, 8 ff. Bādarāyaṇa refers to Kārṣṇājini in BS III, 1, 9. Śaṅkara rejects a special role of "morality" (*caraṇa, ācāra*) in this context; on "ritual and moral works," see above, n. 35.

143. Cf. BSBh III, 1, 24 ff. The duplication of the *jīvas*, or rather the allocation of "guest jīvas," is repeated when the vegetable is eaten and appropriated by a human being or an animal (BSBh III, 1, 26). Rāmānuja and other later commentators agree with Śaṅkara on the basic issues of this interpretation.

144. Cf. Śaṅkara's commentary on *Aitareya Upaniṣad* II, 1:the world as providing manifold facilities ("seats") suitable for the manifold living beings to experience their karmic results (*anekaprāṇikarmaphalopabhogayogyānekādhiṣṭhānavad*); and BSBh II, 2, 1 (*Works* III, 221): the world as "suitable for the enjoyment of the results of various works" (*nānākarmaphalopabhogayogya*); see also above, n. 41.

145. Worldly bondage itself is of the nature of means and ends (*sādhyasādhanalakṣaṇo bandhaḥ*); BUBh III, 2, intr.; *Works* I, 792).

146. Cf. Gauḍapāda, *Māṇḍūkyakārikā* IV, 56: *yāvad dhetupalāveśaḥ, saṃsāras tāvad āyataḥ*. According to the tradition of Advaita Vedānta, Gauḍapāda was the teacher of Śaṅkara's teacher Govinda.

147. In Buddhism, Nāgārjuna has accomplished a radical "consummation" and transcendence of the idea of karma; cf. his *Madhyamakakārikā*, ch. 17. It is well known that Gauḍapāda was strongly influenced by the philosophy of Nāgārjuna.

148. Cf. BSBh I, 1, 5 (*Works* III, 28): *na-īśvarād anyaḥ saṃsārī*. On awareness in plants according to the *Yogavāsiṣṭha*, see W. Slaje, "Bewusstsein und Wahrnehmungsvermögen von Pflanzenaus hinduistischer Sicht." *Der orientalische Mensch und seine Umwelt*, ed. B. Scholz. Graz, 1989, 149–169.

CHAPTER 10

Homo Hierarchicus: The Conceptualization of the Varṇa System in Indian Thought

Introduction

1. There is an old and oft-repeated assertion that classical Indian philosophy does not concern itself with social matters. This view, which seems to agree with the Indian tradition's basic "division of labor" between the soteriological and trans-social orientation of philosophical thought on the one hand and the socially committed sciences of *artha* and *dharma* on the other, has been evaluated and interpreted from a variety of perspectives.[1] The tradition of the Advaita Vedānta, which has been portrayed as the very culmination of Hindu thought, appears to lend especially clear and unequivocal support to the truth of this assessment.

On the other hand, proponents of what has become known as the Neo-Vedānta have argued that this supposed shortcoming actually hides a rich potential of untapped positive possibilities and that the Advaita Vedānta in particular has direct relevance for the social and political problems of our time: that it alone is capable of providing a metaphysically based ethical orientation that would be acceptable to modern thought and appropriate to the current situation in the world. No matter how one may assess the meaning and actual political weight of this claim, the "practical," politicizing Vedānta has had a significant role to play in the philosophical self-representation of modern India. It merits a more serious scholarly attention than it has thus far been accorded, apart from a few promising exceptions. Directly related to this, the question as to the "social relevance" of classical Indian philosophy should also be posed anew—but without simply taking for granted the above-mentioned "division of labor," nor with a preconceived agenda of social and ideological critique. Instead, we should focus on those socially relevant statements that may indeed be found in the Indian philosophical texts, while admitting that these are scattered and isolated cases. There is no denying that India has never had a tradition of political and social philosophizing comparable to that reaching from Plato's idea of the state to the Marxist program of a "secularization" of philosophy.[2] Yet social themes have occasionally been taken up within the context of philosophical discourse, and philosophical terms and perspectives have been applied to social matters. The significance of these references cannot be assessed on a quantitative basis alone: even in their isolation, and as marginal phenomena within Indian philosophical literature, they are expressions of important attitudes and presuppositions of Indian philosophy, and symptoms of its social and historical role.

The conception of the four principal castes (*varṇa*) is the most obvious and significant point of reference for our investigation, and for this reason, the following pages will focus upon this conception. Drawing in particular upon the literature of the Hindu systems of the first millenium A.D., we shall compile philosophical testimony on this subject and examine how the *varṇa* structure of society has been portrayed, analyzed, and rationalized within the context of cosmological, metaphysical, and epistemological discussions.

There has never been a full survey of the texts that pertain to this subject, whether by historians of Indian philosophy or the historians of the Dharmaśāstra, and the following discussion can not and does not have any pretension to fill this gap. This notwithstanding, the passages which shall be presented and discussed below may be considered exemplary and should provide us with a textual basis sufficient for assessing the most important problems and developmental lines.[3]

2. The present chapter deals with theoretical concepts and constructs. It does not address the question to what extent these concepts correspond to social and historical realities; i.e., it does not deal with caste as an actual phenomenon. What this chapter discusses may, in fact, seem even more theoretical, abstract and removed from the realities of social life than what we find in the

Dharmaśāstra literature. The critique of brahminical schemes and constructions which É. Senart and many others have raised with regard to the Dharmaśāstras may seem to be even more appropriate when it comes to the philosophical reconstructions of the varṇa structure.[4]

Indeed, we are dealing with theoretical speculations and constructions; yet these are constructions and conceptualizations developed by traditional Indian theorists. Unlike the interpretations and paradigms of modern Western theorists, they are not only ideas about, but also symptoms and components of the multi-layered Indian tradition. They may not provide us with much factual information about the social reality of traditional India; nonetheless, they are its products and reflections.

The chapter discusses traditional Indian conceptualizations and rationalizations of the varṇa system of society, i.e., of a supposedly natural and inherent hierarchy among human beings. The "homo hierarchicus" is just a segment of the pervasive hierarchy of living beings, which extends "from Brahmā to the tufts of grass" (*brahmādistambaparyanta*). The Indian authors use a variety of terms to characterize this hierarchy of human, subhuman and superhuman forms of life, for instance *tāratamya* ("gradation"), *uccanīcabhāva* ("high and low status"), and *utkarṣāpakarṣa* ("superiority and inferiority").[5] This hierarchy involves different levels of merit and demerit (*dharma, adharma*), pleasure and pain (*sukha, duḥkha*), and of the "manifestness of knowledge, sovereignty, and so forth" (*jñānaiśvaryābhivyakti*); and it provides different stations of *saṃsāra*, i.e., of karmic reward and punishment.[6] Some authors suggest that mankind alone, and no other species of living beings, is subdivided into further classes characterized by mutual "superiority and inferiority" (*utkarṣāpakarṣa*).[7] In addition to such vertical hierarchies, we also find "horizontal" schemes of hierarchy, that is, concentric circles of increasing distance from a dharmic center. The brahmins would place themselves and the other "twice-born" (*dvija*) castes, as well as the orthodox followers of the Veda, in the central region, while the śūdra class with its innumerable subdivisions and bastardizations, as well as all more or less heterodox sects, would be seen as more or less removed or "external" (*bāhya, bāhyatara*) in relation to this center of legitimacy and orthodoxy.[8]

3. The title of this chapter does not imply that it is an attempt to defend L. Dumont's classical and controversial book against its Anglo-American critics. Nonetheless, it does support in its own way what Dumont calls "the main idea" of his book, that is, "the idea of hierarchy separated from power."[9] Regardless of all problems that social and cultural anthropologists may find with this idea, the world-view that is presupposed or articulated in our philosophical sources is indeed inherently hierarchical.

There is no need for us to speculate on the origin of the caste system, on the original meaning and function of the terms *varṇa* and *jāti*, or on "the relationship between the caste system as it can be directly observed, and the classical theory of the varṇas."[10] However, a few general terminological observations will be useful. Many scholars have emphasized the fundamental differences between *jāti* and *varṇa*, and they have argued that "caste" should be avoided as a translation for *varṇa*. A. L. Basham says that the "indiscriminate use" of "caste" for both *varṇa* and *jāti* is "false terminology," and he adds: "All ancient Indian sources make a sharp distinction between the two terms."[11] While Basham's call for terminological caution is certainly appropriate, his claim that the two terms were sharply distinguished in the classical texts is untenable as a general statement. As a matter of fact, for most of the philosophical sources to be discussed in this chapter the terminological distinction is virtually negligible.

Unlike *varṇa*, the term *jāti* does not play a noticeable and thematically relevant role in Vedic literature. It does appear in the Dharmaśāstra literature, beginning with the Dharmasūtras and older verse texts. In these works, it is neither simply a synonym of *varṇa*, nor clearly and consistently distinguished from it. Manu and other authorities refer frequently to the "norms of the jātis" (*jātidharma*), usually in conjunction with the "norms of the regions and families" (*deśadharma, kuladharma*); it does not seem likely that these are references to the four varṇas.[12] Yājñavalkya mentions *varṇa* and *jāti* side by side, as separate or at least separable phenomena.[13]

Yet from an early time, there was at least a partial overlap, together with much interaction and "osmosis." Āpastamba's *Dharmasūtra* uses *jāti* in the sense of *varṇa*.[14] In later texts, this is a more or less familiar phenomenon. As stated earlier, the *Manusmṛti* has usages of *jāti* that imply a distinction from *varṇa*; and Manu X, 4 states that (unlike the *jāti*) the number of *varṇa* is strictly limited to four. Nonetheless, other verses of the same text use *jāti* to refer to the four *varṇa* and, even more conspicuously, *varṇa* to refer to the unlimited number of other "castes" or "races" (*jāti*). For instance, X, 31 uses the word *varṇa* with regard to the "inferior" (*hīna*) groups which result from bastardization; in other verses, the two terms seem to be interchangeable.[15]

The commentators deal with this terminological situation in different ways. In a number of cases, they explain the term *jāti* by referring to the four *varṇa*, i.e., the brahmins etc.[16]; in other cases, they note that *varṇa* is used in the sense of certain subspecies or intermediate groups within the human species (*manuṣyajāti, manuṣyāvāntarajāti*).[17] There are, however, more specific and thematically relevant statements which explain the jātis as mixed castes, such as the *murdhāvasikta* (of brahmin fathers and kṣatriya mothers) or *ambaṣṭha* (of brahmin fathers and vaiśya mothers).[18] This does not necessarily imply that *jāti* is used as a technical term; some authors state that, in addition to "mixed castes," it may also refer to "women" (*strī*) and other groups.[19] At any rate, the texts do not recognize any independent "jāti system," apart from the four varṇas. The theory of "mixed castes" is an attempt to derive all other hereditary social formations from the varṇa system. Such derivation involves a basic ambiguity: Should the "mixed castes" be added to or subsumed under the four varṇas? Do they constitute mere subspecies, or new, additional species, which are genetically derived from, but not included in the varṇa system? The answers may vary, and they are often more or less elusive.[20] While it may be true that the theory of caste mixture "was used to refer real *jāti* to the varṇas,"[21] the instances of "mixed castes" mentioned in the texts are not necessarily more factual than the four varṇas.

4. The philosophical sources which will be discussed in this chapter do not pay much attention to the "mixed castes," or to the distinction between *jāti* and *varṇa*. They deal with the conceptual framework of the four normative and theoretical "castes" which they may call both *jāti* and *varṇa*. In using the term *jāti* for this purpose, they obviously exploit the fact that it means not only "birth" or "species," but was also widely used in grammatical and philosophical literature as a term for "universals," as opposed to particular, individual entities (*vyakti*, etc.).

In the context and for the purpose of this presentation, the term "caste" shall be utilized in the sense of the theoretical notion of varṇa. Although this deviates from current terminological usage, it is not only convenient, but may also remind us of the fact that, in spite of all differences, the varṇa system is, indeed, the prototype for important aspects of the "real" castes.

The textual references found in the following presentation could have been easily augmented. For this, the literature produced by the orthodox traditions of the Pūrvamīmāṃsā and Uttaramīmāṃsā would be of great and obvious importance. In addition, the adaptations of the Mīmāṃsā arguments by the Dharmaśāstra commentators, for instance Medhātithi, would have to be considered.[22] The topic has continued to play its role in modern traditionalistic pandit literature. Among the relevant sources, the *Dharmapradīpa* by Anantakṛṣṇa Śāstrin, Sītārāma Śāstrin and Śrījīva Bhaṭṭācārya deserves particular attention. However, Sanskrit pandits are also found among the advocates of a non-hereditary, ethical and characterological interpretation of the varṇa system.[23]

In the later history of Nyāya and Vaiśeṣika, epistemological and ontological discussions concerning the status of the four varṇas are a somewhat marginal, though certainly not negligible phenomenon. There are even some—hitherto unpublished—monographs in this area, for instance the *Brāhmaṇatvajātivāda*, the *Brāhmaṇatvajātivicāra* and the *Brāhmaṇatvavāda*; manuscripts of these anonymous texts are found in the collection of the Sanskrit University Library (Sarasvatī Bhavana) in Benares.[24] The topic has also been discussed in the sectarian theistic traditions, primarily in the literature of the Vaiṣṇava Vedānta schools. Apart from the numerous *Brahmasūtra* commentaries produced by these schools,[25] we have to mention some direct and specific adaptations of Pūrvamīmāṃsā texts and procedures. Veṅkaṭanātha (also known as Vedāntadeśika), one of the chief representatives of Rāmānuja's Śrīvaiṣṇava school, provides a remarkable example in his *Seśvaramīmāṃsā*, i.e., a theistic adaptation and interpretation of Jaimini's *Mīmāṃsāsūtra*; he discusses the ontological and epistemological status of the varṇas in detail and reproduces Kumārila's arguments from the *Tantravārttika*.[26]

On the other hand, the opponents of brahminical orthodoxy, in particular the Jainas and Buddhists, have paid a great deal of attention to this issue. After the demise of Buddhism in India, the Jainas continued their vigorous attacks against the hereditary varṇa system and, more specifically, against the idea of real "caste universals." The great Jaina dialectician Prabhācandra (eleventh century) epitomizes this tradition of critique in two elaborate sections of his *Nyāyakumudacandra* and his *Prameyakamalamārtaṇḍa*.[27] Even within the Hindu tradition, the attempts of the brahmins to establish their hereditary rank as a quasi-biological species were questioned and ridiculed.[28] However, traditional Advaita Vedānta did not take part in this critique. Its non-dualistic metaphysics has generally not affected its orthodox and conservative position with regard to social norms; this includes its acceptance of the four varṇas as legitimate and authoritative structures of the world of appearance. It has been left to the Neo-Vedānta to proclaim and exploit the social and political potential of nondualism.[29]

Antecedents of the Philosophical Varṇa Theories

5. The present context precludes any discussion of the factual origins of the caste system or the problems of its later historical development and its actual role within Indian society. Concerning its documentation and interpretation in the mythological, cosmological, and ritual texts of the early period and its theoretical explication in the Dharmaśāstra, we may refer to the available standard works, in particular the presentation by P. V. Kane,[30] as well as the older yet still useful compilations of J. Muir[31] and A. Weber.[32] Nevertheless, it seems fitting to include at least a few basic remarks about those aspects of the *varṇa* conception that became important for later philosophical debates, and in particular for the debates between Buddhists and Hindus.

As exemplified by the concept of the brahmin, the cosmic and the social, the ethical norm and the supposed "biological" fact, have been combined within the four varṇas since they were listed in the cosmogonic hymn Ṛgveda X, 90. This is in keeping with a world view whose key concepts interweave aspects of a normative and factual, and an ethical and physical nature. The doctrine of karma and rebirth, which was gradually consolidated, came to provide a natural framework for this approach.[33] And yet the literature from the Brāhmaṇa period also contains a number of terms which indicate that these various aspects and meanings were being distinguished from one another. For example, we find the brahmin who was characterized as such solely as a result of his ancestry or his fulfillment of purely formal functions (*jātibrāhmaṇa; brahmabandhu*) being contrasted with the brahmin who was distinguished by his adequate knowledge and action and who had realized the full sense of his being a brahmin in this manner.[34] In other words, a distinction was made between the ethical and the hereditary aspects, which were conceptually juxtaposed and occasionally contrasted. What is more, the significance of hereditary legitimation occasionally appears to have been secondary,[35] although it would be going too far to see such scattered and often ambivalent passages as evidence of any far-reaching mobility or a predominantly ethical and characterological understanding of the caste system—as the Neo-Vedānta frequently does.

The critique by the Buddhists has to be seen against this background. Their "ethicizing" interpretation of the caste concepts was not a radical innovation. Instead, they drew upon aspects that had long been present in the spectrum of meaning of these concepts, but did so in a manner which credited the ethical aspect with the primary and more intrinsic meaning while playing this against the other aspects. It was here that the coexistence and occasional competition between the ethical/normative and the factual/hereditary aspects first came to be a problem; instead of being coordinated with one another, a sharp contrast began to be made between what was considered to be relevant and irrelevant. As a result, the caste distinctions themselves were ultimately called into question, and the traditional criteria subjected to fundamental criticism.[36]

The concept of *svadharma*, which may be found in some of the later Upaniṣads and in particular in the Bhagavadgītā, offered a way out of this problematic situation.[37] This concept assigns great weight to the ethical motif while simultaneously maintaining and defending the hereditary legitimation of caste membership. The hereditary and the ethical aspects remain distinct and even stand in contrast to one another while being related in such a way that there was no direct competition and confrontation, a procedure that skirts the danger of weakening the hereditary aspect. There is a different ethical appraisal of behavior for each of the four hereditary stages. In other words, each person should prove himself according to his hereditary position. Thus, while a "good" śūdra may be ethically "better" than a "bad" brahmin, this ethical hierarchy cannot change the fact that a brahmin will always remain a brahmin and a śūdra a śūdra.[38] The respecting of this hereditary affiliation and the avoidance of intermingling (*saṃkara*) is, in keeping with the concept of svadharma, in itself a standard and even a fundamental condition of ethical conduct: it is better to perform the duties appropriate to one's station poorly than to fulfill those of another well.[39]

In Patañjali's *Mahābhāṣya*, the problems of reference and differentiation which arise in connection with the "coexistence" of ethical and biological aspects in the concept of varṇa appear as topics of linguistic and epistemological reflection. In a section of the *Tatpuruṣāhnika* (on Pāṇini II, 2,6:*nañ*) that discusses the function of the particle *a-* in such forms as *abrāhmaṇa*, the possibility is considered that the nominal meaning to which the particle of negation refers in such a case is to be understood in the sense of an aggregation of properties (*guṇasamudāya*), i.e., that the *a-* here signifies a deficiency or incompleteness. Such an interpretation would also explain the applicability of the remainder of the compound, i.e., - *brāhmaṇa*, for a share of those properties whose entirety makes up the full meaning of the word *brāhmaṇa* would be retained in its composition with the negative particle *a*. Here, several external criteria of identification (*gaura, śucyācāra, piṅgala, kapilakeśa*, i.e., light-colored, of faultless conduct, brown-eyed, with reddish-brown hair) are added to such traditional "components of meaning" as asceticism (*tapas*), erudition (*śruta*), and legitimate birth (*yoni*).[40] According to this interpretation, any vaiśya who possesses certain ethical or physiological characteristics would be considered to be just as much a "partial brahmin" as a person whose "brahminness" was solely the result of his descent from brahmin parents. On the whole, however, this discussion remains noncommittal and can hardly be seen as an expression of social critique. At no time does the conceptual status of the brahmin etc. appear endangered, and the fact that there are certain problems and exceptions is not considered to be an occasion for questioning the fundamental validity of the caste system or the reliable identifiability of caste membership: as a result of ancient tradition, people know how to distinguish a brahmin from a non-brahmin in daily life. Such physical features as hair and skin color, as well as peculiar forms of livelihood, are still considered valid criteria, while more penetrating questions concerning the authenticity or demonstrability of brahminness, etc., are not posed.[41]

A completely different level of reflection on this problem is developed in the Mīmāṃsā, and in particular by Kumārila. Here, as a later section of this chapter will show, the Buddhist challenge was met in full. The ethical and factual connotations were distinguished from one another in a much more resolute manner, and the priority of the hereditary legitimation was developed with a previously unknown conceptual rigor. Here, safeguarding the caste concept against the ambivalences that resulted from the combination of various semantic components and against the dangers of mobility and variability became an important motivating factor.

In general, the discussions of the varṇa system within traditional Hindu philosophy were largely apologetical and remained reactions to criticism and challenges from without. In accordance with the different stages of development and the fundamental systematic positions of the Indian philosophical schools, a variety of metaphysical, cosmological, and epistemological concepts and theories were placed in the service of this essentially apologetic task.

The Varṇa System and the Guṇa Theory

6. Of all the theories that may be found in classical Indian philosophy, the doctrine of the three *guṇa*, the three basic forces of the dynamic primordial matter (*pradhāna*) or nature (*prakṛti*) from which the visible world periodically develops, has been most widely applied to non-philosophical questions. This Sāṃkhya theory was developed from pre-philosophical and mythological sources and offered a potentially universal, and, indeed, frequently utilized principle for classifying and explaining empirical phenomena; often completely detached from the remaining doctrines of Sāṃkhya, it was applied in a variety of ways in cosmology, psychology, medicine, dietetics, poetics, etc. The guṇa theory was especially popular for classifying and characterizing living beings (especially humans) and their patterns of behavior. Similarly, it could also be used as a means for discussing, justifying, and reinterpreting existing classifications and typologies. It is not surprising, then, that it also became linked in certain ways with the most significant of these classifications, that based upon the varṇa structure of society.

In the classical Sāṃkhya texts from the first millenium A.D. (i.e., in particular in Īśvarakṛṣṇa's *Sāṃkhyakārikā* and the corresponding commentaries) few explicit opinions are to be found; and—as these texts are concerned with fundamental cosmological, metaphysical, and soteriological questions—this was probably not to be expected. Yet one passage, *Sāṃkhyakārikā* v. 53, is worthy of mention:

> *aṣṭavikalpo daivas, tairyagyonyaś ca pañcadhā bhavati,*
> *mānuṣyaś ca-ekavidhaḥ, samāsato bhautikaḥ sargaḥ.*

("The divine domain of evolution has eight types, the animal five, the human one; this, in short, is the evolution of living beings.")

Directly after this verse (v. 54), this enumeration is supplemented by a hierarchical arrangement based upon the distribution of the three guṇas. Now it would certainly be incorrect to draw more far-reaching conclusions from the characterization of the human race as "uniform" (*ekavidha*). Yet, it should be noted that no matter what other assumptions may have been made about the subdivisions of the human race, these were not elevated to the rank of primary cosmological and biological relevance (as occurs in the often-cited Ṛgveda hymn X.90 and in the numerous texts which concur with this). The view of man in his unity and distinction, which tended to recede in later Indian thought, still appeared to possess a certain self-evident validity within the natural philosophy of the *Sāṃkhyakārikā*.

In this context, it is interesting to consider some of the various ways in which commentators have reacted to this passage: in the richest and possibly oldest available commentary, the anonymous *Yuktidīpikā*, the word *ekavidha* is explicated through the comment that there are no subspecies (*jātyantarānupapatteḥ*).[42] But the *Māṭharavṛtti* and the *Sāṃkhyasaptativṛtti* (which has recently been published and which has obvious affinities with the *Māṭharavṛtti*) limit themselves to the statement that the human race (which the verse characterizes as uniform) reaches from the brahmin to the caṇḍāla on the basis of the equality of characteristics (*liṅga*), i.e., primarily their visual appearance.[43] Vācaspati's remark that this characterization of the human race as uniform simply disregards the subdivisions into subspecies, brahmins, etc. is an obvious attempt to temper its tone.[44]

In any case, one can hardly speak of any explicit social reference in the classical Sāṃkhya; nor do we find any explicit applications of the three *guṇa* to the theory of caste. The situation is different in pre- and post-classical Sāṃkhya, as well as in other texts—both older and more recent—that are either directly or indirectly related to the Sāṃkhya.

In this context, much, and much that is controversial, has been said about the most famous of those early texts that utilized Sāṃkhya concepts, the Bhagavadgītā. Let us present a few basic observations which are directly relevant to our topic.

Referring to passages such as IV, 13,[45] which state that the institution of the four varṇas follows the distribution of the guṇas and "works" (*karman*) and speaking of the role of the guṇa theory in the Bhagavadgītā in general, modern Hinduism has often advanced the thesis that the hereditary view of the caste system has here given way to an ethical or characterological view. S. Radhakrishnan, who tends to draw parallels between the Bhagavadgītā and the Buddhist *Dhammapada* with respect to other questions as well, has been an emphatic spokesmen for this view. Here, the concept of svadharma appears to provide additional support for this ethicizing interpretation.[46]

It is very symptomatic of the literary character and the historical role of the Bhagavadgītā that this work has also been subjected to completely opposite interpretations. That is, it has also been cited as an authoritative document which provides support for the traditional hereditary explication of the four varṇas. Such modern traditonalist pandits as Vāsudeva Śāstrin Abhyaṅkara and Durgāprasāda Dviveda have cited the passages in the Bhagavadgītā that deal with svadharma, etc., as evidence *for* the hereditary view and *against* the ethicizing corruption of the caste concept, for they assume that hereditary caste membership and the social roles traditionally ascribed to the castes also correspond to the true and metaphysical being of the individuals concerned.[47] Of course, the Bhagavadgītā is distinguished by its avoidance of categorical and exclusive statements and its general tendency towards reconciliation, synthesis, and ambivalence. For this reason, we should not expect it to explicitly play off the various meanings or aspects of the varṇa concept or claim exclusive validity for one meaning or one aspect. At the same time, it is clear that the fundamental hereditary meaning of caste membership remains unquestioned, and is in fact defended in a subtle, conciliatory, and very accommodating manner against the ethicizing meaning represented by Buddhism; in the opening chapters, the mixing of the castes (*varṇasaṃkara*) is repeatedly referred to as a threatening phenomenon.[48] Classifications made on the basis of ethical or characterological criteria appear alongside of and within the biological and hereditary arrangement of the castes without replacing or even endangering it.[49] Here, it is obvious that we can no longer speak of any naive and unreflected coexistence among the meanings and aspects such as may be found in the older texts, and especially those dating from the pre-Buddhist period. The ethical and biological/hereditary aspects overlap and merge, albeit in a manner that clearly presupposes the confrontation between the meanings which the Buddhists brought about. The concept of *svadharma* (i.e., the duties that result for a person from his position in life) appears to allow a great deal of room for the ethical aspect while simultaneously securing and stabilizing the traditional, hereditary structure as the very context and foundation for ethical valuation; according to the doctrine of rebirth and retributive causality (*saṃsāra; karman*, etc.), the caste rank results from previous existences and does not necessarily reflect one's current moral achievements. The "distribution of the guṇas and the works" (*guṇakarmavibhāga*) referred to in the above-cited passage IV,13 is doubtlessly to be understood within the context of the doctrine of saṃsāra.[50]

7. The manner in which the term *karman* was applied to the four castes is revealingly ambivalent: while "works" in the sense of ethically relevant behavior (*ācāra*) are ascribed to the two higher varṇas (*brāhmaṇa, kṣatriya*), "works" in the sense of types of livelihood or employment are associated with the two lower varṇas (*vaiśya, śūdra*).[51] The reasons behind this practice are easy to understand: since ancient times, the status of the brahmin, and to a lesser extent that of the kṣatriya, has been associated with such characteristic virtues as wisdom, honesty, and self-discipline. These values were reserved for the higher castes, and could not also be assigned to the lower castes as their appropriate norms (svadharma); for these lower castes, especially the śūdras, were associated with such ethically negative attributes as an impure way of life, licentiousness, and dullness—attributes hardly suitable to be assigned or recommended as norms or duties. Accordingly, the only alternative was to refer to the means of occupation—whose faithful fulfillment could open up the dimension of "ethical" values—to give meaning to the concept of svadharma for the lower castes. For this reason, while a śūdra could indeed be a "good" śūdra, his caste-bound achievements could not help him to attain the peculiar ethical potential that belongs (i.e., is "innate") to the brahmin (*brahmakarma svabhāvajam*; XVIII, 42).

A clear paraphrase of this point of view may be found in the rhetorical question posed by a nineteenth century pandit, "Soobajee Bapoo," who asked whether a mule, no matter how hardworking he is (i.e., who performs his functions as a mule as perfectly as he can) can ever become a horse.[52]

It is remarkable that the central statements made in the Bhagavadgītā about the svadharma were also utilized in the law book of Manu.[53] Moreover, Manu also made use of the guṇa theory in order to lend a metaphysical and cosmological emphasis to his hierarchical classification of all living beings. This is a "mixed hierarchy" like those so typical in the "presystematic" texts. Manu introduces us to the following beings, arranged in an ascending order determined by the relative distribution of the three guṇas- *sattva, rajas,* and *tamas*:[54] Plants (*sthāvara*), worms (*kṛmi*), turtles, śūdras, barbarians (*mleccha*), lions, birds, hypocrites (*dāmbhikāḥ puruṣāḥ*), and *piśāca* demons are dominated chiefly by *tamas*; wrestlers (*malla*), actors (*naṭa*), kṣatriyas, great debaters (*vādayuddhapradhāna*), and gandharvas are dominated chiefly by *rajas*; ascetics (*yati*), certain brahmins (*vipra*), stars (*nakṣatra), ṛṣi, deva, Brahmā, dharma,* the *mahān* (i.e., the cosmic *buddhi,* "knowledge"), and even *avyakta* (i.e., non-manifested "nature" itself) are dominated chiefly by *sattva.* Manu's list clearly intermingles a number of aspects and criteria; his categories are partly ethical, characterological, mythological, biological/cosmological, or refer to occupation. Within the sphere of human existence, the four varṇas are not considered as a comprehensive and exclusive principle of classification and subordination (the vaiśya are not mentioned at all). And Manu simply ignores the fact that much overlapping and blending occurs in his list (this "overlapping of the genera," *jātisaṃkara* in the logical sense, was meticulously avoided by the later systematic philosophers).

There are a number of other examples in which the four varṇas appear within comprehensive hierarchies and evolutionary series, for instance in the Mahābhārata or in the Brāhmaṇas (specifically in the "table of creation" used in the *agnicayana* ritual and first quoted by A. Weber).[55] The question whether the *varṇa* system was originally included in these hierarchies or added at a later time shall not be dealt with here. The passage from the *Śukānupraśna* chapter of the Mahābhārata, which, in a series of progressive dichotomies leads from basic biological categories to the concept of the true brahmin who knows brahman, is on a different conceptual level and reminiscent of the diheretic procedure found in Plato's *Sophist* and *Politicus*.[56] Enumerations that proceed from biological or essentially cosmological categories to ethical concepts, eventually culminating in the concept of the true brahmin as the genuine sage or the true knower of the Veda, have a tradition that may be traced from the *Śatapathabrāhmaṇa* to numerous more recent texts.[57]

Returning now to our subject of how the guṇa theory has been utilized to explicate the varṇa system, it remains to be noted that the three guṇas were not only applied within a context of general and comprehensive hierarchies, but also particularly and individually to the four varṇas, sometimes in conjunction with the doctrine of caste colors.[58] Here, of course, difficulties, or inconvenience at the very least, arose from the fact that a threefold schema was being used to explicate and justify a group of four and that, quite generally, attempts were being made to link two schemas which originated from independent (and in fact divergent) sources.[59]

One seemingly obvious solution to this conflict, yet one which was nevertheless surprising within the Indian context, was proffered by the *Anugītā* in the Mahābhārata; it applies the guṇas to just three varṇas, assigning *tamas* to the śūdra, *rajas* to the kṣatriya, and *sattva*, the highest guṇa, to the brahmin; the vaiśya has no part in this process.[60] Now it would certainly be wrong to expect that a derivative text such as the *Anugītā* would critically and autonomously apply philosophical and cosmological concepts to social conventions, and thus attempt a critical reconstruction and reform of the varṇa system along the lines suggested by the metaphysics of the guṇas, and many other passages leave no doubt that the *Anugītā* never seriously calls the number of the four varṇas into question.[61]

Other authors have used other means in their attempts to reconcile that discrepancy which the Anugītā clearly avoids through mere omission. Often, the vaiśya was endowed with a combination of rajas and tamas and the other varṇas with "pure" guṇas.[62] Durgāprasāda Dviveda, whom we have already mentioned, proceeded in a somewhat different fashion, and further elevated the position of the brahmin. In his view, the brahmin is defined through *sattva* alone, the kṣatriya through rajas and sattva, the vaiśya through rajas and tamas, and the śūdra through tamas alone or through tamas and rajas.[63]

P. T. Raju's attempt to depict Plato's threefold psychological and social scheme of λογιστικόν, θυμός, and ἐπιθυμία as an analogy to such applications of the three guṇas is not convincing.[64] Instead, it underscores a fundamental difference. For Plato develops a comprehensive rational construction that considers social and political questions in a manner that deliberately distances itself from existing conventions; among the guṇa theorists, on the other hand, we find a cosmological scheme being coordinated with a social order that was considered to be as natural as the cosmos itself. There is no contrast here between a "natural" and a "positive" or merely conventional order. The guṇa theory was not used to question or criticize the varṇa system. To be sure, the concepts sattva, rajas, and tamas do serve to recall the ethical and characterological aspects of the varṇa system as opposed to its hereditary connotations; and in fact, modern authors have often used these concepts to explicate the four principal castes in the sense of psychological and physiological types.[65] Yet no criteria were developed for empirically determining and unambiguously distinguishing among these types and, therewith, for a practically feasible division of society independent of the hereditary order, and the readiness for alternatives often remained verbal. Even S. Radhakrishnan, one of the most persuasive spokesmen for an interpretation of the four varṇas based upon character and vocation and not upon hereditary group membership, admitted: "Since we cannot determine in each individual case what the aptitudes of the individuals are, heredity and training are used to fix the calling."[66] When viewed against this background, the position of such a traditional scholar as Durgāprasāda Dviveda appears more consistent: he considers the application of the three guṇas to be merely another way of specifying what is by definition implied in the hereditary membership in a caste; and such hereditary membership alone is able to provide reliable testimony about the true, metaphysical, guṇic disposition of a person, which is never really accessible to independent, empirically oriented criticism or verification.[67]

Castes as Real Universals

8. Another philosophical device that has been drawn upon in interpreting and discussing the caste system is the realistic concept of universals (*sāmānya, jāti*). While this did not achieve the popularity of the doctrine of the three guṇas, its many metaphysical, linguistic, and epistemological ramifications assured it a greater importance in the philosophical discussions of the classical period. The theory of real universals received its most distinctive treatment in the Nyāya and Vaiśeṣika, and in this version, it became a classical target for Buddhist criticism. Yet it also played a very notable role in the Mīmāṃsā, in particular with respect to the present topic. Before we take up the manner in which the concept of *sāmānya* was applied to the theory of castes, it seems appropriate to make a few remarks about its peculiar systematic role within the Vaiśeṣika and on its historical role during the classical period.

Most probably in connection with linguistic considerations and initially in a more or less undifferentiated manner, the realistic concept of *sāmānya* or *jāti* was at first concerned with the problem of the one-in-many, of what particular entities may have in common, of the identical and enduring meaning of words. That which is common and universal is one, indivisible, subject to no change or decay, yet inherent in many changing individuals. However, the development of thought about this topic soon led to a distinction between what were considered to be real universals and other, merely accidental, "additional qualities" (*upādhi*). While this does not amount to an equivalence of the concepts of sāmānya and jāti with the Western concept of essence, they nevertheless served to demarcate what was substantial and constitutive from accidental attributes and merely temporal and extrinsic functions. In this sense, the actual sāmānya is that which makes a concrete individual thing what it is: a horse (*aśva*) is what it is insofar as "horseness" (*aśvatva*) is inherent in it, while a cow is what it is insofar as "cowness" (*gotva*) is inherent in it. On the other hand, "cookness" (*pācakatva*) is merely an "additional quality," but not a real type and factor of identity. The sāmānyas thus signify structures of the universe, biological species, and other basic forms within the real, empirical world that remain unaffected by the periodic destructions of the world and always reappear at the beginning of a new epoch. For this reason, and in the face of the ancient cosmological associations of the varṇa doctrine, it would seem natural that the four castes were also viewed in the sense of such invariable prototypes.

Yet the old Vaiśeṣika and Nyāya texts did not portray the four varṇas as universals. To be sure, the caste hierarchy, both in itself and as an integral component of dharma, was unambiguously and unequivocally accepted. In his mythical/philosophical description of the regeneration of the world after its disintegration into atoms at the beginning of a new epoch, Praśastapāda makes it clear that he attributes a cosmological status to the system of the four varṇas. And in fact, he does this with much greater decisiveness than the classical Sāṃkhya. He even includes a clear allusion to the *Puruṣasūkta*, although in contrast to the Ṛgveda, he does not speak of an original cosmogonic act, but rather of a recurrent event. At the beginning of each new world period, souls (*ātman*) are assigned to these social archetypes, as well as to other forms of life, in accordance with their unredeemed karma from the preceding world period.[68]

In Nyāya and Vaiśeṣika texts from the ninth and tenth centuries, we find that the interpretation and discussion of the varṇa theory within the context of the doctrine of universals had become a familiar and common theme. Here as well, the epistemological orientation which prevailed in the discussions of this period is in the foreground; that is, the discussions primarily revolve around questions as to how, within the context of the doctrine of the means of knowledge (*pramāṇa*), each of the varṇas may be safely recognized as such and distinguished from one another and how the view that the castes are determined by real universals may be epistemologically justified. Since the Vaiśeṣika and subsequently the Nyāya claimed that the universals (*sāmānya*) are demonstrable in perception as the data of "mere intuition" (*ālocanamātra, nirvikalpakapratyakṣa*), the question of perception also had to be posed with respect to caste universals. And when countering objections from the Buddhists and others, it was essential to consider the relation between direct perception and that indirect knowledge which was acquired through "instruction" (*upadeśa*) and genealogical tradition.

9. In his *Nyāyamañjarī* (ninth century), Jayantabhaṭṭa notes that a person initially requires "instruction" and genealogical knowledge if he is to be able to ascertain the caste membership of a particular individual—at the very least, one has to have learned the meanings of the corresponding words. Afterwords, however, one merely has to use one's perceptual abilities in order to identify a person as a member of a particular caste. The fact that learning is the prerequisite of this act does not, as he emphasizes, call into question the results of perception as such. Must not a person similarly first be instructed about the meaning of the word "cow" before he is able to identify a cow as such? According to this line of reasoning, linguistic instruction is merely the external preparation for a perceptual act, a preparation that does not in any way detract from the validity of the results of that act: just as that which a person perceives after he has reached the top of a mountain does not lose its status as content of perception (merely because it requires such preparation).[69] While Jayanta does mention another position, namely, that a brahmin can be identified merely on the basis of his distinguished appearance even without prior genealogical instruction, he does not seem to concur with this view.[70]

In a later section of his *Nyāyamañjarī*, Jayanta resumes the discussion of the perceptibility of "caste universals," and once again, he cites the simile of the view from the mountain, which he has obviously borrowed from Kumārila's *Tantravārttika*.[71]

The fact that the perception of a brahmin, as opposed to the seeing of a cow, does not presuppose a one-time learning alone but also a genealogical inquiry that must be made for each case, was not considered a difficulty to be taken seriously. On this point, the Vaiśeṣika commentator Śrīdhara (tenth century) was even more explicit. While admitting that the "brahminness" (*brāhmaṇatva*) of a brahmin is not perceived as easily and directly as the "cowness" (*gotva*) of a cow, he considers the difference merely one of degree. By being taught about the ancestry of a person, we learn to see him in the correct way, yet this does not detract from the authenticity of such seeing.[72] Similarly, in order to be able to distinguish between the classes or "castes" of precious gems, one must have previously acquired a certain expertise in this field.[73] Śrīdhara' epistemological confidence was not shaken by the critics who pointed out that the possible marital unreliability of brahmin women could endanger the legitimate descent of the offspring and the authenticity of the universal "brahminness."[74]

The notion of real "caste universals" is generally taken for granted by later Vaiśeṣika commentators, although it is not an extensively debated topic in their works. An anonymous commentary on the Vaiśeṣikasūtra which was written some time after Udayana, possibly around 1200, resolutely dismisses all arguments against the real existence and perceptibility of a universal *brāhmaṇatva*, and it concludes: "This is not so, since (the universal brahminness) is, indeed, established through sense perception expressed in (the recurrent observation) 'this is a brahmin, this (too) is a brahmin.' Otherwise, such universals as cowness would also be eliminated" (*tan na, brāhmaṇo 'yam brāhmaṇo 'yam iti pratyakṣād eva tatsiddheḥ. anyathā gotvāder api vilayāt*).[75]

As could be expected, the Buddhist philosophers took up positions against these arguments of the adherents of the Nyāya and Vaiśeṣika. Examples of this may be found in Śāntarakṣita's *Tattvasaṃgraha*, Kāmalaśīla's accompanying commentary *Tattvasaṃgrahapañjikā*,[76] and the extensive linguistic and epistemological discussions in Prajñākaragupta's *Pramāṇavārttikabhāṣya* (also known as the *Vārttikālaṅkāra*).[77] Prajñākaragupta in particular discusses the relationship between "instruction" (*upadeśa*) and perception (*pratyakṣa*) that was also dealt with by Jayanta and Śrīdhara. In his view, however, no matter how this relationship is interpreted, there is no way to determine the reality and genuineness of caste universals, and especially of brahminness. In addition to these epistemological and "criteriological" questions, basic problems of definition associated with the doctrine of the four varṇas are repeatedly touched upon.[78]

10. In general, the Nyāya and Vaiśeṣika philosophers did not consider the defense and analysis of the varṇa system to be their main task. The majority of the texts simply take it for granted, and they do not discuss it explicitly. Those that do typically limit themselves to a few brief remarks or allusions.[79] Quite obviously, this topic is not really intrinsic to the Nyāya and Vaiśeṣika. The situation was different in the Mīmāṃsā, a system whose apologetic motivation is straightforward and which, as a whole, represents an attempt to develop a comprehensive explanation and defense of the Vedic dharma. It was especially Kumārila (seventh century), the leading philosophical systematizer of the Mīmāṃsā, who appropriated the concept of universals as an apologetic device for discussing the subject of caste. In contrast, the second major school of the Mīmāṃsā, which follows Kumārila's rival Prabhākara, developed some exemplary arguments for criticizing such applications of the concept of universals. Śrīdhara's discussion seems to be inspired by and based upon the positive as well as negative arguments produced by these two schools of Mīmāṃsā. The passage from the *Nyāyakandalī* discussed earlier does not go in any significant way beyond those ideas and arguments we find in the works of Kumārila on the one hand and in a representative text of the Prābhākara school, Śālikanāthamiśra's *Prakaraṇapañcikā*, on the other.[80]

In a number of passages in Kumārila's main works, i.e. the *Ślokavārttika* and the *Tantravārttika*, it is either explicitly stated or implicitly assumed that the four varṇas are determined by real universals and thus "ontologically" different from one another, and that caste membership is metaphysically prior to all ethical, occupational and characterological criteria. In the reification and hypostatization of the universals (*jāti, sāmānya*), Kumārila does not go as far as the classical Vaiśeṣika; his universals occur *in rebus* and are related to their substrates in an identity-in-difference relationship. Nevertheless, they are real, eternal prototypes. Kumārila's predecessors, in particular Śabara and the so-called Vṛttikāra, introduced the topic of universals under the title *ākṛti*, "form," "shape." According to Śabara's testimony in his commentary on *Mīmāṃsāsūtra* I, 1, 5, the Vṛttikāra taught that such "forms" are directly perceived (*pratyakṣa*), not inferred (*sādhya*). The Nyāya, on the other hand, distinguished between *ākṛti* and *jāti*. According to Gautama's *Nyāyasūtra* II, 2, 65(68), the "form" or "shape" manifests the universal and its characteristic marks (*ākṛtir jātiliṅgākhyā*). Both of these positions imply difficulties, as far as the identification of "caste universals" is concerned. Are there any distinctive visible forms (*ākṛti, ākāra*) or configurations (*saṃsthāna*) that could support the assumption that different universals, real generic properties, inhere in the brahmins and kṣatriyas? Obviously, they do not differ from each other in the same conspicuous manner in which a horse differs from an elephant. This is an observation which was sufficiently familiar to the opponents of the varṇa system.[81]

In his commentary on *Nyāyasūtra* and *Nyāyabhāṣya* II, 2, 65(68), Uddyotakara notes that not all universals are indicated by "forms" (*na punaḥ sarvā jātir ākṛtyā liṅgyate*). Kumārila goes further than this. He claims that the Mīmāṃsā concept of *ākṛti*, since it is used as a synonym of *jāti* or *sāmānya*, i.e. as general term for "universal," has no connotation of "form," "shape" or "configuration" at all.[82] Both in the *Ākṛtivāda* of the *Ślokavārttika* and in the *Ākṛtyadhikaraṇa* of the *Tantravārttika*, he argues vigorously for the conceptual dissociation of "form"/"shape" and "universal". This has obvious and significant implications for his theory of caste universals.

In the *Tantravārttika*, Kumārila remarks somewhat casually that the brahmins and the other castes have heads, hands, etc., that are quite similar in shape, and that they are usually the object of nondiscriminating perception; nevertheless, the caste distinctions can be ascertained on the basis of memories concerning the lineage of the parents.[83] In the *Ślokavārttika*, he states that different types of criteria may serve to identify real generic properties and the distinctive classes to which they belong, for instance color in the case of gold and copper, smell and taste in the case of sesame oil and melted butter, the shape in the case of a pot, and birth or descent (*yoni*) in the case of the brahmin and the other castes. All this does not affect Kumārila's basic premise that ultimately the universals or generic properties themselves should be perceptible; reliance on these criteria is just the manner of accomplishing such perception.[84] Vācaspati adopts this argumentation for his *Nyāyavārttikatātparyaṭīkā*, while commenting on *Nyāyasūtra* II, 2, 65(68) and on Uddyotakara's remark that not all universals are indicated by forms; Vācaspati, too, insists that universals such as brahminness are to be manifested by one's lineage (*brāhmaṇatvādijātis tu yonivyaṅgyā*). Of course, unlike the other criteria, the criterion "descent" involves genealogical information and recollection. Kumārila does not deny this; but in his view, it is no fundamental difference. It simply means that the identification of caste universals is less direct and requires more preparation than that of other universals.

11. The passage most significant for our topic may be found at the beginning of the *Tantravārttika* (on Sūtra I, 2, 2). In his typically free and independent matter, Kumārila discusses an opposing opinion (*pūrvapakṣa*) which is presented in the Mīmāṃsāsūtra and the corresponding commentary of Śabara. This concerns the view that the *arthavāda* passages of the Vedas are irrelevant and devoid of authority. One of the reasons for this given by the *pūrvapakṣin* is that the *arthavāda* passages and other passages evidently contradict the results of perception. One of the examples given by Śabara is the following Vedic sentence: "We do not know whether we are brahmins or non-brahmins."[85] The assumption behind the use of this example is that such a statement (ignoring its incompatibility with other passages) contradicts the knowledge of the difference between brahmins and non-brahmins that is generally familiar in daily life. For Kumārila, this remark provides a starting point for a discourse on the "ontological" status and the recognizability of the four varṇas. Here, more than defending the meaning and the authority of the Brāhmaṇa passage cited by Śabara against those who would simply deny or doubt the caste theory, he defends it against those among its adherents who have a naive and unclarified understanding of the varṇa concept, and who depend too greatly upon external features of behavior or visual appearance for identifying the castes. On this occasion, Kumārila demonstrates his thorough grasp of the definitional and epistemological problems associated with the subject as well as his recognition of the difficulties of genealogical derivation; for he actually stresses precisely these problems and difficulties, thereby lending further weight to his claim that it is quite possible to defend in an age of increased criticism and rational argumentation both the dharma and the varṇa system that is integrated therein. In developing his arguments in this section, Kumārila abstains from any clear or direct attack upon an opposing viewpoint that is clearly marked as such. Instead, he presents a kind of dialogue in which he gradually articulates and clarifies his own position.[86] It is important to remember that here Kumārila is commenting upon a pūrvapakṣa passage—although he goes far beyond the starting point offered by Śabara, for he does not merely paraphrase the pūrvapakṣa, but also appends his own critical opinion thereto. In order to fully understand this discussion, one other point must be considered as well: the philosophical Mīmāṃsā was concerned with securing the authoritativeness of the Vedic revelation and the sacred tradition (*śruti, śāstra, āgama*) within the framework provided by the doctrine of the means of knowledge (*pramāṇa*); in other words, the intention was to place the Veda alongside of the other means of knowledge (perception, inference etc.) as a source of knowledge in its own right capable of conveying contents which would otherwise be inaccessible.[87] The problem of the four varṇas should also be seen in this light: to what extent are they objects of the Vedic revelation, and to what extent are they accessible to and demonstrable through the worldly means of knowledge and normal human experience (*lokaprasiddha*)? Kumārila's position is carefully considered: while arguing that the varṇas are essentially accessible to the domain of worldly knowledge, he adds that the śruti nevertheless retains a helpful and important role for discovering their true nature.[88] According to his commentators as well as his opponents, Kumārila took it for granted that the four varṇas are determined by real universals. No special emphasis was laid upon this assumption.[89]

Kumārila begins with the thesis that the castes may be demonstrated through normal human knowledge. What is the nature of this knowledge? Is it sensory perception? Is it really possible to argue that the class membership of a brahmin (i.e., his determination by means of the universal "brahminness") can be ascertained through sensory perception in the same manner as the class membership of a tree (i.e., its determination by means of the universal "treeness")? In the case of the brahmin, of course, we must first be told the facts of his ancestry. Yet in order to be able to identify a tree as such, must we not first be told about the meaning of the word "tree" as well?[90] Kumārila himself states explicitly that these two examples differ in more than just one respect. In the case of the tree, we have the impression of an entity that may be distinguished and identified on the basis of certain features of appearance that are independent of any knowledge of the appropriate word. Yet since such external features as conduct or occupation are unreliable because there is no way to be certain that a member of a particular caste will adhere to the duties he has been assigned, the same does not hold true in the case of the brahmin.[91] According to the doctrine which Kumārila develops in the *Ślokavārttika*, however, external features such as these are not the only means for determining universals. A knowledge of genealogical relationships may also serve this purpose. This argument, in turn, leads into the problem of the possible unfaithfulness of brahmin women. At first, Kumārila simply states that one should not argue against a rule by citing its exceptions. Yet he does not fail to add that extramarital liaisons with men from the same standing are not problematic, and that the Smṛti has reliable rules available for cases of actual bastardization as well as rules for reassigning a lineage to a "pure" caste after a number of generations.

Yet none of these arguments are really able to call the existence and recognizability of the castes into question; using a simile which (as we have noted earlier) will appear again in Jayanta's *Nyāyamañjarī*, Kumārila states that that which is perceived after one has reached the top of a mountain does not lose its perceptual character as a result.[92] His commentator Someśvara adds the general observation that non-perceivability does not result from the fact that something is difficult to apprehend. The difference between a male and a female Kokila (a type of Indian cuckoo) only gradually enters into the realm of perception; and so is it with the differences between the castes as well: it becomes possible to perceive these differences because we are initially aided by a genealogical knowledge based upon memory and uninterrupted tradition.[93] Elsewhere, Kumārila compares the identification and distinction of castes with the distinction of correct and incorrect Sanskrit words. In both cases, tradition, recollection, and learning are necessary before the appropriate determinations can be made through simple acts of perception. Knowing how to distinguish castes is like mastering the Sanskrit language.[94] The assumption is that, just as in the case of the expert gemmologist, the process requires a certain noncommunicable expertise or initiation.

12. Several key remarks follow. According to Kumārila, the alleged or real contradiction between the Vedic statement quoted by Śabara and the results of perception, which provides the starting point for the entire discussion, is pertinent to those who wish to derive brahminness, etc. from behavior. In his opinion, however, there is no justification for deriving caste distinctions from behavior. Instead, we have to assume that the brahmins etc. are already established in their identity, for only on this basis can the behavioral norms to which they are subject be applied to them.[95] If their brahminness was a consequence of their behavior, then a vicious circle would result; it would be possible that the behavior of a person would render him a brahmin at one moment and a śūdra at the next, provided that he was not (reflecting the fact that some actions are ambivalent) both at the same time. In Kumārila's view, reducing the castes to the status of temporary and ambivalent functions and behaviors would be destructive as well as absurd. The Vedic provisions concerning a particular caste could not be applied, and stable social and religious rules would be impossible. Only when a person *is* a brahmin, a kṣatriya, etc., can he be told what his duties are as such. Someone *is* a brahmin only to the extent that the universal *brāhmaṇatva* is inherent in him. Such an essential property cannot be added later; its acquisition must coincide with the event of entering into existence, i.e., with birth itself. Brahminness cannot be reduced to an aggregation of virtues, such as asceticism, nor can it be reduced to any disposition that arises as a result of such virtuous behavior; and it cannot be manifested thereby.[96] A brahmin's identity, like that of the member of any other caste, is rooted in his ancestry. For this reason, any knowledge of this identity must be founded upon genealogical relationships, although it may (ideally) also be attained through perception. In this way, Kumārila ruled out the possibility of an ethicizing reinterpretation or reduction of the four varṇas as well as all caste mobility. Nothing on earth can affect one's caste membership, for this has a status of metaphysical stability.[97] It remains inaccessible to merely extrinsic criteria yet is not completely cut off from the domain of perception and argumentation. Kumārila's interpretation and defense of the four varṇas conforms exemplarily with his program of defending the tradition of the Veda (i.e., primarily the Brāhmaṇas) in an age of critical reflection and discussion while simultaneously saving it from the grip of autonomous rationality. Here again, we find a philosophy of the Vedic dharma that has produced its own complex and subtle epistemology and whose apologetic and restorative aims are nevertheless easily recognizable.

Kumārila's discussion in the *Tantravārttika* suggests that he was already in a position to look back upon a tradition of philosophical discussions which had considered this subject from a number of perspectives. An epistemological discussion about different ways to grasp the "universals" or "forms" (*ākṛti*) can be found as early as Patañjali's *Mahābhāṣya*, and this work in turn makes reference to still older sources. Patañjali also notes that *jāti* is that which is obtained by birth (*jananena yā prāpyate, sā jātiḥ*).[98] Later commentators have found in Patañjali's work explicit references to the problem of the relationship between direct perception and verbal instruction (*upadeśa*).[99] By this time, the terminological coincidence between *jāti* as "caste" and as "genus" or "universal" was obviously quite familiar, and the conceptual association of "universals" and "castes" should have been a natural step. There is, indeed, evidence that this connection had been made long before Kumārila's time. Our most important source is Bhartṛhari (ca. A.D. 500), who is in turn indebted to Pantañjali and other older authorities. In general, Bhartṛhari's work has been of great importance for Kumārila.

Bhartṛhari discusses the status of the *brāhmaṇa* in several sections of his *Vākyapadīya*, for instance in the *Vṛttisamuddeśa* of the third Kāṇḍa, which resumes and expands Patañjali's explication of the term *abrāhmaṇa.*[100] In the *Jātisamuddeśa, brāhmaṇatva* appears repeatedly as a familiar example of a "universal" (*jāti*).[101] To be sure, Bhartṛhari's understanding of universals is different from the static realism of the Vaiśeṣika; for him, they are potentialities or powers (*śakti*) of the dynamic "word-brahman" (*śabdabrahman*). Nevertheless, it was easy for Kumārila to combine this with his own adaptation of the Vaiśeṣika theory of universals. There are various other, more specific references in the *Vākyapadīya*. Just as Śrīdhara centuries later, Bhartṛhari mentions those experts who can identify precious stones or metals. They, too, exemplify the refinement of perception through training and practice. In the same verse, he states that superhuman beings (*asmadviśiṣṭa*) can perceive universals directly by means of all sense organs.[102] In his long and remarkable commentary on this verse, Helārāja refers specifically to the perception of "caste universals" and claims that "something analogous to the dewlap," i.e. to the criterion of the universal "cowness" (*gotva*), must exist (and be accessible to superhuman perception) as far as "brahminness" (*brāhmaṇatva*), etc., are concerned, although it may be utterly imperceptible for us.[103] The idea of a superhuman awareness of caste universals which does not depend on recollection and instruction (*smṛti, upadeśa*) has become a familiar assumption in theistic circles. We find it, for instance, in the *Seśvaramīmāṃsā* of Rāmānuja's follower Veṅkaṭanātha (i.e., Vedāntadeśika, fourteenth century).[104]

This notwithstanding, Kumārila appears to have been the first to give this "application" its radical and explicit character and to combine it with a comprehensive philosophical defense of the Vedic dharma. And in his assertion that brahminness does not issue from an aggregation of ascetism or other properties, he also appears to allude to the passage in the *Mahābhāṣya* which, as we saw earlier, refers to a verse of unknown origin that deals with precisely this question of "aggregation" (*samudāya*)—admittedly in a manner which Kumārila was no longer able to accept.[105] In any case, it may be said that to a large degree, Kumārila's discussion became the starting point for the subsequent debate not only in Mīmāṃsā, but also in Nyāya and Vaiśeṣika.

13. In general, Kumārila introduces numerous methodological and philosophical innovations in his endeavor to restore the allegedly original sense of the Vedic *dharma* and to defend it against innovations; he may, indeed, be considered as one of the most independent thinkers of the classical tradition. His relationship to Śabara is known to have been much freer than that of his great rival Prabhākara, whose own traditionalism frequently had radical and "innovative" consequences as well and whose own attempts to articulate the Vedic tradition in the medium of classical philosophy offers a revealing counterpart to Kumārila's technique. The ways in which he approached the question of caste provides us with a good example to illustrate this.

The school of the Prābhākaras, known to us primarily through its presentation by Śālikanāthamiśra, attempted to develop a defense of the *varṇāśramadharma* which did not depend upon Kumārila's interpretation of the four principal castes as real universals: in their view, the existence of genealogical relationships and the traditional knowledge of these sufficed to make the Vedic rules applicable.[106] They saw no reason to seek recourse in questionable philosophical constructions. There are no human groups which are determined by and distinguishable through real universals; in fact, there are no real universals at all below the sāmānya or jāti of "humanness" (*puruṣatva*), that corresponds to the one essential form (*ākāra*) shared by men and women, brahmins and śūdras. There is no determinable "form" nor anything like it that can serve as a sign of the generic differentiation between the brahmin and the kṣatriya. In contrast to the Bhāṭṭamīmāmsā school founded by Kumārila, the Prābhākara school did not abandon the premise that "form" and visible similarity are essential features of genuine universals.[107] In Śālikanātha's opinion, no practice, preparation, or instruction could help one further: since there is no real universal "brahminness," it cannot be manifested as a datum of perception. He dismisses Kumārila's argument that a person's experience in the domain of smell will eventually aid him to visually grasp the difference between melted butter and sesame oil, arguing that this amounts to a mere manipulation of the concept of perception; in reality, we are dealing with an implicit inference.[108]

The alleged caste universals are nothing but "additional qualifications" (*upādhi*), i.e., extrinsic roles and functions which are admittedly sanctioned by tradition but do not fundamentally differ from such occupational epithets as "cook-ness" (*pācakatva*), the "additional qualification" most frequently mentioned in the discussion of the subject of universals. Brahminness, etc., means nothing other than descent from a particular lineage (*santativiśeṣaprabhavatva*), and lineages do not require any theoretical or metaphysical explanation, since they are generally familiar and established through traditional usage (*lokata eva prasiddhāḥ*). There is no need to hypostasize caste universals in order to justify the use of such words as "brahmin," etc., or the applicability of the specific Vedic rules for a caste. In this context, Śālikanātha takes up the problem of the marital faithfulness of brahmin women, a topic that enjoyed some popularity among Buddhist critics of the caste system. However, he does not consider this to pose any serious danger to the fundamental reliability of the traditionally accepted genealogical relationships, and dismisses the problem as an artificial scepticism with no serious impact upon the traditional knowledge and behavior of men.[109] Whereas Kumārila attempts to provide an independent metaphysical and epistemological basis, the Prābhākaras limit themselves to sanctioning what tradition already accepts. At first glance, this procedure may appear naive and unreflected, yet the fact that they avoid a metaphysical construction like Kumārila's in itself amounts to a philosophical statement. Śālikanātha's arguments against Kumārila reveal an intellect sharpened on Buddhist criticism while his use of the term *upādhi* indicates a linguistic and epistemological position concerning this subject that was precise and radical in its own way.

Kumārila's school of the Mīmāṃsā represents the mainstream of traditional Vedic/brahminic orthodoxy. In contrast, Prabhākara and his followers remained outsiders, and they were even suspected by the orthodoxy of an intended or unintended alliance with Buddhism. Kumārila himself found a one-sided yet poignant way to express philosophically what was intrinsic and special in the Hindu dharma as compared to Buddhism and other "heterodoxies." This may be seen in the manner in which he presented the varṇa system and the rigorous fashion in which he anchored the identity of the castes in real universals, thereby removing it from any change, mobility, or reduction to criteria of ethical standards and the quality of behavior. His position and procedure with respect to the question of caste has clear echoes in several discussions in the modern traditionalist pandit literature and in the arguments against reformers and reinterpreters contined therein. Vāsudeva Śāstrin Abhyaṅkara has utilized them to counter the "idle chatter" (*pralāpa*) of those "moderns" (*ādhunika*) who wish to relate or even reduce the meaning of caste terms to behavior and who assert that a person can change his caste status and become a brahmin merely by virtue of his behavior.[110] In this context, Abhyaṅkara also speaks of the Bhagavadgītā, emphasizing that the "behavior essential to the brahmin" (*brahmakarma svabhāvajam*) referred to in verse XVIII,42 can in no way be utilized to justify an ethicizing explanation: such forms of behavior as moderateness, etc., are not meant to be factors that first create brahminness, but are solely duties that apply to it.[111] Brahminness, etc., can only be attained through birth. It is a genuine and real universal (Abhyaṅkara speaks of *jāti* and *jātisāmānya*), on the same footing as the biological species. Even if their outer forms are similar, brahmins, kṣatriyas, etc. are as different from one another as lions are from elephants. There can be no caste mobility.[112]

Abhyaṅkara's argumentation is noteworthy for its trenchancy and terseness, but is not unique with regard to its implications. In his *Cāturvarṇyaśikṣā*, Durgāprasāda Dviveda uses essentially the same arguments, namely, that the four varṇas are constituted in a manner that is prior to all behavior, and in his eyes, this means that they must be determined by real universals.[113] "Soobajee Bapoo," the pandit who completed the 1839 edition of the *Vajrasūcī* for L. Wilkinson (and who used the occasion to include some critical remarks of his own in his *Taṅka*, or "Tunku"), argues along essentially the same lines that Kumārila developed in such an exemplary manner.[114]

Non-Dualism and the Varṇa System

14. While the philosophical theories we have been discussing thus far have played no great roles in the social and political discussions of modern India, the philosophy of Advaita Vedānta has often been associated with social and political topics; it has even been claimed that it affords a metaphysical basis for practical ethical demands and programs. This has occurred in particular within the widespread movement loosely referred to by the term Neo-Vedānta, and it has had significant effects upon both the public culture of India and the manner in which India has presented itself to the rest of the world. It would not be difficult to compile a list of literally hundreds of statements asserting that the Advaita Vedānta has social relevance for India as well as a more fundamental relevance for the future of all mankind. It has been associated with, and even utilized to "derive," such concepts as tolerance, equality, peaceful coexistence, brotherhood, internationalism, the community of nations, democracy, and social and economic justice—as well as nationalism and anarchy.[115] We encounter such phrases as "Vedantic socialism" (Ramatirtha), "political Vedantism" (Aurobindo), etc.; we hear of "collective economic liberation on an idealistic (i.e., Vedāntic) basis";[116] we are even informed that the Vedānta is capable of providing us with "food, shelter and clothing" or of protecting us from the hydrogen bomb.[117]

These proponents of Advaita Vedānta assume that its monistic metaphysics can be reconciled without difficulty with the political ideas of the French revolution, the Enlightenment's notions of autonomy, and the socialist ideal of justice; moreover, they suggest that the only prerequisite that must be fulfilled to ensure its practical effects is a correct insight into this metaphysics. "The Vedāntic thought, if pursued honestly, is sure to give us a socialistic pattern of society wherein no distinction on the ground of colour, sex, caste, religion or age can be located."[118] "Domestic, social, political or religious salvation of every country lies in Vedānta carried into effect."[119] While one may feel inclined to see in such statements a caricature of the Neo-Vedānta program, their basic tendency accords with other statements couched in more careful terms which have been expressed time and again by more important and representative persons in the public and cultural life of modern India, e.g., S. Radhakrishnan, C. Rajagopalachari, and K. M. Munshi.

M. S. Golwalkar summarized the line of reasoning (which he propounded as a principle of his own nationalistic political movement) that lies at the heart of the claims that the Advaita has social and political applicability in the following way:

> The 'I' in me, being the same as the 'I' in the other beings, makes me react to the joys and sorrows of my fellow living beings just as I react to my own. This genuine feeling of identity born out of the community of the inner entity is the real driving force behind our natural urge for human unity and brotherhood. Thus it is evident that world unity and human welfare can be made real only to the extent the mankind realises this common Inner Bond.[120]

Serious attempts at providing a philosophical rationale for political and social action have been linked with various forms of political rhetoric which utilizes Vedāntic terminology for the purpose of propagating practical goals. An example of this is provided by one of the pioneers of Neo-Vedānta, Svami Vivekananda, a pragmatic visionary and orator who knew how to adjust his words to fit his situation and audience. Vivekananda became the successor of Ramakrishna (i.e., Gadadhar Chatterji, 1836–1886), whom Indians as well as Westerners have celebrated as the very symbol of modern Hinduism and the living Vedānta. Ramakrishna is seen as the incarnation of a universal yet never abstract synthesis and tolerance, and as the confirmation of the true potential of Hinduism, which could only become visible through the encounter with the West. Because he is portrayed as the representative of this "true" and universalized

Hinduism, he simultaneously appears as the very representative of religion itself and as the embodiment of a Hinduized notion of fulfillment capable of taking up and neutralizing the view expressed by many missionaries that Christianity represented the true fulfillment of all religions. In this role, Ramakrishna served Vivekananda as a model for political activity as well as social reform. It must be emphasized, however, that the motivation of practical and social responsibility which was so important for Vivekananda was unimportant to Ramakrishna himself, who would at best have greeted it with mild irony. To be sure, Ramakrishna was of the opinion that one should not disregard the social world; yet he stated that one should always understand that, ultimately, there was nothing which could or had to be done for it.[121]

In contrast, Vivekananda and his successors were certain that not only could the Vedānta become "practical" but that it had to become practical if it was to fulfill its possibilities. They assumed that it alone, as the philosophy of absolute unity and the converging point of all religions, philosophies, and ideologies, was capable of providing a solid metaphysical foundation and an effective motivation for ethical demands and practical goals. Apart from Vivekananda, the most representative spokesman for this message was S. Radhakrishnan, who served in a number of both national and international offices. Radhakrishnan represented the "idea of fulfillment" in an exemplary and especially conciliatory and impressive manner, arguing that the Vedānta is "not *a* religion, but religion itself in its most universal and deepest significance."[122] He saw it as providing the framework and goal for a future synthesis of all religions and philosophies and, therewith, for the resolution of ideological and political differences and the solution of social problems. Here, the basic assumption is that Śaṅkara's doctrine concerning the absolute identity of the real in brahman must find its correspondence in a social attitude concerned with unity, equality, and reconciliation, and that it should also have fundamental effects upon the understanding of caste differences. Radhakrishnan was of the opinion that the Upaniṣadic formulas of unity, and especially the *tat tvam asi* ("that art thou") characterized the "basic principle of all democracy"; and he assures us: "Śaṅkara's philosophy was essentially democratic."[123]

15. In the face of such claims, we must ask to what extent (if at all) Śaṅkara and traditional Advaita Vedānta provide a basis for socially applying the metaphysics of nondualism and for formulating a principle of equality that would have social and political dimensions. Once again, the question of caste will occupy the focus of our attention.

Scholars have repeatedly noted that Śaṅkara's position was conservative, although they have occasionally done this with regret or consternation.[124] In this context, the most important passage may be found in Śaṅkara's commentary on Brahmasūtra, I, 3, 34–38. Naturally, this is a passage the representatives of the Neo-Vedānta tend to pass over without comment. Here, Śaṅkara discusses the "right" or "mandate" (*adhikāra, adhikāritā*) to study the Vedas. Essentially, this revolves around the question as to whether the śūdras should be allowed to study the Vedic revelation and, therewith, be admitted to the indispensable starting point for the liberating and saving knowledge of brahman. Śaṅkara's position is clear and, in its detail and rigor, goes far beyond the sūtra text he is commenting upon. In his view, the śūdras may not be admitted to the study of the Vedas; they are to be excluded from the textual and educational access to the absolute unity of reality in the same way that (as the teachings of the Pūrvamīmāṃsā maintain) they are to be excluded from carrying out the Vedic ritual sacrifices. Śaṅkara presupposes that the varṇa system is based upon birth and physical family membership, and he makes it clear that the metaphysical unity of the real cannot in any way be taken as a premise of social and religious equality in an empirical sense.[125]

To support his position, Śaṅkara cites a number of passages from the śruti and the smṛti; and he refers to the frequently-cited rule in Gautama's Dharmaśāstra which states that a śūdra who illegitimately listens to Vedic texts should have his ears filled with molten tin or varnish (*trapu, jatu*).[126] Śaṅkara discusses at great length a comment by his *pūrvapakṣin* that in the śruti and smṛti cases are reported in which śūdras did indeed attain absolute knowledge; specifically, he refers to the cases of Jānaśruti in the *Chāndogya Upaniṣad* and of Vidura in the *Mahābhārata*. Śaṅkara makes use of an etymologizing reinterpretation of the word *śudra* and assumes that in rare exceptions *smṛti* texts (which are not prohibited for the śūdras) are also capable of imparting liberating knowledge. He also discusses the story of Satyakāma Jābāla (Chāndogya Upaniṣad IV,4ff.) in a manner both noteworthy and instructive. The representatives of the Neo-Vedānta usually consider this story of a young man who does not know who his father was and is classified by his teacher Haridrumata Gautama as a brahmin by virtue of his honesty to be an example of an ethical, characterological, nonhereditary view of the varṇa system. Śaṅkara, on the other hand, does not interpret Satyakāma's honesty as the cause and defining factor of his brahminness, but as a mere indicator of his hereditarily legitimate membership in the brahmin caste.[127]

Such a modern author as Deussen was not the first to claim that there is a discrepancy between the metaphysics of all-encompassing unity and the insistence upon strict hereditary barriers in the social domain and even in religious and soteriological matters. We may also find this view expressed within the Indian tradition; a very succinct example has been provided by Rāmānuja, Śaṇkara's great rival.[128] Rāmānuja's position concerning the question of admittance to the study of the Vedas was essentially the same as Śaṇkara's, and he does not fault Śaṅkara for not drawing any social consequences from his metaphysical position; instead, he questions the legitimacy of a metaphysics that appears to be a priori incapable of providing a basis for the varṇa system and which poses a potential danger to the dharma. He asks how a person who considers brahman to be the sole, exclusive, and in itself completely undifferentiated reality can have any basis for denying the śūdras access to salvation. If all individuals have always been in truth part of the one, all-encompassing brahman, and if the only real concern is with becoming aware of this truth, of realizing it within one's own self-awareness, what reasons could there possibly be for excluding a śūdra who has the ability and the willingness to attain such self-awareness? Furthermore, Rāmānuja considers the assertion that this liberating self-awareness may only be attained through "hearing" (*śravaṇa*), i.e., on the basis of an "awakening" through the Vedic texts, to be unjustified—and to be completely unjustifiable within the context of Advaita Vedānta. Yet even if one acceded to this assumption, was it not possible that a śūdra might accidentally hear one of the "great sayings" (*mahāvākya*) of the Upaniṣads, such as the *tat tvam asi*, and thereby be directed towards final liberation? Moreover, why should someone who has attained the liberating knowledge of unity and has thus transcended the ritual rules and social conventions exclude a śūdra from sharing this knowledge with him? In short, Rāmānuja is arguing that Śaṅkara's position offers no basis for excluding the śūdras from the study of the Vedas and from liberating knowledge.

For the Advaita Vedāntins, these and similar problems are ultimately irrelevant, and they get around them by means of a conception that Rāmānuja could not accept. Their doctrine of the "twofold truth" posits a distinction between truth in its absolute sense (*paramārtha*) and truth in the conventional, relative sense of empirical life (*vyavahāra*), juxtaposing the two without mediation or mutual adjustment. For this reason, they did not consider it necessary to "adjust" or reconcile the absolute (i.e., the unity of brahman) with the relative and ultimately unreal world of spatiotemporal particulars and interpersonal relations. All the same, some Advaitins exhibit an undeniable tendency towards formulations which are more conciliatory than those contained in Śaṅkara's *Brahmasūtrabhāṣya*, a tendency to mitigate the rigor of the social demarcations by referring to the unity of the absolute. Śaṅkara's disciple Sureśvara, for example, emphasized the identity of the "viewer" (*draṣṭṛ*), that is, the absolute subject, in Brahmā (as well as in the brahmin) and in the caṇḍāla.[129]

16. Even in many of those texts which are ascribed to Śaṅkara himself, absolute unity is explained and affirmed by referring to the irrelevancy of social distinctions; according to the short tracts *Svātmanirūpaṇa* and *Daśaślokī* (whose authenticity is admittedly quite uncertain), Śaṅkara would have stated that the castes (*varṇa*), stages of life (*āśrama*), etc. have ceased to have meaning for him.[130] The so-called "minor Upaniṣads," in particular those groups known as the "Saṃnyāsa Upaniṣads" and the "Sāmānya Vedānta Upaniṣads," contain a number of similar tersely formulated statements. For example, the *Nāradaparivrājaka Upaniṣad* describes the knower of the Vedānta as one who is "beyond the castes and stages of life" (*ativarṇāśramin*), while the *Maitreya Upaniṣad* looks down upon the "deluded ones whose behavior is linked to the castes and the stages of life" (*varṇāśramācārayutā vimūḍhāḥ*).[131] The *Nirālamba Upaniṣad* states that the castes cannot be ascribed to the skin, or the blood, or the flesh, or the bones, or even the ātman itself, but are merely a product of *vyavahāra*, the practical conventions of life.[132]

The *Vajrasūcī Upaniṣad*, whose age and authenticity is admittedly very obscure, goes especially far in this respect. This text, which S. Radhakrishnan later included in his collection of "principal Upaniṣads," caused some sensation in the nineteenth century. It exhibits important parallels to a polemic Buddhist treatment of the caste system, the *Vajrasūcī* attributed to Aśvaghoṣa. It refutes a number of attempts to define the brahmin, especially those that refer to birth and social function, and finally asserts that the true brahmin can only be determined by his knowledge of brahman.[133]

Yet such statements, which do indeed explicitly declare that the hereditary differences between the castes are ultimately irrelevant, must always be seen in connection with the doctrine of the twofold truth. The caste differences are irrelevant only in the light of the absolute unity of the absolute, but not with respect to interpersonal relationships, and there is no suggestion of translating the metaphysical unity into social equality. The knower of brahman is "beyond the castes" because he is beyond all empirical distinctions whatsoever; the distinctions between father and son, human and animal, etc. are just as irrelevant for him as are the distinctions between the castes. He who has transcended the castes and the stages of life through his knowledge of brahman has been "liberated from space and time" (*deśakālavimukta*) and is "free of creation" (*prapañcarahita*) as well.[134] If, as we may read in the *Bṛhadāraṇyaka Upaniṣad*, the father is ultimately not a father, the mother is not a mother, and the worlds are not worlds, then obviously the caṇḍāla cannot really be a caṇḍāla and the brahmin cannot be a brahmin. Since, in the view of the Advaita, everything below the unity of brahman may be traced back to cosmic illusion (*māyā*), the castes are "unreal" only because the entire world in which they are found is "unreal."[135]

Thus the fact that the castes are invalid in an absolute sense does not imply that they have been negated in a "worldly" sense or that the rules concerning their mutual relations may be disregarded. As we have already seen in our discussion of Śankara's notion of *adhikāra*, the right to liberating knowledge, there can be no mention of any empirical equality, even with respect to the organized forms of religious life and the access to salvation.

The *Vedāntasāravārttikarājasaṃgraha*, a text whose attribution to Sureśvara is at least questionable, appears to form an exception in this regard, since it does in fact imply equality in the access to knowledge and thus to liberation (*vidyādhikāritā*) "for all castes" (*sarvajātiṣu*)—to the extent that they are endowed with the capacity for self-awareness (*bodha*).[136] Yet aside from the fact that this text appears to be somewhat isolated within the tradition of the Advaita Vedānta, it should be noted that this assertion of equality is strictly soteriological. In other words, it refers only to the possibility of liberation from the world, but not to the status within the world.

The Indian schools display some freedom and variation with respect to the question of equality in soteriological matters, a fact which in the eleventh century even attracted the attention of the Islamic traveler to India, al-Bīrūnī.[137] As is generally known, the sectarian theistic schools usually exhibit more openness and flexibility than the classical orthodox systems. One sectarian system well capable of competing philosophically with the Advaita Vedānta, the Pratyabhijñā doctrine of Kashmir Śaivism, explicitly opens itself to all persons, regardless of their caste membership or other status.[138] Even within the sectarian traditions, one should not overestimate the concrete social applications and the historical effects of such equality with respect to soteriological matters. Yet they display a greater willingness to consider the commitment to a particular doctrinal system and a particular path to liberation as a unifying and equalizing factor. The willingness to revoke the normally valid and generally unquestioned social barriers for the more radical forms of religious life, above all, for "renunciation" (*saṃnyāsa*), is particularly far-reaching.

17. Yet even with regard to such special areas of social life as *saṃnyāsa*, the "orthodox" Advaita Vedāntins tend to be cautious and conservative. The freedom conceded to the "renouncer" (*saṃnyāsin*) and even the liberated *jīvanmukta* is carefully channeled. Even in negation and in renunciation, he remains bound to that same order from which he is freeing himself. For the existence and fundamental validity of this order constitutes the precondition for the possibility of liberating oneself from it. Only a person who is entitled to study the Vedas and to carry out the Vedic sacrifices can be entitled to liberate himself from these. The saṃnyāsin continues to draw his legitimation from that very dharma from which he is liberating himself.[139] And just as the access to renunciation and liberation is limited, so also are there rules of behavior (concerning the practice of asking for alms, etc.) and distinctions between different groups of renouncers to be adhered to within saṃnyāsa; only the highest of these groups, the *paramahaṃsa*, is permitted a greater degree of freedom. In interpreting "liberation while alive" (*jīvanmukti*), the strict representatives of Advaita Vedānta (who adhere most closely to Śaṅkara) also make a point of stating that such transcendence of the social and dharmic domain does not jeopardize the social status quo and its basic structure, the system of the four varṇas. Sureśvara stresses that a person who is truly liberated during his lifetime will never exhibit "uncontrolled behavior" (*yatheṣṭācaraṇa*), while his commentator Jñānottama remarks that such a person automatically continues to behave in accordance with his human nature as well as his caste membership. In this way, those radical sectarians (especially Śaivites) and other alleged jīvanmuktas who violate the rules of traditional social behavior (and, therewith, the dharma) are excluded from the domain of true and legitimate "liberation while alive." The possible consequences of the transcendence of all social norms that is implied in the concept of liberation (*mukti*) have thus been neutralized.[140]

In summary, we may say that in the "orthodox" Advaita Vedānta, the assumption of the absolute unity *in* liberation remains linked to an uncompromising adherence to an unequal, caste-bound access to it. In general, any intermingling of the two levels of truth, any "application" of the absolute (*paramārtha*) to the empirical and conventional (*vyavahāra*), is avoided. A basic metaphysical indifference with respect to questions of interpersonal and social relationships appears in conjunction with a decisively conservative attitude on the empirical level. Here, as well as in other matters of vyavahāra, (i.e., in nonultimate matters) the Advaitins follow Kumārila's Pūrvamīmāṃsā. In accordance with their basic orientation, they do not make any independent efforts to render the varṇa system metaphysically and epistemologically respectable.

It is obvious that the social and political argumentation of the Neo-Vedānta has not simply been borrowed from the teachings of the classical Advaita Vedānta or from the tradition of classical Indian philosophicizing in general. And the claim that the Advaita contains an implicit practical potential, and that this potential is, as it were, waiting to be actualized and carried out, deserves serious, but also critical attention. Since Rammohan Roy, there have been numerous, sometimes deeply committed, sometimes merely rhetorical attempts to put the metaphysics of nondualism to ethical and political use, that is, attempts to relate the levels of the absolute and the empirical or conventional which were separated by classical Vedānta and make them fruitful for one another.[141] Yet the fundamental problem of "mediating" between the metaphysical, all-encompassing unity and a socially and politically realizable equality was frequently ignored.[142]

Ramakrishna, the apolitical inspirer of the Neo-Vedānta, spoke in his graphic, metaphorical language (which was certainly not intended to have any social or political significance) of some basic difficulties that any ideology of "practical" or "political" Vedānta has to face. In doing so, he displayed a religious common sense that most of his successors lack. In his parable of the elephant, he tells of a young student of Advaita Vedānta who places so much trust in the doctrine of the identity of all things within God that he fails, in spite of the warnings of its driver, to avoid an approaching elephant which he consistently identified with God. Seriously injured, he must be lectured by his master that although everything is indeed a manifestation of God, he should have nevertheless heeded to the equally divine words of the elephant driver.[143]

Ramakrishna also used a famous metaphor of water that contrasts the unity of this thirst-quenching substance with the irrelevant multiplicity of its names. In this way, he wished to illustrate the unity of the divine and the truth in the face of the multitude of confessions and religions.[144] This metaphor has become so popular among the proponents of the Neo-Vedānta that Ramakrishna's use of another water metaphor has frequently been overlooked. As he notes, the scriptures assert that water is a form of God (and, we may add, a manifestation of his unity). Yet only some of this water is suitable for religious purposes; other water is suitable for washing the face, and still other water is only suitable for cleaning plates or dirty clothes.[145]

Epilogue: Dharma and Mutual Sustenance

18. The oldest extant presentation of the fourfold division of society into *brāhmaṇa, kṣatriya, vaiśya*, and *śūdra* is found in the cosmogonic hymn Ṛgveda X, 90, the so-called *Puruṣasūkta*. For the later Indian advocates of the *varṇa* system, this text (which may be relatively late and somewhat retrospective within the Ṛgveda itself) provides one of the most authoritative pieces of scriptural evidence and support. It illustrates the idea of the *homo hierarchicus* in a most memorable and exemplary fashion; in a sense, it anticipates and supersedes its later formulations:

> *yat puruṣaṃ vyadadhuḥ, katidhā vyakalpayan?*
> *mukhaṃ kim asya, kau bāhū kā ūrū pādā ucyete?*
> *brāhmaṇo 'sya mukham āsīd bāhū rājanyaḥ kṛtaḥ,*
> *ūrū tad asya yad vaiśyaḥ, padbhyāṃ śūdro ajāyata.*

"When (the gods) divided Puruṣa (i.e., the primeval cosmic entity), into how many parts did they apportion him? What was his mouth (and head)? Which were his arms? Which (objects) are said to be his thighs and feet? The brahmin was his mouth, the kṣatriya was installed as his arms; what is known as the vaiśya were his thighs; the śūdra originated from his feet."[146]

However, it is not only the idea of the *homo hierarchicus*, or of a hierarchic structure of society, which these verses convey. They also associate the four castes with an organic structure, and they evoke the idea of coherence and mutual support within a living totality. Modern defenders of an idealized varṇa structure have repeatedly referred to this connotation. For instance, S. Radhakrishnan states that in the *Puruṣasūkta* "the different sections of society are regarded as the limbs of the great self." He adds: "Human society is an organic whole, the parts of which are naturally dependent in such a way that each part in fulfilling its distinctive function conditions the fulfillment of function by the rest, and is in turn conditioned by the fulfillment of its function by the rest. In this sense the whole is present in each part, while each part is indispensable to the whole".[147]

The idea of interdependence and mutual supplementation has also appealed to Roberto de'Nobili (1577–1656), the great Jesuit missionary who has been called the first Western Sanskrit scholar.[148] Yet in "orthodox" Hindu thought and literature, including the majority of those sources which we have discussed in the preceding pages, it does not play a very visible and significant role. It is virtually absent in the apologetics of the Pūrvamīmāṃsā and the Nyāya-Vaiśeṣika. In these systems, as well as in the more rigid Dharmaśāstra texts, the mutual separation of the castes is emphasized more strongly than their mutual rapport. For a somewhat different picture, we have to turn to other sources.

In a general and implicit sense, the idea of cosmic balance, and of the mutual support and supplementation of the various parts of nature and society seems to be present in a variety of religious, philosophical, and legal texts, for instance, in the Mahābhārata and in several Upaniṣads. More specifically, we hear about the mutual support of brahmins and kṣatriyas, gods, humans, and animals, etc.[149] However, explicit theoretical expositions of this idea are less frequent. They occur, above all, in Sāṃkhya and Yoga texts, for instance, in the *Yuktidīpikā* and the *Jayamaṅgalā*, two commentaries on Īśvarakṛṣṇa's *Sāṃkhyakārikā*.[150] The most interesting presentation is found in Vyāsa's *Yogabhāṣya*, together with the so-called *Yogasūtrabhāṣyavivaraṇa* attributed to Śaṅkara.

Vyāsa's commentary on *Yogasūtra* II, 28 deals with the theory of "nine causes" (*nava kāraṇāni*) or types of causation, which has parallels in Buddhist thought.[151] The last type of cause in the list is called *dhṛti*, "support," "sustenance." Vyāsa explains it as follows: "The body is the cause of sustenance for the sense organs; and these support this (body). The elements sustain the bodies, the bodies support each other; and animal, human, and divine bodies support all entities, because there has to be mutual support."[152]

The *Vivaraṇa* explains in more detail how humans, animals, and gods are supposed to support each other, and how they contribute to the sustenance of all other entities in the world. In addition, the text notes: *evaṃ varṇāśramāṇām apy anyonyopakāreṇa dhṛtikāraṇatvaṃ, parasparopāśrayeṇa hi jagad akhilam api dhriyate* ("In this way, the castes and stages of life also sustain each other, since they are useful for each other. Indeed, the entire world is upheld through mutual dependence.")[153] A. Wezler says that according to this passage "the four *varṇas* and the four *āśramas* support and thus sustain each other mutually, that none of them is able to get along without the others." He emphasizes that such mutuality and interdependence distinguishes this passage from other texts which suggest a more "unilateral" dependence of social groups and formations, for instance, the dependence of the other three stages of life (*āśrama*) on the productive "householder" (*gṛhastha*).[154]

19. Mutual support and upholding appear as fundamental conditions for the preservation of the natural and social world. Interdependence is a pervasive principle which is both factual and normative. All entities in the world, in particular living beings and different social groups, have to support each other actively or passively. Self-preservation is impossible without mutual support and sustenance. On the other hand, the mutuality of support and sustenance presupposes meaningful differentiation. Natural species and social groups cannot support and supplement each other if they are not sufficiently different from one another.

The word *dhṛti*, which is used in the presentation of the "nine causes," has a close etymological kinship with *dharma*. Both terms are derived from the root *dhṛ*, "to uphold," "sustain." Although this derivation cannot account for the semantic complexities of *dharma*, it is by no means negligible, especially with regard to its more ancient usages. *Dharma* is, indeed, associated with "upholding." As we have noted earlier in this book, the term refers originally "to the primeval cosmogonic 'upholding' and opening of the world and its fundamental divisions, and then to the repetition and human analogues of the cosmogonic acts in the ritual, as well as the extension of the ritual into the sphere of social and ethical norms. Subsequently, there is increasing emphasis on the 'upholding' of the social and religious status quo, of the distinction between hereditary groups and levels of qualification (i.e., the *varṇāśramadharma*), and on the demarcation of the *ārya* against the *mleccha*."[155] Upholding the structure and the basic divisions of the social and natural world, and upholding one's own identity in a system of mutual balance—this is at least part of the semantic range of dharma, and it is probably part of its most ancient and original meaning.

This idea of mutuality in the Sāṃkhya-Yoga concept of *dhṛti* seems to preserve connotations of the Vedic dharma which are missing, or at least much less conspicuous, in the supposedly more "orthodox" explanations of the Pūrvamīmāṃsā and the Nyāya-Vaiśeṣika. As we have seen, both the Nyāya-Vaiśeṣika and the Mīmāṃsā approach the Veda from a certain distance. Their ideas of the

Veda, and of the Vedic dharma, are not "real extensions" ("prolongements réels")[156] of Vedic life and thought. And in general, those who present themselves as the most orthodox and uncompromising guardians of the sanctity and authority of the Veda are not necessarily closest to its spirit. Here as in other areas of Indian thought, the role of the Veda is ambiguous and elusive.

Chapter 10: Notes

1. Two classical examples of such critique are provided by Hegel and Max Weber; cf. *India and Europe*, ch. 6 (on Hegel); M. Weber, *Die Wirtschaftsethik der Weltreligionen. II: Hinduismus und Buddhismus*. Tübingen, 1921 (seventh reprint: 1988), 142 ff. (trans. H.H. Gerth and D. Martindale: *The Religion of India*. New York, 1968, 144 ff.).

2. While Kauṭilya's *Arthaśāstra* contains an elaborate methodology of politics and administration, it can hardly be classified as a system of political philosophy.

3. For an earlier German version of this chapter, see *Nachrichten der Akademie der Wissenschaften in Göttingen*. Philologisch-historische Klasse. 1975, No. 9 (published 1976).

4. Cf. R. Lingat, *The Classical Law of India*, trans. from the French by J.D.M. Derrett. Berkeley, 1973, 36 ff.

5. See, for instance, Śaṅkara, BSBh I, 1, 4 (*Works* III, 13 f.); Manu X, 42 (*utkarṣaṃ ca-apakarṣaṃ ca*) and commentaries; Anantakṛṣṇa Śāstrin et al., *Dharmapradīpa*. Calcutta, n.d. (Preface: 1937), 67 f.

6. Cf. BSBh I, 1, 4 (*Works* III, 13 f.); I, 3, 30 (*Works* III, 129).

7. Cf. Bhāruci on Manu X, 42 (ed. J. H. Dave. Bombay, 1982, 307): *evaṃ ca saty eṣa varṇavibhāga utkarṣāpakarṣasambandho manuṣyaviṣaya eva draṣṭavyaḥ, na gavādiṣu*).

8. Cf. Manu X, 30 f.; Medhātithi on Manu II, 6 (ed. J.H. Dave, 168).

9. Cf. L. Dumont, *Homo Hierarchicus. The Caste System and Its Implications*. Complete revised English edition. Chicago, 1980, XXXV; Dumont finds this idea "generally rejected" by the majority of his reviewers.

10. *Homo Hierarchicus*, 72.

11. A. L. Basham, *The Wonder That Was India*. New York, 1959, 148.

12. Manu VIII, 41 adds the norms and customs of the "guilds" (*śreṇi*) to this list: Gītā I, 43 associates the destruction of *jātidharma* and *kuladharma* with the "mixture of varṇas" (*varṇasaṃkara*).

13. Cf. Yājñavalkya II, 69: *yathājāti yathāvarṇam*; II, 206: *daṇḍapraṇayanaṃ kāryaṃ varṇajātyuttarādharaiḥ*.

14. Cf. Āpastamba II, 6, 1: *jātyācārasaṃśaye*; G. Bühler, *Sacred Laws of the Āryas*, part 1 (Sacred Books of the East) translates: "If he has any doubts regarding the caste and conduct . . . ." Cf. also L. Dumont (see above, n. 7), 73: "Far from being completely heterogeneous, the concepts of varṇa and *jāti* have interacted, and certain features of the osmosis between the two may be noticed."

15. See, for instance, Manu X, 5; 27.

16. Cf. Kullūka, Nandana, Nārada and others on Manu VIII, 41.

17. Cf. Medhātithi on Manu X, 4; Nandana on Manu X, 27; see also Kullūka's statement that caste mixture or bastardization can produce a new *jāti* comparable to a mule, but no new varṇa (on Manu X, 4: *saṃkīrṇajātīnāṃ tv aśvataravan mātāpitṛjātivyatiriktajātyantaratvān na varṇatvam*).

18. See, for instance, Mitramiśra, *Vīramitrodaya*, and Vijñāneśvara, *Mitākṣarā*, on Yājñavalkya II, 69 (ChSS, 497; 502) and II, 206 (ChSS, 682; 684).

19. Cf. Mitramiśra, *Vīramitrodaya* on Yājñavalkya II, 69 (ChSS, 497).

20. Cf. *India and Europe*, 180; and on mixed castes in general: H. Brinkhaus, *Die altindischen Mischkastensysteme*. Wiesbaden, 1978.

21. L. Dumont (see above, n. 7), 71. In this connection, Dumont also notes the "the classical texts described in terms of varṇa what must surely have been a caste system in embryo."

22. Cf. Medhātithi on Manu X, 5; see also P.V. Kane, "The Tantravārttika and the Dharmaśāstra Literature." *Journal of the Bombay Branch of the Royal Asiatic Society*, N.S. 1 (1925), 95–102.

23. Calcutta, n.d. (Preface: 1937); the protection of the hereditary identity of Hinduism against reinterpretations and "new sects" (*nūtanasaṃpradāya*) is one of the main goals of the book, and the problem of castes (*jāti*) is its major topic; see 63–187: *Jātitattvaprakāśa*. As an example of a basically ethical and characterological interpretation, we may mention Maheśvarānanda Giri, *Cāturvarṇyabhāratasamīkṣā*, 2 vols. Bombay, 1963–1968. This work cites the *Vajrasūcī Upaniṣad* (vol. 1, 22–25; see below, n. 133) and shows the influence of Neo-Vedānta.

24. Cf. *A Descriptive Catalogue of the Sanskrit Manuscripts* (*Vivaraṇapañcikā*), Sanskrit University Library (Sarasvatī Bhavana), vol. 8: Nyāya-Vaiśeṣika Mss. Varanasi, 1962, Nos. 34 017; 33 731; 31 393.

25. On Rāmānuja, see below, n. 128. Problems concerning the perception and identification of castes, especially "brahminness" (*brāhmaṇya*), are also discussed by Rāmānuja's predecessor Yāmuna; cf. *Āgamaprāmāṇya*, ed. and trans. J. A. B. van Buitenen. Madras, 1971, 66; 103. Yāmuna (ca. 1000) is obviously familiar with the Mīmāṃsā arguments on this topic.

26. Cf. *Seśvaramīmāṃsā and Mīmāṃsāpādukā* by Vedāntadeśika, ed. U. T. Viraraghavacarya. Madras, 1971, 144–151 (on MS I, 2, 2); see also below, n. 104. Veṅkaṭanātha/Vedāntadeśika discusses not only the theory of caste universals, but also the application of the guṇa theory to the varṇa system; cf. *Seśvaramīmāṃsā*, 149 f. On Vallabha's version of the Mīmāṃsāsūtra, see G. H. Bhatt, "Vallabhācārya's Text of the Jaimini Sūtras II. 1." *Journal of the Oriental Institute* (Baroda) 2 (1952), 68–70.

27. Cf. *Prameyakamalamārtaṇḍa* (commentary on Māṇikyanandin's *Parīkṣāmukha*), ed. Mahendra Kumar. Second ed., Bombay, 1941; especially 482–487 (482: *etena nityaṃ nikhilabrāhmaṇavyaktivyāpakaṃ brāhmaṇyam api pratyākhyātam. na hi tat tathābhūtaṃ pratyakṣādipramāṇataḥ pratīyate*); *Nyāyakumudacandra* (commentary on Akalaṅka's *Laghīyastraya*), 2 vols., ed. Mahendra Kumar. Bombay, 1938–1941; especially vol. 2, 767–779 (*brāhmaṇatvajātivicāra*).

28. See, for instance, Kṣemendra, *Darpadalana*, ch. 1 (examples of false genealogical pride).

29. Cf. *India and Europe*, 234; 240 ff. Traditional Advaita Vedānta does not try to apply non-dualism in ethics; instead, it sees ethical conduct either as a prerequisite or as a natural concomitant of non-dualistic spiritual realization. According to *Vivekacūḍāmaṇi*, v. 37, those who have attained this realization are inherently beneficial, "just as the spring season" (*vasantavad*). This echoes Mahāyāna Buddhist ideas.

30. Cf. P. V. Kane, *History of Dharmaśāstra*, 5 vols. Poona, 1930–1962; especially vol. 2, 19–164.

31. Cf. Muir I, for a useful presentation of source materials.

32. See A. Weber, "Collectanea über die Kastenverhältnisse in den Brāhmaṇa und Sūtra." *Indische Studien* 10 (1868), 1–160.

33. Cf. *India and Europe*, 322 f.; myths about the origination of the non-brahminical castes due to karmic deterioration are not unusual; see Mahābhārata XII, 181, 10–20.

34. Cf. A. Weber, "Collectanea" (see above, n.32), 97 ff.

35. Cf. Weber, "Collectanea," 70 f.; 97 ff.; see also W. Rau, *Staat und Gesellschaft im alten Indien*. Wiesbaden, 1957, 4; 62 ff.; against Weber, Rau claims that the hereditary varṇa system did not take shape in the period of the Brāhmaṇas, but only in the period of the Sūtras. However, Rau's references seem to deal with exceptions rather than with the general norm. Ethical interpretations which presuppose an underlying hereditary system are more common in the epics; see, e.g., Mahābhārata III, 206, 12 (*vṛttena hi bhaved dvijaḥ*); and O. Strauss, "Ethische Probleme aus dem Mahābhārata" (first published 1911). *Kl. Schr.*, ed. F. Wilhelm. Wiesbaden, 1983, 11–153; especially 148 ff.

36. The following Suttas of the Pali canon contain critical references to the varṇa system: *Aggañña, Ambaṭṭha, Sāmaññaphala* and *Soṇadaṇḍa* in the *Dīghanikāya*; *Assalāyana* and *Madhura* in the *Majjhimanikāya*; *Vāseṭṭha* in the *Suttanipāta*. Several Buddhist texts in Sanskrit radicalize the critique, for instance the *Śārdūlakarṇāvadāna* in the *Divyāvadāna* (ed. E. B. Cowell and R. A. Neil. Cambridge, 1886; ed. separately S. K. Mukhopadhyaya. Santiniketan, 1954) and the *Vajrasūcī* falsely attrib-

uted to Aśvaghoṣa; for editions of this text, see A. Weber, "Über die Vajra-sūcī (Demantnadel) des Açvaghoṣa." *Abhandlungen Preuss. Ak. Wiss.* Berlin, 1859, 205–264 (with German trans.); S. K. Mukherjee, "The Vajrasūcī of Aśvaghoṣa." *Visva-Bharati Annals* 2 (1949), 125–184 (with English trans.); *Vajrasūcī*, ed. R. P. Dwivedi (with paraphrase and notes in Hindi). Varanasi, 1985.

37. On *dharma* and *svadharma*, cf. *India and Europe*, ch. 17.

38. Cf. Bhagavadgītā I, 41 ff.

39. Gītā III, 35: *śreyān svadharmo viguṇaḥ paradharmāt svanuṣṭhitāt*; see also XVIII, 47 (and Manu X, 97): *varaṃ svadharmo viguṇo, na pārakhyaḥ svanuṣṭhitaḥ.*

40. Cf. *The Vyākaraṇa-Mahābhāṣya*, ed. F. Kielhorn; third ed. by K. V. Abhyankar, vol. 1. Poona, 1962, 411:

tapaḥ śrutaṃ ca yoniś ca-ity etad brāhmaṇakāraṇam/
tapaḥśrutābhyāṃ yo hīno jātibrāhmaṇa eva sa.

tathā gauraḥ śucyācāraḥ piṅgalaḥ kapilakeśa ity etān apy abhyantarān brāhmaṇye guṇān kurvanti.

41. The application of the word *brāhmaṇa* to persons who do not have the hereditary legitimation remains ultimately confined to cases of doubt and inadequate information; see *Mahābhāṣya*, vol. 1, 411 f.: *jātihīne saṃdehād durupadeśāc ca brāhmaṇaśabdo vartate.*

42. See *Yuktidīpikā*, ed. R. C. Pandeya. Delhi, 1967, 137.

43. Cf. *Sāṃkhyakārikā with Māṭharavṛtti*, ed. V. P. Sarma. Benares, 1922; on v. 53: *tulyaliṅgatvād brāhmaṇādicaṇḍālāntaḥ; Sāṃkhyasaptativṛtti* (V_1), ed. E. A. Solomon. Ahmedabad, 1973, 68: *tulyaliṅgatvād brāhmaṇādiś caṇḍālāntaḥ.*

44. Cf. *Sāṃkhyatattvakaumudī* on v. 53: *brāhmaṇatvādyavāntarajātibhedāvivakṣayā.*

45. Gītā IV, 13: *cāturvarṇyaṃ mayā sṛṣṭaṃ guṇakarmavibhāgaśaḥ.*

46. Radhakrishnan has published annotated editions amd translations of both works; see also *The Hindu View of Life*. London, 1968 (first ed.: 1927), 86: "Caste is a question of character."

47. See below, n. 110–113.

48. Cf. Gītā I, 41 ff.; see also III, 24 f. (avoidance of mixture, *saṃkara*, and maintenance of the social order, *lokasaṃgraha*).

49. See, for instance, Gītā VII, 16.

50. Cf. Śaṅkara on Gītā IV, 13.

51. Cf. Gītā XVIII, 41 ff.; IV, 13; see also D. P. Vora, *Evolution of Morals in the Epics*. Bombay, 1959, 129. There are, of course, also types of livelihood and occupation associated with the two highest castes; but they are not mentioned in the Gītā passage XVIII, 41 ff.

52. Cf. *Vajrasūcī*, ed. A. Weber (see above, n.36), 236.

53. See Gītā III, 35; XVIII, 47; and Manu X, 97; for *svadharma*, see also Gītā II, 31; 33; Maitrī Upaniṣad IV, 3; Gītā XVIII, 45 f. has *svakarman*.

54. Manu XII, 42–52.

55. See Mahābhārata XII, 200; especially 31 ff. (on the four varṇa); cf. also A. Weber, "Collectanea" (see above, n.32), 7. We may also recall Ṛgveda X, 90.

56. Mahābhārata XII, 229, 12–25.

57. Cf. A. Weber, "Collectanea," 97; among later texts, see, e.g., *Vivekacūḍāmaṇi*, v. 2.

58. On "caste colors," cf. Mahābhārata XII, 181, 5; A. Weber, "Collectanea," 10 f.: Ps.-Śaṅkara, *Sarvasiddhāntasaṃgraha* XI, 48.

59. The coordination of the three guṇas with the "human goals" (*puruṣārtha*) creates analogous problems. It is easy as long as the older

group of three goals (*trivarga*) without *mokṣa* is involved; Manu XII, 38 correlates *kāma* with *tamas, artha* with *rajas* and *dharma* with *sattva*. It becomes, however, more complex when *mokṣa* is added; cf. Bhagavan Das, *The Science of Social Organization,* vol. 1. Second ed., Adyar, 1932, 78.

60. Cf. *Anugītā* XXIV, 11; the text is found within the Mahābhārata XIV, 16–51.

61. Cf. *Anugītā* XX, 43, which refers to three twice-born castes and presupposes the śūdras as the fourth varṇa. The vaiśyas are also omitted in Manu XII, 42–52.

62. Cf. K. Damodaran, *Indian Thought.* New York, 1967, 482 (referring to K. M. Munshi, *Foundations of Indian Culture*, 68: "energy/inertia"); P. T. Raju, *The Philosophical Traditions of India.* London, 1971, 209: "activity/lethargy."

63. Cf. *Cāturvarṇyaśikṣā vedadṛṣṭyā sametā.* Lucknow, 1927, 2.

64. *The Philosophical Traditions of India.* London, 1971, 209.

65. See, for instance, Vinoba Bhave, *Talks on the Gītā.* New York, 1960, 191 ff.

66. *The Hindu View of Life.* London, 1968, 79.

67. See above, n. 63.

68. Cf. PB, 48 f.; 272 f.

69. Cf. NM, 204: *na hi yad giriśṛṅgam āruhya gṛhyate, tad apratyakṣam.*

70. NM, 204: *upadeśanirapekṣam api cakṣuh kṣatriyādivilakṣaṇāṃ saumyākrtiṃ brāhmaṇajātim avagacchati-ity eke.*

71. Cf. NM, 389; on Kumārila's usage of the simile of the mountain, see below, n. 92.

72. See NK (in PB), 13: *tadā brāhmaṇo 'yam iti pratyakṣeṇa-eva pratīyate.*

73. Ibid. The reference to precious stones appears natural for an Indian author of that period, since these, too, were divided into "castes" (*brāhmaṇa*, etc.); cf. R. Garbe, *Die indischen Mineralien* (*Naraharis Rājanighaṇṭu 13*). Leipzig, 1882, 81. Kumārila refers to expert jewelers in his TV on MS I, 3, 25; on Bhartṛhari, see below, n. 102.

74. Here, of course, one may refer to Manu's view that an illegitimate child would reflect the defects and the low status of the father in its behavior; cf. Manu X, 60 ff.

75. See *Vaiśeṣikadarśana of Kaṇāda with an Anonymous Commentary*, ed. A. Thakur. Darbhanga, 1957, 14 f. (on VS I, 2, 7).

76. Cf. TS, v. 1554 ff. (with commentary).

77. Ed. Rāhula Sāṅkṛtayāyana. Patna, 1953 (Tibetan Sanskrit Works Series); see especially 10 ff.; also 209 f.; 530.

78. Cf. *Pramāṇavārttikabhāṣya*, especially 10 ff.; also 209 f.; 530.

79. See, for instance, Bhāsarvajña, NBhūṣ, 311 (in connection with problems of inference); Laugākṣi Bhāskara, *Tarkakaumudī*, ed. M. N. Dvivedin. Bombay, 1886 (Bombay Sanskrit and Prakrit Series), 21; Keśavamiśra, *Tarkabhāṣā*, ed. D. R. Bhandarkar. Poona, 1937 (Bombay Sanskrit and Prakrit Series), 33 (perception of a *brāhmaṇa*).

80. See below, n. 83 ff.; 106 ff.

81. Cf. the *Vajrasūcī* (see above, n. 36); the same type of argument has also been attributed to the materialists; see Kṛṣṇamiśra, *Prabodhacandrodaya*, ed. and trans. S. K. Nambiar. Delhi, 1971, 38 (II, v. 18): *tulyatve vapuṣāṃ mukhādyavayavair varṇakramaḥ kīdṛśo*. . . .

82. Cf. ŚV, 438 (*Vanavāda*, v. 16): *ākṛtir jātir eva-atra saṃsthānaṃ na prakalpyate*; 385 (*Ākṛtivāda*, v.3): *jātim eva-ākṛtiṃ prāhur, vyaktir ākriyate yayā*; and 388 (v. 18): *sāmānyam ākṛtir jātiḥ śaktir vā*.

83. Cf. TV on MS I, 3, 25: *tulyaśiraḥpāṇyādyākāreṣv api saṃkīrṇalokadṛṣṭigrāhyeṣu brāhmaṇādiṣu mātāpitṛsambandhasmaraṇād eva varṇavivekāvadhāraṇam bhavati*.

84. Cf. ŚV, 439 f. (*Vanavāda*, v. 22–30). In v. 29, Kumārila notes that conduct (*ācāra*) indicates the presence of *brāhmaṇatva* only if it is properly supervised by a king (*rājānupālita*). In v. 30, he emphasizes that the pervasive inherence of the universals in their substrates cannot be refuted since it is directly perceived (*pratyekasamavetatvaṃ dṛṣṭatvān na virotsyate*); and such perceptibility may well be "dependent on the knowledge of the parents" (*mātāpitṛjñānāpekṣa*; see Pārthasārathi on this passage, with reference to TV).

85. Śabara on MS I, 2, 2: *na ca-etad vidmo vayaṃ brāhmaṇā vā smo 'brāhmaṇā vā iti*; cf. *Gopatha Brāhmaṇa* I, 5, 21: *na vayaṃ vidmo yadi brāhmaṇā smo yady abrāhmaṇā smo; Maitrāyaṇī Saṃhitā* I, 4, 11 (ed. L. von Schroeder, vol. 1, 60): *na vai tad vidma yadi brāhmaṇā vā smo 'brāhmaṇā vā*. The reference *Taittirīya Brāhmaṇa* II, 1, 2, given by the editors of TV, is incorrect.

86. The commentator Someśvara feels occasionally compelled to state explicitly that Kumārila is, indeed, presenting his own view; cf. NSudhā, 10: *āśaṅkitā svābhiprāyam āviṣkaroti*.

87. Cf. E. Frauwallner, *Materialien zur ältesten Erkenntnislehre der Karmamīmāṃsā*. Vienna, 1968; see also above, ch. 2.

88. Someśvara tries to clarify Kumārila's somewhat ambiguous reliance on both perception and authoritative instruction; see NSudhā, 14: *pratyakṣāvagatisambhavād anyatra śāstravyāpāro na-aṅgīkṛtaḥ, iha tu tadasambhavāc chāstraviṣayatvaṃ na-ayuktam . . . nanv ākārasāmyena kvacid api brāhmaṇyādivivekasya pratyakṣeṇa-avagatyasambhavāt sarvatra-āgamagamyatvam eva-aṅgīkāryam ity āsaṅkāṃ nirākurvan upasaṃharati*.

89. Someśvara, NSudhā, 10, states that it is necessary to assume something that is universally present in all individual brahmins and forms the content of the notion "brahmin" (*tasmāt sarveṣu brāhmaṇeṣu anusyūtaṃ pratyekasamavetaṃ brāhmaṇapratyayaviṣayabhūtaṃ kiṃcid avaśyam eṣṭavyam*); on p. 11, he adds that universals such as brahminness, which are to be known through such special pervasive notions, cannot be denied (*tasmāt samānākāreṣv api piṇḍeṣu vilakṣaṇabrāhmaṇapratyayavedyabrāhmaṇyādijātir na-apahnotuṃ śakyate*).

90. For the following discussion, see TV, 4 ff. (on MS I, 2, 2). The *siddhānta* section (on MS I, 2, 7 ff.) does not address this issue at all.

91. As Kumārila notes in the *Ślokavārttika*, conduct would be a valid criterion only under proper supervision; see above, n.84.

92. See above, n. 69 ff.; cf. also Someśvara, NSudhā, 12: *na ca durjñānatvamātreṇa-apratyakṣatvaṃ śaṅkyam.*

93. See TV, 6: *darśanasmaraṇapāramparyānugṛhītapratyakṣagamyāni brāhmaṇatvādīni.*

94. Cf. TV, 217 (on MS I, 3, 27):
āditaś ca smṛteḥ siddhaḥ pratyakṣeṇa-api gamyate/
sādhvasādhuvibhāgo 'yaṃ kuśalair varṇabhedavat.

See also above, n. 73, on the case of the expert jewelers.

95. Cf. TV, 6: *siddhānāṃ hi brāhmaṇādīnām ācārā vidhīyante.*

96. Cf. TV, 7: *na tapaādīnāṃ samudāyo brāhmaṇyam, na tajjanitaḥ saṃskāraḥ, na tadabhivyaṅgyā jātiḥ.*

97. According to Kumārila, there is no loss of brahminness etc. in the strict and literal sense. Authoritative statements which seem to indicate that a brahmin sinks to the level of a śūdra due to certain types of misconduct can only mean that he is deprived of particular rights and responsibilities. Critics of the varṇa system sometimes use the loss of caste status as an argument against its hereditary nature; see, for instance, the *Vajrasūcī.*

98. Cf. *Mahābhāṣya* on IV, 1, 63; V, 3, 55; and above, n. 40.

99. Nāgeśa makes explicit reference to *upadeśa*; cf. *Patañjali's Vyākaraṇa-Mahābhāṣya: Tatpuruṣāhnika,* ed. with trans. by S. D. Joshi and J. A. F. Roodbergen. Poona, 1973, 118 f.

100. Cf. VP III/14, 250 ff.; and K. A. Subramania Iyer, *Bhartṛhari.* Poona, 1969, 390 ff.; 397 ff. On *abrāhmaṇatva*, see also Kumārila, ŚV, 402 ff. (*Apohavāda*, v. 13–30).

101. Cf. VP III/1, 44:

brāhmaṇatvādayo bhāvāḥ sarvaprāṇiṣv avasthitāḥ/
abhivyaktāḥ svakāryāṇāṃ sādhakā ity api smṛtiḥ.

Helārāja paraphrases: *brāhmaṇatvakṣatriyatvādayaḥ sāmānyaviśeṣāḥ*. Cf. also VP III/1, 28 (*brāhmaṇatvādi*).

102. Cf. VP III/1, 46.

103. Cf. *VP with the commentary of Helārāja*. Kāṇḍa III, part 1, ed. K. A. Subramania Iyer. Poona, 1963, 51–55; especially 55: *brāhmaṇatvādiṣv asti kiṃcit sāsnādisthānīyam upavyañjanam asmākaṃ param atīndriyam.*

104. Cf. *Seśvaramīmāṃsā* (see above, n. 24), 151: *ataḥ īśvaramaharṣiprabhṛtīnāṃ pratyakṣaṃ brāhmaṇyādikam.*

105. See above, n. 40; 90.

106. For the following discussion, cf. Śālikanāthamiśra, *Prakaraṇapañcikā* (with *Nyāyasiddhi* by Jayapurinārāyaṇa), ed. A. Subrahmanya Sastri. Benares, 1961, 100–103.

107. *Prakaraṇapañcikā*, 101: *na hi kṣatriyādibhyo vyāvartamānaṃ sakalabrāhmaṇeṣv anuvartamānam ekam ākāram aticiram anusandadhato 'pi budhyante.* In his preceding rejection of a highest universal "beingness" or "reality" (*sattā*; cf. 97ff.), Śālikanātha also refers to a lack of "similarity."

108. See ibid., 101: *na hi tadānīṃ cākṣuṣasya saṃvedanasya viṣayātirekaḥ, kiṃ tv anumānam eva tatra sarpiṣaḥ.*

109. Ibid., 102: *kathaṃ punas tajjanyatvam eva śakyam avagantum, strīṇām aparādhasambhavāt. sambhavanti hi puṃścalyo striyaḥ pariṇetāraṃ vyabhicarantyaḥ.* The *Vajrasūcī* (ed. A. Weber, 220; 232; see above, n. 36) epitomizes the manner in which the Buddhist critics exploit this issue.

110. Cf. *Dharmatattvanirṇaya*, ed. Mārulakara. Poona, 1929 (Ānandāśrama Sanskrit Series), 18 ff.

111. Ibid., 18: *na hi tatra śamādikaṃ karma brāhmaṇatvajātiprayojakatvena-uktam, kiṃ tu brāhmaṇatvajātiprayojyatvena.*

112. Ibid., 19: *tathā ca janmasiddhā jātir, na kvāpi kathamapi nivartate.*

113. Cf. *Cāturvarṇyaśikṣā vedadṛṣṭyā sametā*. Lucknow, 1927, 198 f. also 1: *aśvādivaj jātiguṇakriyābhir vibhinnabhāvātiśayaṃ prapannāḥ.*

114. Cf. *Vajrasūcī*, ed. A. Weber (see above, n.36), 237; 239; 252.

115. See S. L. Malhotra, *Social and Political Orientations of Neo-Vedantism*. Delhi, 1970, VII f.

116. See G. C. Dev, *Idealism and Progress*. Calcutta, 1952, 440 ff.; also his *The Philosophy of Vivekananda and the Future of Man*. Dacca, 1963, 96 f. ("Gospel of Emancipation of Common Man").

117. See S. Joshi, *The Message of Shankara*. Allahabad, 1968, 177; R. N. Vyas, *The Universalistic Thought of India*. Bombay, 1970, V.

118. R. N. Vyas, *Universalistic Thought*, 16.

119. Ramatirtha as cited by H. Maheshwari, *The Philosophy of Swāmī Rāma Tīrtha*. Agra; 1969, 169.

120. *Bunch of Thoughts*. Bangalore, 1966, 5f.; on the idea of a "practical Vedānta," see also *India and Europe*, 239 ff. (specifically on Vivekananda).

121. Ramakrishna often compared the world to a worthless "hog plum"; cf. *The Gospel of Sri Ramakrishna*, trans. Nikhilananda. Madras, 1969 (first ed.: 1944), 379; 903. In his *Karmayoga* (ch. 5, conclusion), Vivekananda himself still cited Ramakrishna's metaphor of the "dog's tail" to illustrate the incorrigibility of the world.

122. *The Hindu View of Life*. London, 1968, 18; see also *India and Europe*, 409.

123. Cf. *The Hindu View of Life*, 87; *History of Philosophy, Eastern and Western*. London, 1952–1953, vol. 1, 447.

124. See, for instance, P. Deussen, *Das System des Vedānta*. Second ed., Leipzig, 1906, 63 ff. (trans. Ch. Johnston: *The System of the Vedānta*. Chicago, 1912, 60 ff.).

125. On Śaṅkara's concept of *adhikāra*, see above, ch. 3, § 12 ff. Further statements on castes are found in BUBh I, 4, 6; 14; II, 4, 5 (castes and superimposition); TUBh II, 6, 1.

126. Cf. BSBh I, 3, 38; see also Gautama XII, 4.

127. Cf. BSBh I, 3, 37; in the Upaniṣad itself, the situation is somewhat ambiguous. The story of Satyakāma is also cited and discussed by several Dharmaśāstra commentators; see, for instance, Medhātithi and Govindarāja on Manu X, 5.

128. See Rāmānuja's *Śrībhāṣya* on BS I, 3, 34–38.

129. See *Naiṣkarmyasiddhi* II, 88; cf. also Śaṅkara, BUBh II, 4, 5.

130. Cf. *Svātmanirūpaṇa*, v. 139: *varṇāsramarahito 'ham varṇamayo 'ham; Daśaślokī*, v. 2: *na varṇā na varṇācāradharmāḥ*. Both texts are found in: *Minor Works of Śaṅkarācārya*, ed. Bhagavat. Second ed., Poona, 1952.

131. Cf. *The Minor Upaniṣads*, ed. F.O. Schrader, vol. 1: *Saṃnyāsa-Upaniṣads*. Madras, 1912. 193: 112.

132. *Nirālamba Upaniṣad*, v. 10 (in: *The Sāmānya-Vedānta-Upaniṣads*, ed. Mahadeva Sastri. Adyar, 1921).

133. See *The Principal Upanishads*, ed. and trans. S. Radhakrishnan. London, 1953. A. Weber (see above, n. 36) saw the *Vajrasūcī Upaniṣad* (which he ascribed to Śaṅkara) as the model for the Buddhist *Vajrasūcī*; according to S.K. Mukherjee, the Buddhist text is the original. It has been generally overlooked that a version of the *Vajrasūcī Upaniṣad* was already published and translated into Bengali by Rammohan Roy in 1821; see *Rāmamohana-Granthāvalī*, ed. B.N. Bandyopādhyāya and S. K. Dāsa. Calcutta, n.d. (1959), section 4, 43–48. According to Rammohan, the text is by Mṛtyuṃjaya; this can hardly

be Mṛtyuṃjaya Vidyālaṅkāra, Rammohan's teacher and, later on, opponent.

134. Cf. *Maitreya Upaniṣad*; in: *The Minor Upaniṣads* (see above, n. 131), 114 f.

135. Cf. *Bṛhadāraṇyaka Upaniṣad* IV, 3, 22; see also Śaṅkara, USG I, 15 ff. (freedom of the *ātman* from caste distinctions); and the following statement by Madhusūdana Sarasvatī: *varṇāśramādivyavahārasya mithyājñānamūlatvena mithyātvam* (*Siddhāntabindu*, ed. P. C. Divanji. Baroda, 1933, Gaekwad's Oriental Series, 41).

136. Published in *A Descriptive Catalogue of the Sanskrit Manuscripts in the Tanjore Mahārāja Serfoji's Sarasvatī Mahāl Library*, ed. P. P. S. Sastri, vol. 13. Srirangam, 1931, No. 7736; see especially v. 11 f.

137. Cf. *Alberuni's India*, trans. E. C. Sachau. London, 1910 (and many reprints), vol. 1, 104.

138. Cf. Abhinavagupta, *Īśvarapratyabhijñāvimarśinī* IV, 2, 3; ed. M. Kaul Shastri. Bombay, 1921 (Kashmir Series of Texts and Studies), vol. 2, 276: *na-atra jātyādyapekṣā kācit.*

139. Cf. P. Olivelle, "A Definition of World Renunciation." *Wiener Zeitschrift für die Kunde Südasiens* 19 (1975), 75–83.

140. Cf. P. Hacker, *Schüler Śaṅkaras*, 105; but see also *Vivekacūḍāmaṇi*, v. 542.

141. See *India and Europe*, 205 f.; 212; 239 ff.; 251 ff.

142. There were, of course, important representatives of modern Indian thought who denied or questioned the ethical and social applicability of non-dualism; in the nineteenth century, Debendranath Tagore (Ṭhākur) and Dayānanda Sarasvatī were among the critics of Śaṅkara's Advaita Vedānta.

143. *The Gospel of Sri Ramakrishna*, trans. Nikhilananda. Madras, 1969 (first ed.: 1944), 8 f.

144. *The Gospel*, 204; for a somewhat different version, see 374 f.

145. *The Gospel*, 9.

146. Ṛgveda X, 90, 11-12.

147. See S. Radhakrishnan, *The Hindu View of Life*. London, 1968, 107.

148. See *India and Europe*, ch. 3; S. Arokiasamy, *Dharma, Hindu and Christian, according to Roberto de Nobili*. Rome, 1986, 289 ff.; 292.

149. See, for instance, *Bṛhadāraṇyaka Upaniṣad* I, 4, 10, on the interaction of animals, humans, and gods; see also the concept of *lokasaṃgraha*, as used in Bhagavadgītā III, 20.

150. See P. Chakravarti, *Origin and Development of the Sāṃkhya System of Thought*. New Delhi, second ed., 1975, 218 ff.

151. See A. Wezler, "On the *varṇa* System as Conceived of by the Author of the Pātañjala-Yoga-Śāstra-Vivaraṇa." *Dr. B. R. Sharma Felicitation Volume*, Tirupati, 1986, 172–188; specifically p. 185, note 14. A. Wezler deserves credit for having drawn our attention to the remarkable statements in the Vivaraṇa.

152. The Sanskrit text reads as follows: *dhṛtikāraṇaṃ śarīram indriyāṇām, tāni ca tasya. mahābhūtāni śarīrāṇām, tāni ca parasparam. sarveṣām tairyagyonamānuṣadaivatāni ca parasparārthatvāt.*

153. See YSBhV, 210 f. (on YS and YBh II, 28).

154. See A. Wezler, "On the *varṇa* System," 180 f.

155. See above, ch. 1; and *India and Europe*, 332.

156. See above, ch. 1; and L. Renou, *Le destin*, 3.

Abbreviations

Ak. Wiss. (Lit.)	Akademie der Wissenschaften (und der Literatur).
A Thousand Teachings	*A Thousand Teachings. The Upadeśasāhasrī of Śaṅkara.* Trans. with introduction and notes by S. Mayeda. Tokyo, 1979.
Beweisverfahren	H. Brückner, *Zum Beweisverfahren Śaṃkaras. Eine Untersuchung der Form und Funktion von dṛṣṭāntas im Bṛhadāraṇyakopaniṣadbhāṣya und im Chāndogyopaniṣadbhāṣya des Śaṃkara Bhagavatpāda.* Berlin, 1979 (Diss. Marburg).
BS (Bh)	*Brahmasūtra (Bhāṣya).*
BU	*Bṛhadāraṇyaka Upaniṣad.*
BUBh(V)	*BU Bhāṣya (Vārttika).*
ChSS	Chowkhamba Sanskrit Series.
Dasgupta I-V	S.N. Dasgupta, *A History of Indian Philosphy*, 5 vols. Cambridge, 1922–1955 (several reprints).
Diss.	Ph.D. dissertation.
GBh	*Gītābhāṣya.*
GOS	Gaekwad's Oriental Series.
India and Europe	W. Halbfass, *India and Europe: An Essay in Understanding.* Albany, 1988.
L'autorité du Veda	G. Chemparathy, *L'autorité du Veda selon les Nyāya-Vaiśeṣikas.* Louvain-la-Neuve, 1983.

Le destin — L. Renou, *Le destin du Veda dans l'Inde*. Paris, 1960 (Études védiques et pāṇinéennes, vol. 6).

Kl. Schr. — *Kleine Schriften*.

MK — *(Mūla) Madhyamakakārikā* (by Nāgārjuna).

MS — *Mīmāṃsāsūtra*.

Muir I-V — J. Muir, *Original Sanskrit Texts on the Origin and History of the People of India*. 5 vols. New Delhi, 1976 (reprints of the partly revised and enlarged editions, London, 1870–1874).

Naiṣk. — Sureśvara, *Naiṣkarmyasiddhi*.

NBh — *Nyāyabhāṣya* (by Vātsyāyana Pakṣilasvāmin).

NBhūṣ — Bhāsarvajña, *Nyāyabhūṣaṇa*, ed. Yogīndrānanda. Benares, 1968.

ND — *Nyāyadarśana*; see NV; NVT.

NK — *Nyāyakandalī* (by Srīdhara); see PB.

NM — *The Nyāyamañjarī of Jayanta Bhaṭṭa*, ed. S. N. Śukla, 2 vols. Benares, 1934–1936 (Kashi Sanskrit Series).

NS — *Nyāyasūtra*.

NSudhā — Someśvara, *Nyāyasudhā* (commentary on Kumārila's *Tantravārttika*), ed. Mukunda Śāstrī. Benares, 1909 (ChSS).

NV; NVT — *Nyāyavārttika* by Uddyotakara; *Nyāyavārttikatātparyaṭīkā* by Vācaspati; *Adhyāya* 1 (if not marked otherwise) quoted from: *Nyāyadarśana* (ND) of Gautama, ed. A. Thakur. Darbhanga, 1967 (includes *Adhyāya* 1 of Udayana's *Pariśuddhi*); for

	the remaining parts, cf. NV, ed. V. P. Dvivedin. Calcutta, 1914 (Bibliotheca Indica); NVT, ed. R. S. Drāviḍa. Benares, 1925–1926 (Kashi Sanskrit Series).
Pariśuddhi	(*Nyāyavārttikatātparya-*) *Pariśuddhi* by Udayana, ed. A. Thakur; see NV; NVT.
PB	*The Bhāṣya of Praśastapāda*, together with the *Nyāyakandalī* (NK) of Śrīdhara, ed. V.P. Dvivedin. Benares, 1895 (Vizianagram Sanskrit Series; reprint Delhi, 1984 under the title: *The Praśastapāda Bhāshya*).
PTS	Pali Text Society.
Schüler Śaṅkaras	P. Hacker, *Untersuchungen über Texte des frühen Advaitavāda*. 1: *Die Schüler Śaṅkaras*. Wiesbaden, 1951 (Ak. Wiss. Lit. Mainz, 1950, No. 26).
SK	*Sāṃkhyakārikā* (by Īśvarakṛṣṇa).
Studien	T. Vetter, *Studien zur Lehre und Entwicklung Śaṅkaras*. Vienna, 1979.
s. v.	sub verbo ("under the word").
ŚV	Kumārila, *Ślokavārttika* with the commentary *Nyāyaratnākara* by Pārthasārathi Miśra, ed. Dvārikadāsa Śāstrī. Benares, 1978 (Prācyabhāratī Series).
TS	*Tattvasaṃgraha* (by Śāntarakṣita).
TUBh (V)	*Taittirīya Upaniṣad Bhāṣya* (*Vārttika*).
TV	Kumārila, *Tantravārttika* in: *Mīmāṃsādarśana*, ed. K. V. Abhyaṅkara and K. S. Jośī. Poona, second ed., 1970 (vol. 1: on MS I, 2, 1–II, 1, 49; Ānandāśrama Sanskrit Series).

US — *Śaṅkara's Upadeśasāhasrī*, crit. ed. with introduction and indices by S. Mayeda. Tokyo, 1973 (USG, US II: *Upadeśasāhasrī, Gadyabandha*).

v. — verse.

VP — Bhartṛhari, *Vākyapadīya* (cited according to the edition by W. Rau, Wiesbaden, 1977, or as indicated).

VS — *Vaiśeṣikasūtra* (cited according to the edition by Jambuvijaya, Baroda, 1961, or as indicated).

Works I–III — *Works of Śaṅkarācārya in Original Sanskrit*, Delhi. I: Ten Principal Upaniṣads with Śāṅkarabhāṣya, reprint 1978 (originally Delhi, 1964); II: Bhagavadgītā with Śāṅkarabhāṣya. reprint 1978 (of the second ed. by Bhagavat, Poona, 1929); III: Brahmasūtra with Śāṅkarabhāṣya, n.d. (unacknowledged reprint of the edition by V. S. Paṇśīkar, Bombay, 1915).

YBh — *Yogabhāṣya* (by Vyāsa).

YD — *Yuktidīpikā*, ed. R. C. Pandeya. Delhi, 1967.

YS — *Yogasūtra.*

YSBhV — *Pātañjala-Yogasūtra-Bhāṣya-Vivaraṇam of Śaṅkara-Bhagavatpāda*, ed. P. S. Rama Sastri and S. R. Krishnamurti Sastri. Madras, 1952 (Madras Government Oriental Series).

Quotes and references without indication of specific editions follow generally accepted divisions into chapters, verses, etc. The *Mahābhārata* is quoted according to the critical edition begun by V. S. Sukthankar and published in Poona, the *Rāmāyaṇa* according to the Baroda edition prepared by G. H. Bhatt and others. Otherwise, all references are page references.

INDEX

The index lists proper names, as well as a selection of relevant terms, from the text of the book. With the exception of important anonymous works, titles of works are usually not listed. Names and concepts from the notes appear only if they are of special thematic relevance and go beyond the information provided by the text. Names which are found in bibliographical references (i.e., primarily names of modern scholars), have been omitted. Entries do not necessarily appear in the form in which they occur in the text. Some terminological entries refer to exemplary usages only. Subheadings have been generally avoided. All references are page references. Andreas Pohlus (Humboldt University, Berlin) deserves recognition for his contribution to this index.

pratisandhāna, 26, 43n. 15
pratiṣedha, 90, 211, 306
pratītyasamutpāda, 296
Pratyabhijñā doctrine, 384
pratyakṣa, 151, 366f.
pratyaya, 165, 215f., 236n. 63
pratyekabuddha, 65
pravāha, 221, 239n. 91
pravṛtti, 72
prayojana, 243, 247
Preisendanz, K., 122n. 64, 124n. 74
preyas, 49n. 75, 251, 254
prince in the jungle, 262n. 48
proof, 26, 137f.
pṛthaktva, 38
punarāvṛtti, 291
punarbhava, 249
punarjanma, 249
punarmṛtyu, 291
Purāṇas, 3, 6, 59, 73, 88, 271f., 296
Purandara, 293
Pūrṇakalaśagaṇi, 105
puruṣa, 215f., 218, 225, 228, 236n. 63, 253, 268–270, 276, 287n. 43, 309
puruṣabahutva, 225
puruṣabuddhi, 134f.
puruṣamativaicitrya, 71
puruṣārtha, 27, 95, 118n. 35, 236n. 60, 243, 280, 289n. 48, 396n. 59
Puruṣasūkta, 364, 387
puruṣatarka, 64, 135, 147
puruṣatva, 277, 375
Puruṣottamadeva, 105
Pūrvamīmāṃsā, 23, 35f., 38, 58, 60, 69, 72, 92, 94, 143, 147–155, 161, 182, 226, 251, 275–278, 298, 352, 380, 385, 388 f.

Radhakrishnan, S., 52–54, 358, 362, 378f., 383, 387
rāga, 226, 296
Rajagopalachari, C., 378
rajas, 360, 362
Raju, P. T., 362, 397n. 62
Ramakrishna, i.e., Gadadhar Chatterji, 378f., 386
Rāmanātha Śāstrī, S. K., 206–208, 229n. 1
Rāmānuja, 45n. 35, 299, 307, 341, 345, 352, 374, 381 f.
Rāmāyaṇa, 59
Rammohan Roy, 74, 131, 385, 403n. 133
rationality, 32, 131, 178, 182, 280
Rau, W., 284n. 10, 394n. 35
reason, 31, 36f., 39, 58, ch. 5 passim, 209, 219
reason and faith, 132
relativism, relativistic, 111, 281
religion, religions, 8, 15, 51, 100
religion and Hinduism, 7, 51–53
Renou, L., 1–3
representation, 11
revelation, 4, 36f., 39f., 59, ch. 5 passim, 219, 225
(*see also* Vedic revelation)
Ṛgveda, 1, 19n. 15, 41, 353, 357, 364, 387
ritual, ritualism, ritualists, 14, 29, 60, 72, 87–114 passim, 210, 268
roga, 246
ṛṣi, 37f., 48n. 65
ruci, 71, 73
Ruegg, D. S., 66

Śabara, 5, 30, 68f., 89–94, 149, 161, 169, 191n. 100, 210, 275–280, 301–305, 307, 367, 369, 371, 374
śabda, 26, 134
śabdabrahman, 38, 373
śabdādvaita, 203n. 207
śabdanityatva, 44n. 31
śabdapradhāna, 6
śabdatattva, 38
saccidānanda, 255
sadācāra, 96
Sadānanda, 83n. 84, 161
sādhana, 72, 227, 243, 252, 257
sādhanatā, 307, 367
sādhāraṇatva, 214
sādharmyavaidharmya, 200n. 175
sādhya, 149, 168, 170, 251f., 257
sādhyasādhanabhāva, 152f., 170